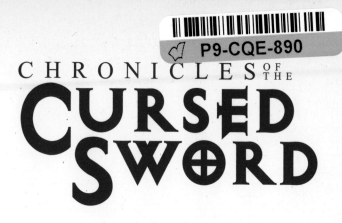

CHRONICLES OF THE CURSED SWORD

Volume 22

Story by
YEO BEOP-RYONG

Art by
PARK HUI-JIN

TOKYOPOP

HAMBURG // LONDON // LOS ANGELES // TOKYO

Chronicles of the Cursed Sword Volume 22
Story By Park Hui Jin & Yeo Beop Ryong

Translation - Ellen Choi
English Adaptation - Matt Varosky
Retouch and Lettering - Star Print Brokers
Production Artist - Lauren O'Connell
Graphic Designer - Colin Graham

Editor - Peter Ahlstrom
Digital Imaging Manager - Chris Buford
Pre-Production Supervisor - Vicente Rivera, Jr.
Production Specialist - Lucas Rivera
Managing Editor - Vy Nguyen
Art Director - Al-Insan Lashley
Editor-in-Chief - Rob Tokar
Publisher - Mike Kiley
President and C.O.O. - John Parker
C.E.O. and Chief Creative Officer - Stu Levy

A ⬤ TOKYOPOP® Manga

TOKYOPOP and ⬤ are trademarks or registered trademarks of TOKYOPOP Inc.

TOKYOPOP Inc.
5900 Wilshire Blvd. Suite 2000
Los Angeles, CA 90036

E-mail: info@TOKYOPOP.com
Come visit us online at www.TOKYOPOP.com

ISBN: 978-1-4278-0149-4

First TOKYOPOP printing: August 2008
10 9 8 7 6 5 4 3 2 1
Printed in the USA

Contents

CHRONICLES OF THE CURSED SWORD

the cast of characters

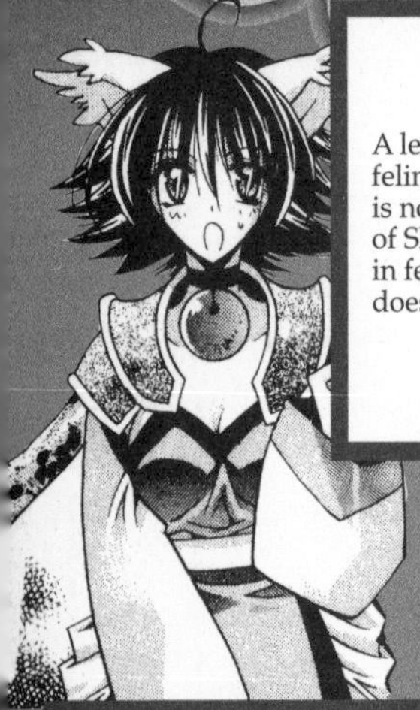

MINGLING

A lesser demon with feline qualities, Mingling is now the loyal follower of Shyao Lin. She lives in fear of Rey, who still doesn't trust her.

THE PASA SWORD

A living sword that hungers for demon blood, but at a great cost—it can take over the user's body and, in time, his soul.

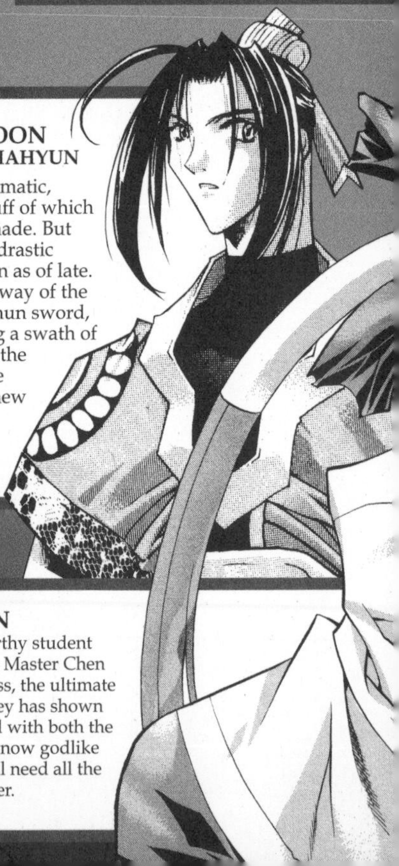

JARYOON
KING OF HAHYUN

Noble and charismatic, Jaryoon is the stuff of which great kings are made. But there has been a drastic change in Jaryoon as of late. Now under the sway of the spirit of the PaChun sword, Jaryoon is cutting a swath of humanity across the countryside as he searches for his new prey: Rey.

SHYAO LIN

A sorceress, previously Rey's traveling companion and greatest ally. Shyao has recently discovered that she is, in fact, one of the Eight Sages of the Azure Pavilion, sent to gather information in the Human Realm. Much to her dismay, her first duty as Rana, the Lady Sohwa, is to kill Rey Yan.

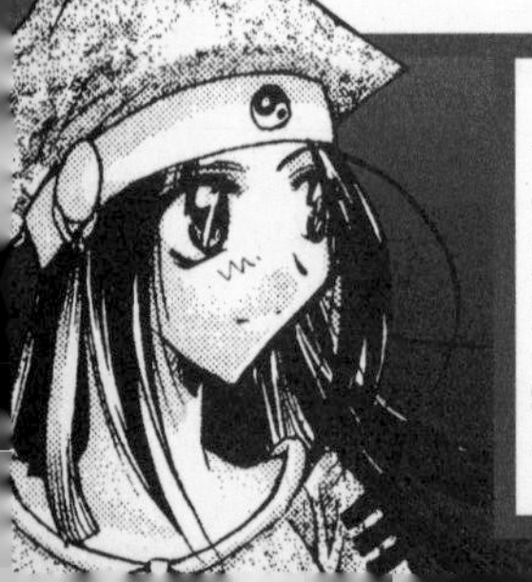

REY YAN

Rey has proven to be a worthy student of the wise and diminutive Master Chen Kaihu. At the Mujin Fortress, the ultimate warrior testing grounds, Rey has shown his martial arts mettle. And with both the possessed Jaryoon and the now godlike Shyao after his blood—he'll need all the survival skills he can muster.

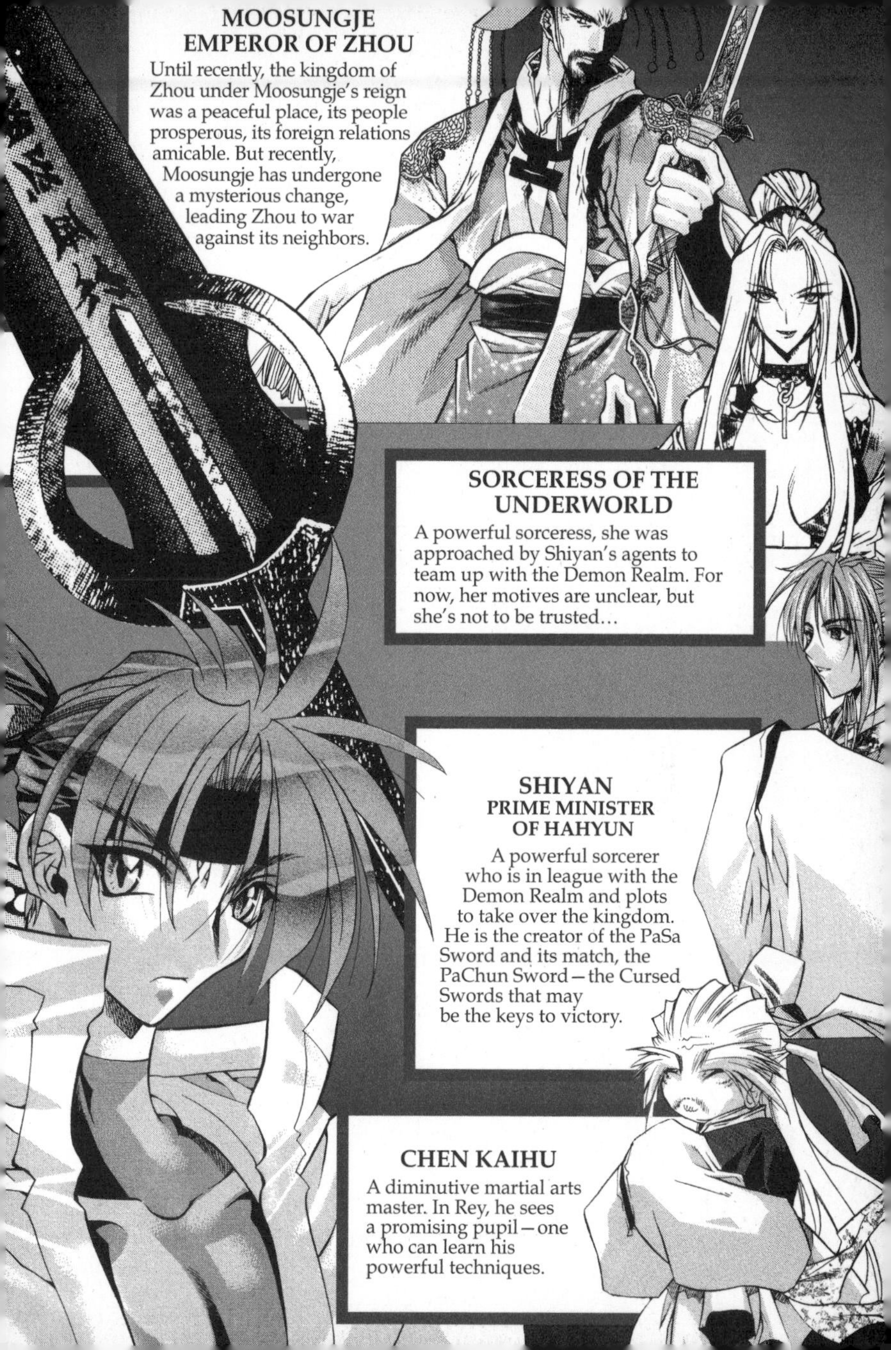
MOOSUNGJE
EMPEROR OF ZHOU
Until recently, the kingdom of Zhou under Moosungje's reign was a peaceful place, its people prosperous, its foreign relations amicable. But recently, Moosungje has undergone a mysterious change, leading Zhou to war against its neighbors.
SORCERESS OF THE UNDERWORLD
A powerful sorceress, she was approached by Shiyan's agents to team up with the Demon Realm. For now, her motives are unclear, but she's not to be trusted…
SHIYAN
PRIME MINISTER OF HAHYUN
A powerful sorcerer who is in league with the Demon Realm and plots to take over the kingdom. He is the creator of the PaSa Sword and its match, the PaChun Sword—the Cursed Swords that may be the keys to victory.
CHEN KAIHU
A diminutive martial arts master. In Rey, he sees a promising pupil—one who can learn his powerful techniques.

Thus Far In...
CHRONICLES OF THE
CURSED SWORD

In an era of warring states, warlords become kings, dynasties crumble, and heroes can rise from the most unlikely places. Rey Yan was an orphan with no home, no skills and no purpose. But when he comes upon the PaSa sword, a cursed blade made from the bones of the Demon Emperor, he suddenly finds himself with the power to be a great hero…

Now Rey has discovered that the Heavenly Realm has chosen the most drastic measure possible in order to keep the Demon Realm from ever attacking them—they plan to seal off the Human Realm, which will result in the end of all life on Earth! To stop this from happening, Rey and an unlikely company of demons, sages, and warriors have managed to destroy two of the towers that will serve as seals, but six still remain and time is running out!

Chapter 84
Jade Tower

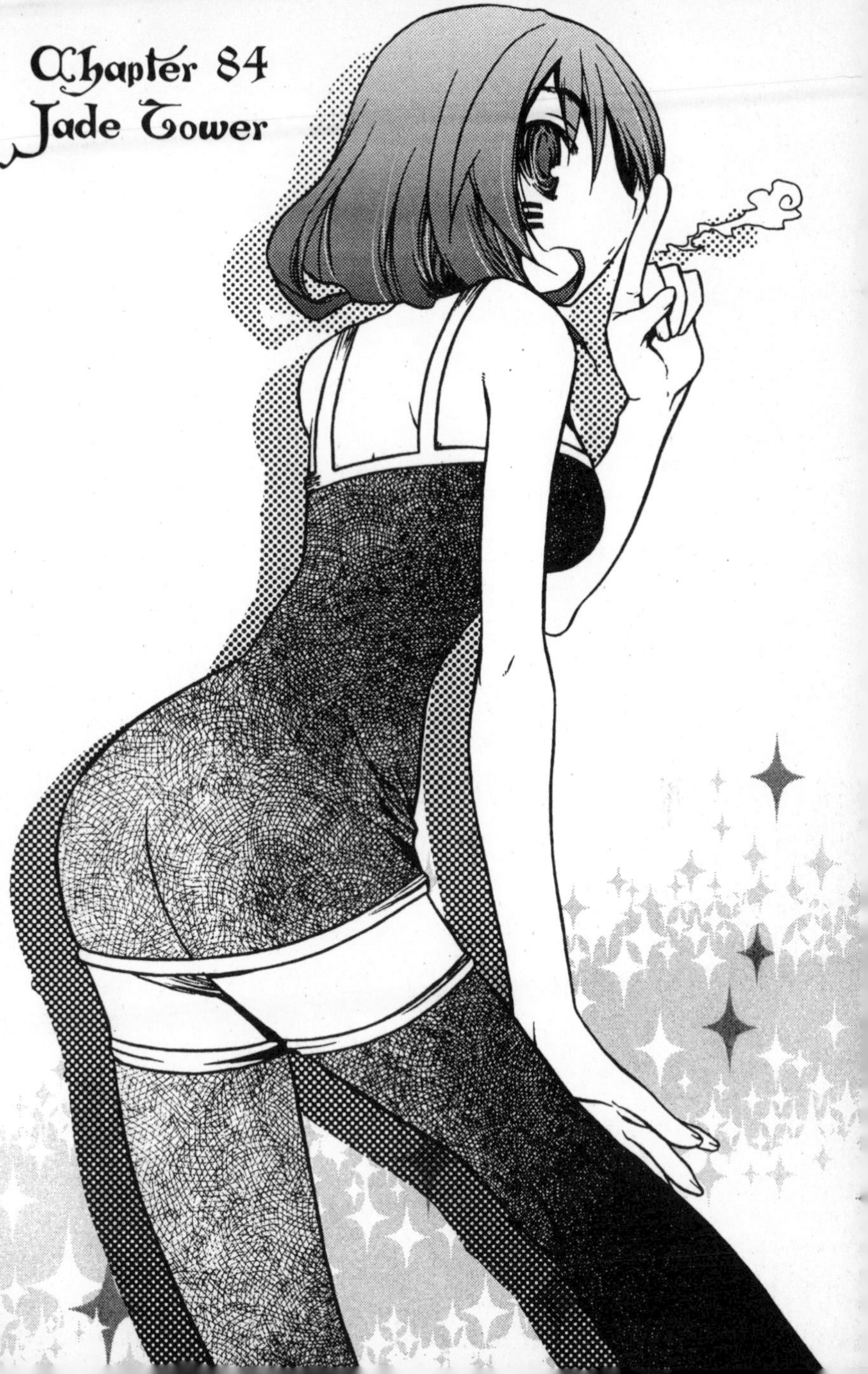

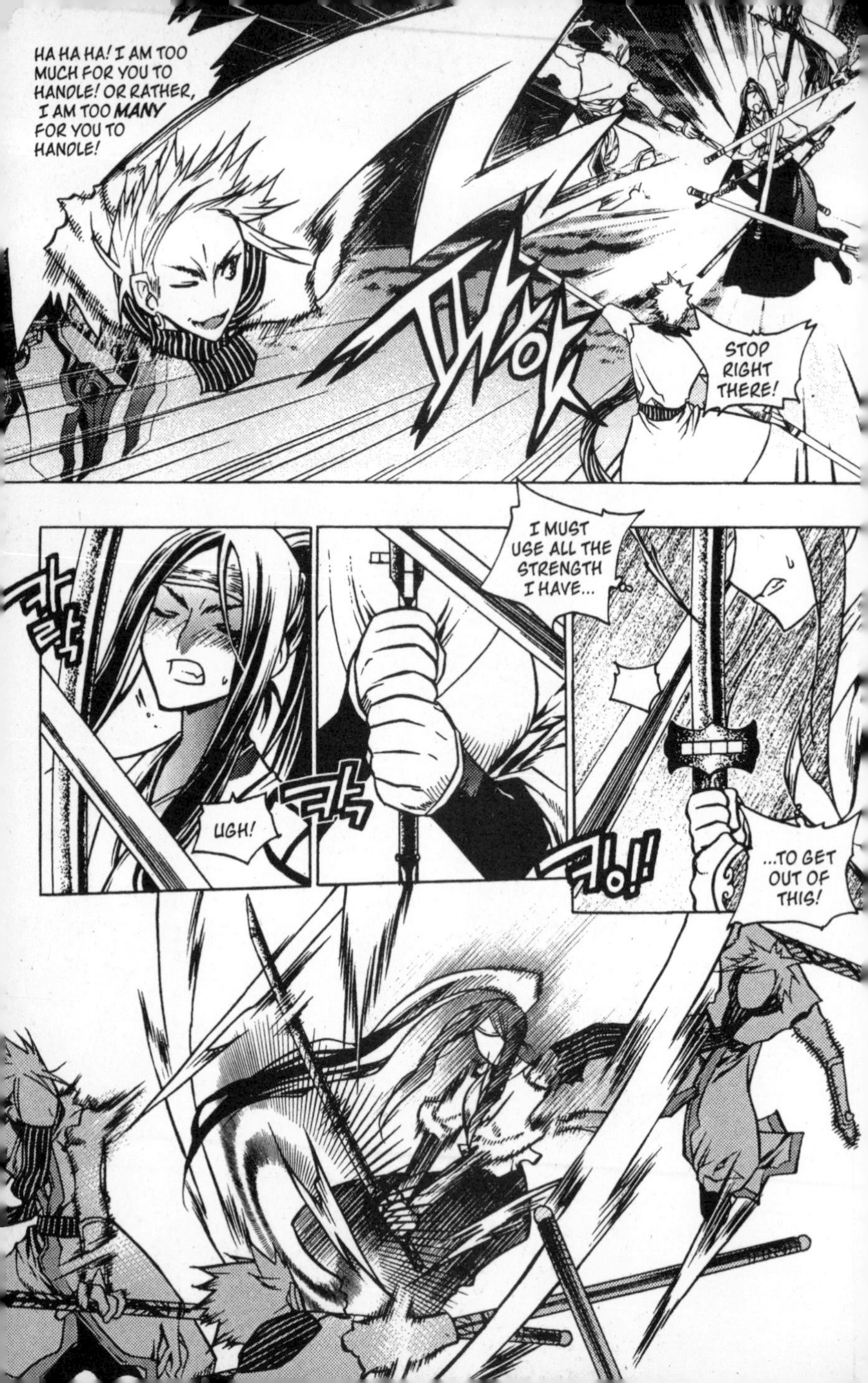
HA HA HA! I AM TOO MUCH FOR YOU TO HANDLE! OR RATHER, I AM TOO MANY FOR YOU TO HANDLE!
TWOK
STOP RIGHT THERE!
UGH!
I MUST USE ALL THE STRENGTH I HAVE...
...TO GET OUT OF THIS!

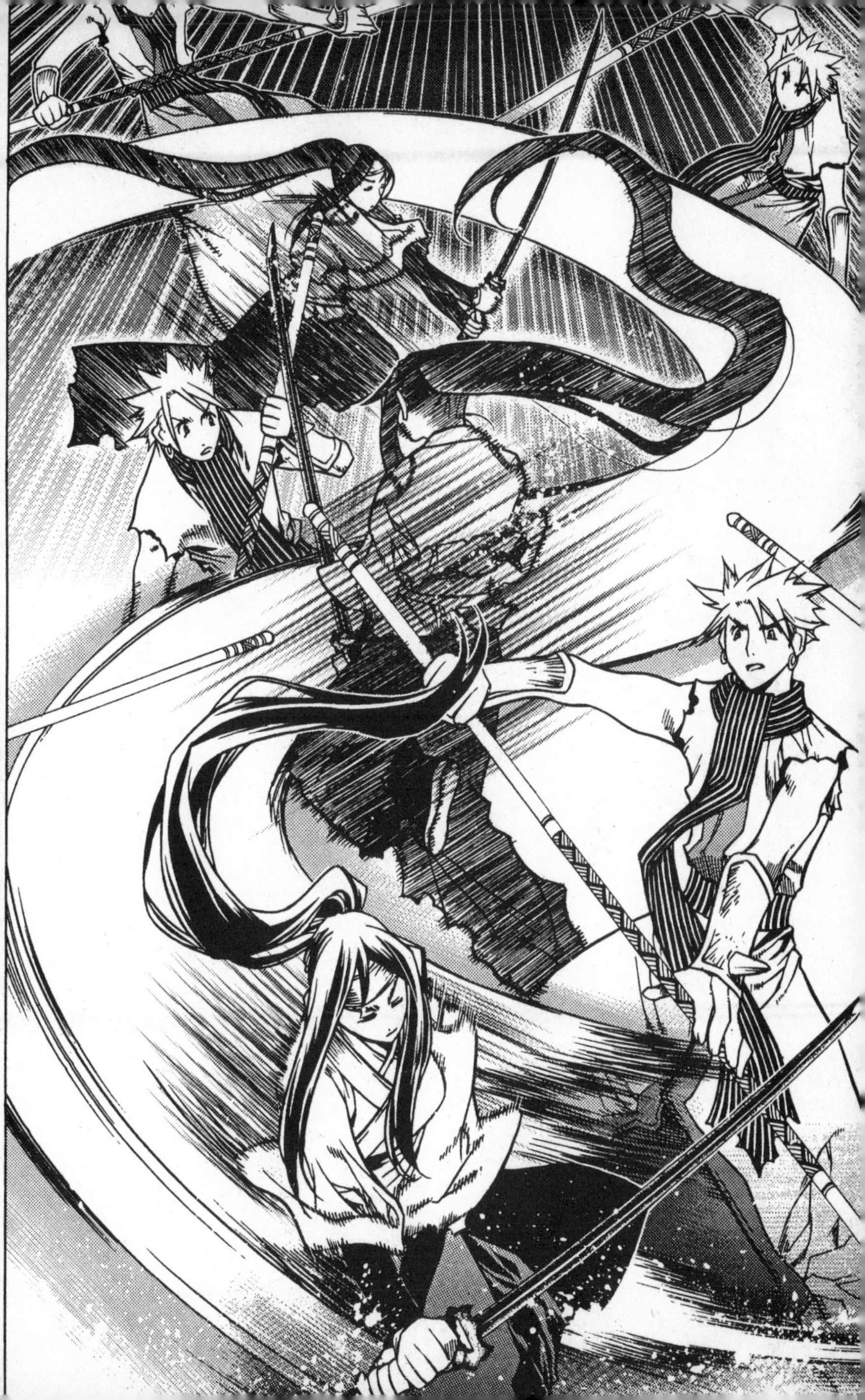

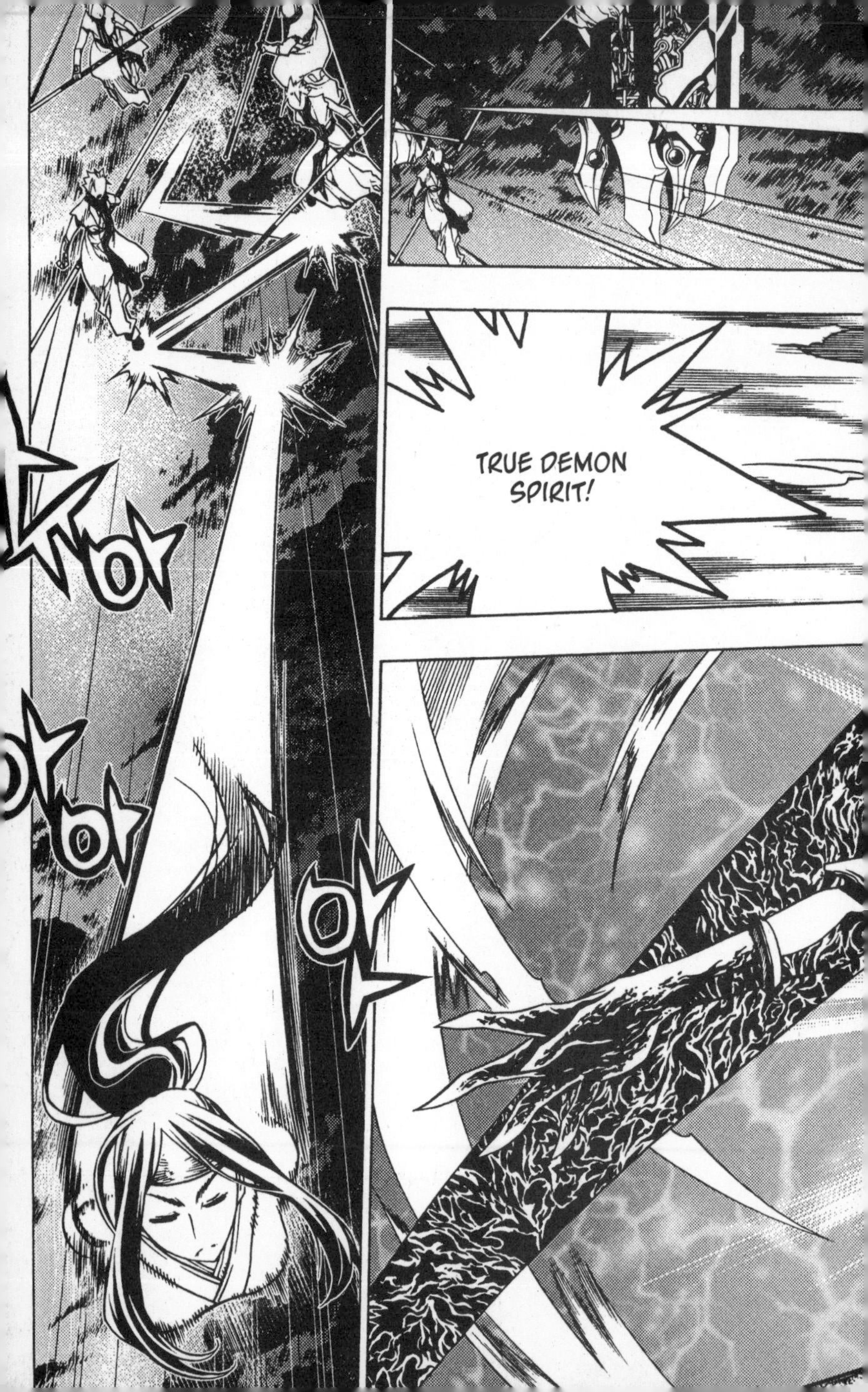
TRUE DEMON SPIRIT!

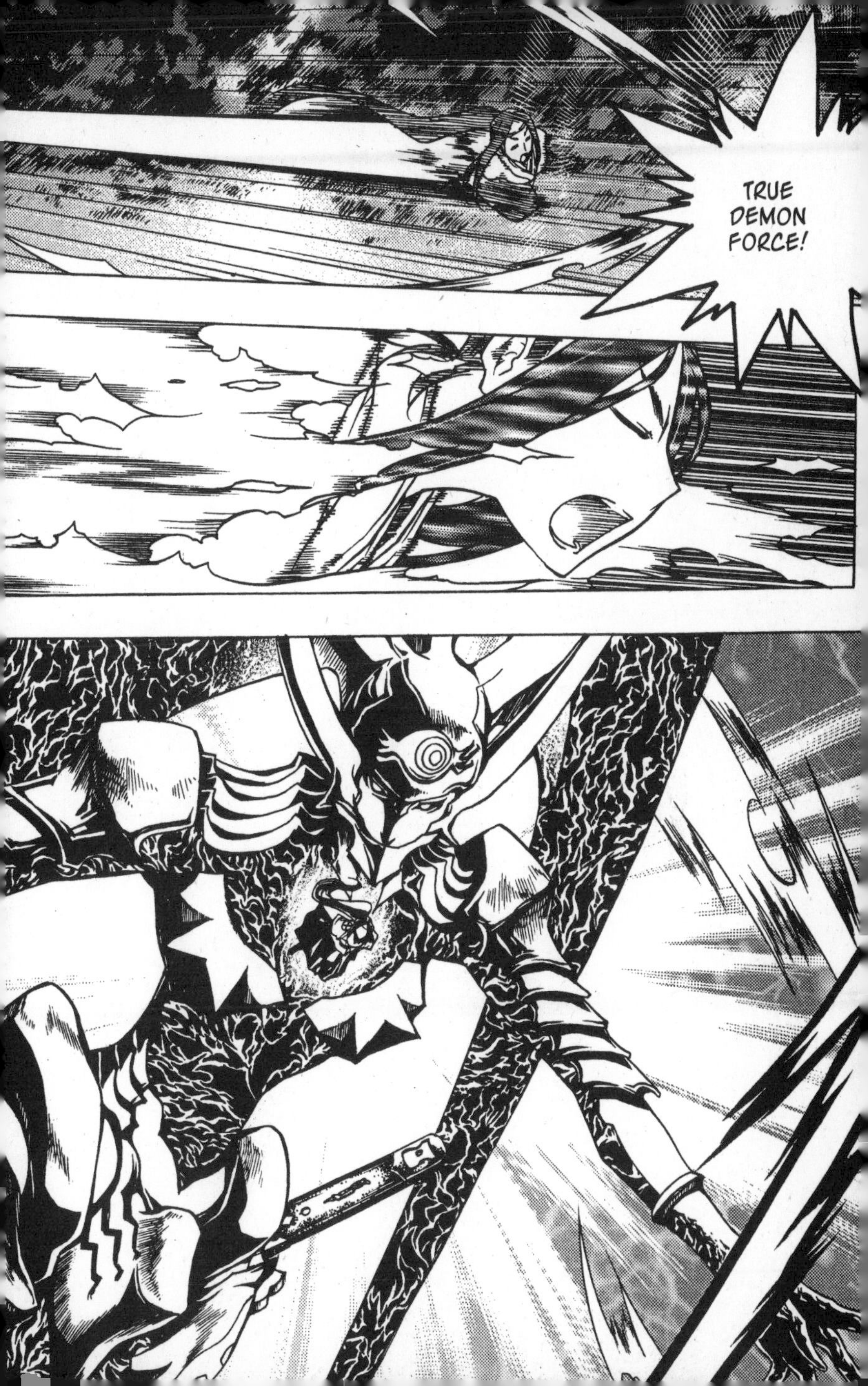
TRUE
DEMON
FORCE!

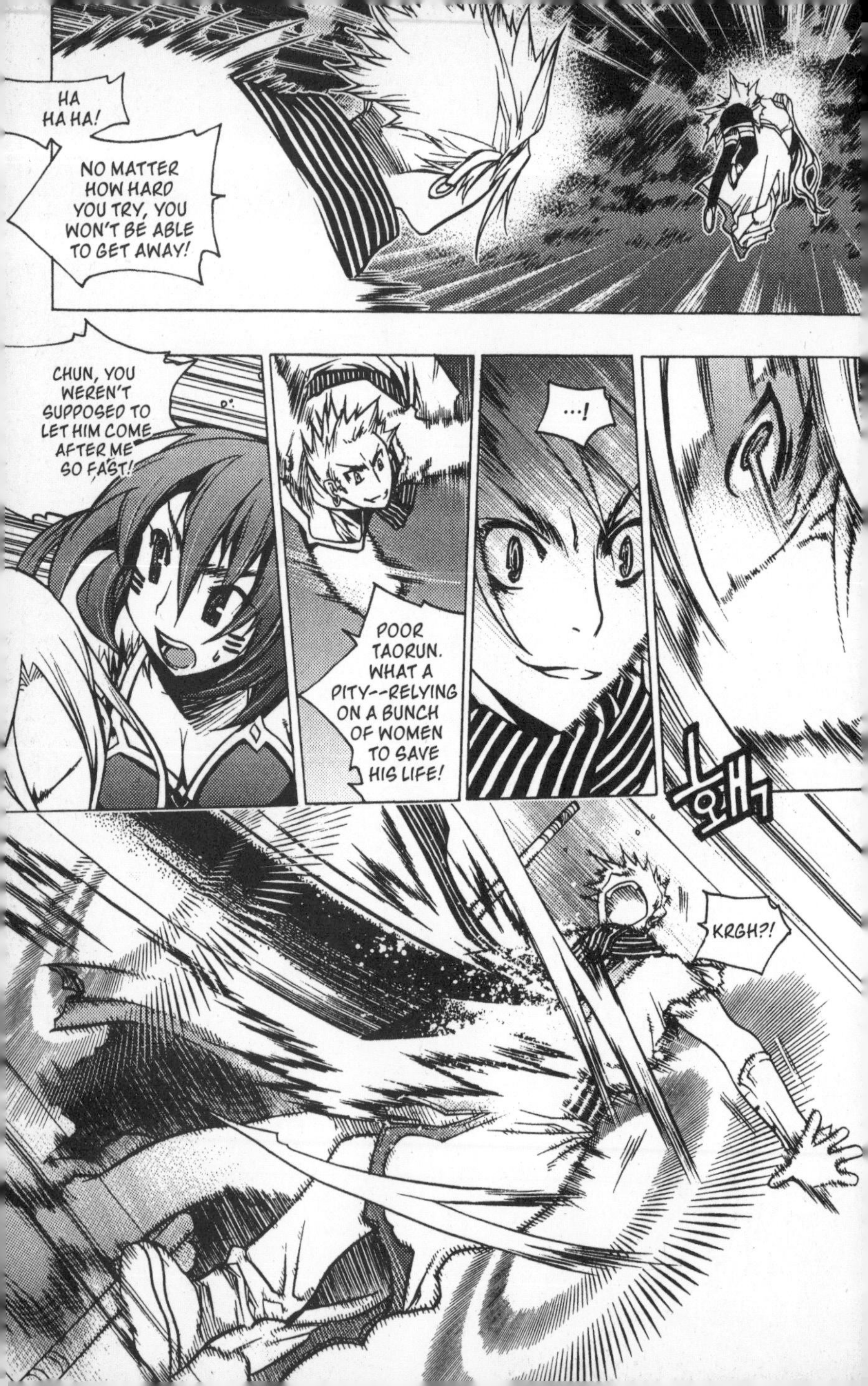
HA HA HA!
NO MATTER HOW HARD YOU TRY, YOU WON'T BE ABLE TO GET AWAY!
CHUN, YOU WEREN'T SUPPOSED TO LET HIM COME AFTER ME SO FAST!
POOR TAORUN. WHAT A PITY--RELYING ON A BUNCH OF WOMEN TO SAVE HIS LIFE!
...!
KRGH?!

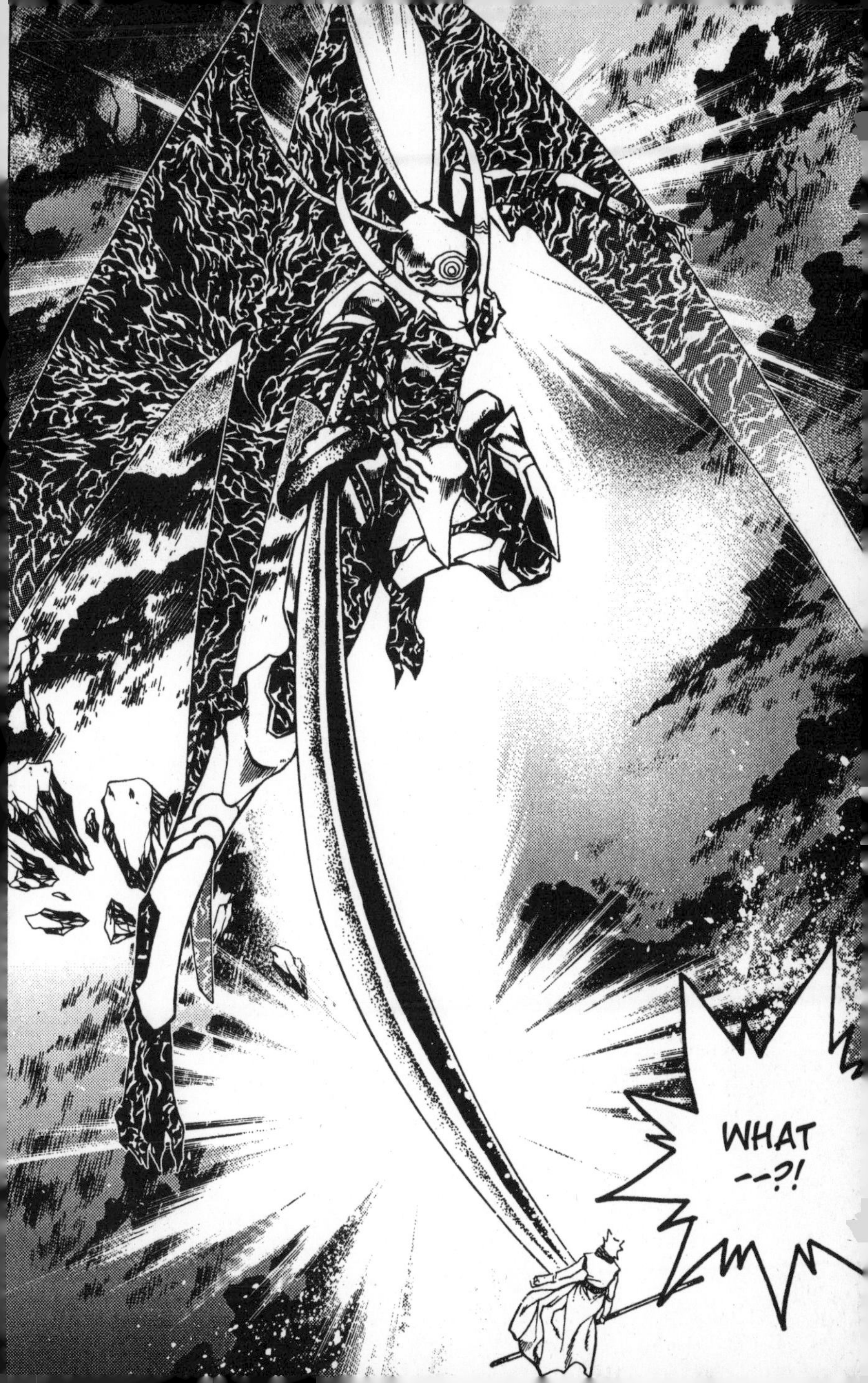
WHAT
--?!

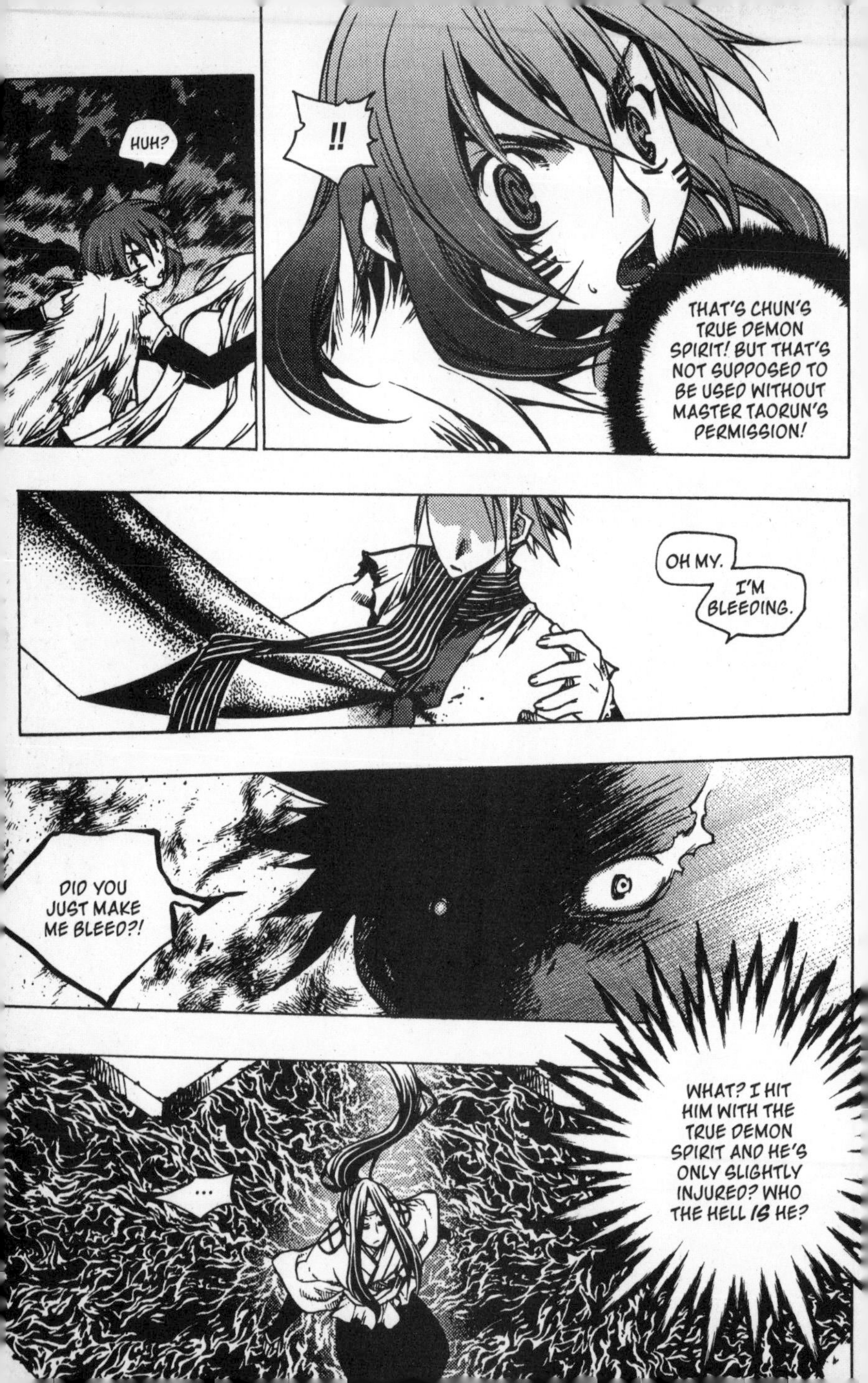
!!
THAT'S CHUN'S TRUE DEMON SPIRIT! BUT THAT'S NOT SUPPOSED TO BE USED WITHOUT MASTER TAORUN'S PERMISSION!
HUH?
OH MY. I'M BLEEDING.
DID YOU JUST MAKE ME BLEED?!
WHAT? I HIT HIM WITH THE TRUE DEMON SPIRIT AND HE'S ONLY SLIGHTLY INJURED? WHO THE HELL *IS* HE?
...

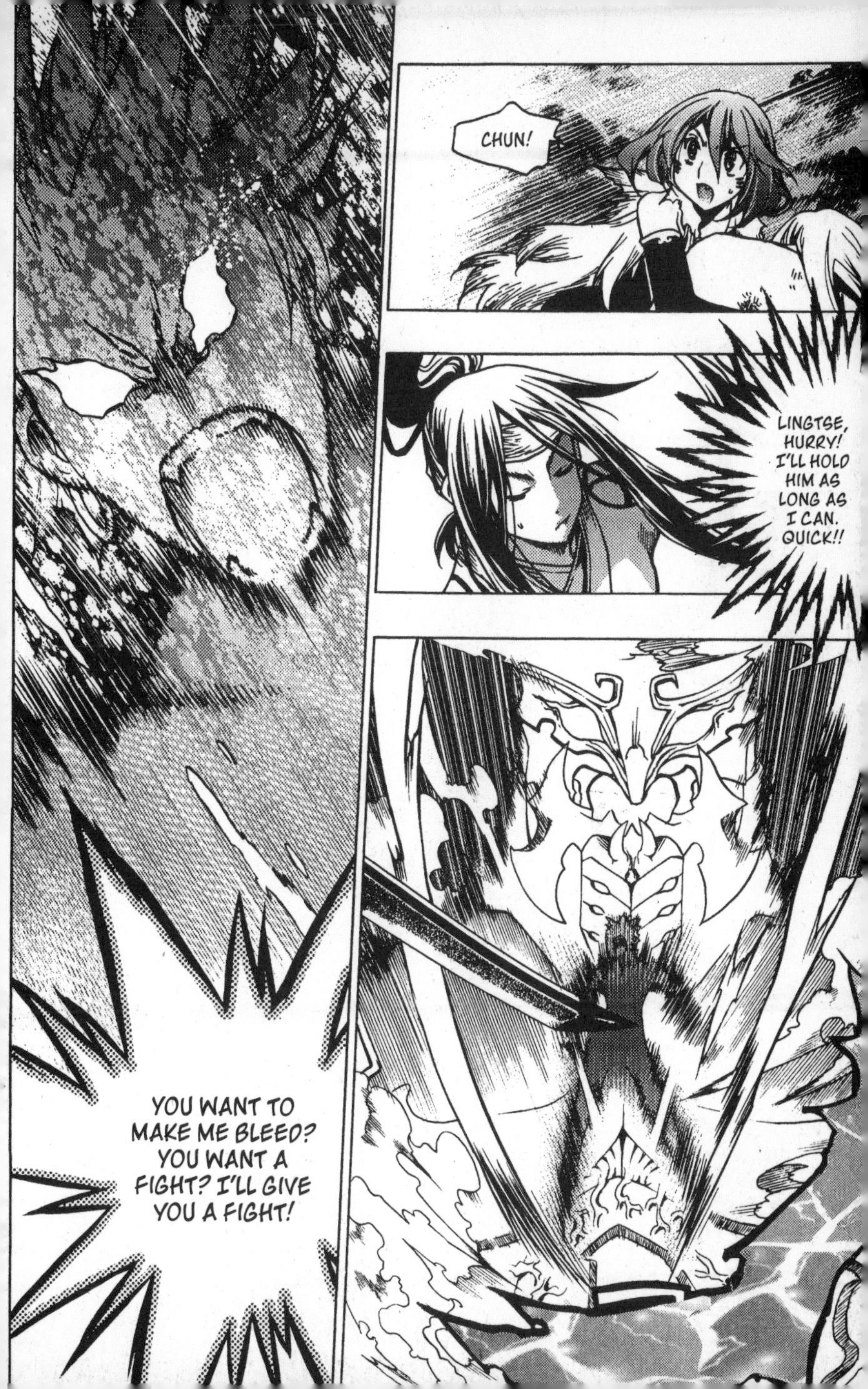
CHUN!
LINGTSE, HURRY! I'LL HOLD HIM AS LONG AS I CAN. QUICK!!
YOU WANT TO MAKE ME BLEED? YOU WANT A FIGHT? I'LL GIVE YOU A FIGHT!

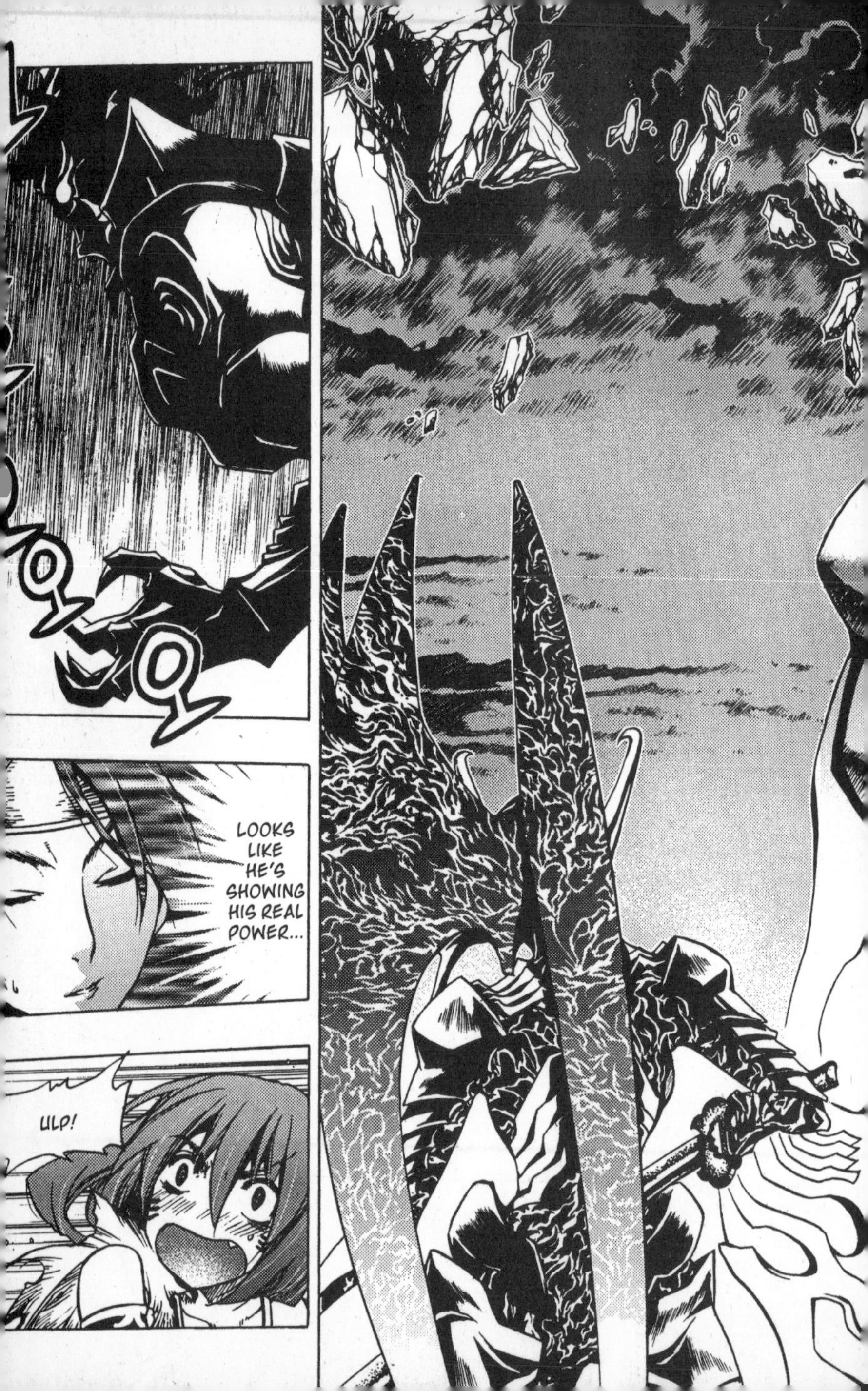
LOOKS LIKE HE'S SHOWING HIS REAL POWER...
ULP!

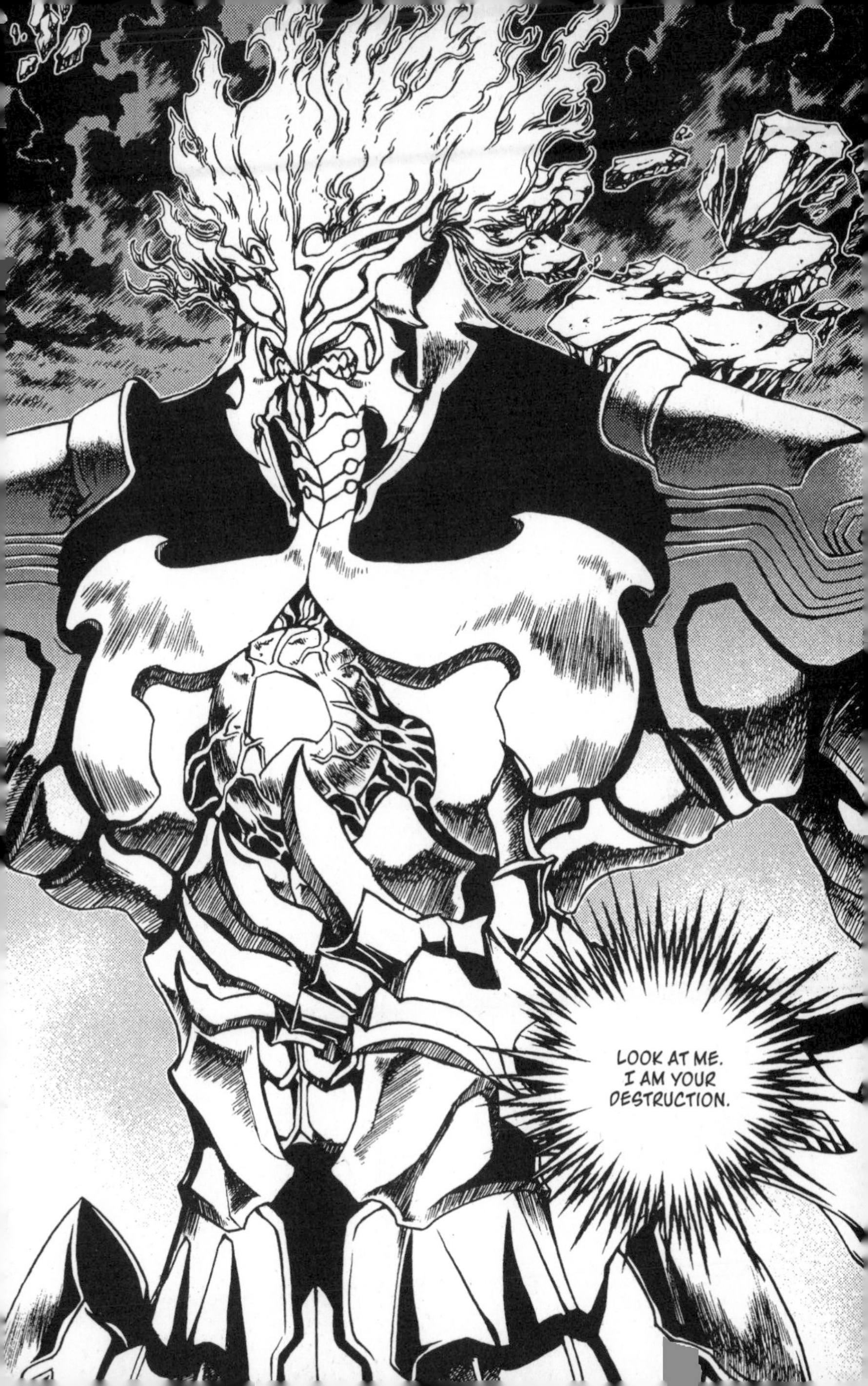
LOOK AT ME.
I AM YOUR
DESTRUCTION.

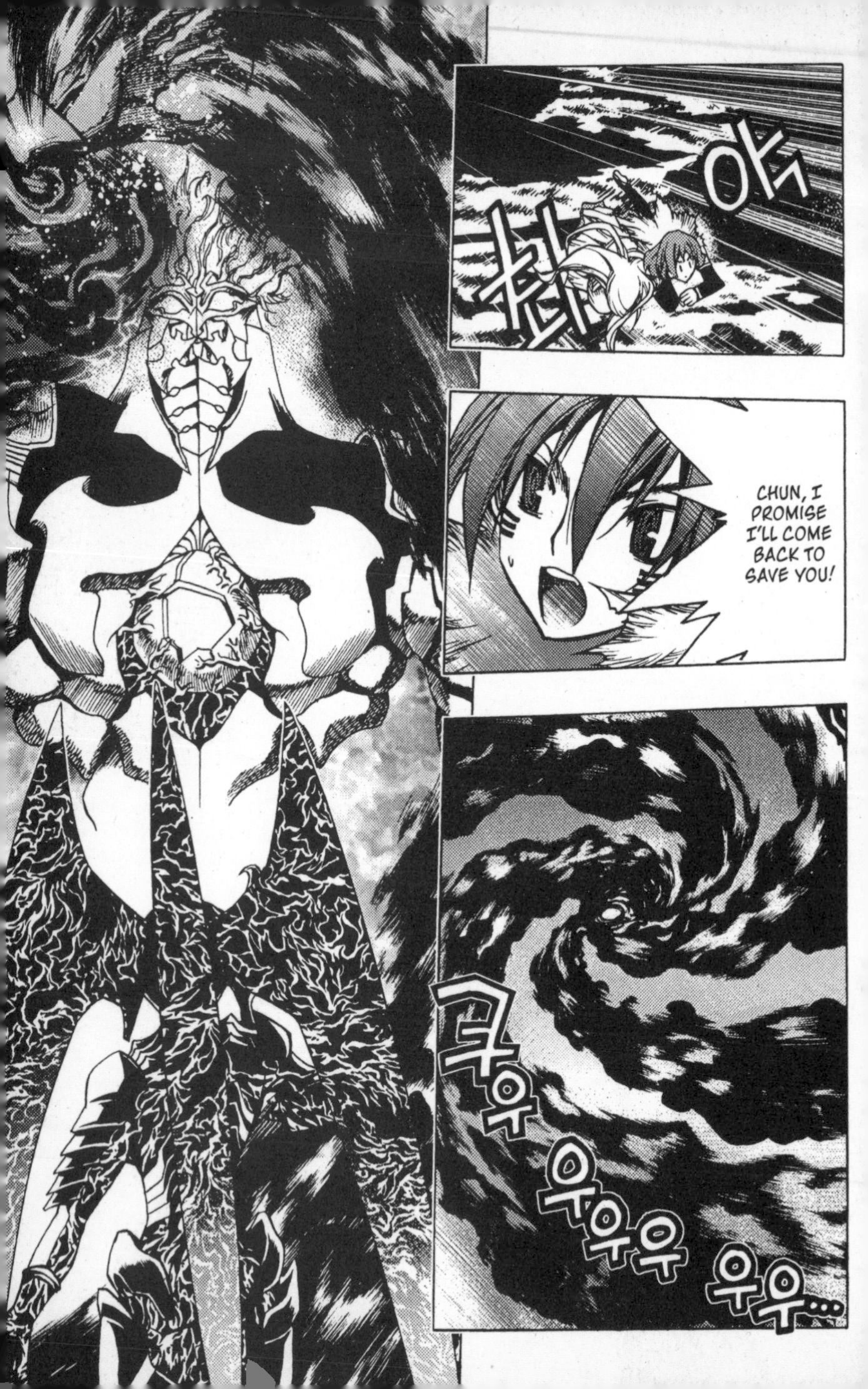
CHUN, I PROMISE I'LL COME BACK TO SAVE YOU!

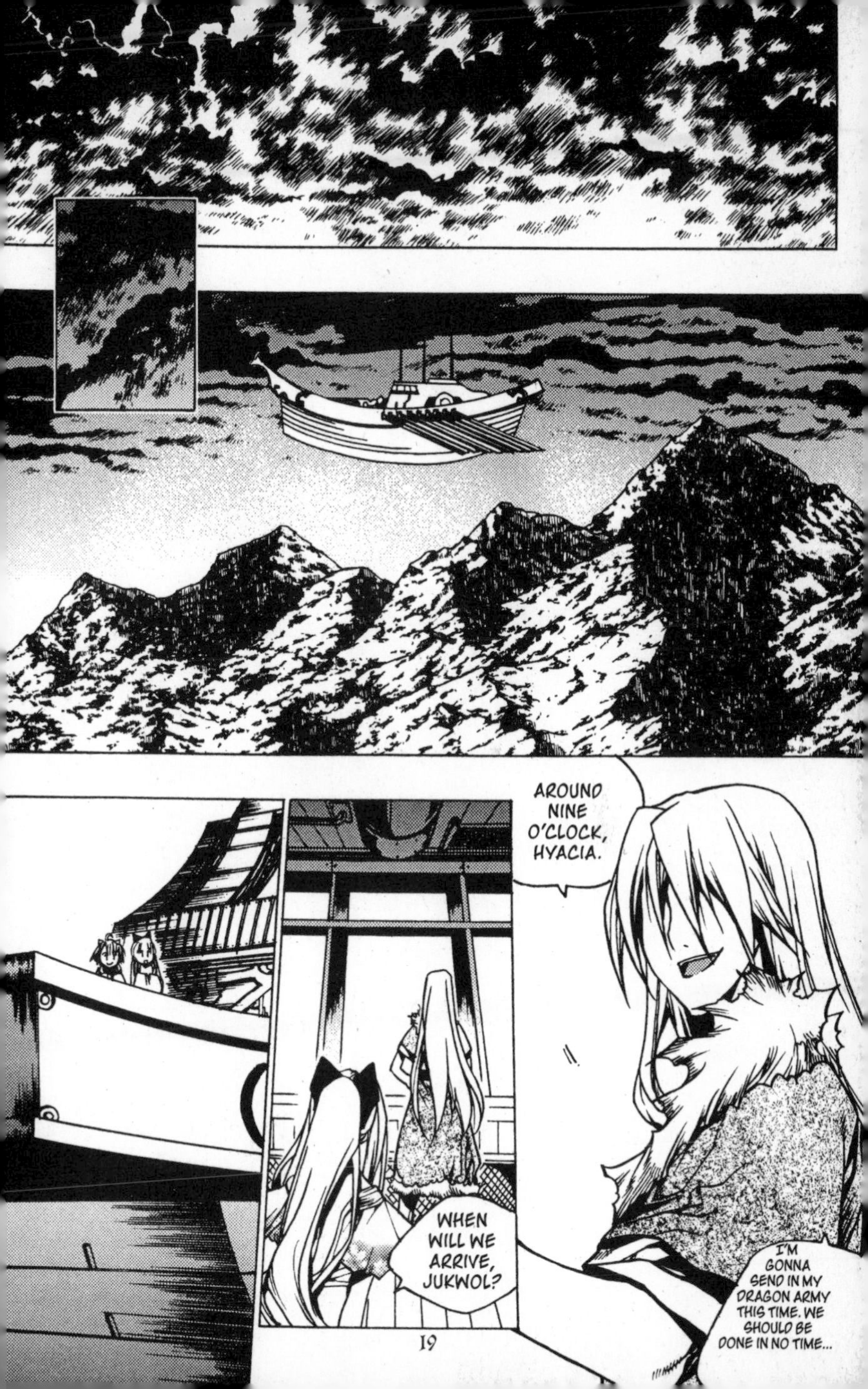
WHEN WILL WE ARRIVE, JUKWOL?
AROUND NINE O'CLOCK, HYACIA.
I'M GONNA SEND IN MY DRAGON ARMY THIS TIME. WE SHOULD BE DONE IN NO TIME...

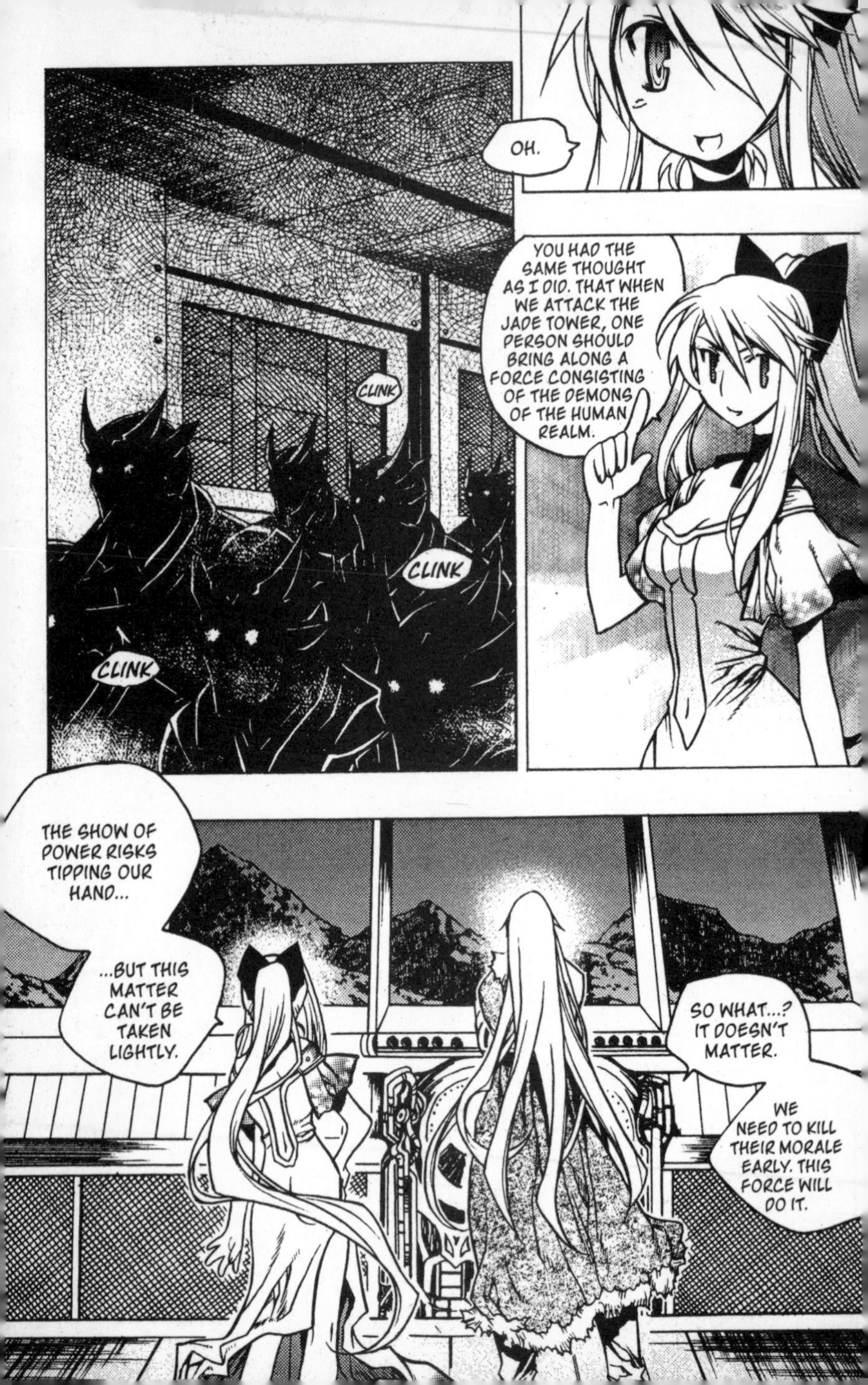
CLINK
CLINK
CLINK
OH.
YOU HAD THE SAME THOUGHT AS I DID. THAT WHEN WE ATTACK THE JADE TOWER, ONE PERSON SHOULD BRING ALONG A FORCE CONSISTING OF THE DEMONS OF THE HUMAN REALM.
THE SHOW OF POWER RISKS TIPPING OUR HAND...
...BUT THIS MATTER CAN'T BE TAKEN LIGHTLY.
SO WHAT...? IT DOESN'T MATTER.
WE NEED TO KILL THEIR MORALE EARLY. THIS FORCE WILL DO IT.

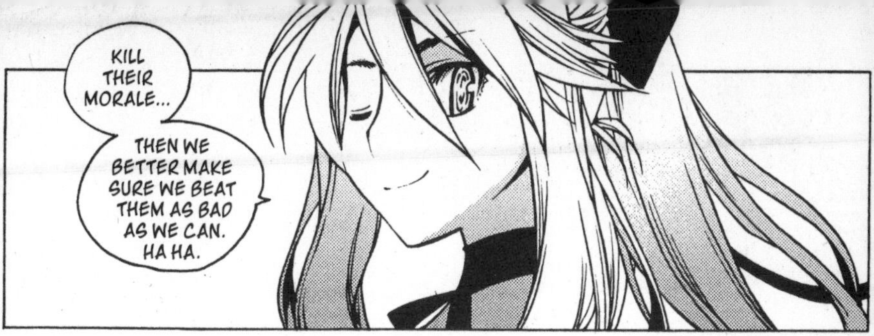
KILL THEIR MORALE...
THEN WE BETTER MAKE SURE WE BEAT THEM AS BAD AS WE CAN. HA HA.
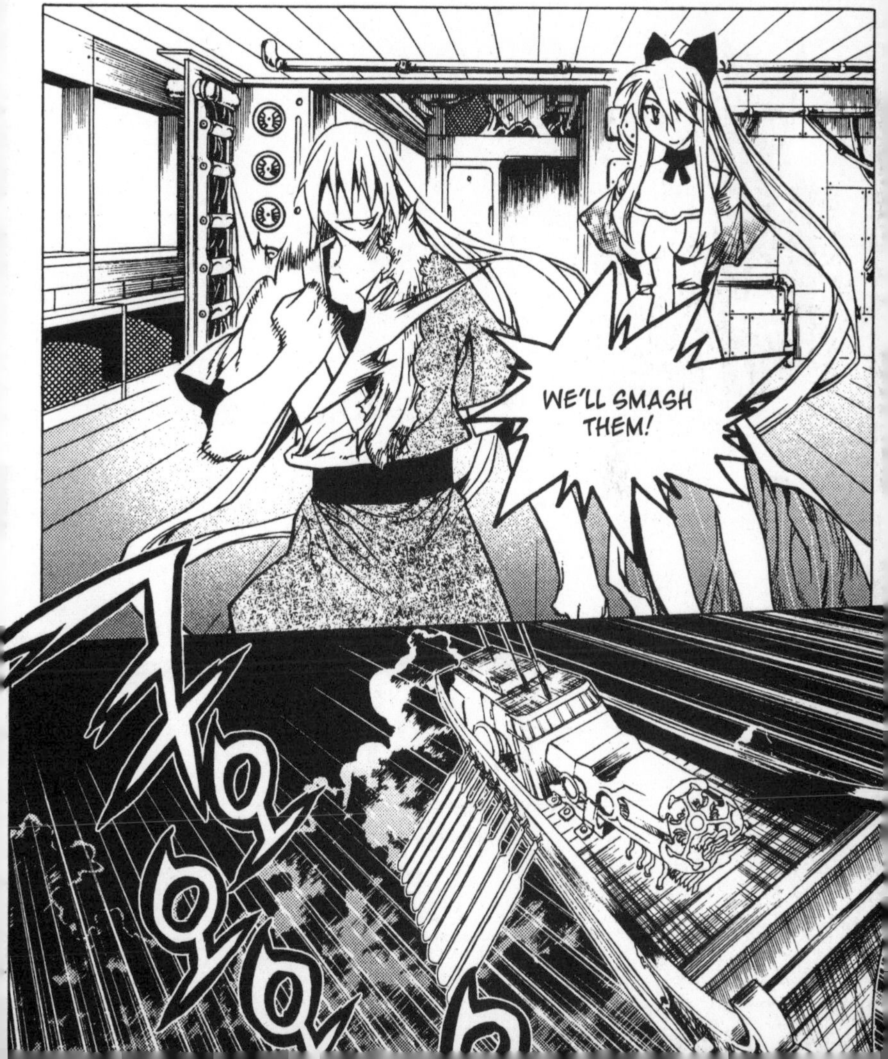
WE'LL SMASH THEM!

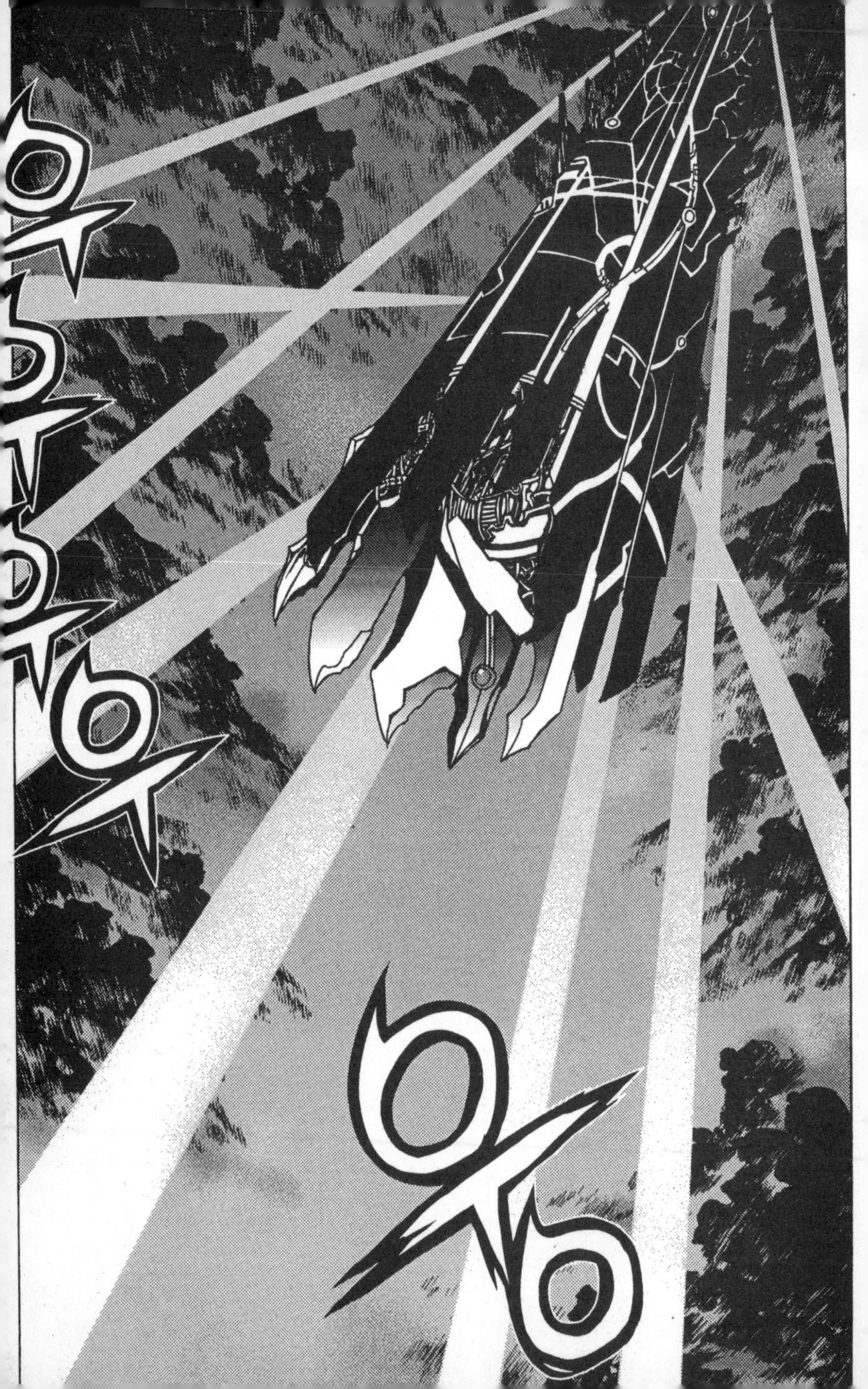

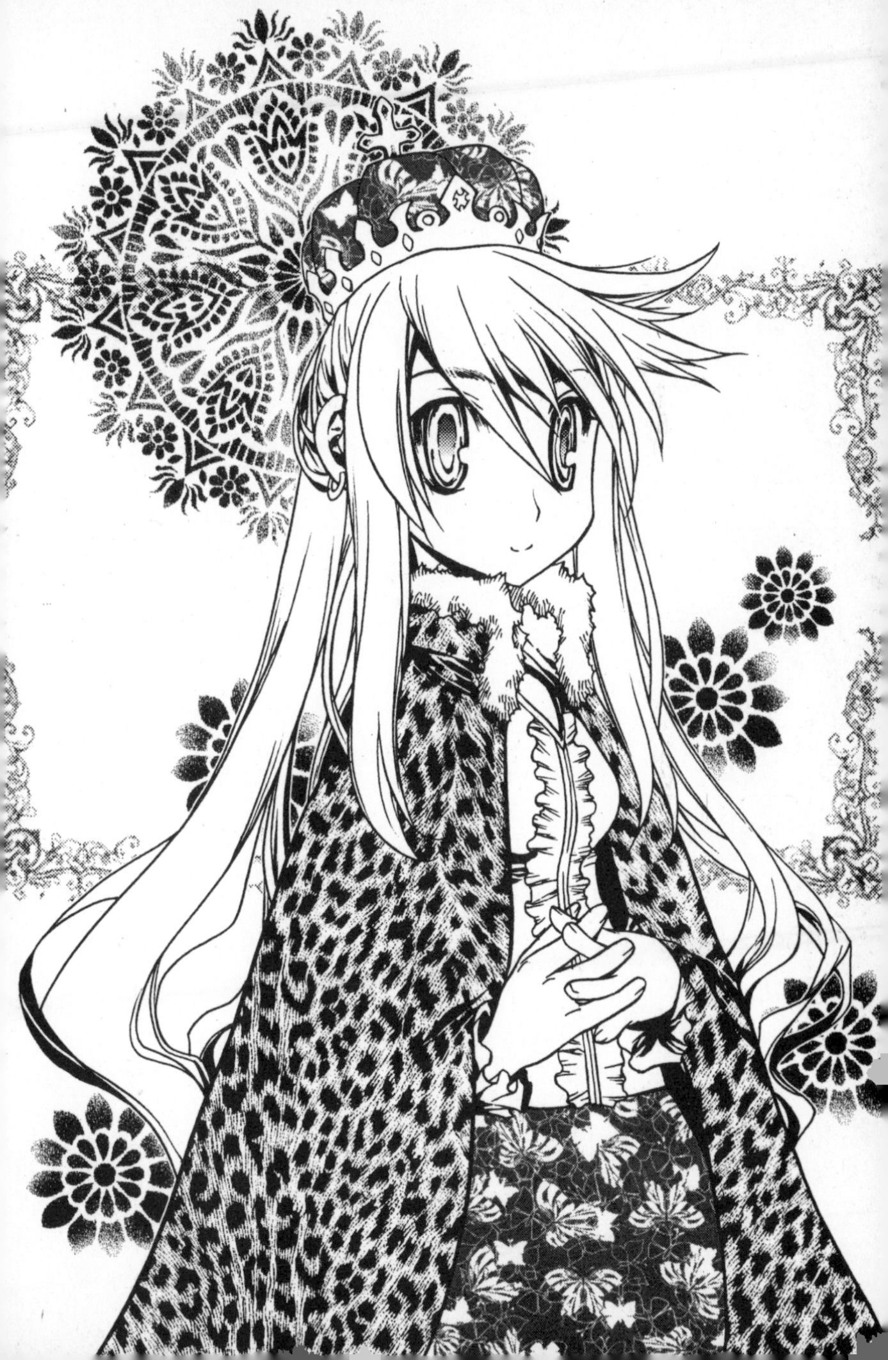

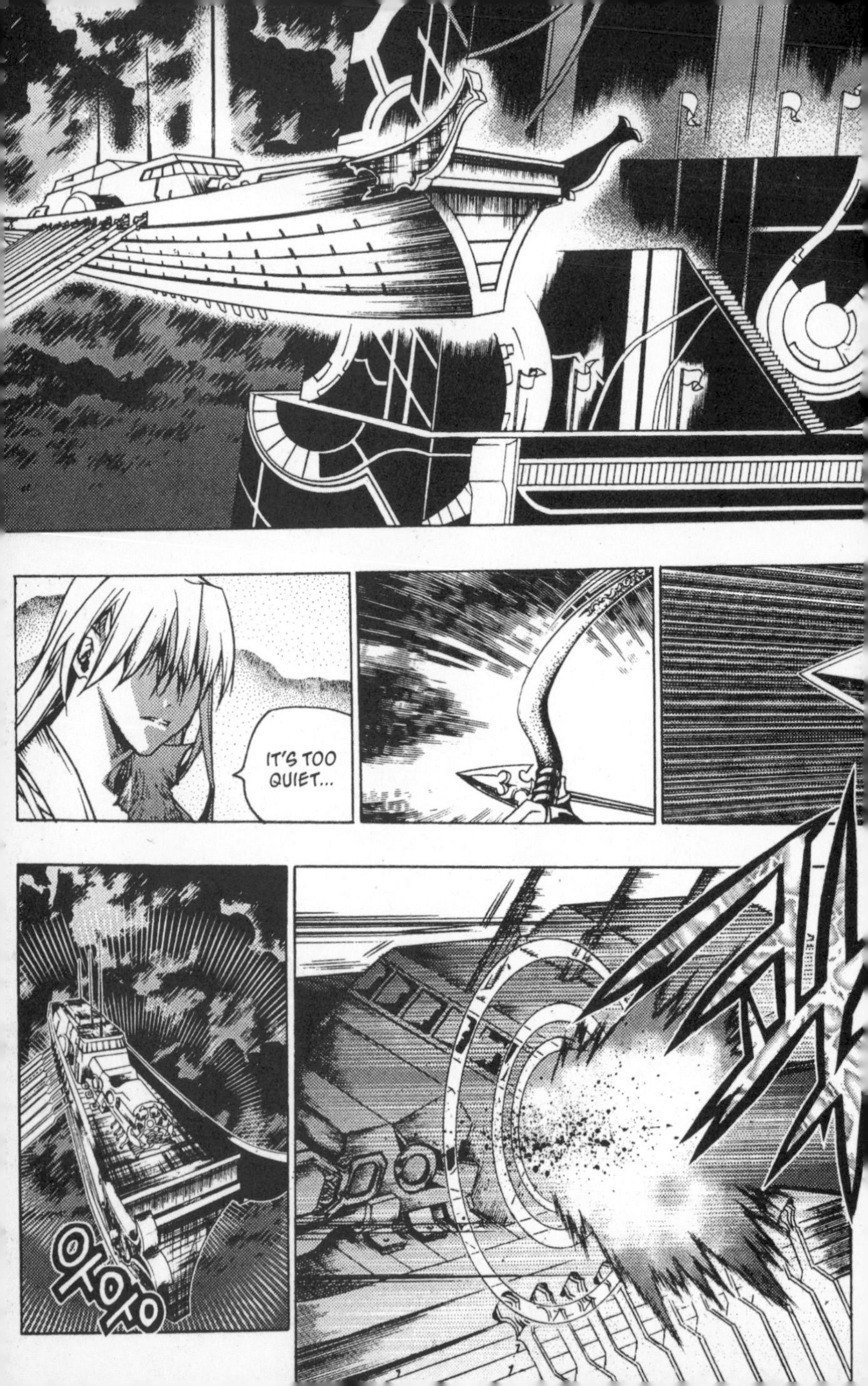
IT'S TOO QUIET...
아아아

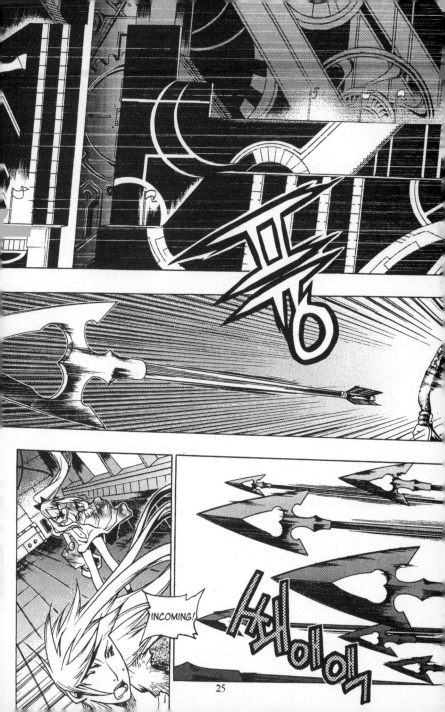

INCOMING!

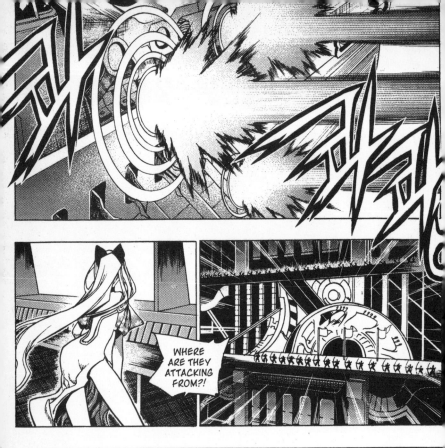

WHERE ARE THEY ATTACKING FROM?!

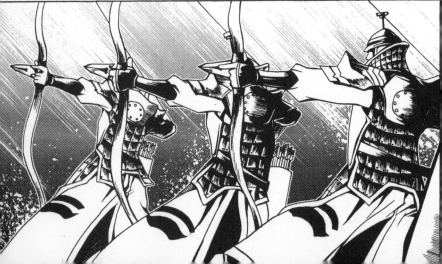

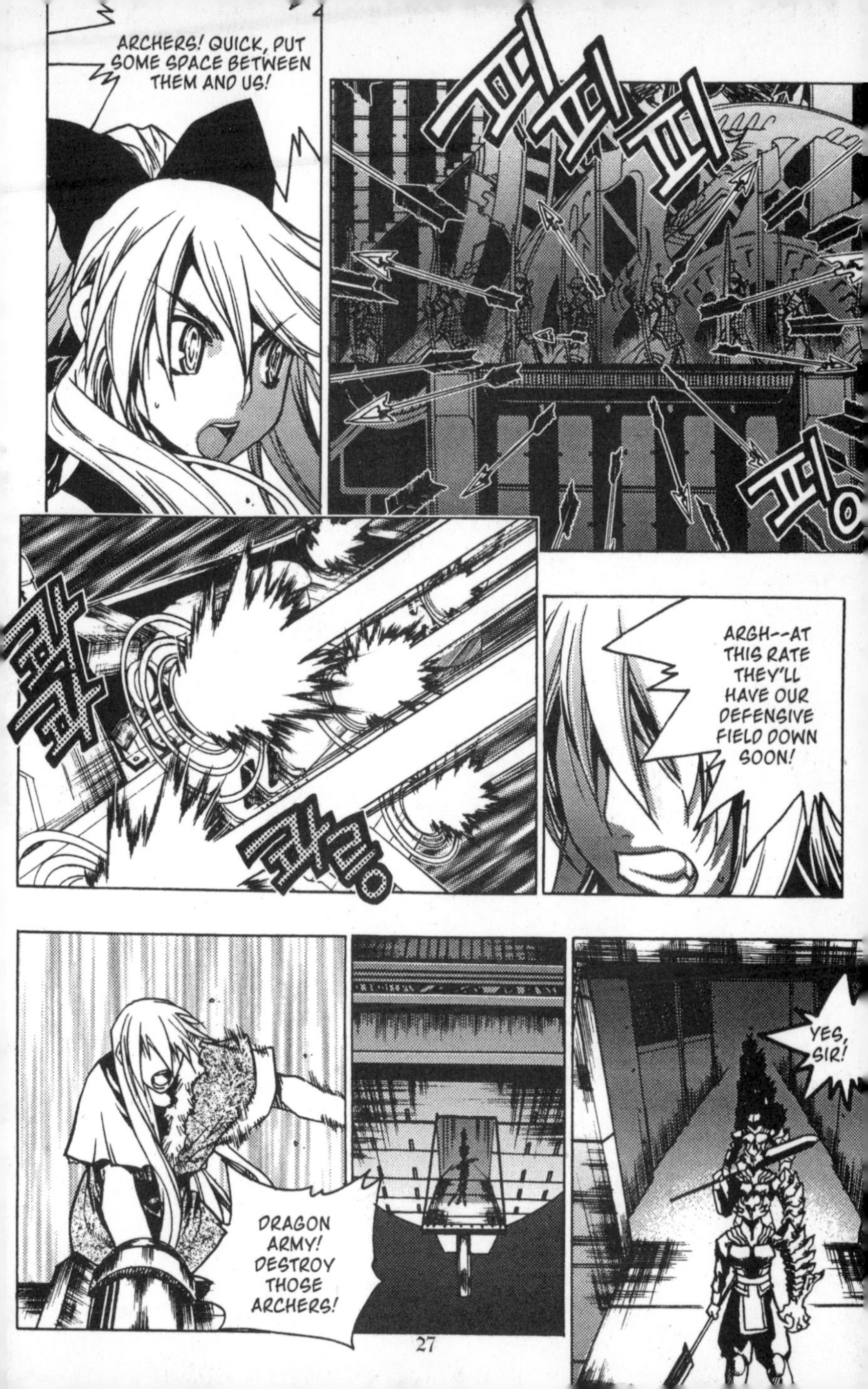
ARCHERS! QUICK, PUT SOME SPACE BETWEEN THEM AND US!
ARGH--AT THIS RATE THEY'LL HAVE OUR DEFENSIVE FIELD DOWN SOON!
DRAGON ARMY! DESTROY THOSE ARCHERS!
YES, SIR!

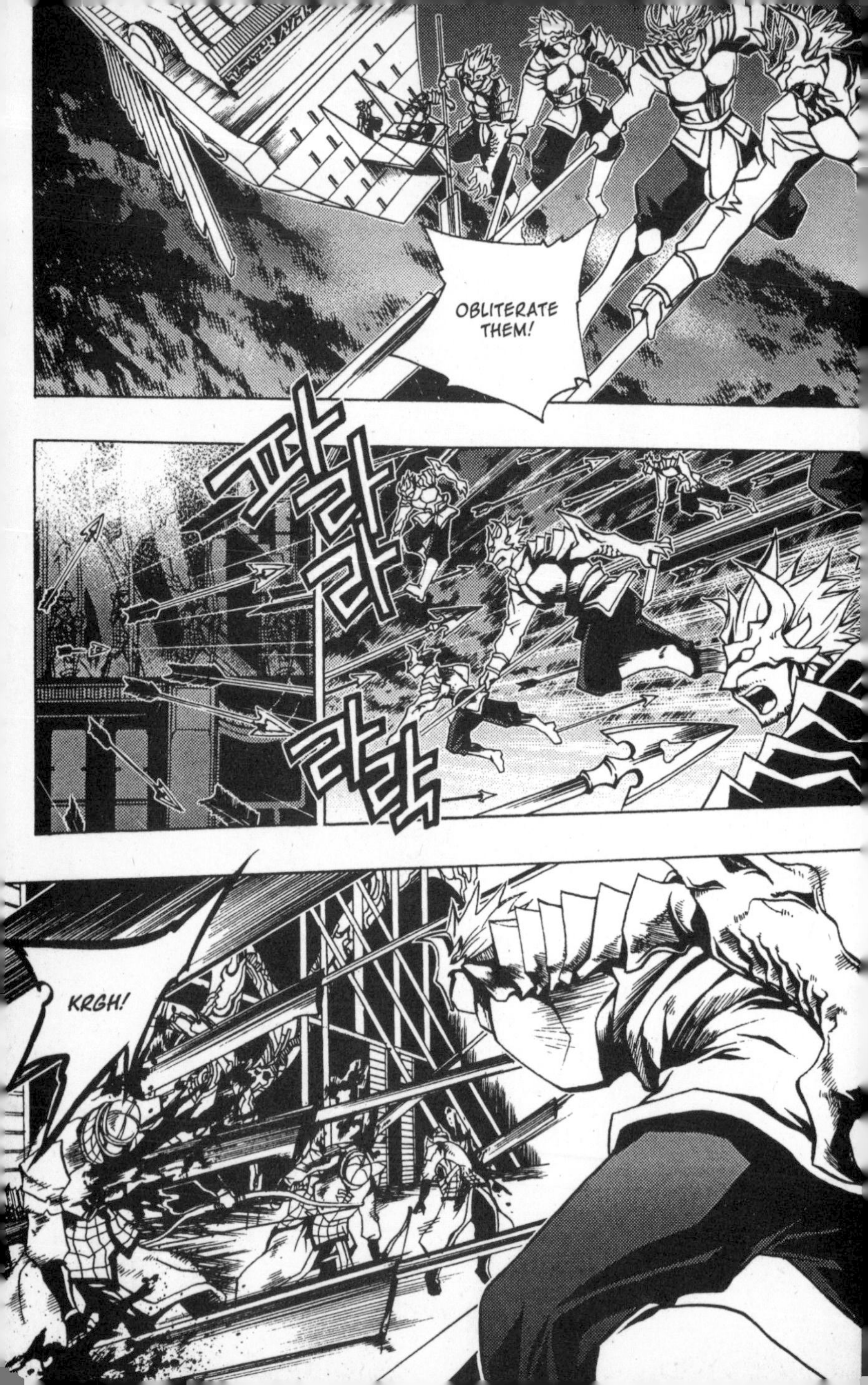
OBLITERATE THEM!
KRGH!

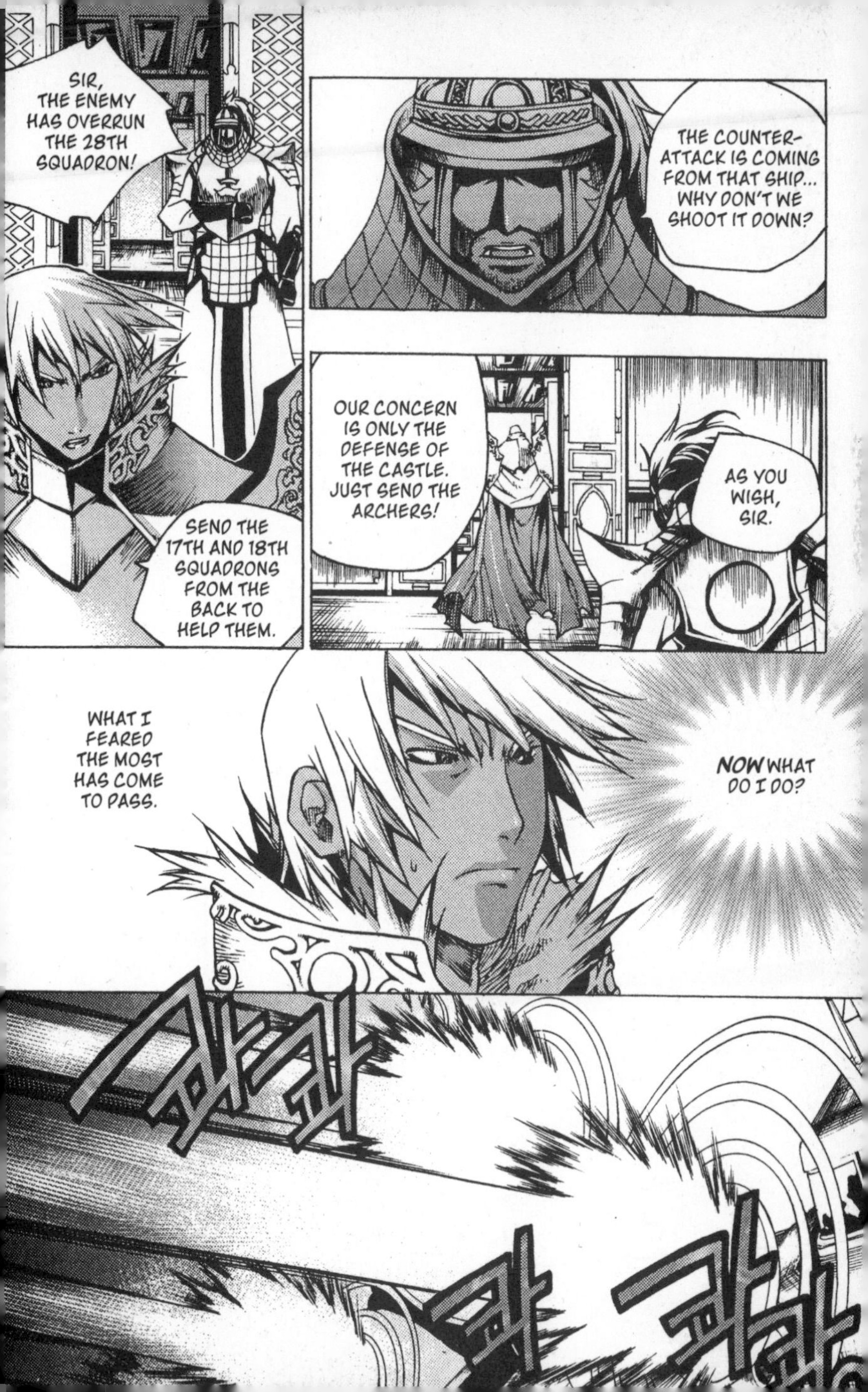
SIR, THE ENEMY HAS OVERRUN THE 28TH SQUADRON!
SEND THE 17TH AND 18TH SQUADRONS FROM THE BACK TO HELP THEM.
THE COUNTER-ATTACK IS COMING FROM THAT SHIP... WHY DON'T WE SHOOT IT DOWN?
OUR CONCERN IS ONLY THE DEFENSE OF THE CASTLE. JUST SEND THE ARCHERS!
AS YOU WISH, SIR.
WHAT I FEARED THE MOST HAS COME TO PASS.
NOW WHAT DO I DO?

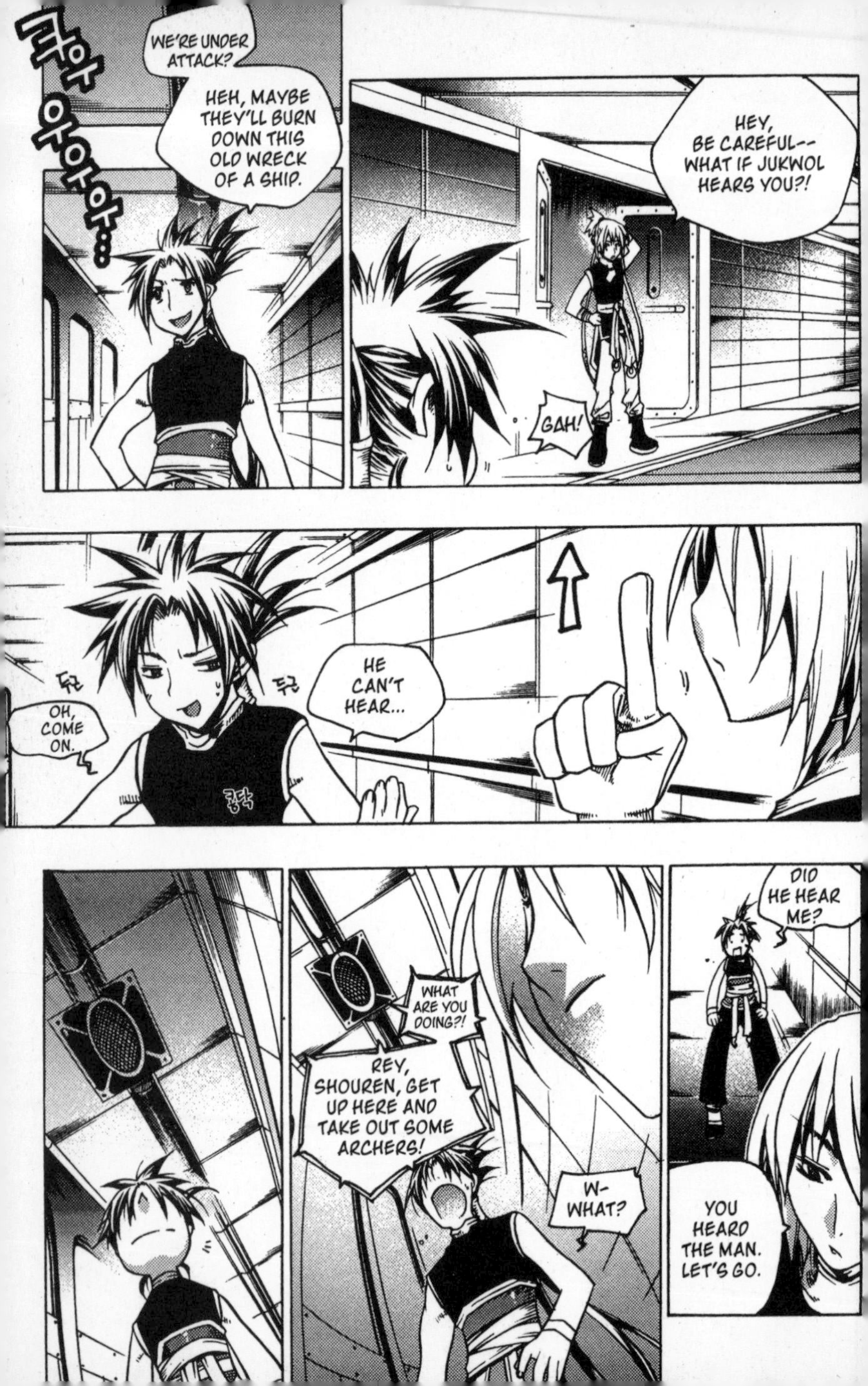
WE'RE UNDER ATTACK?
HEH, MAYBE THEY'LL BURN DOWN THIS OLD WRECK OF A SHIP.
HEY, BE CAREFUL--WHAT IF JUKWOL HEARS YOU?!
GAH!
OH, COME ON.
HE CAN'T HEAR...
WHAT ARE YOU DOING?!
REY, SHOUREN, GET UP HERE AND TAKE OUT SOME ARCHERS!
W-WHAT?
DID HE HEAR ME?
YOU HEARD THE MAN. LET'S GO.

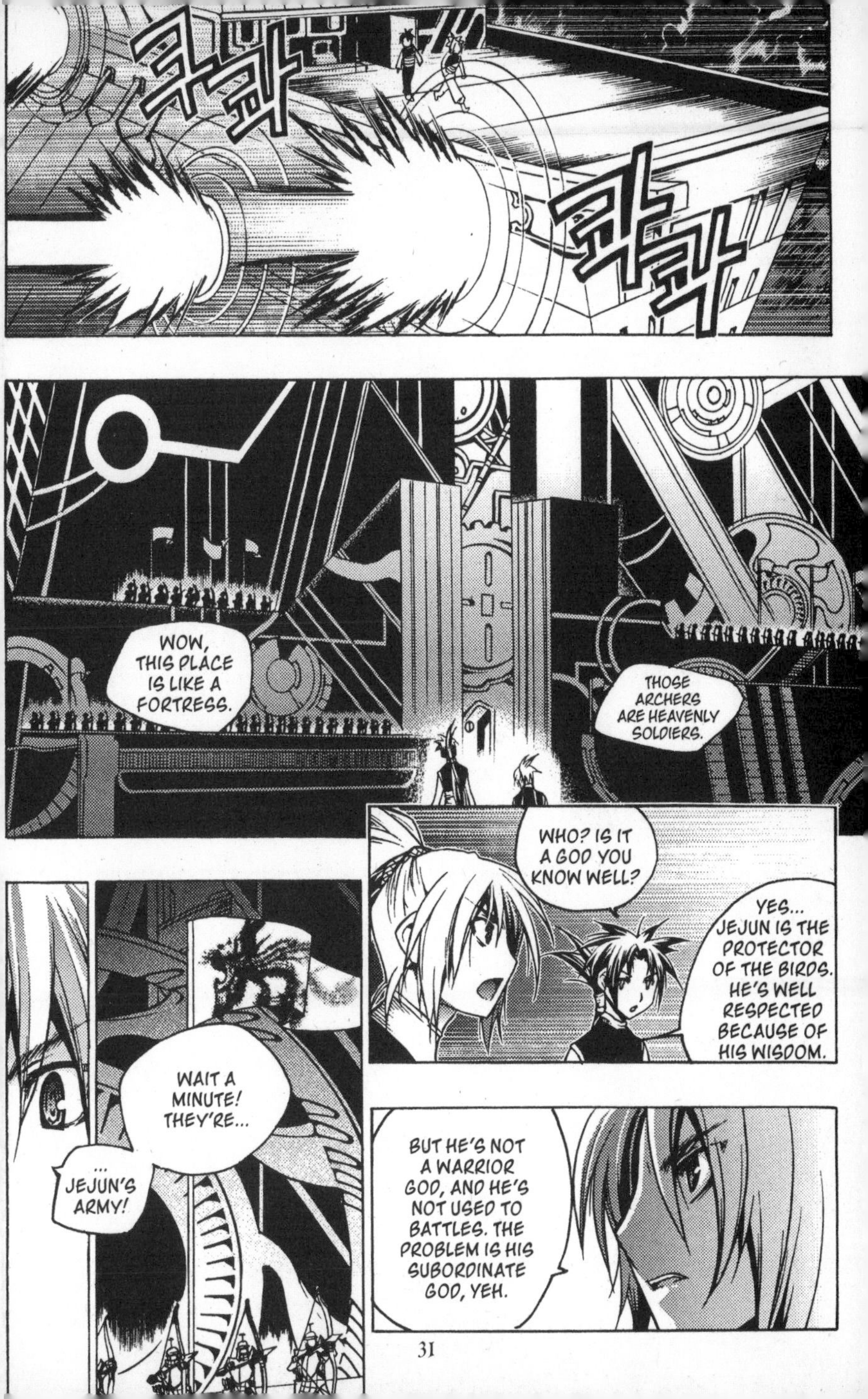
WOW, THIS PLACE IS LIKE A FORTRESS.
THOSE ARCHERS ARE HEAVENLY SOLDIERS.
WAIT A MINUTE! THEY'RE...
... JEJUN'S ARMY!
WHO? IS IT A GOD YOU KNOW WELL?
YES... JEJUN IS THE PROTECTOR OF THE BIRDS. HE'S WELL RESPECTED BECAUSE OF HIS WISDOM.
BUT HE'S NOT A WARRIOR GOD, AND HE'S NOT USED TO BATTLES. THE PROBLEM IS HIS SUBORDINATE GOD, YEH.

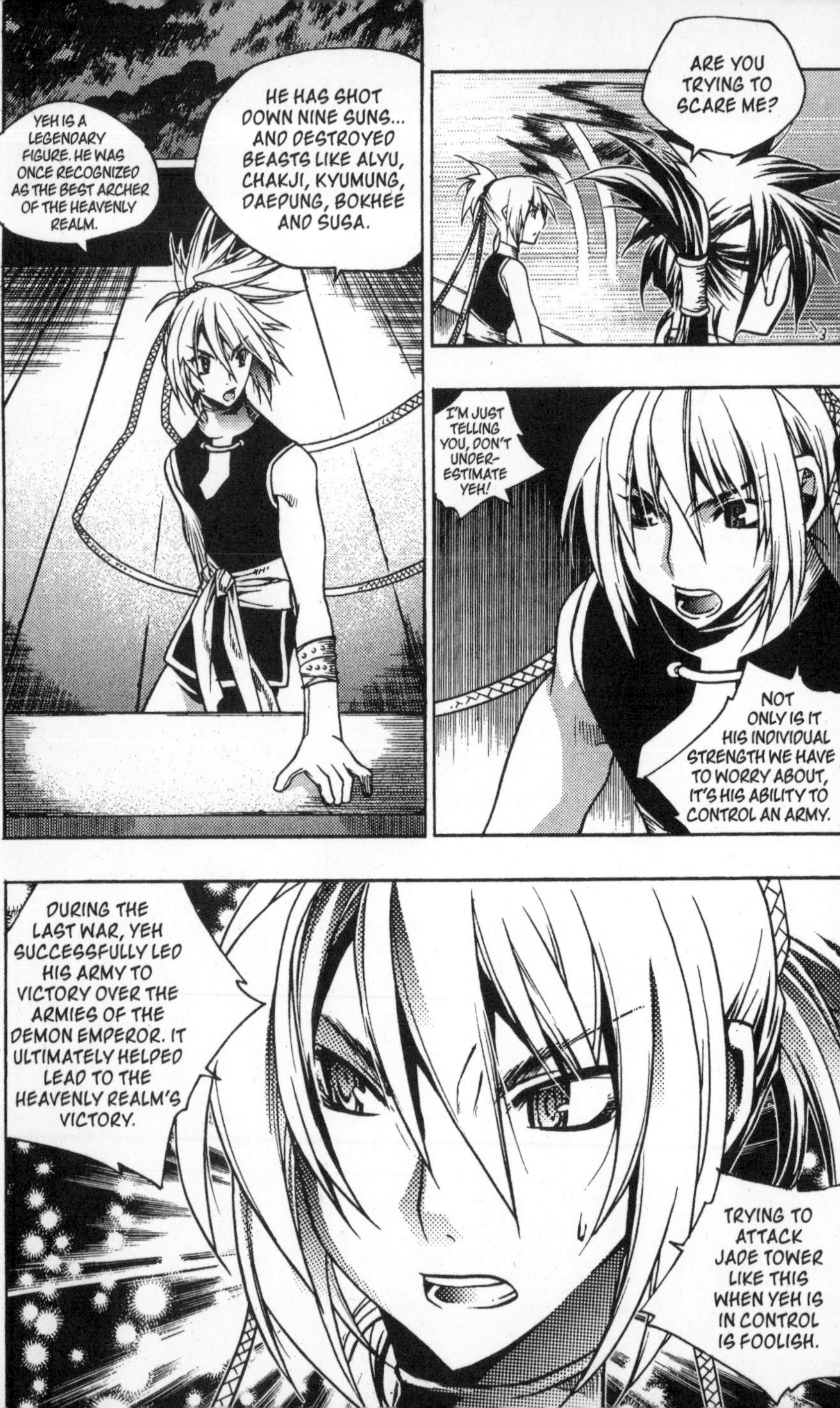
YEH IS A LEGENDARY FIGURE. HE WAS ONCE RECOGNIZED AS THE BEST ARCHER OF THE HEAVENLY REALM.
HE HAS SHOT DOWN NINE SUNS... AND DESTROYED BEASTS LIKE ALYU, CHAKJI, KYUMUNG, DAEPUNG, BOKHEE AND SUSA.
ARE YOU TRYING TO SCARE ME?
I'M JUST TELLING YOU, DON'T UNDER-ESTIMATE YEH!
NOT ONLY IS IT HIS INDIVIDUAL STRENGTH WE HAVE TO WORRY ABOUT, IT'S HIS ABILITY TO CONTROL AN ARMY.
DURING THE LAST WAR, YEH SUCCESSFULLY LED HIS ARMY TO VICTORY OVER THE ARMIES OF THE DEMON EMPEROR. IT ULTIMATELY HELPED LEAD TO THE HEAVENLY REALM'S VICTORY.
TRYING TO ATTACK JADE TOWER LIKE THIS WHEN YEH IS IN CONTROL IS FOOLISH.

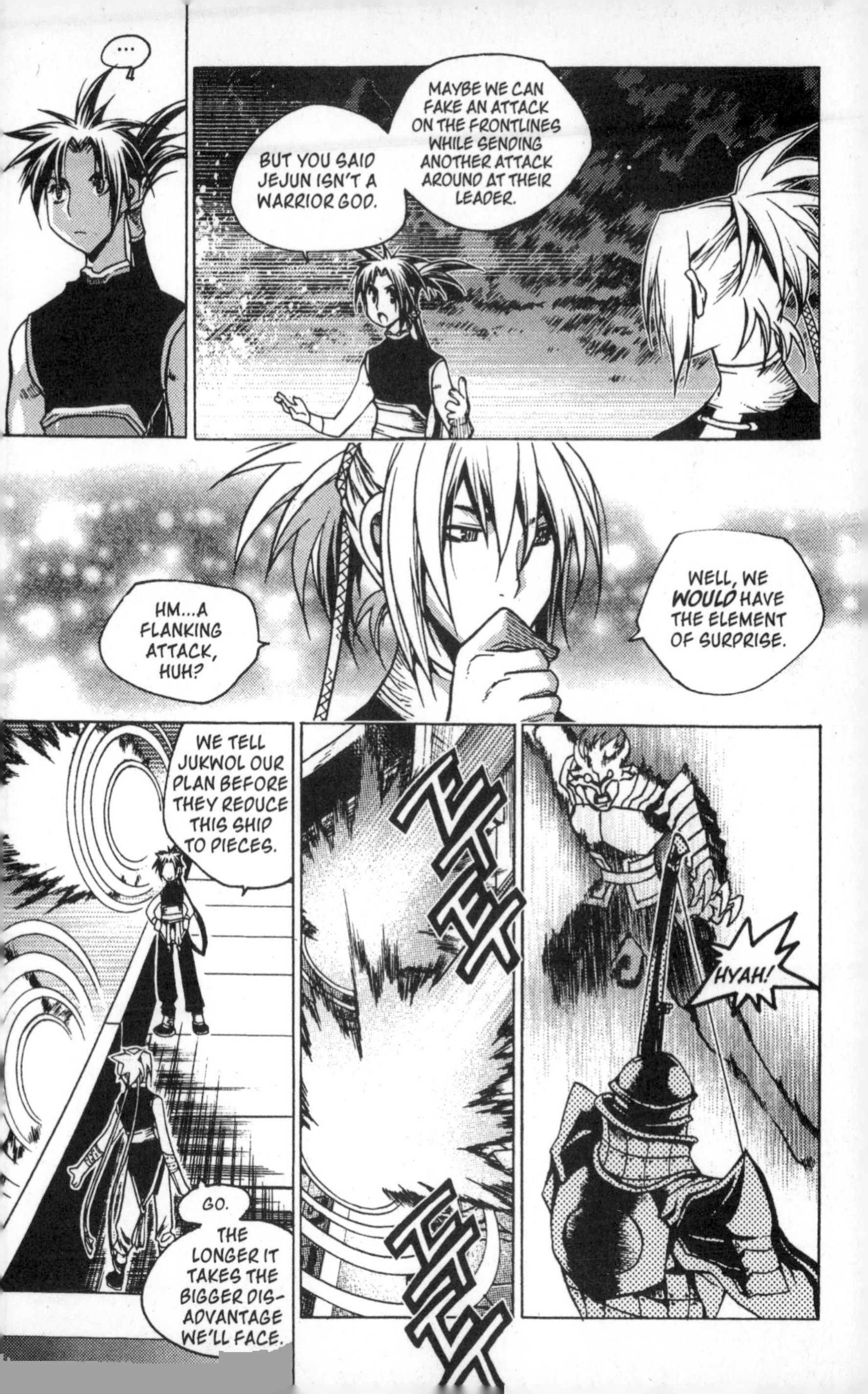
...
BUT YOU SAID JEJUN ISN'T A WARRIOR GOD.
MAYBE WE CAN FAKE AN ATTACK ON THE FRONTLINES WHILE SENDING ANOTHER ATTACK AROUND AT THEIR LEADER.
HM...A FLANKING ATTACK, HUH?
WELL, WE WOULD HAVE THE ELEMENT OF SURPRISE.
WE TELL JUKWOL OUR PLAN BEFORE THEY REDUCE THIS SHIP TO PIECES.
GO.
THE LONGER IT TAKES THE BIGGER DIS-ADVANTAGE WE'LL FACE.
HYAH!

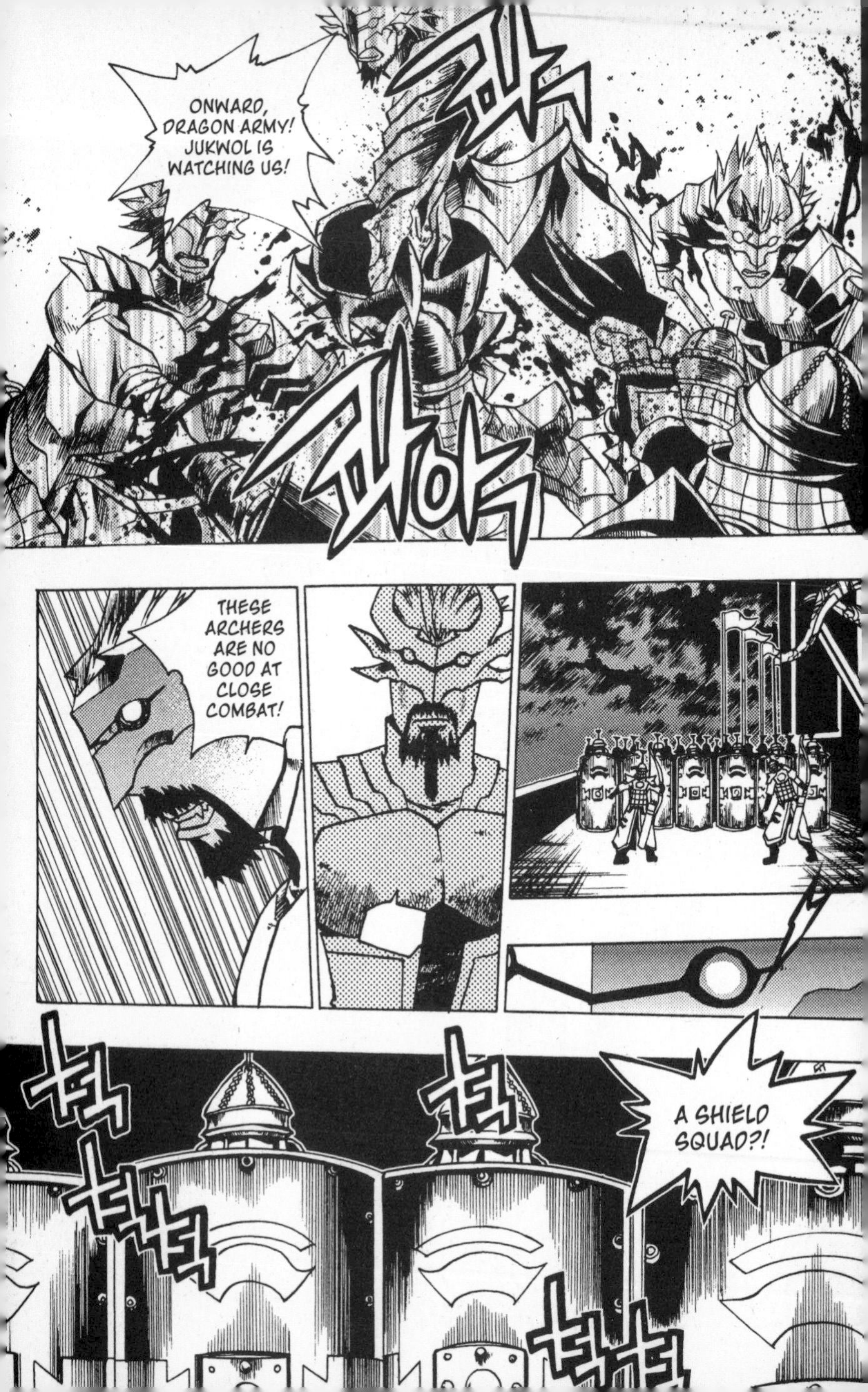
ONWARD, DRAGON ARMY! JUKWOL IS WATCHING US!
THESE ARCHERS ARE NO GOOD AT CLOSE COMBAT!
A SHIELD SQUAD?!

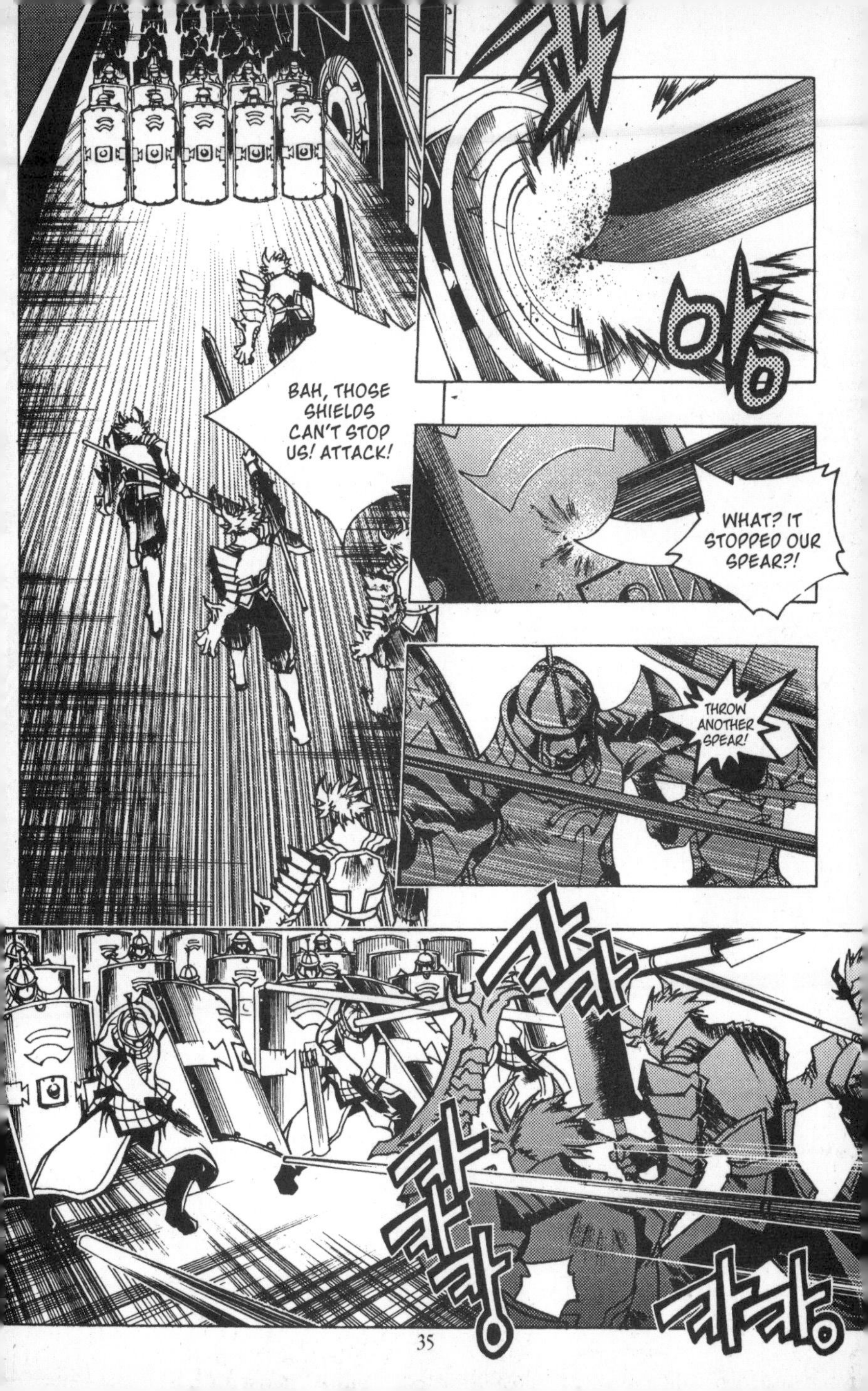
BAH, THOSE SHIELDS CAN'T STOP US! ATTACK!
WHAT? IT STOPPED OUR SPEAR?!
THROW ANOTHER SPEAR!

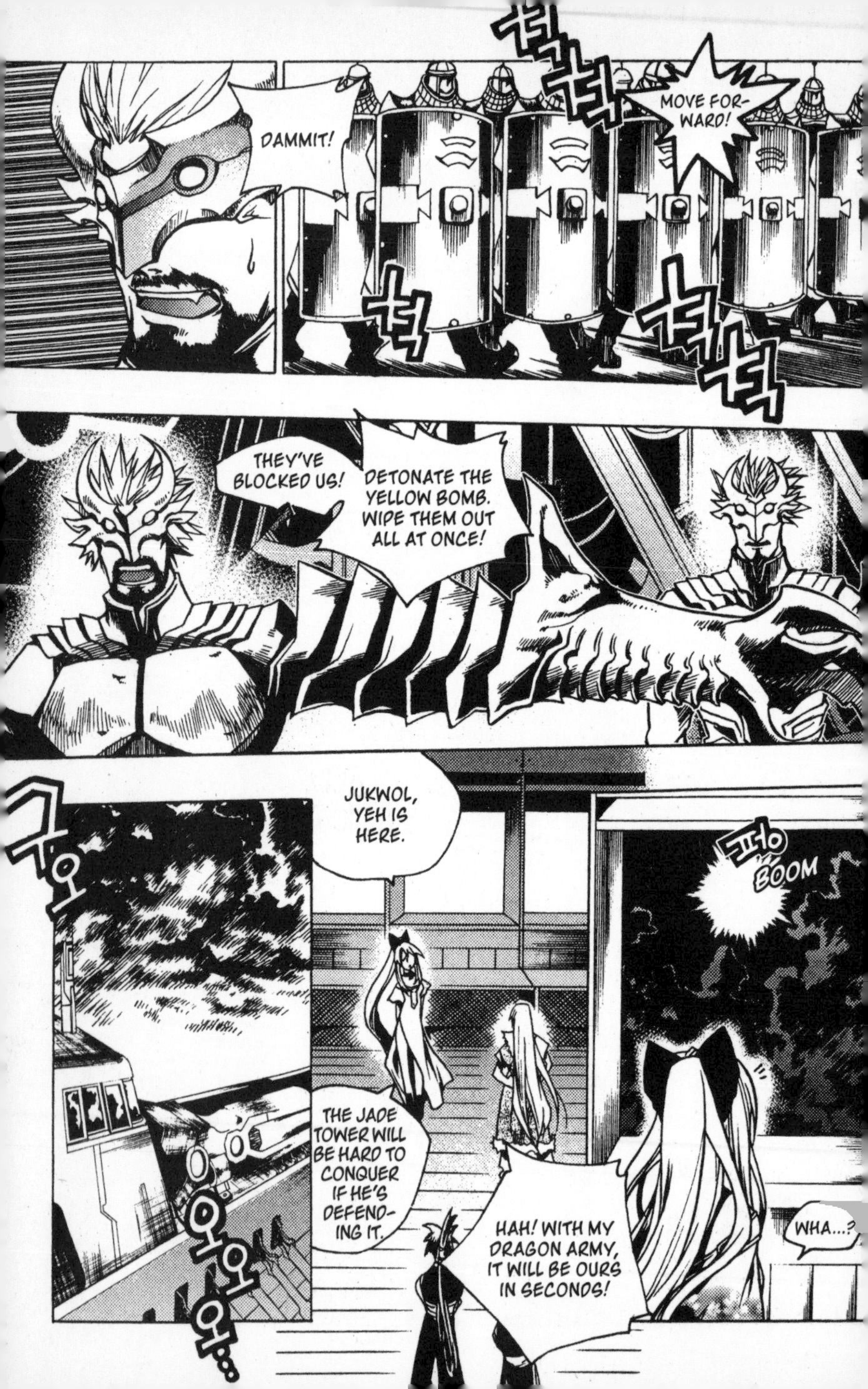
DAMMIT!
MOVE FOR-WARD!
THEY'VE BLOCKED US!
DETONATE THE YELLOW BOMB. WIPE THEM OUT ALL AT ONCE!
JUKWOL, YEH IS HERE.
BOOM
THE JADE TOWER WILL BE HARD TO CONQUER IF HE'S DEFEND-ING IT.
HAH! WITH MY DRAGON ARMY, IT WILL BE OURS IN SECONDS!
WHA...?

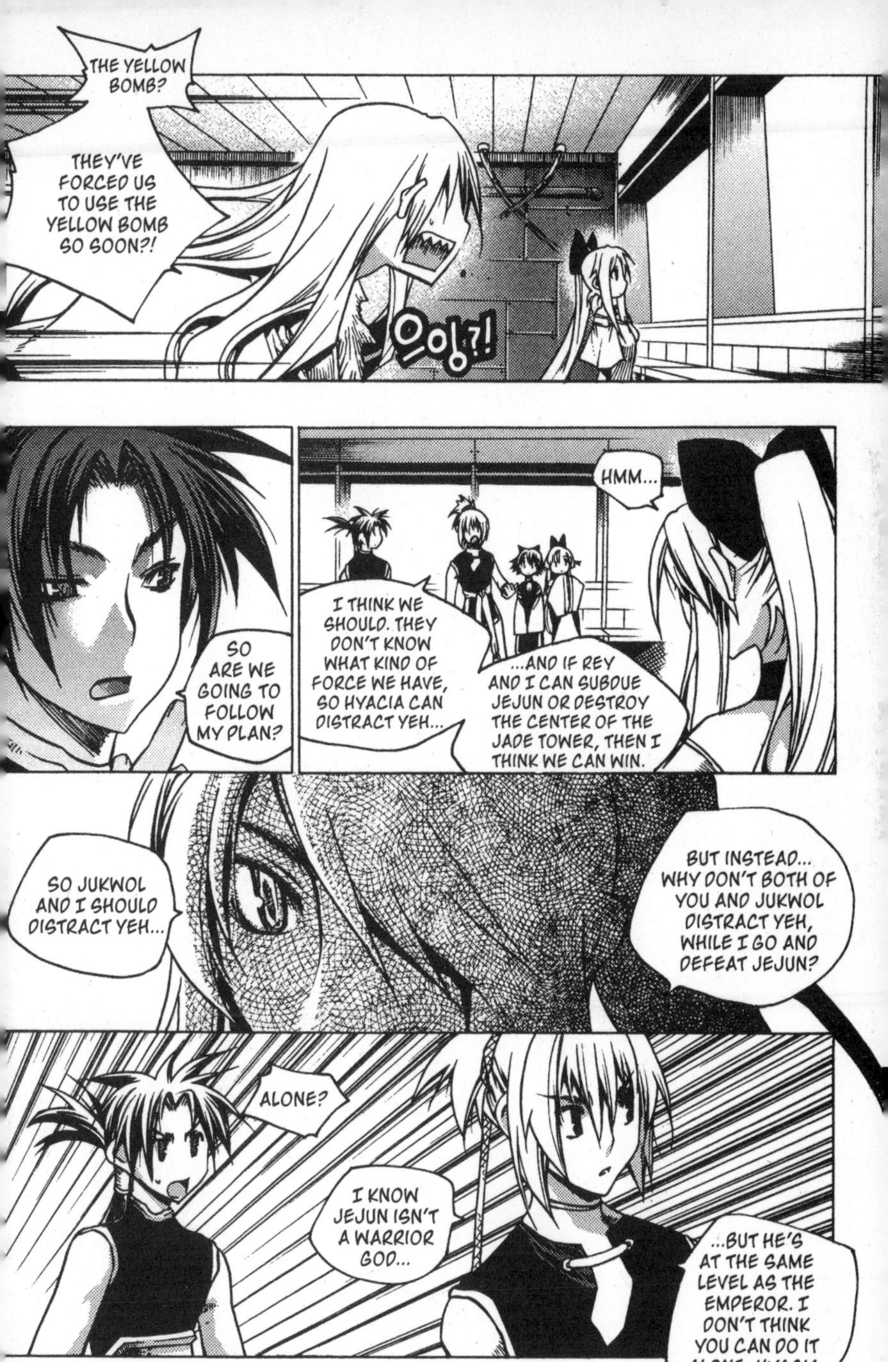
THE YELLOW BOMB?
THEY'VE FORCED US TO USE THE YELLOW BOMB SO SOON?!
으잉?!
SO ARE WE GOING TO FOLLOW MY PLAN?
HMM...
I THINK WE SHOULD. THEY DON'T KNOW WHAT KIND OF FORCE WE HAVE, SO HYACIA CAN DISTRACT YEH...
...AND IF REY AND I CAN SUBDUE JEJUN OR DESTROY THE CENTER OF THE JADE TOWER, THEN I THINK WE CAN WIN.
SO JUKWOL AND I SHOULD DISTRACT YEH...
BUT INSTEAD... WHY DON'T BOTH OF YOU AND JUKWOL DISTRACT YEH, WHILE I GO AND DEFEAT JEJUN?
ALONE?
I KNOW JEJUN ISN'T A WARRIOR GOD...
...BUT HE'S AT THE SAME LEVEL AS THE EMPEROR. I DON'T THINK YOU CAN DO IT ALONE, HYACIA.

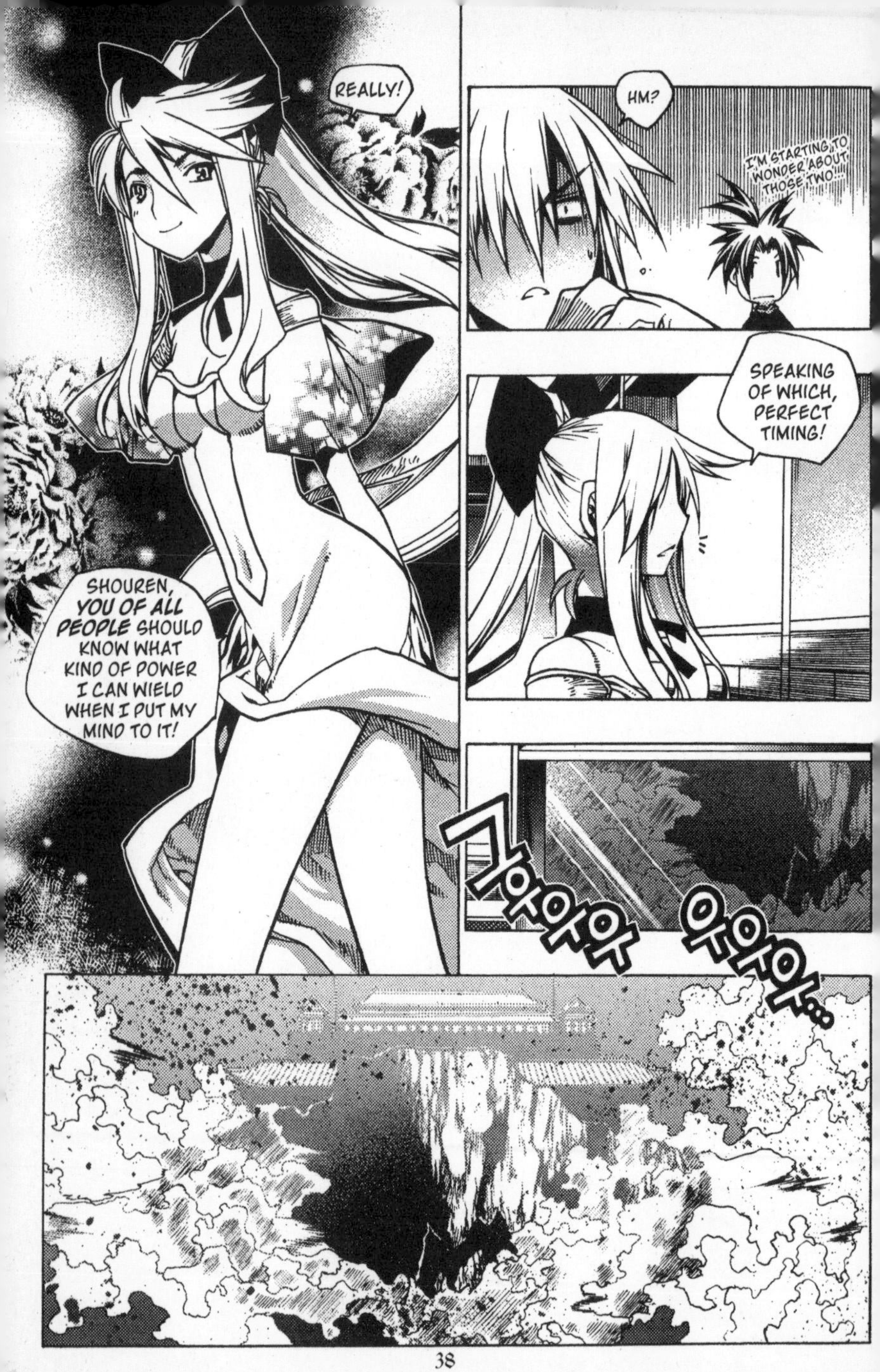
REALLY!
SHOUREN, **YOU OF ALL PEOPLE** SHOULD KNOW WHAT KIND OF POWER I CAN WIELD WHEN I PUT MY MIND TO IT!
HM?
I'M STARTING TO WONDER ABOUT THOSE TWO!!
SPEAKING OF WHICH, PERFECT TIMING!
ZOOOO OOOO...

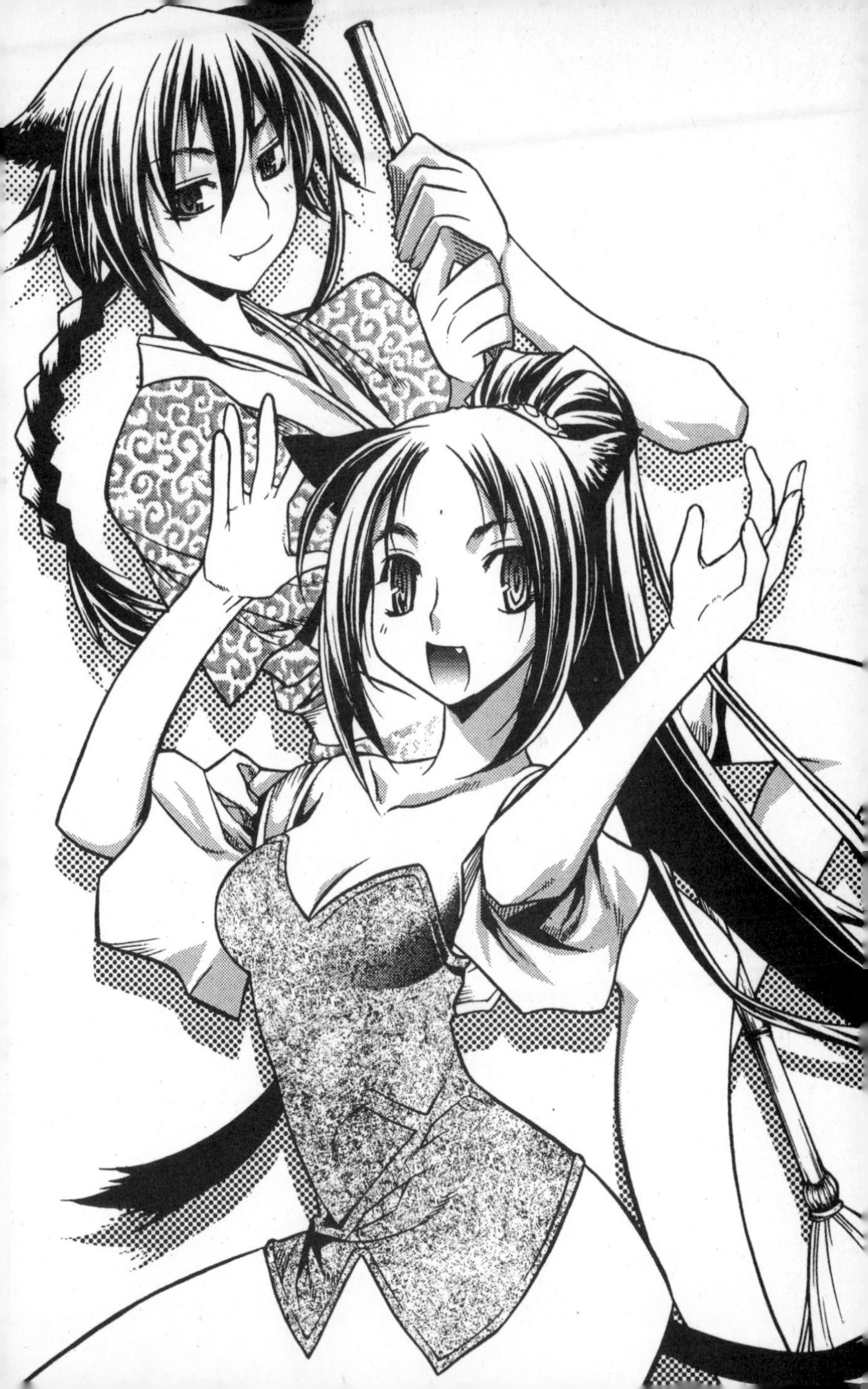

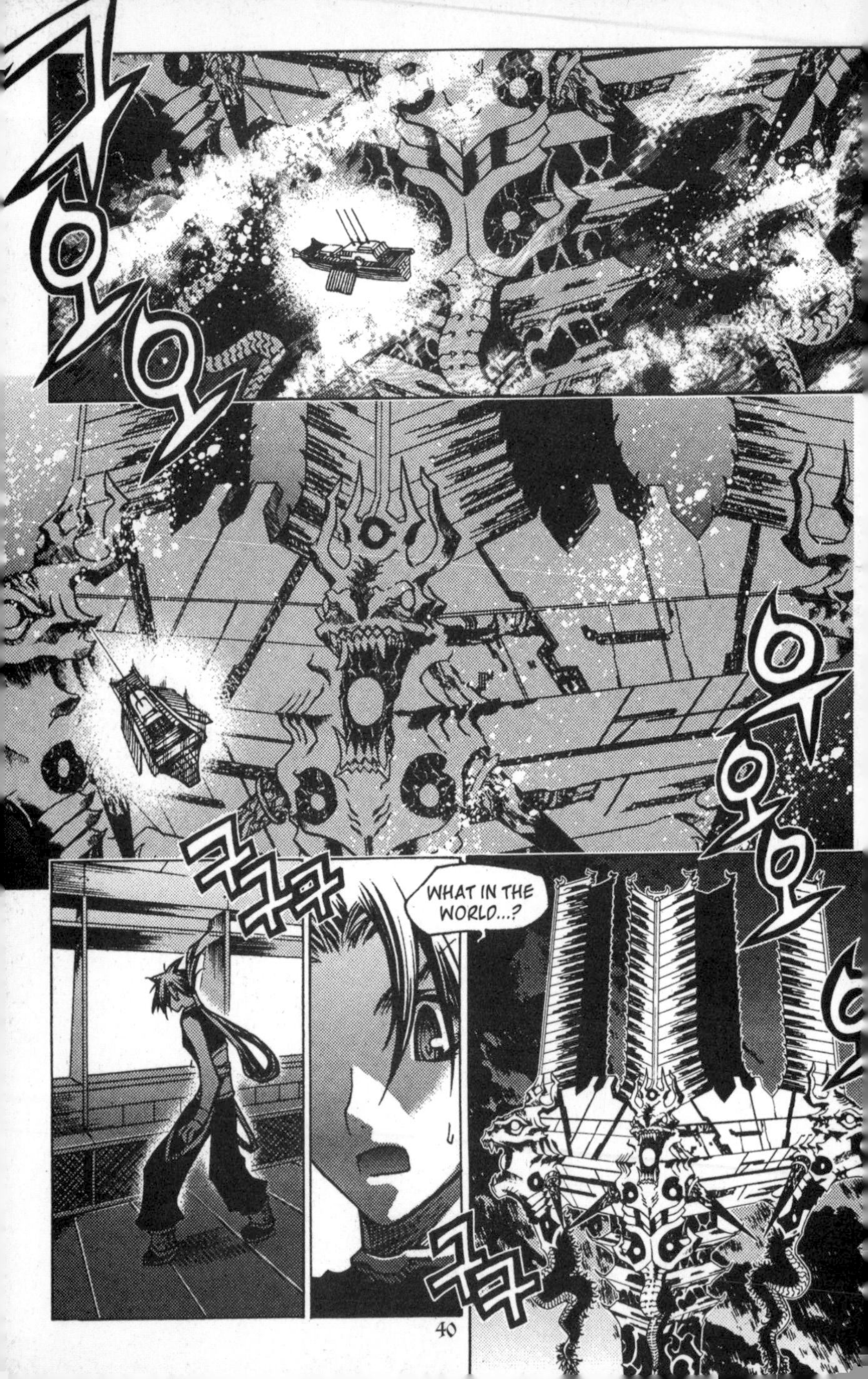
WHAT IN THE WORLD...?

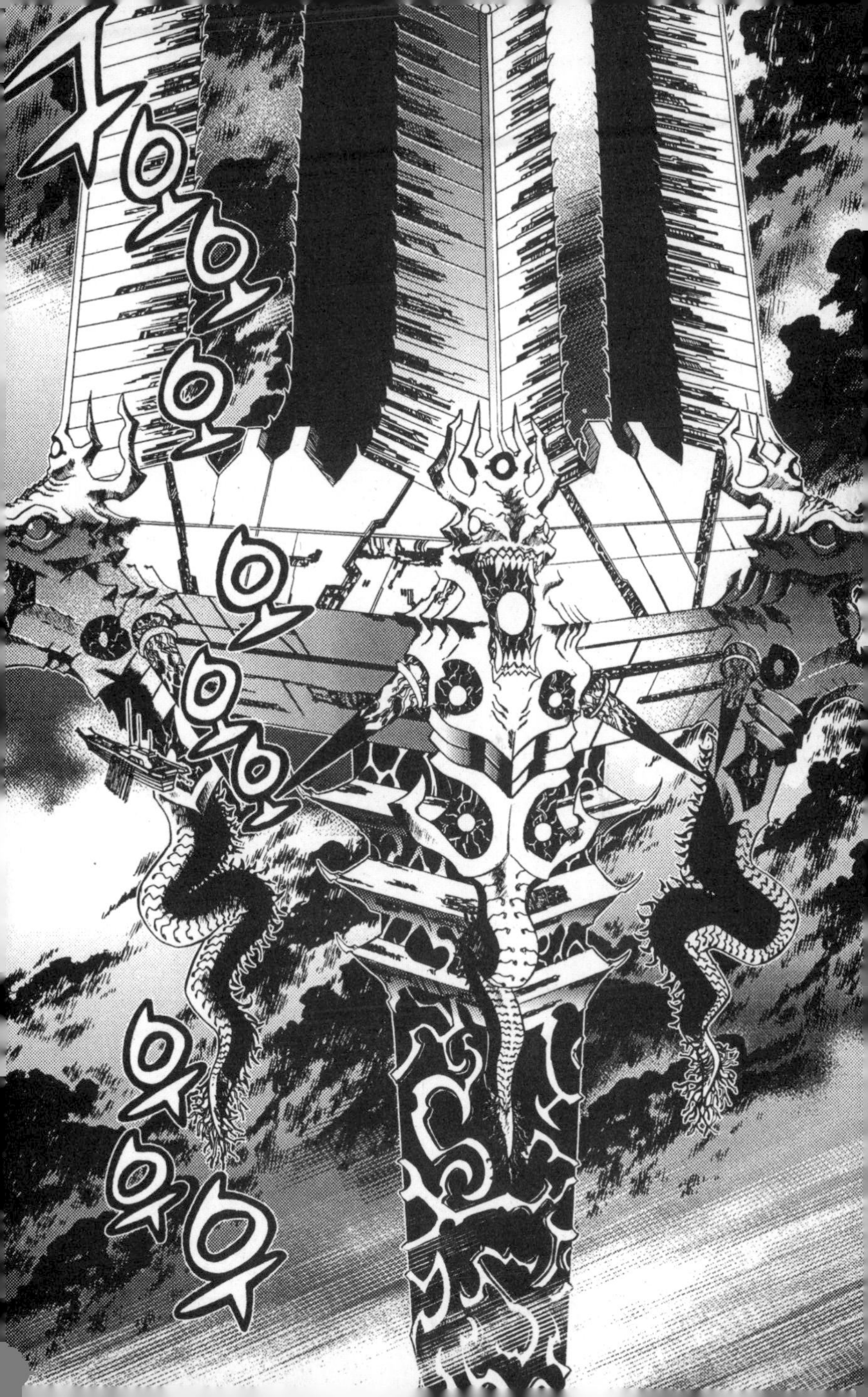
크오오오오오오오오오

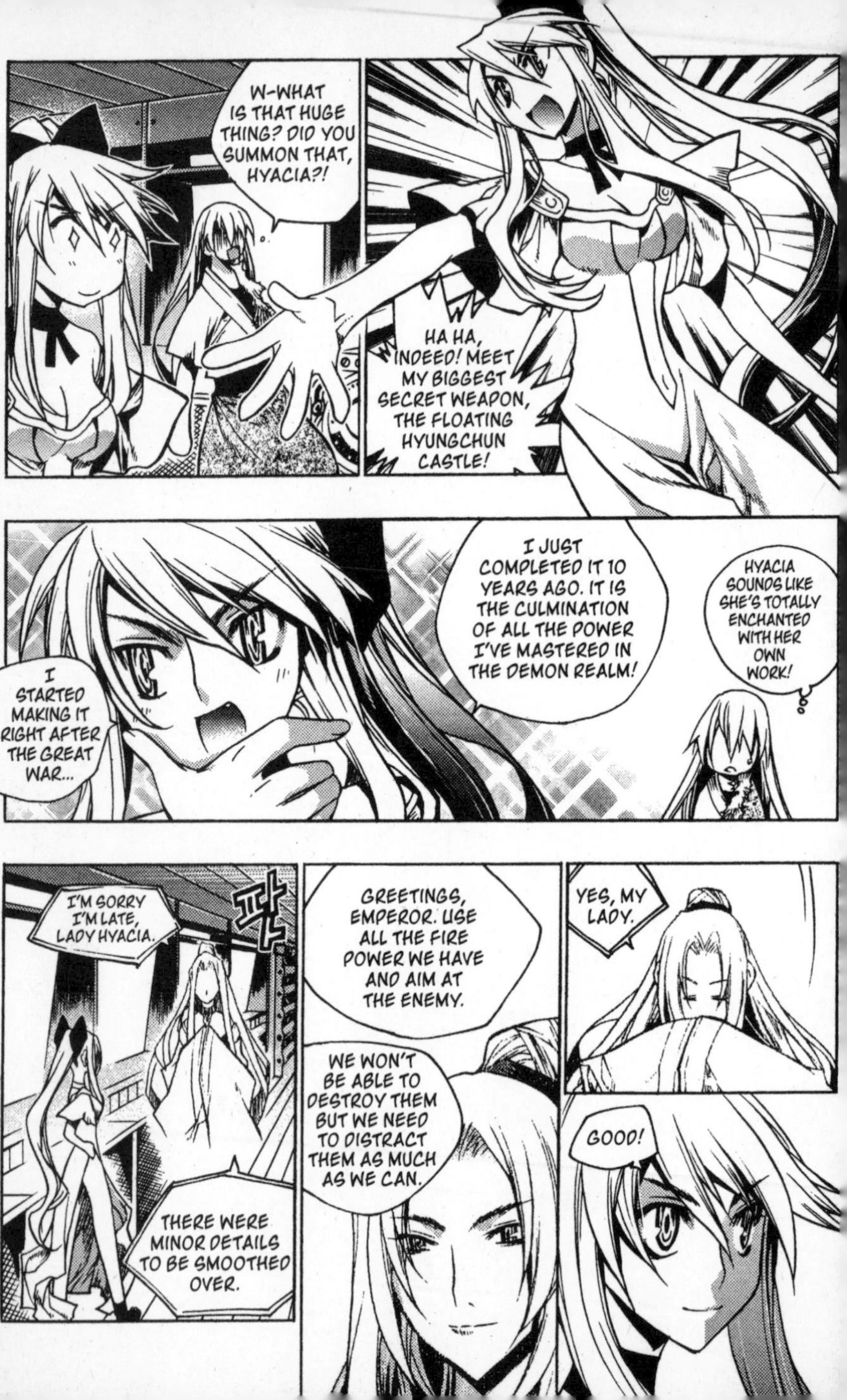
W-WHAT IS THAT HUGE THING? DID YOU SUMMON THAT, HYACIA?!
HA HA, INDEED! MEET MY BIGGEST SECRET WEAPON, THE FLOATING HYUNGCHUN CASTLE!
I STARTED MAKING IT RIGHT AFTER THE GREAT WAR...
I JUST COMPLETED IT 10 YEARS AGO. IT IS THE CULMINATION OF ALL THE POWER I'VE MASTERED IN THE DEMON REALM!
HYACIA SOUNDS LIKE SHE'S TOTALLY ENCHANTED WITH HER OWN WORK!
I'M SORRY I'M LATE, LADY HYACIA.
THERE WERE MINOR DETAILS TO BE SMOOTHED OVER.
GREETINGS, EMPEROR. USE ALL THE FIRE POWER WE HAVE AND AIM AT THE ENEMY.
WE WON'T BE ABLE TO DESTROY THEM BUT WE NEED TO DISTRACT THEM AS MUCH AS WE CAN.
YES, MY LADY.
GOOD!

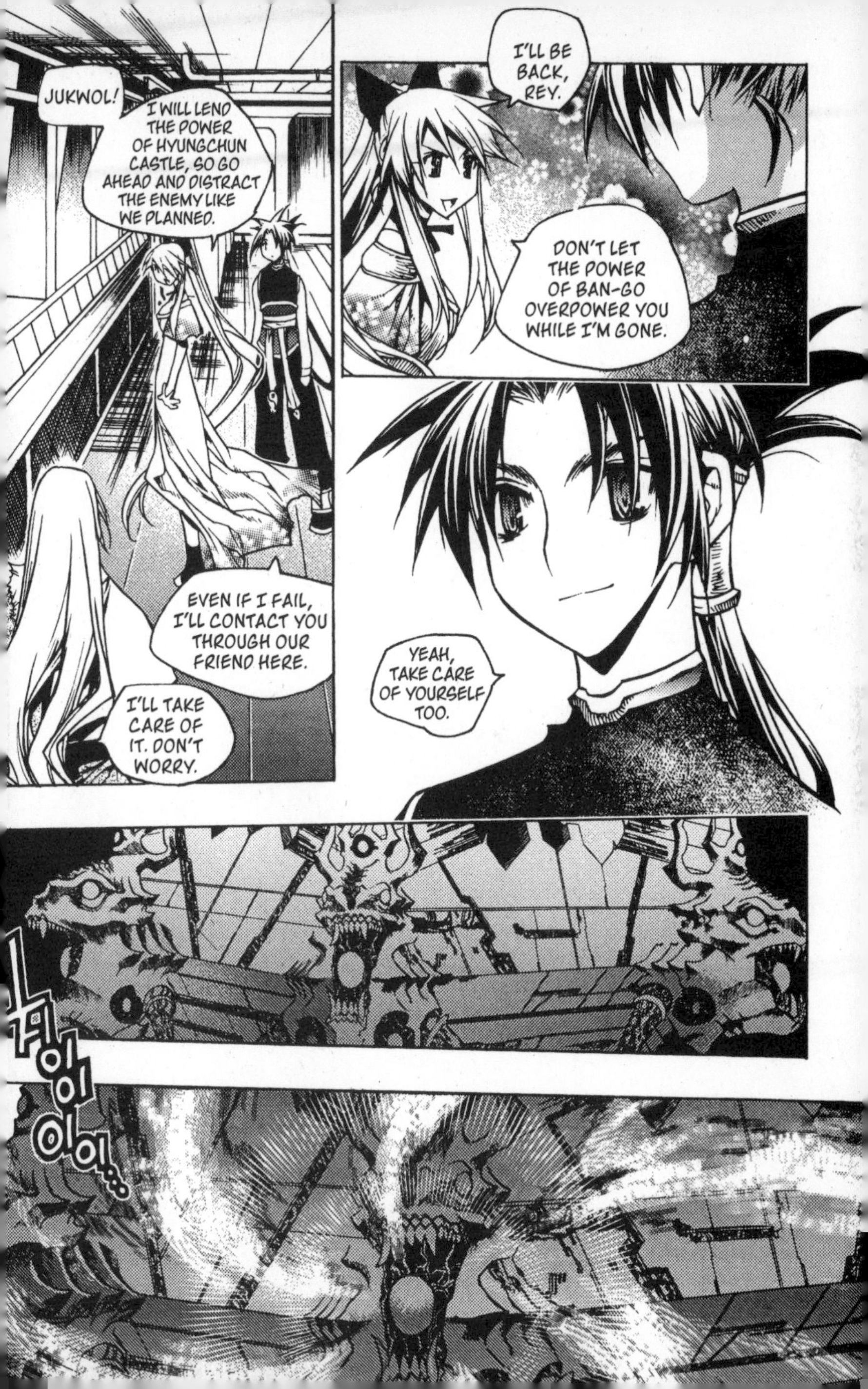
JUKWOL!
I WILL LEND THE POWER OF HYUNGCHUN CASTLE, SO GO AHEAD AND DISTRACT THE ENEMY LIKE WE PLANNED.
EVEN IF I FAIL, I'LL CONTACT YOU THROUGH OUR FRIEND HERE.
I'LL TAKE CARE OF IT. DON'T WORRY.
I'LL BE BACK, REY.
DON'T LET THE POWER OF BAN-GO OVERPOWER YOU WHILE I'M GONE.
YEAH, TAKE CARE OF YOURSELF TOO.

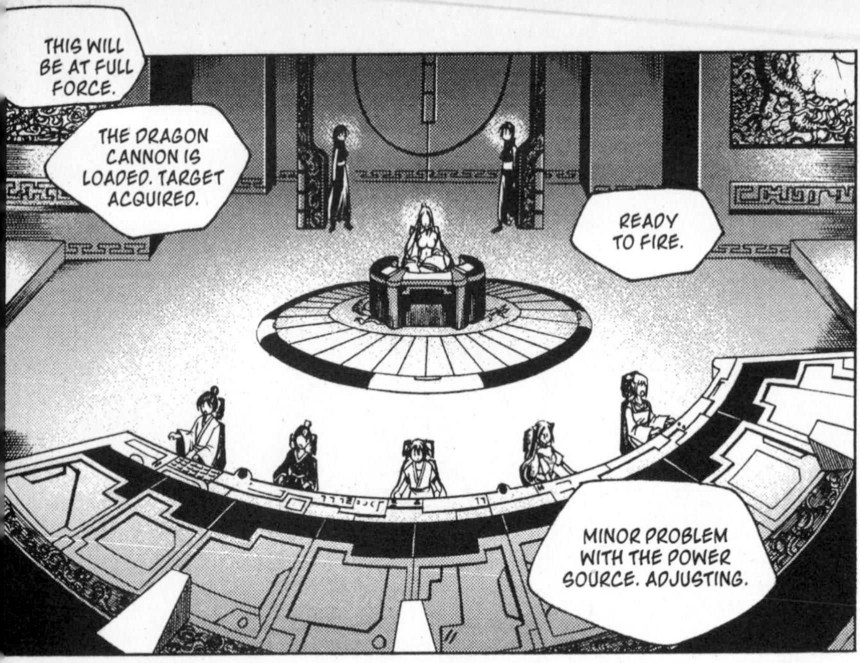
THIS WILL BE AT FULL FORCE.
READY TO FIRE.
THE DRAGON CANNON IS LOADED. TARGET ACQUIRED.
MINOR PROBLEM WITH THE POWER SOURCE. ADJUSTING.
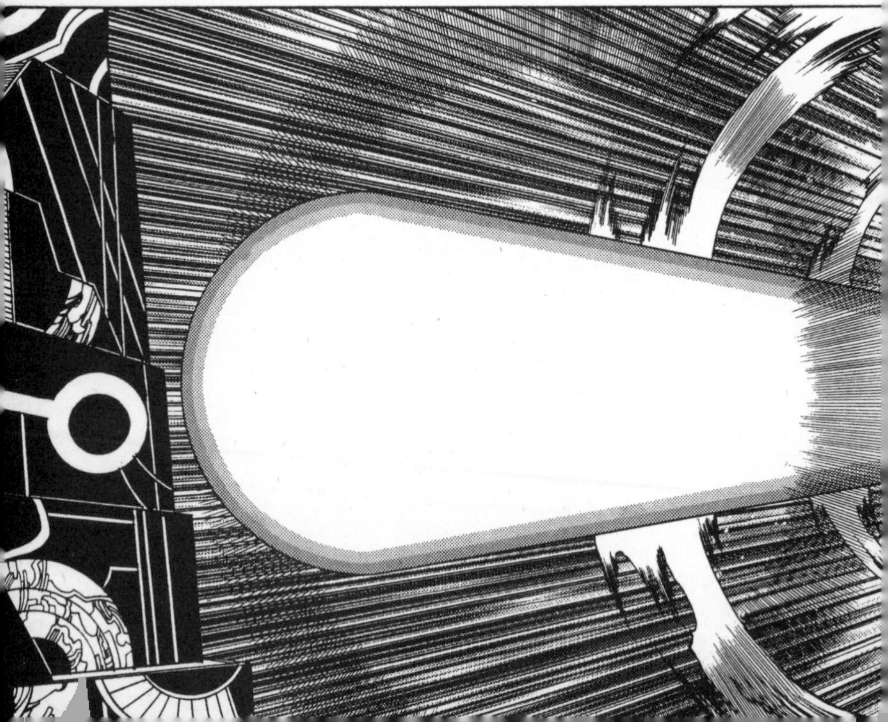

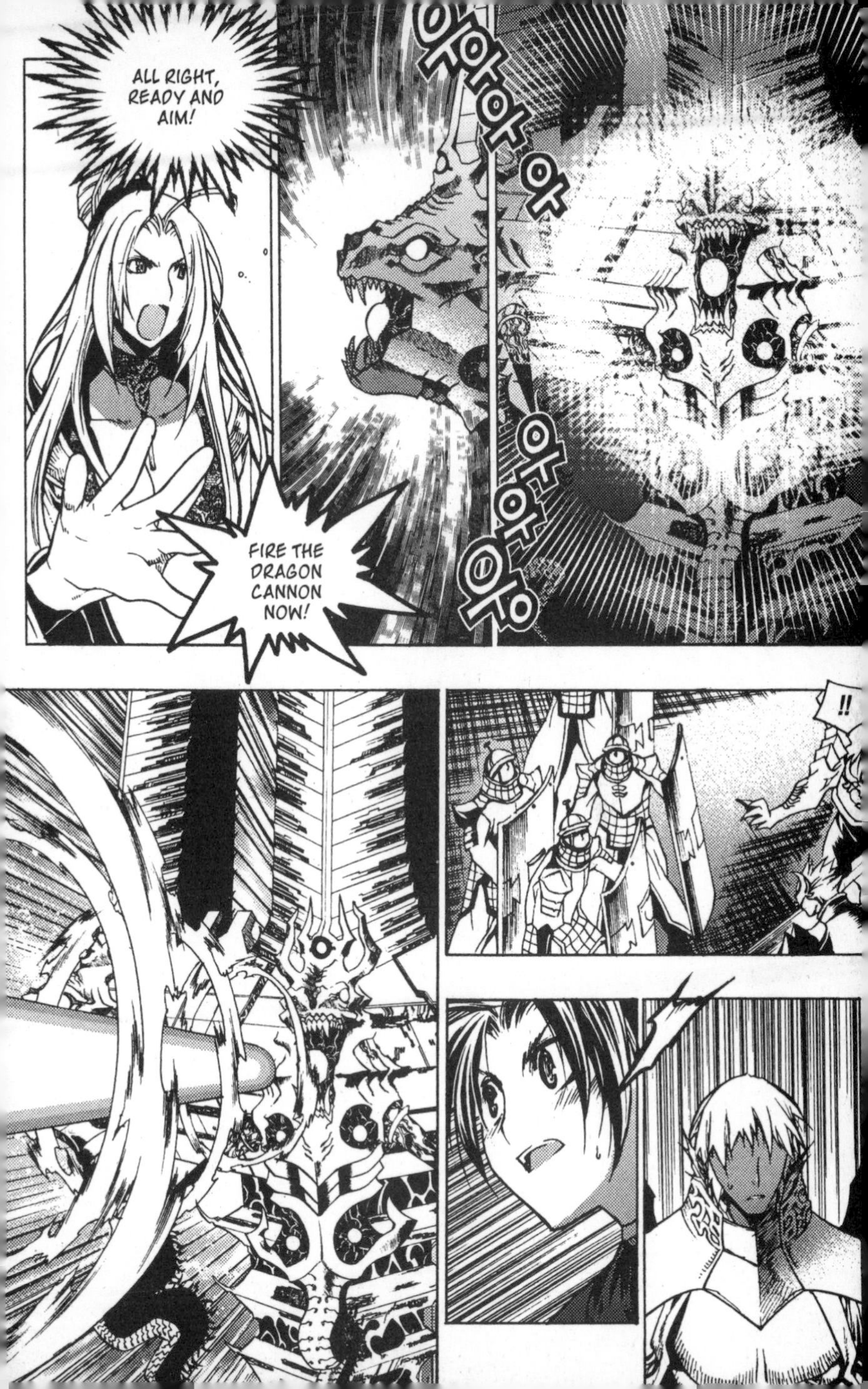
ALL RIGHT, READY AND AIM!
FIRE THE DRAGON CANNON NOW!
!!

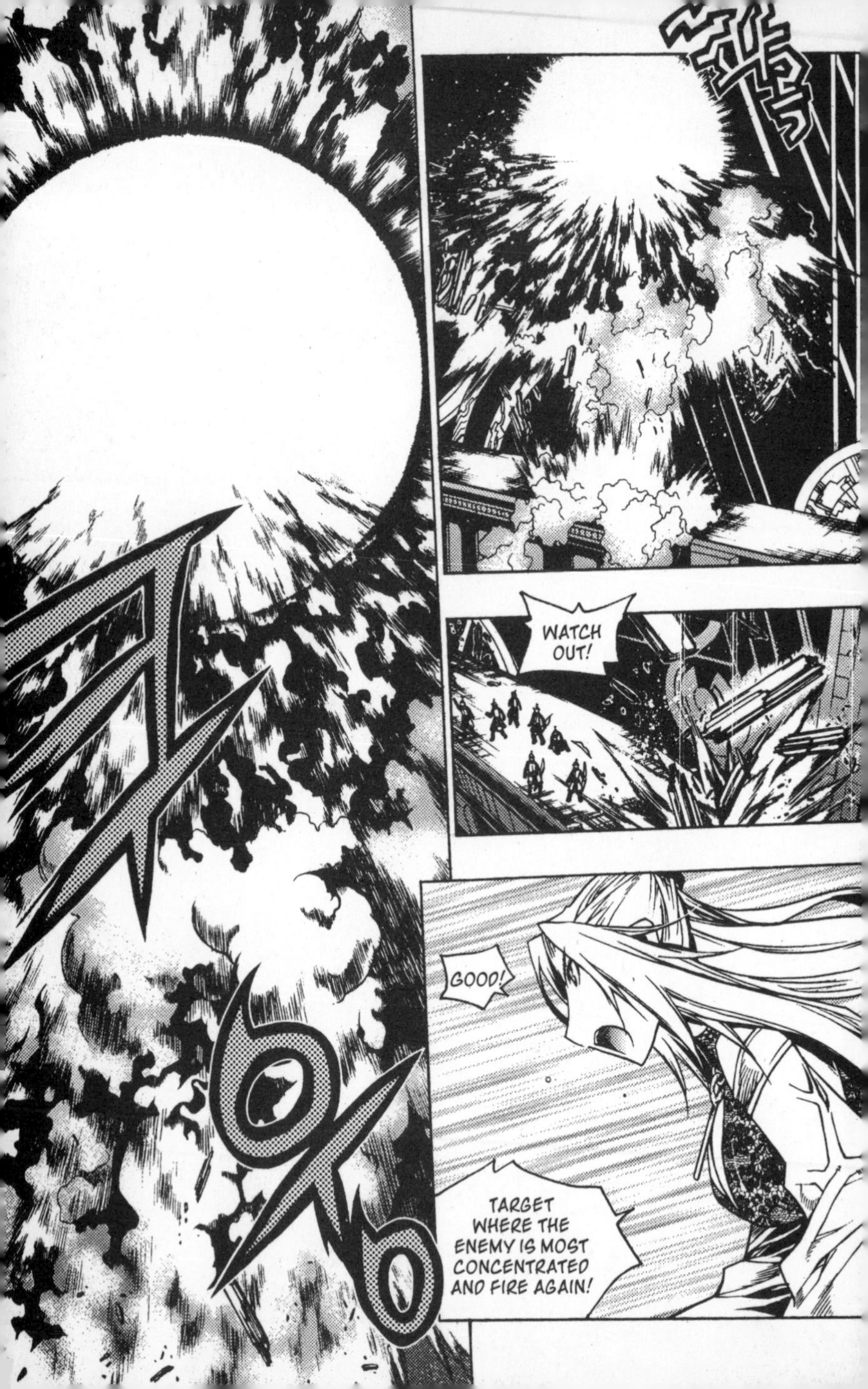
WATCH OUT!
GOOD!
TARGET WHERE THE ENEMY IS MOST CONCENTRATED AND FIRE AGAIN!

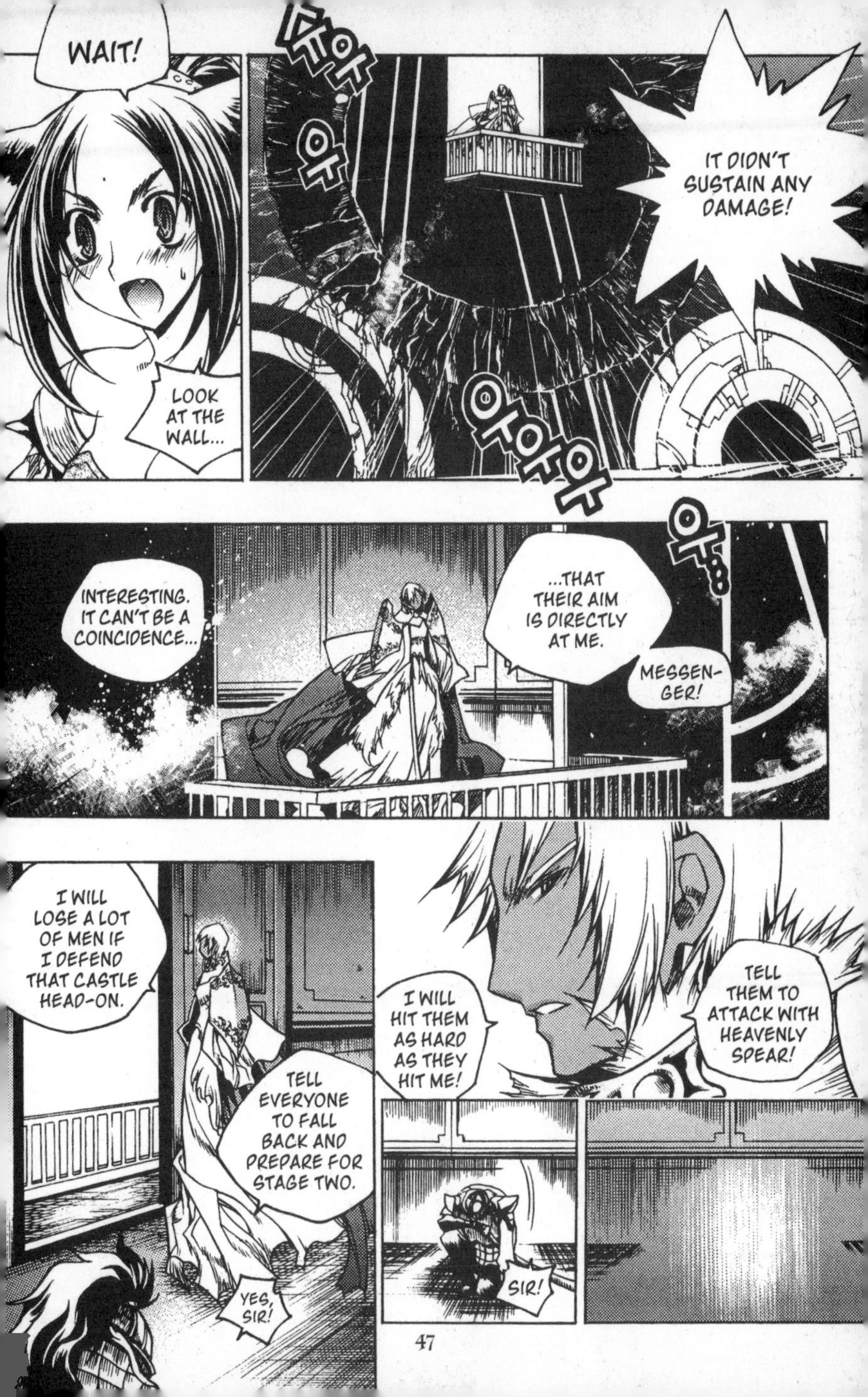
WAIT!
LOOK AT THE WALL...
IT DIDN'T SUSTAIN ANY DAMAGE!
INTERESTING. IT CAN'T BE A COINCIDENCE...
...THAT THEIR AIM IS DIRECTLY AT ME.
MESSENGER!
I WILL LOSE A LOT OF MEN IF I DEFEND THAT CASTLE HEAD-ON.
TELL EVERYONE TO FALL BACK AND PREPARE FOR STAGE TWO.
YES, SIR!
I WILL HIT THEM AS HARD AS THEY HIT ME!
TELL THEM TO ATTACK WITH HEAVENLY SPEAR!
SIR!

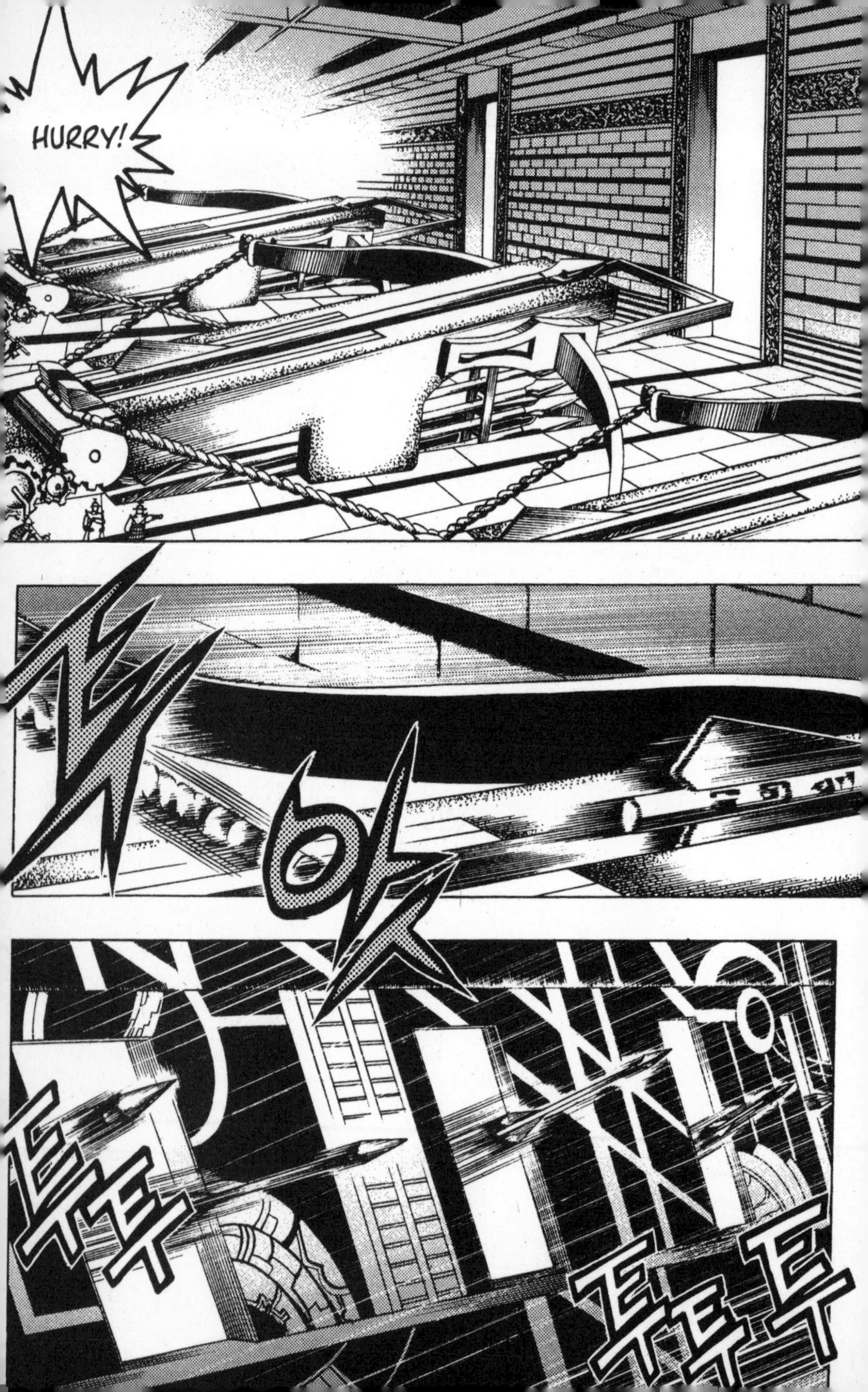
HURRY!

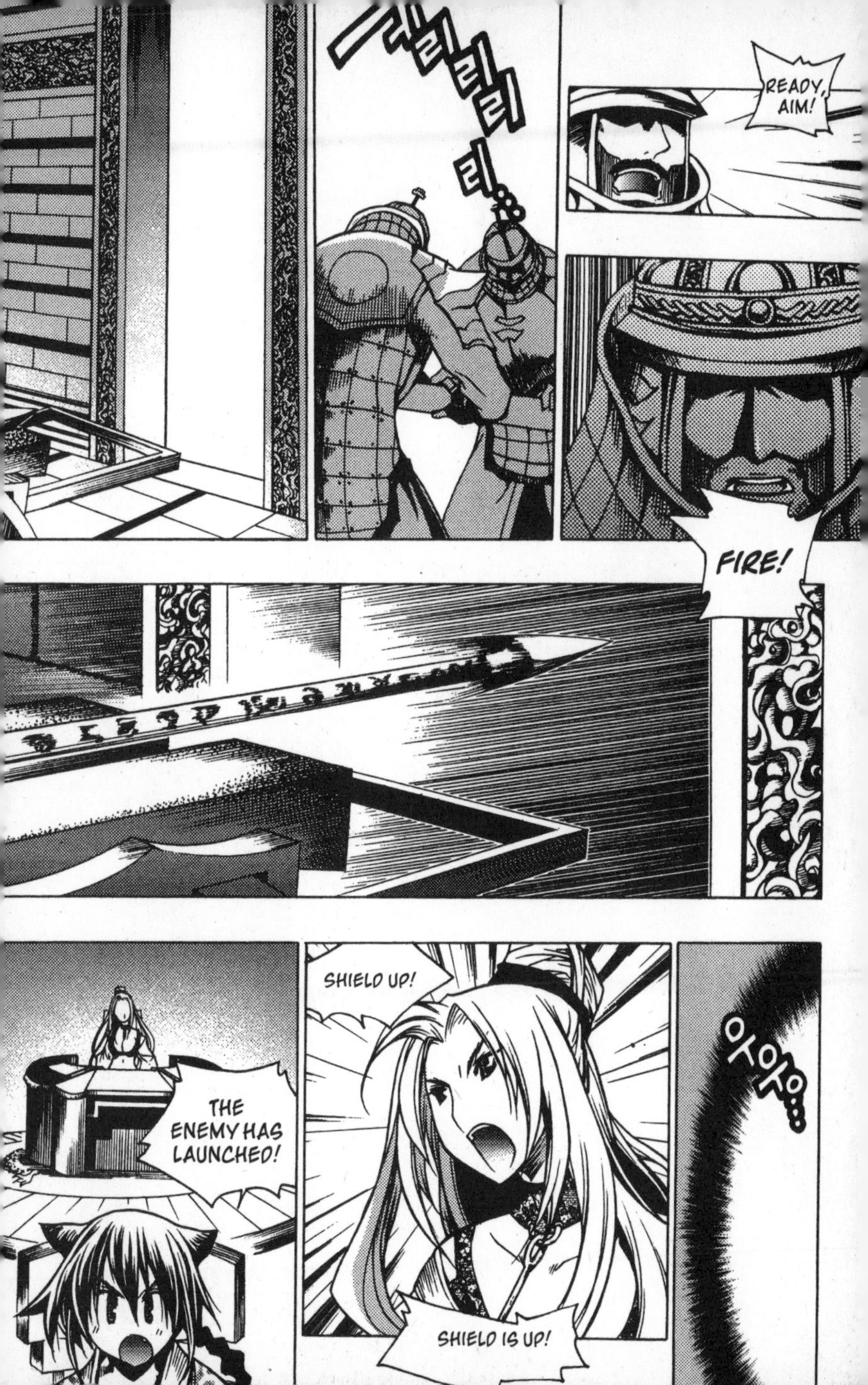
READY, AIM!
FIRE!
THE ENEMY HAS LAUNCHED!
SHIELD UP!
SHIELD IS UP!

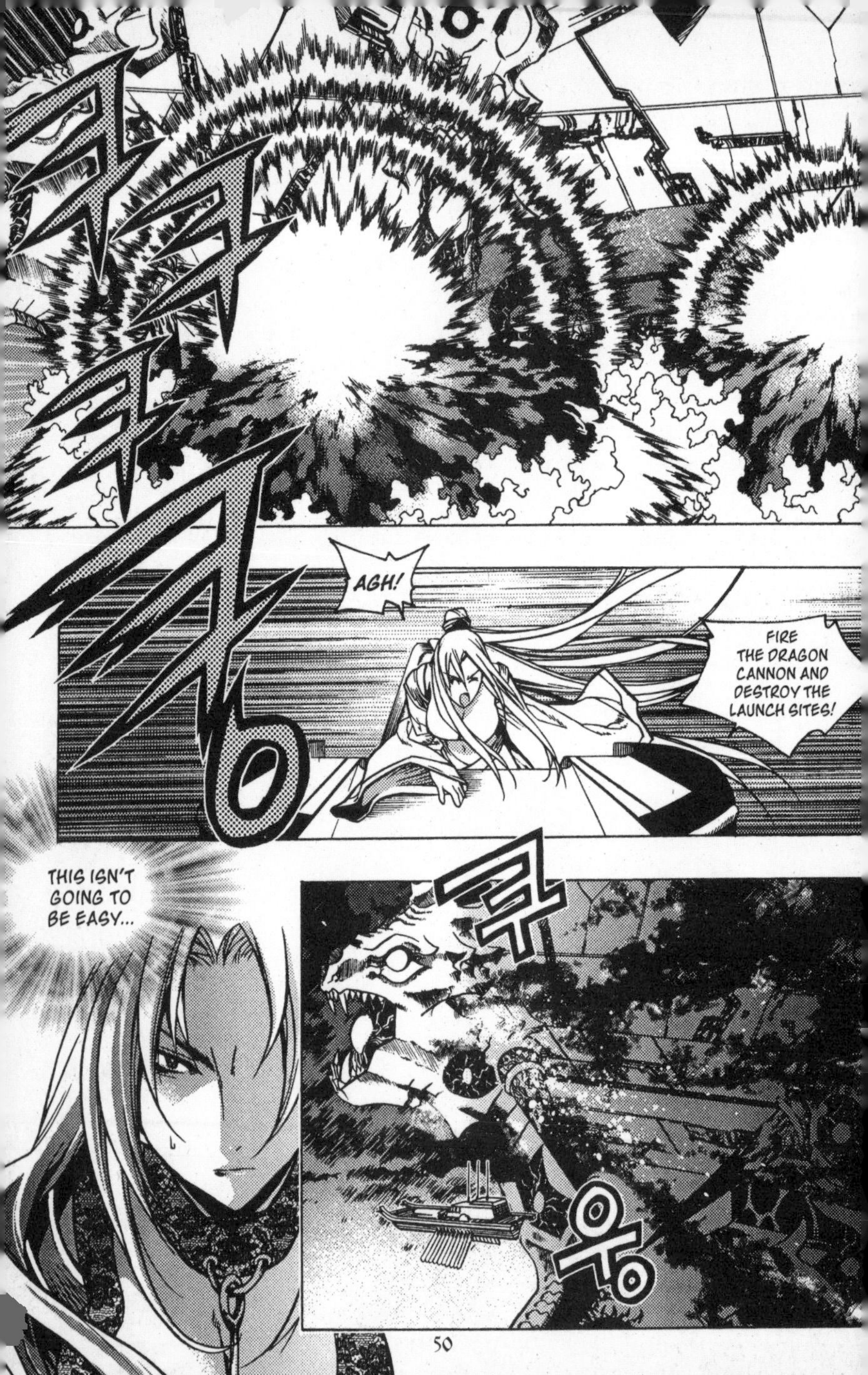
AGH!
FIRE THE DRAGON CANNON AND DESTROY THE LAUNCH SITES!
THIS ISN'T GOING TO BE EASY...

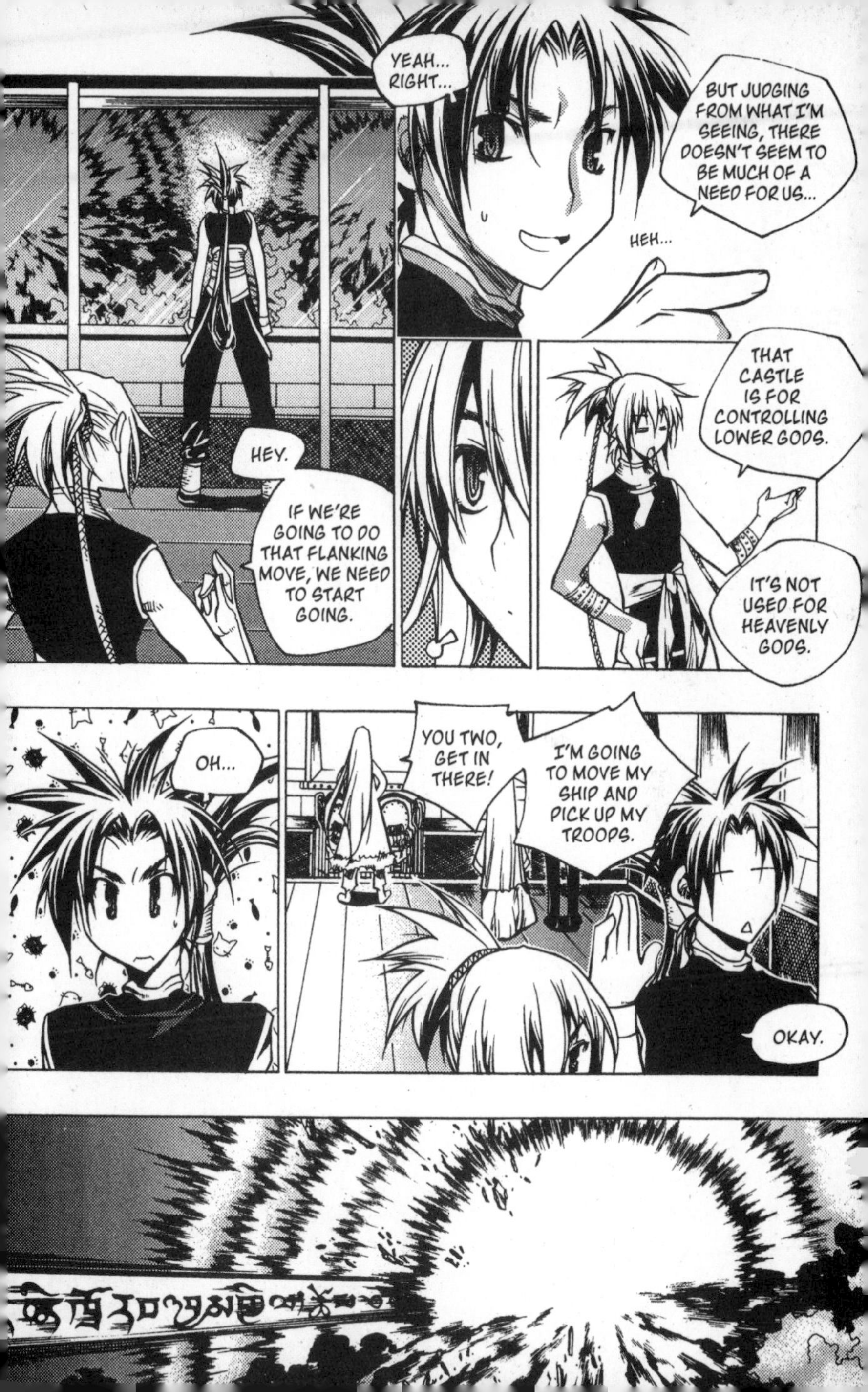
YEAH... RIGHT...
BUT JUDGING FROM WHAT I'M SEEING, THERE DOESN'T SEEM TO BE MUCH OF A NEED FOR US...
HEH...
THAT CASTLE IS FOR CONTROLLING LOWER GODS.
IT'S NOT USED FOR HEAVENLY GODS.
HEY.
IF WE'RE GOING TO DO THAT FLANKING MOVE, WE NEED TO START GOING.
YOU TWO, GET IN THERE!
I'M GOING TO MOVE MY SHIP AND PICK UP MY TROOPS.
OKAY.
OH...

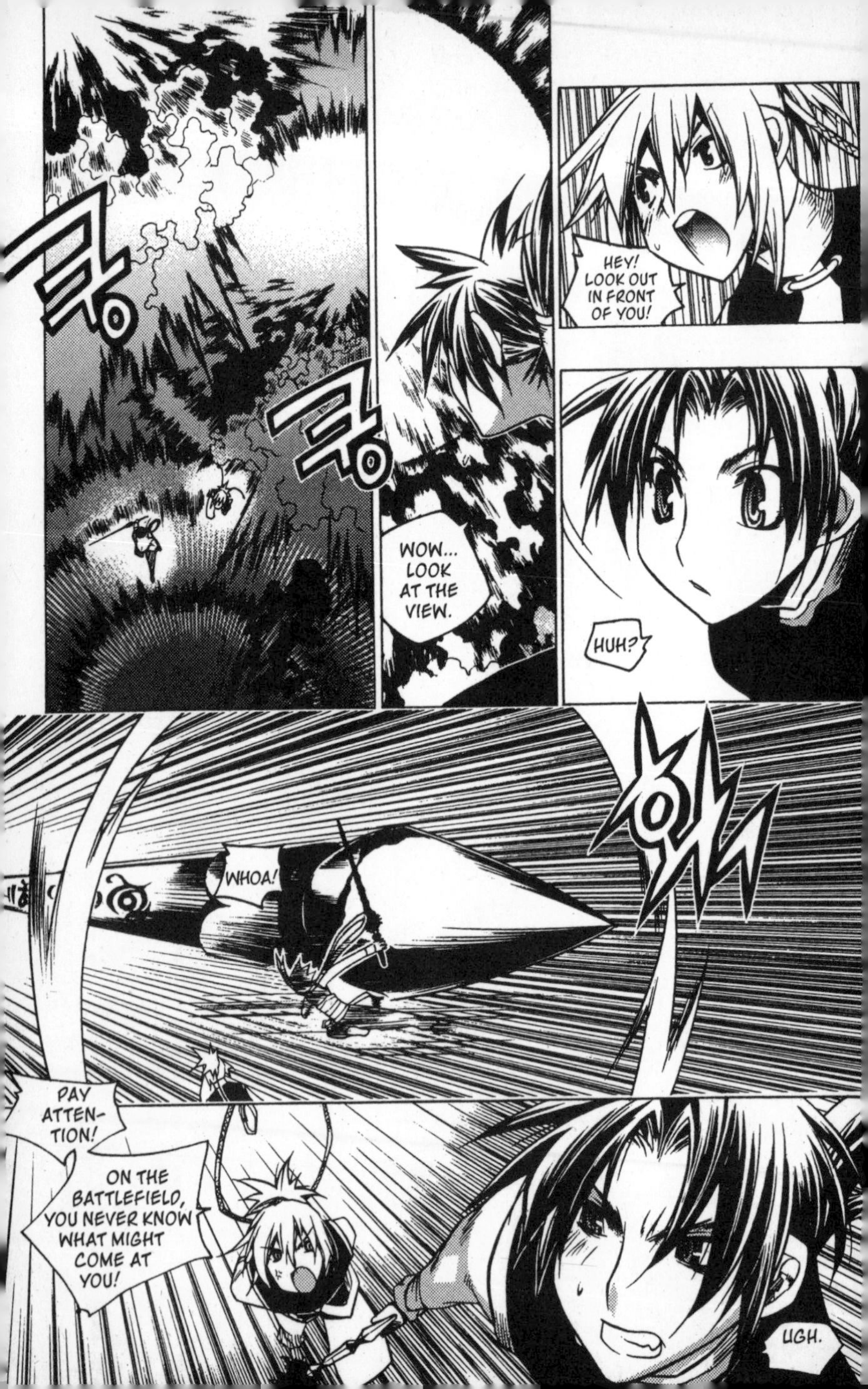
HEY! LOOK OUT IN FRONT OF YOU!
HUH?
WOW... LOOK AT THE VIEW.
WHOA!
PAY ATTEN- TION!
ON THE BATTLEFIELD, YOU NEVER KNOW WHAT MIGHT COME AT YOU!
UGH.

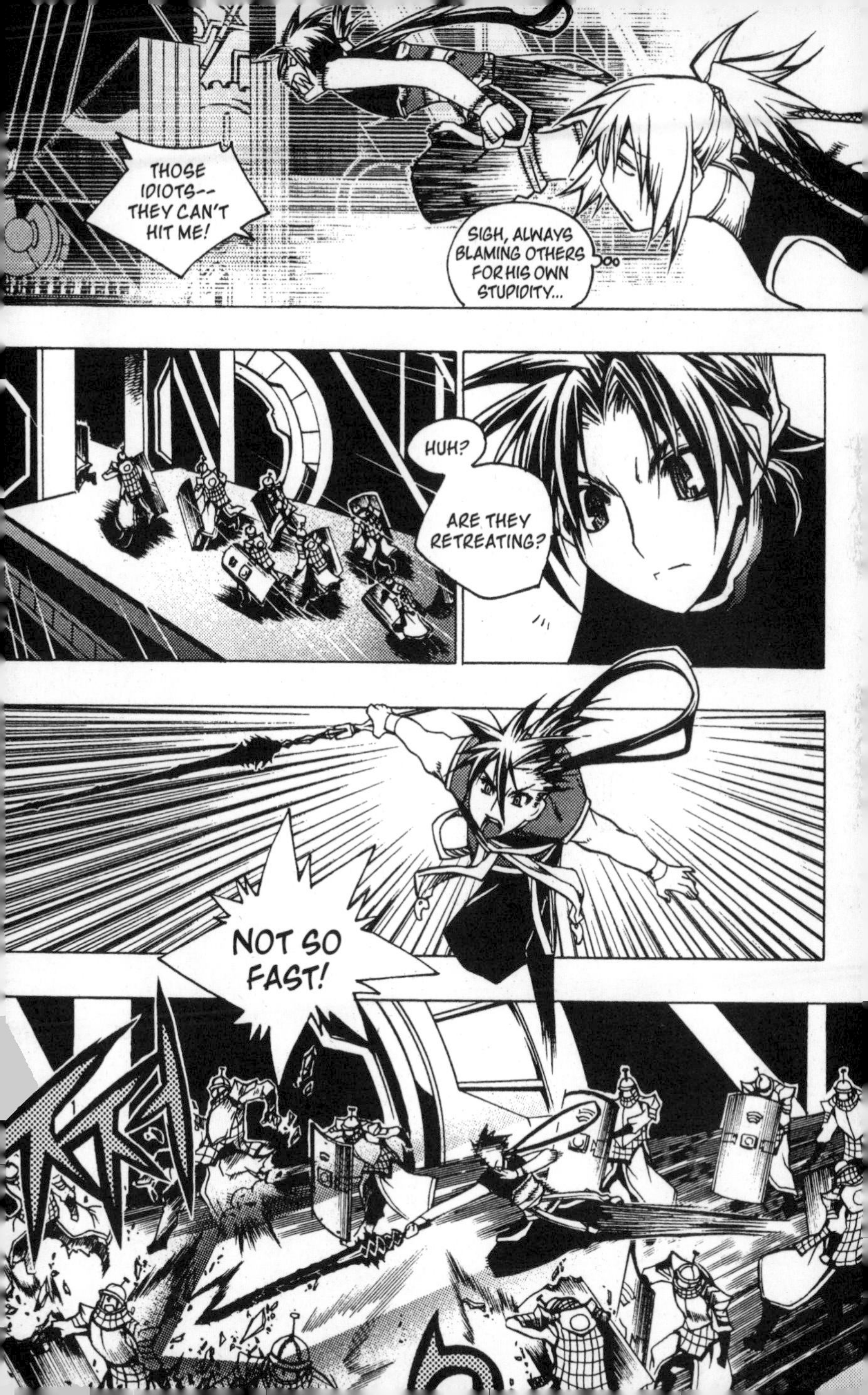
THOSE IDIOTS-- THEY CAN'T HIT ME!
SIGH, ALWAYS BLAMING OTHERS FOR HIS OWN STUPIDITY...
HUH?
ARE THEY RETREATING?
NOT SO FAST!

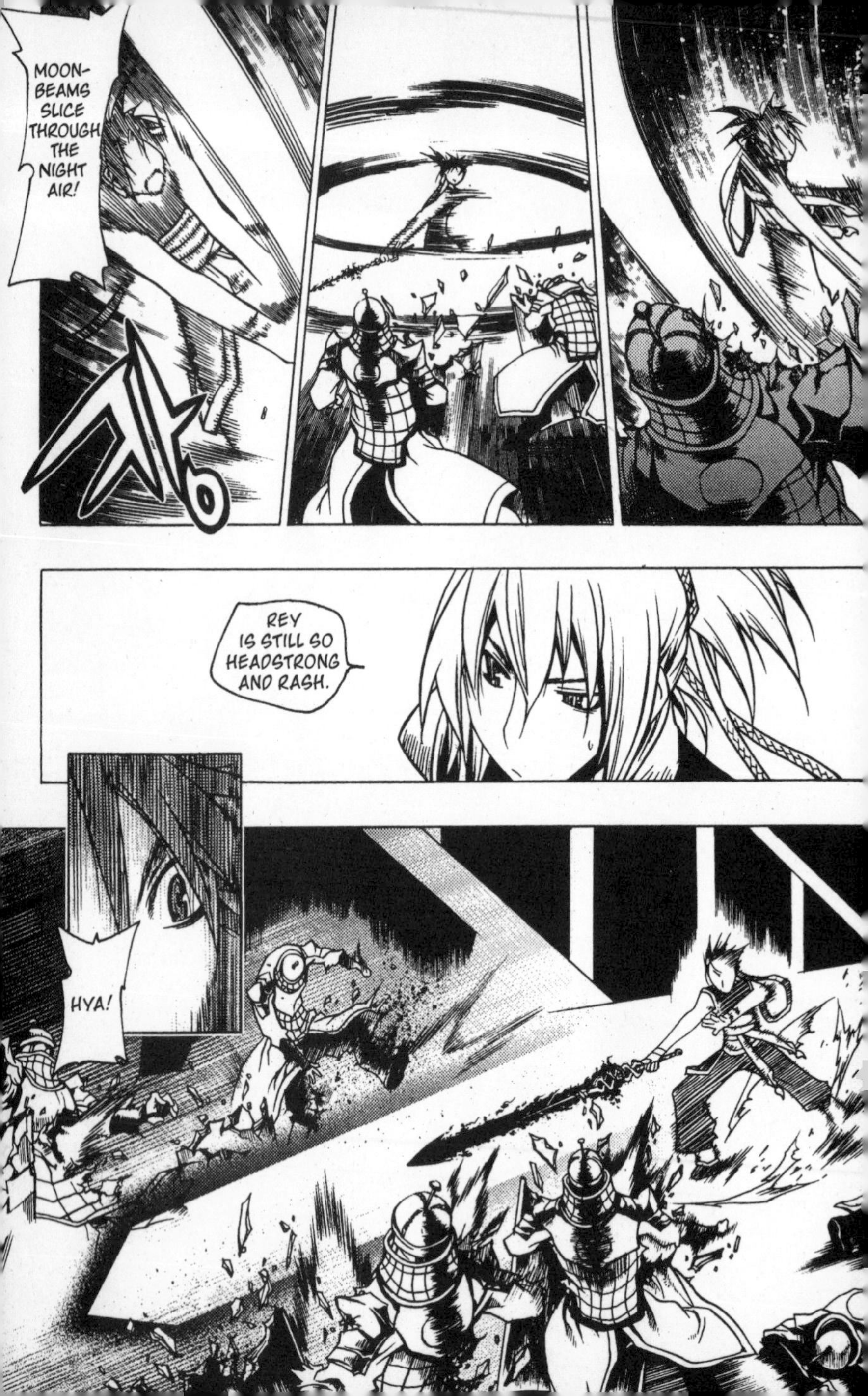
MOON-BEAMS SLICE THROUGH THE NIGHT AIR!
REY IS STILL SO HEADSTRONG AND RASH.
HYA!

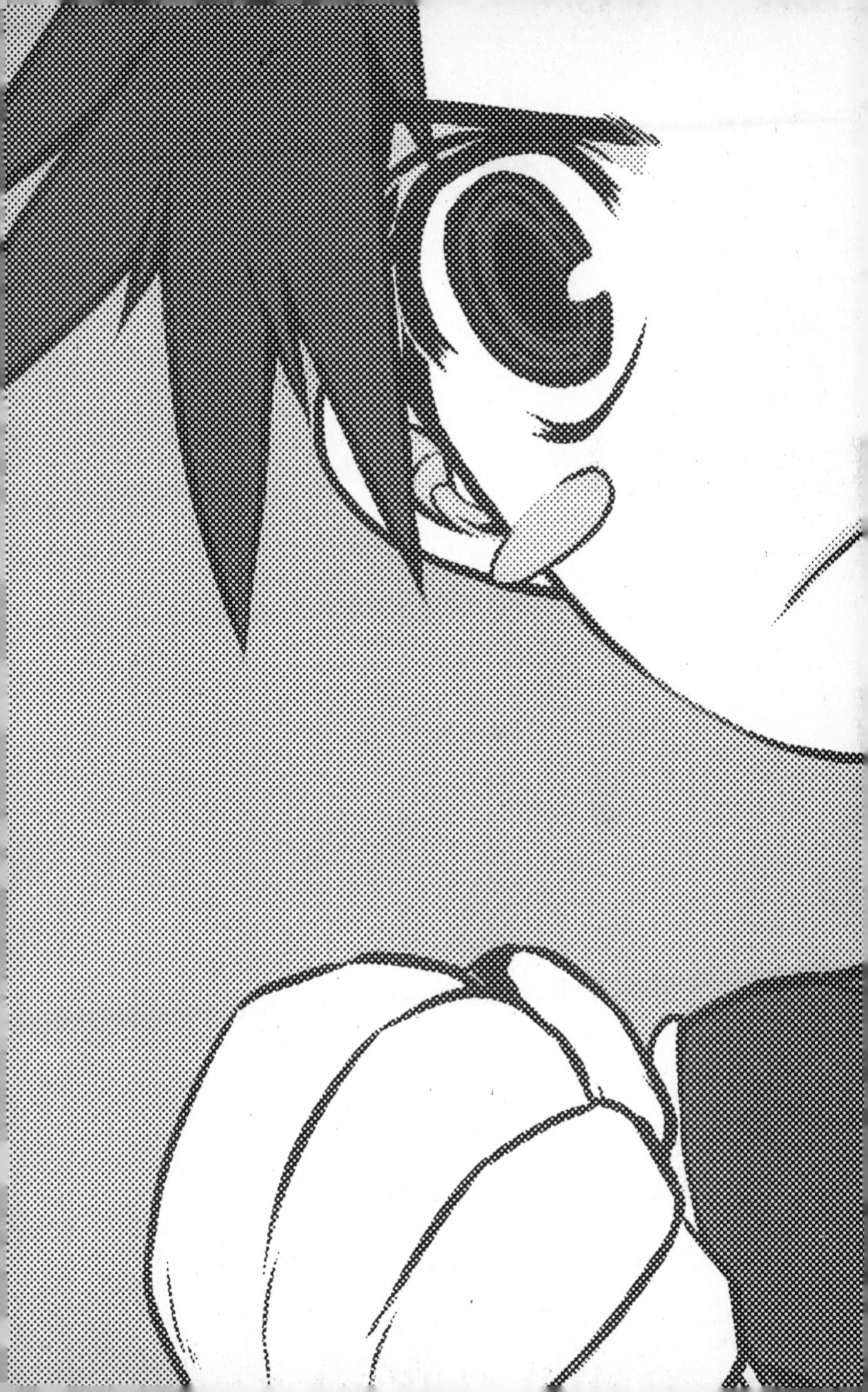

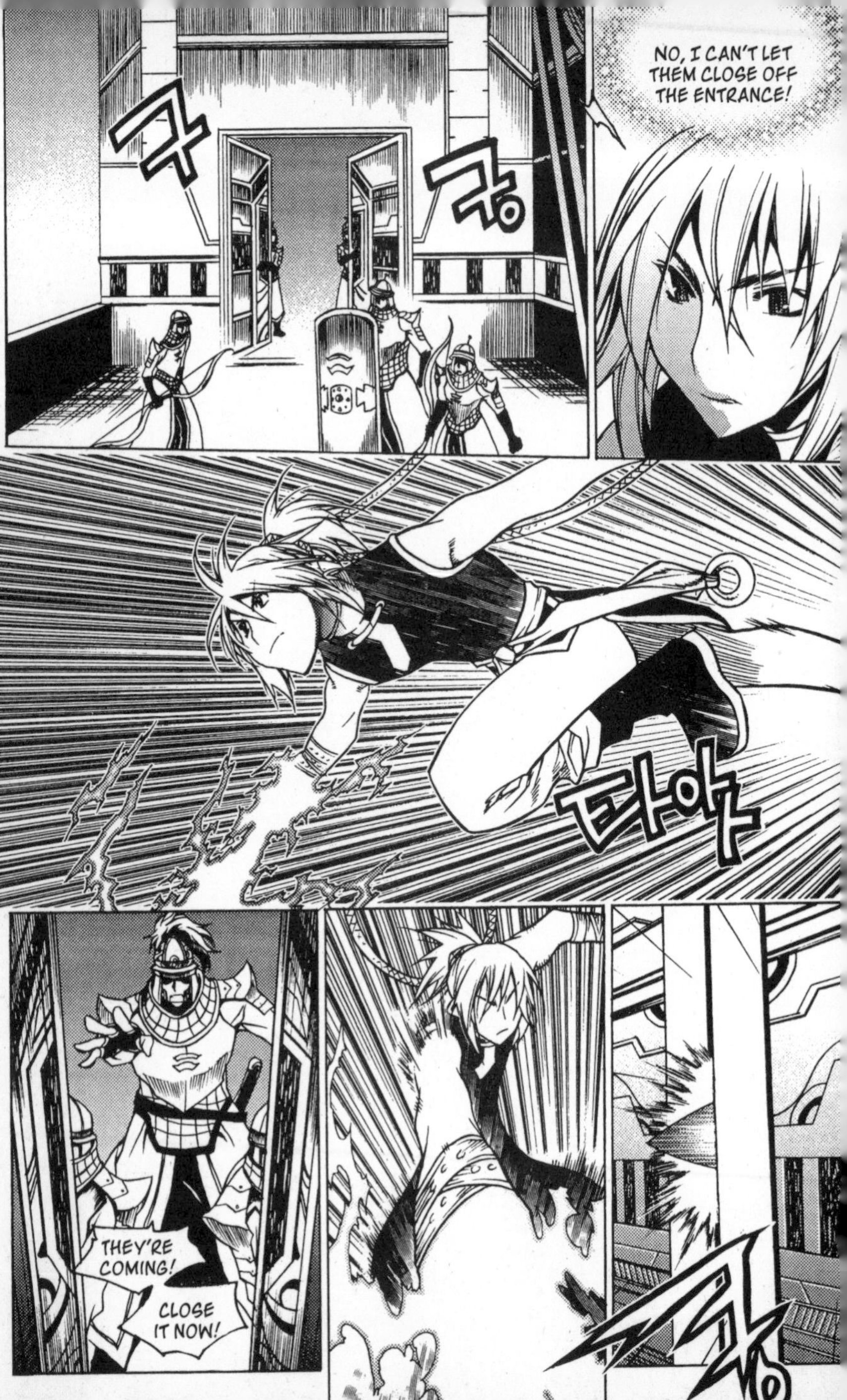
NO, I CAN'T LET THEM CLOSE OFF THE ENTRANCE!
THEY'RE COMING!
CLOSE IT NOW!

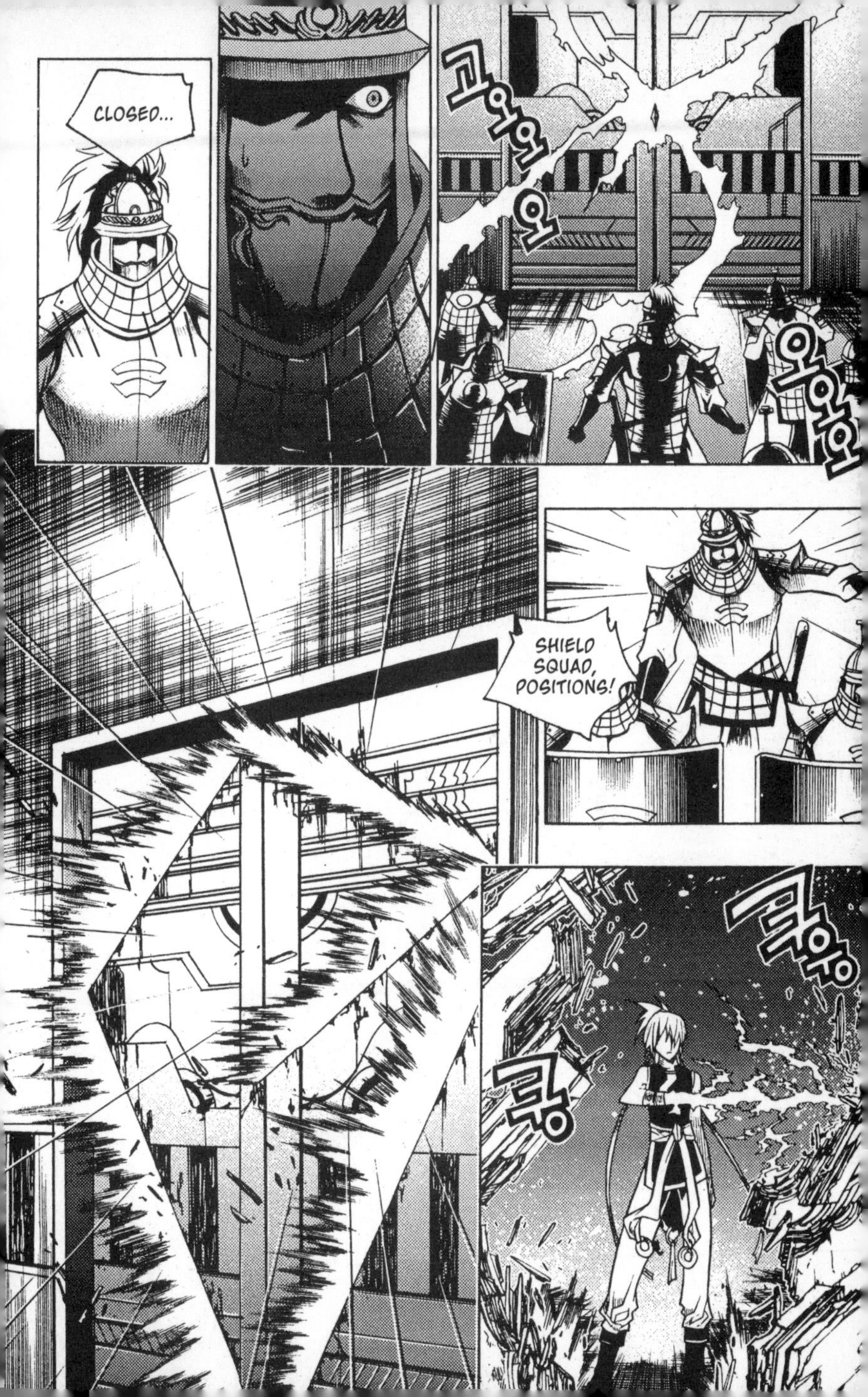
CLOSED...
SHIELD SQUAD, POSITIONS!

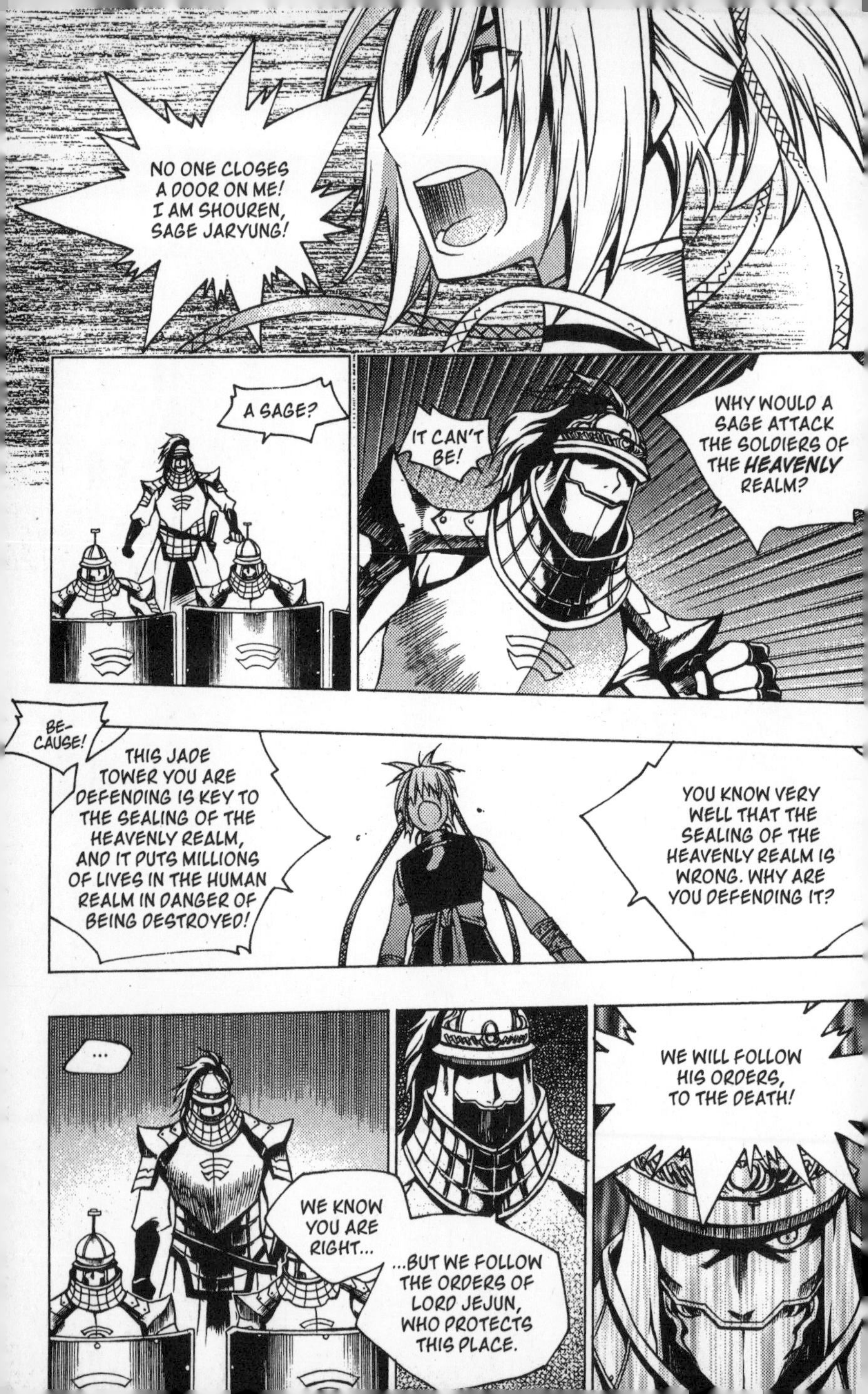
NO ONE CLOSES A DOOR ON ME! I AM SHOUREN, SAGE JARYUNG!
A SAGE?
IT CAN'T BE!
WHY WOULD A SAGE ATTACK THE SOLDIERS OF THE HEAVENLY REALM?
BE-CAUSE!
THIS JADE TOWER YOU ARE DEFENDING IS KEY TO THE SEALING OF THE HEAVENLY REALM, AND IT PUTS MILLIONS OF LIVES IN THE HUMAN REALM IN DANGER OF BEING DESTROYED!
YOU KNOW VERY WELL THAT THE SEALING OF THE HEAVENLY REALM IS WRONG. WHY ARE YOU DEFENDING IT?
...
WE KNOW YOU ARE RIGHT...
...BUT WE FOLLOW THE ORDERS OF LORD JEJUN, WHO PROTECTS THIS PLACE.
WE WILL FOLLOW HIS ORDERS, TO THE DEATH!

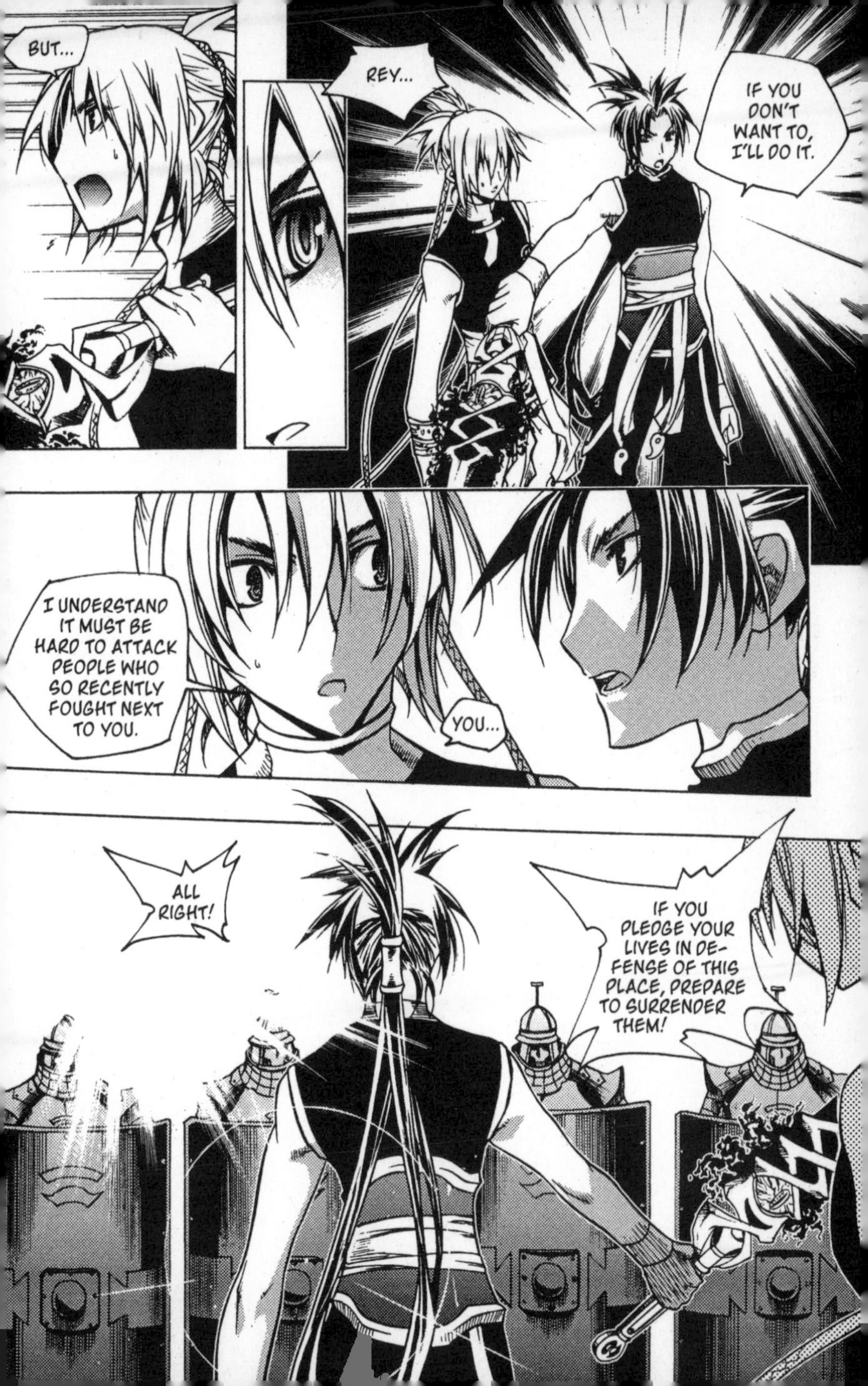
IF YOU DON'T WANT TO, I'LL DO IT.
REY...
BUT...
YOU...
I UNDERSTAND IT MUST BE HARD TO ATTACK PEOPLE WHO SO RECENTLY FOUGHT NEXT TO YOU.
IF YOU PLEDGE YOUR LIVES IN DE-FENSE OF THIS PLACE, PREPARE TO SURRENDER THEM!
ALL RIGHT!

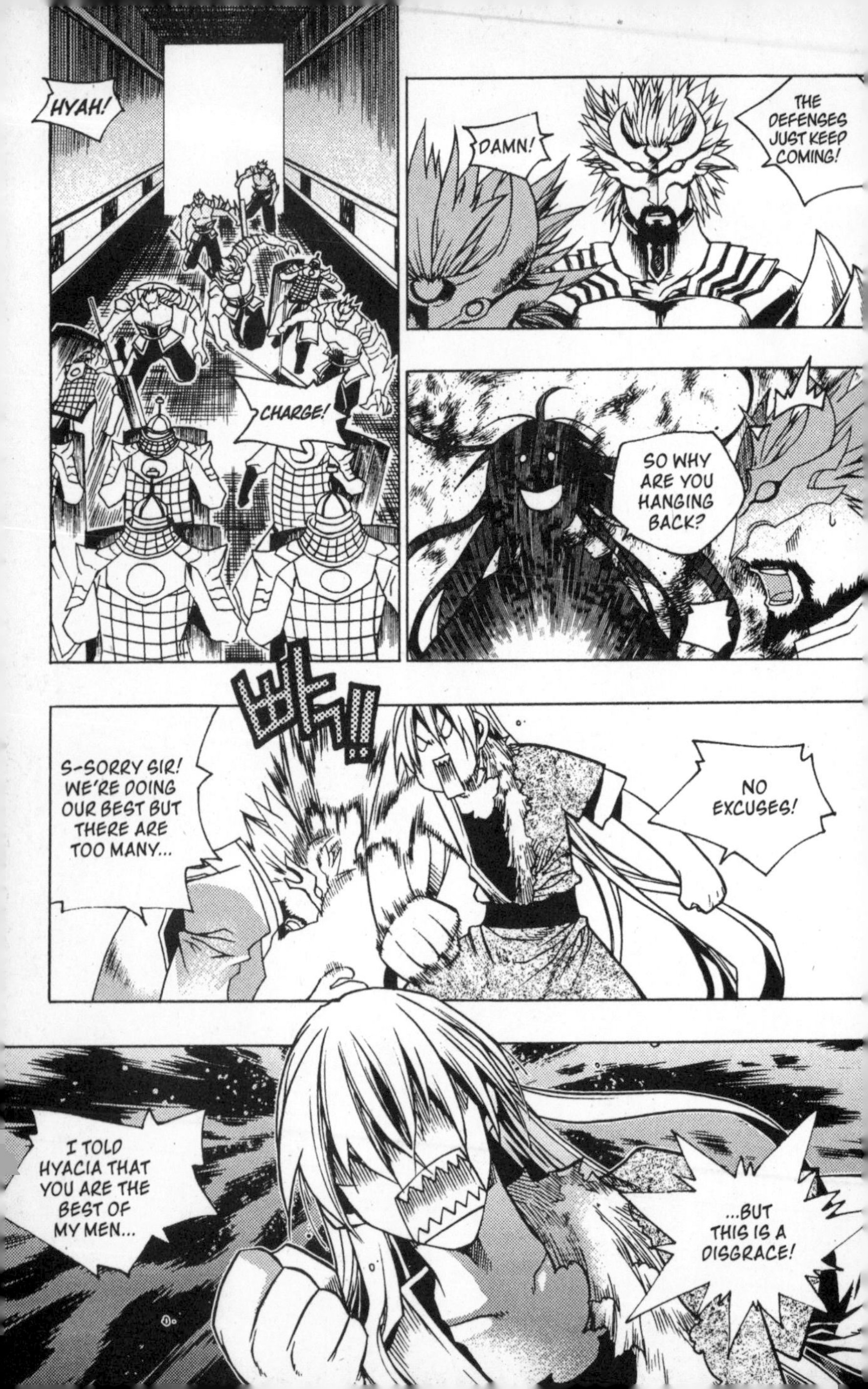
HYAH!
CHARGE!
DAMN!
THE DEFENSES JUST KEEP COMING!
SO WHY ARE YOU HANGING BACK?
빡!!
S-SORRY SIR! WE'RE DOING OUR BEST BUT THERE ARE TOO MANY...
NO EXCUSES!
I TOLD HYACIA THAT YOU ARE THE BEST OF MY MEN...
...BUT THIS IS A DISGRACE!

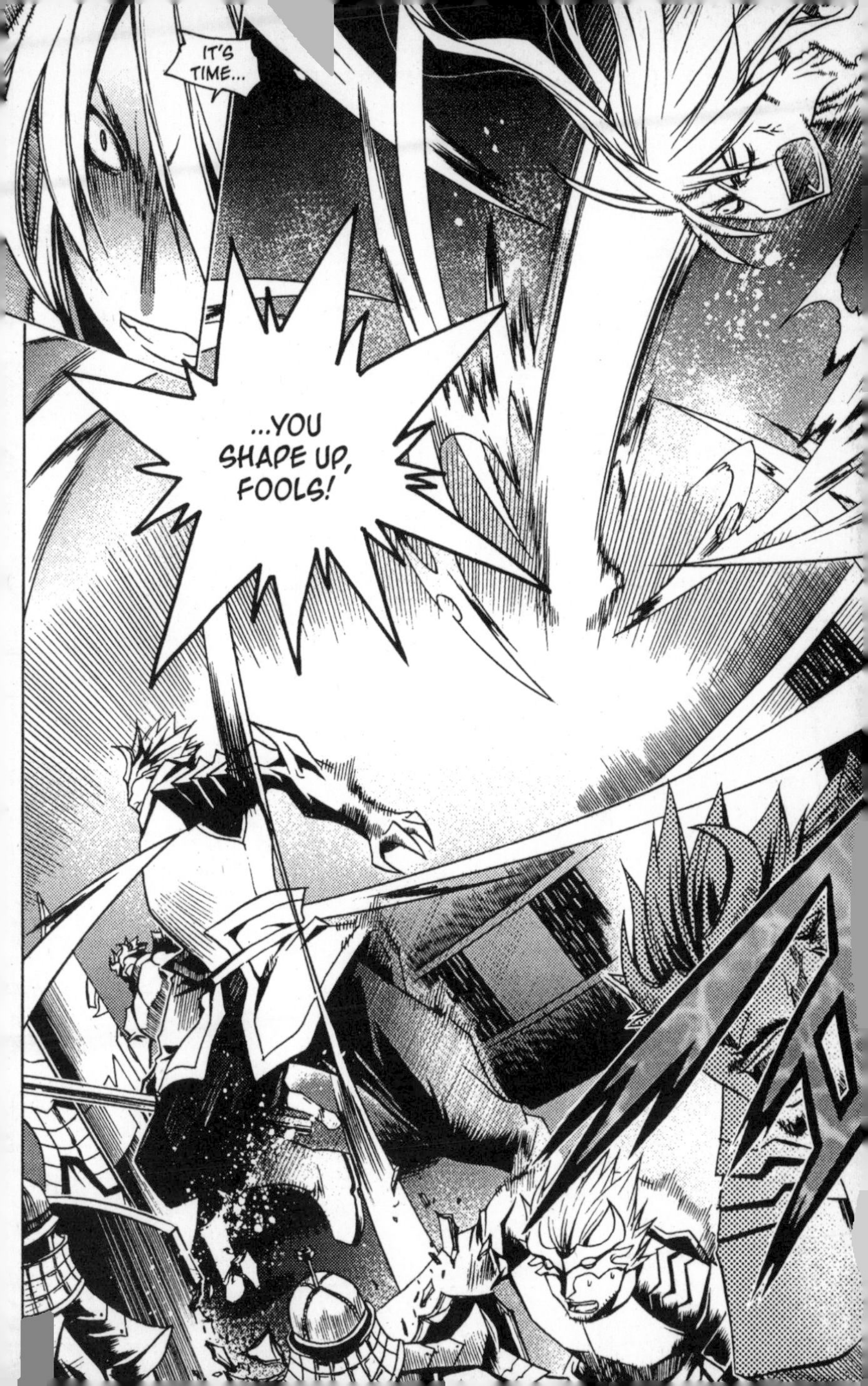
IT'S TIME...
...YOU SHAPE UP, FOOLS!

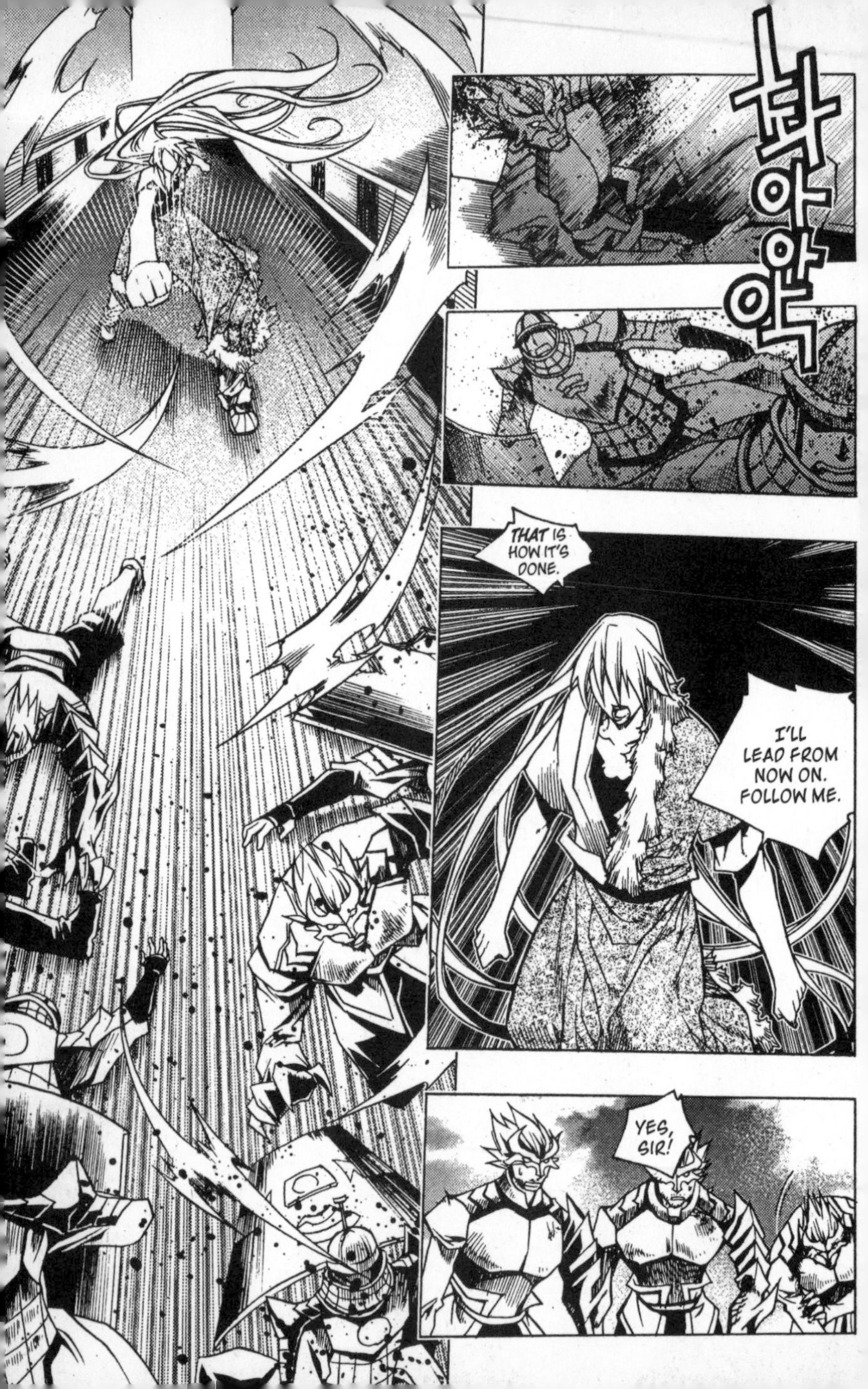

촤아아악
THAT IS HOW IT'S DONE.
I'LL LEAD FROM NOW ON. FOLLOW ME.
YES, SIR!

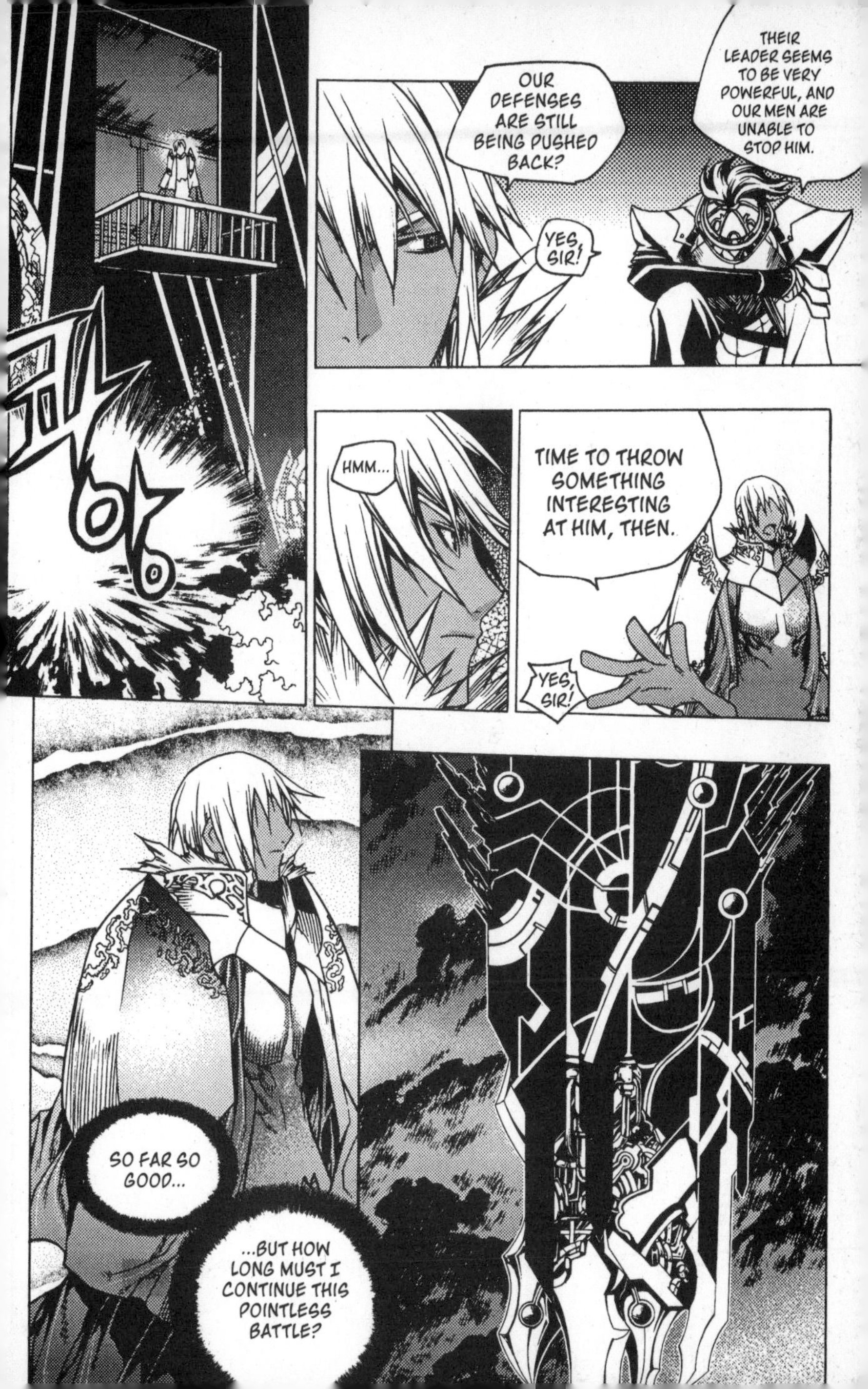
OUR DEFENSES ARE STILL BEING PUSHED BACK?
YES, SIR!
THEIR LEADER SEEMS TO BE VERY POWERFUL, AND OUR MEN ARE UNABLE TO STOP HIM.
TIME TO THROW SOMETHING INTERESTING AT HIM, THEN.
YES, SIR!
HMM...
SO FAR SO GOOD...
...BUT HOW LONG MUST I CONTINUE THIS POINTLESS BATTLE?

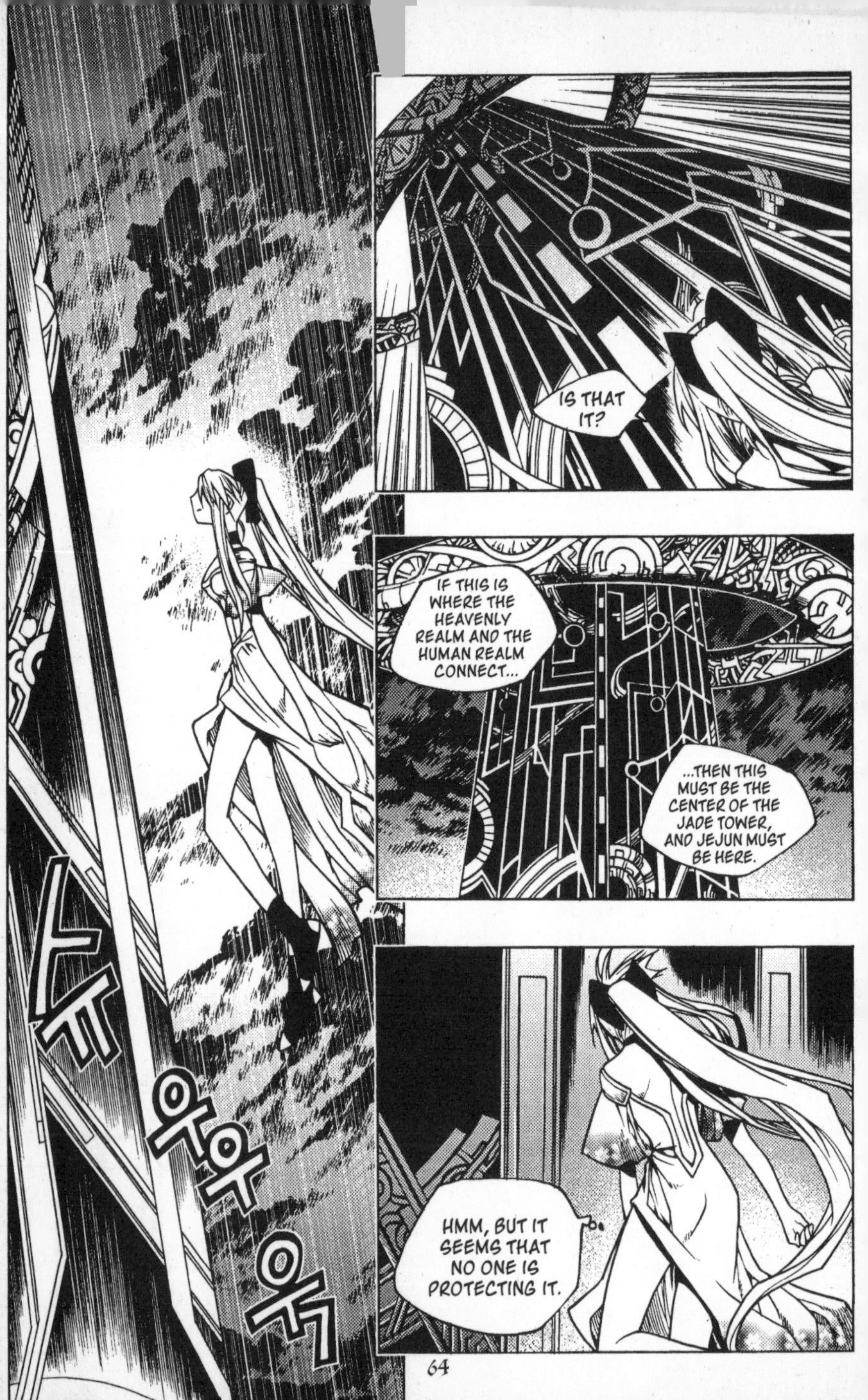
슈우우우
IS THAT IT?
IF THIS IS WHERE THE HEAVENLY REALM AND THE HUMAN REALM CONNECT...
...THEN THIS MUST BE THE CENTER OF THE JADE TOWER, AND JEJUN MUST BE HERE.
HMM, BUT IT SEEMS THAT NO ONE IS PROTECTING IT.

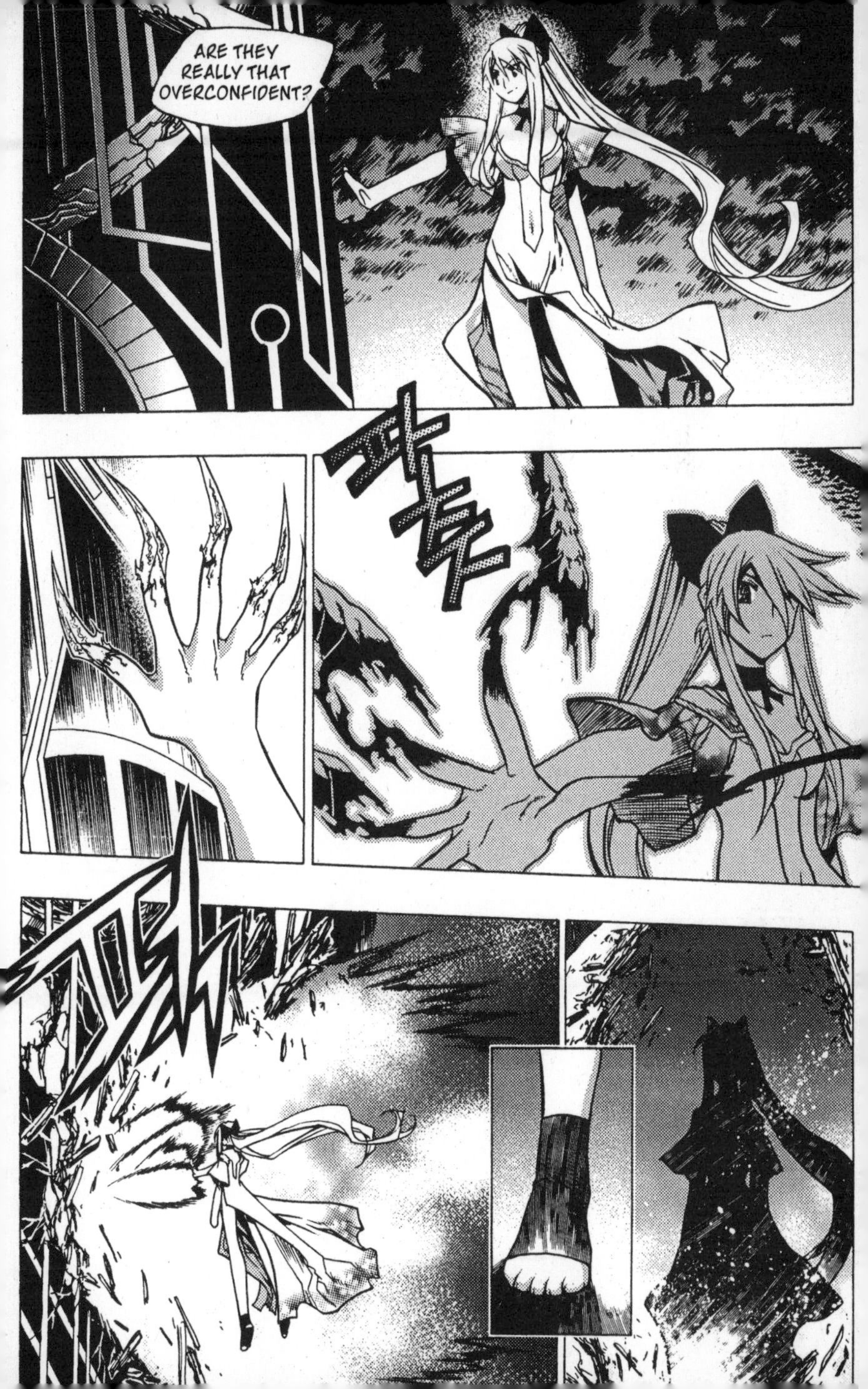
ARE THEY
REALLY THAT
OVERCONFIDENT?

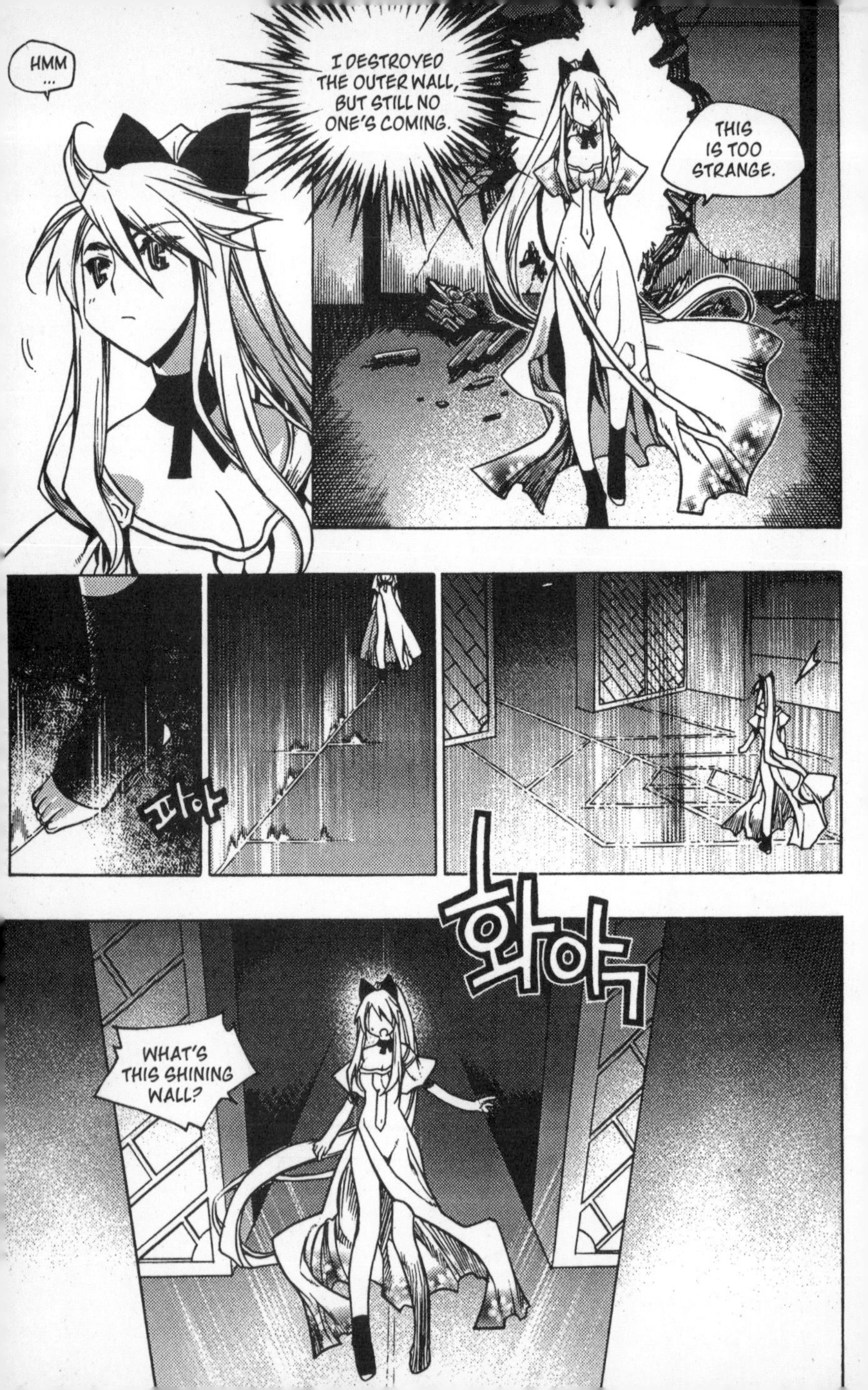
HMM ...
I DESTROYED THE OUTER WALL, BUT STILL NO ONE'S COMING.
THIS IS TOO STRANGE.
파아
화악
WHAT'S THIS SHINING WALL?

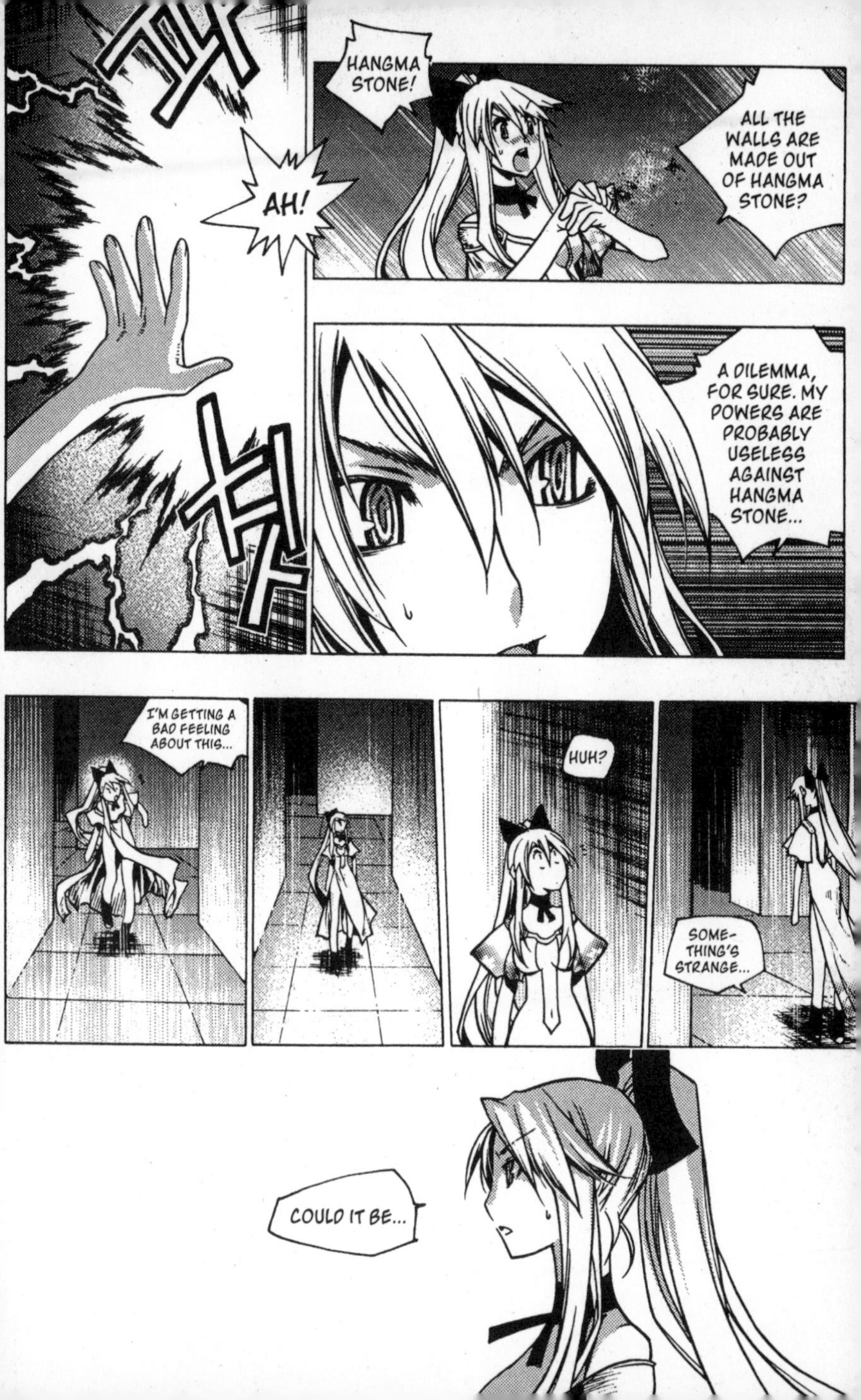
AH!
HANGMA STONE!
ALL THE WALLS ARE MADE OUT OF HANGMA STONE?
A DILEMMA, FOR SURE. MY POWERS ARE PROBABLY USELESS AGAINST HANGMA STONE...
I'M GETTING A BAD FEELING ABOUT THIS...
HUH?
SOME-THING'S STRANGE...
COULD IT BE...

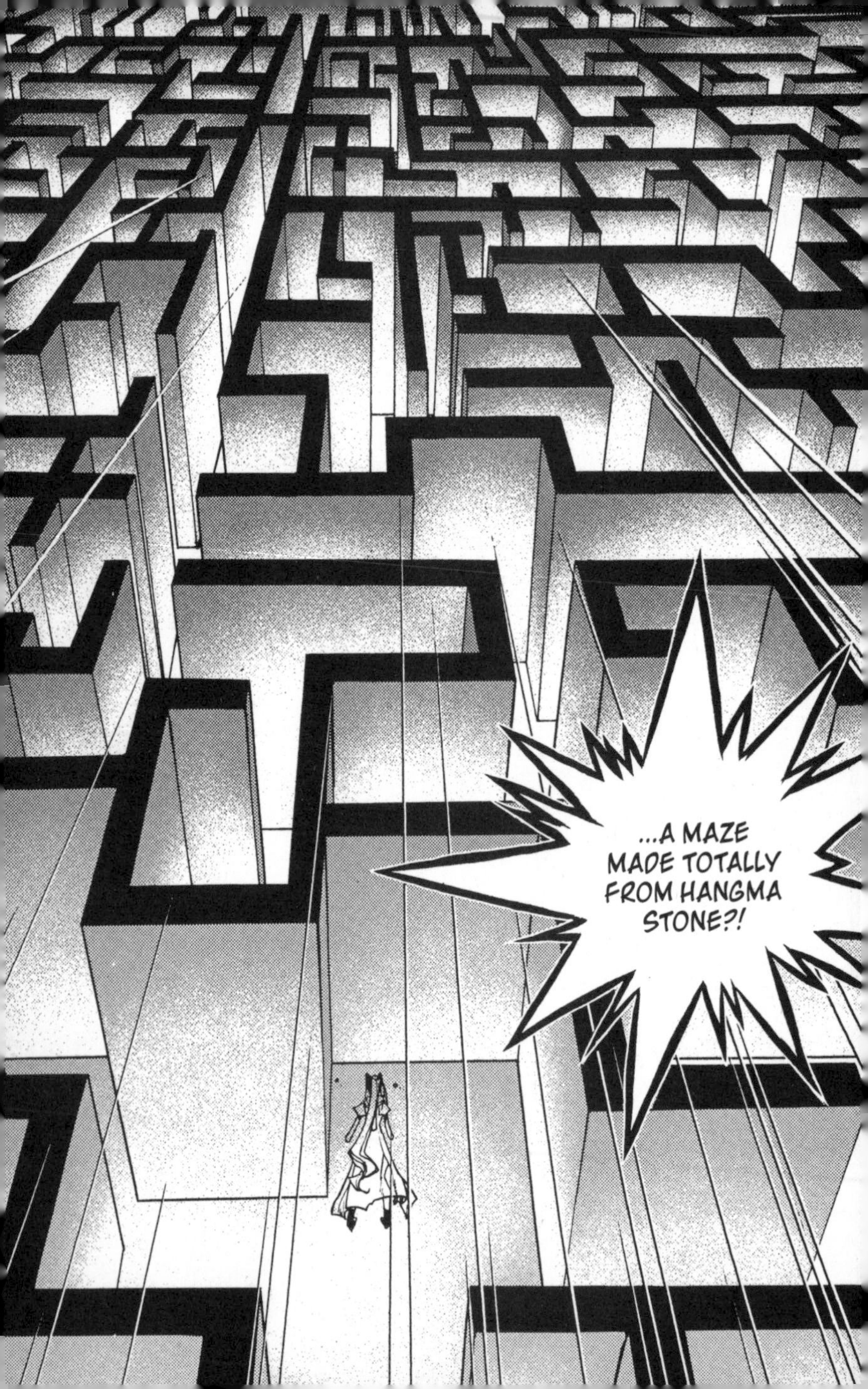
...A MAZE MADE TOTALLY FROM HANGMA STONE?!

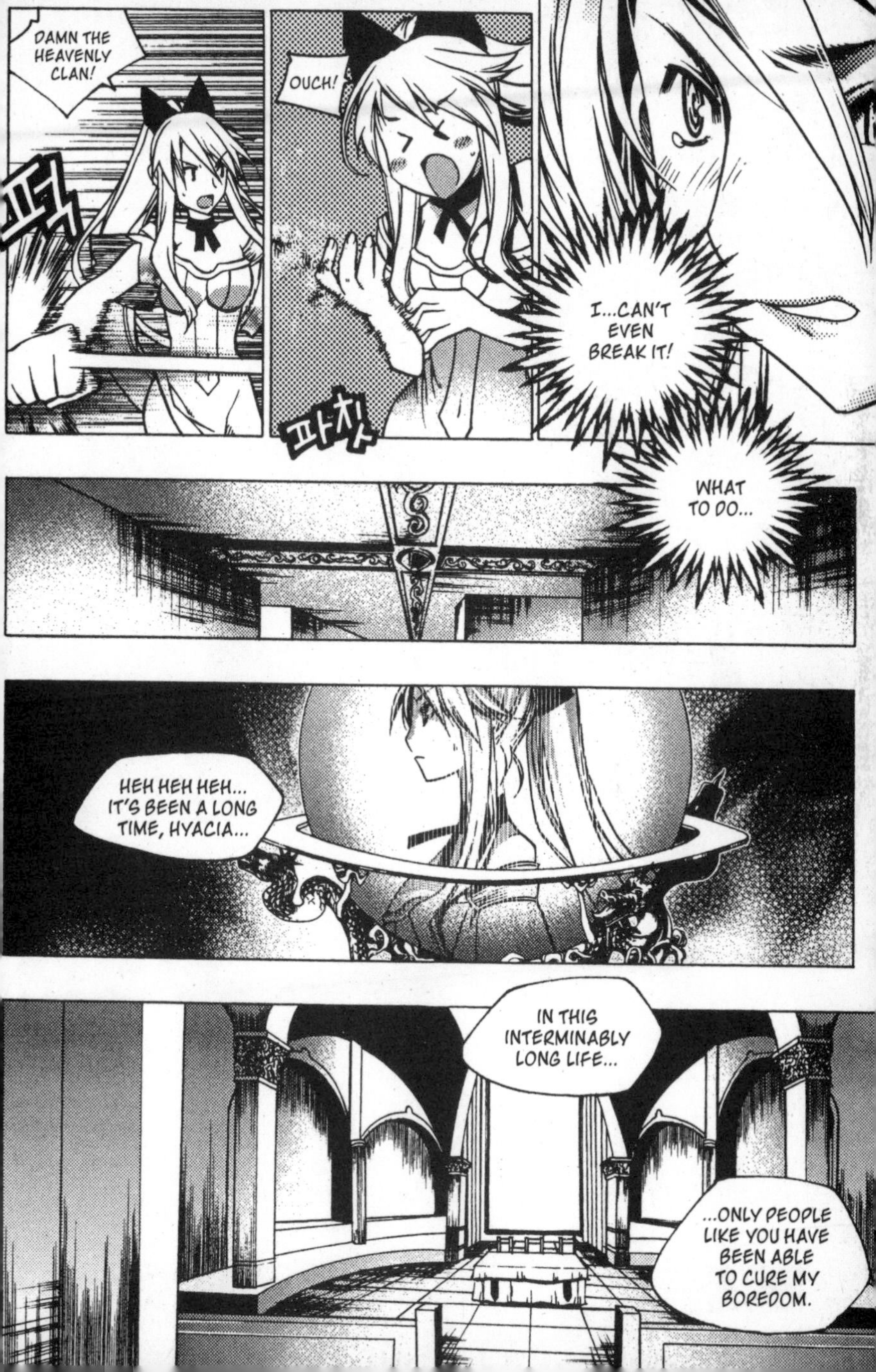
DAMN THE HEAVENLY CLAN!
OUCH!
I...CAN'T EVEN BREAK IT!
WHAT TO DO...
HEH HEH HEH... IT'S BEEN A LONG TIME, HYACIA...
IN THIS INTERMINABLY LONG LIFE...
...ONLY PEOPLE LIKE YOU HAVE BEEN ABLE TO CURE MY BOREDOM.

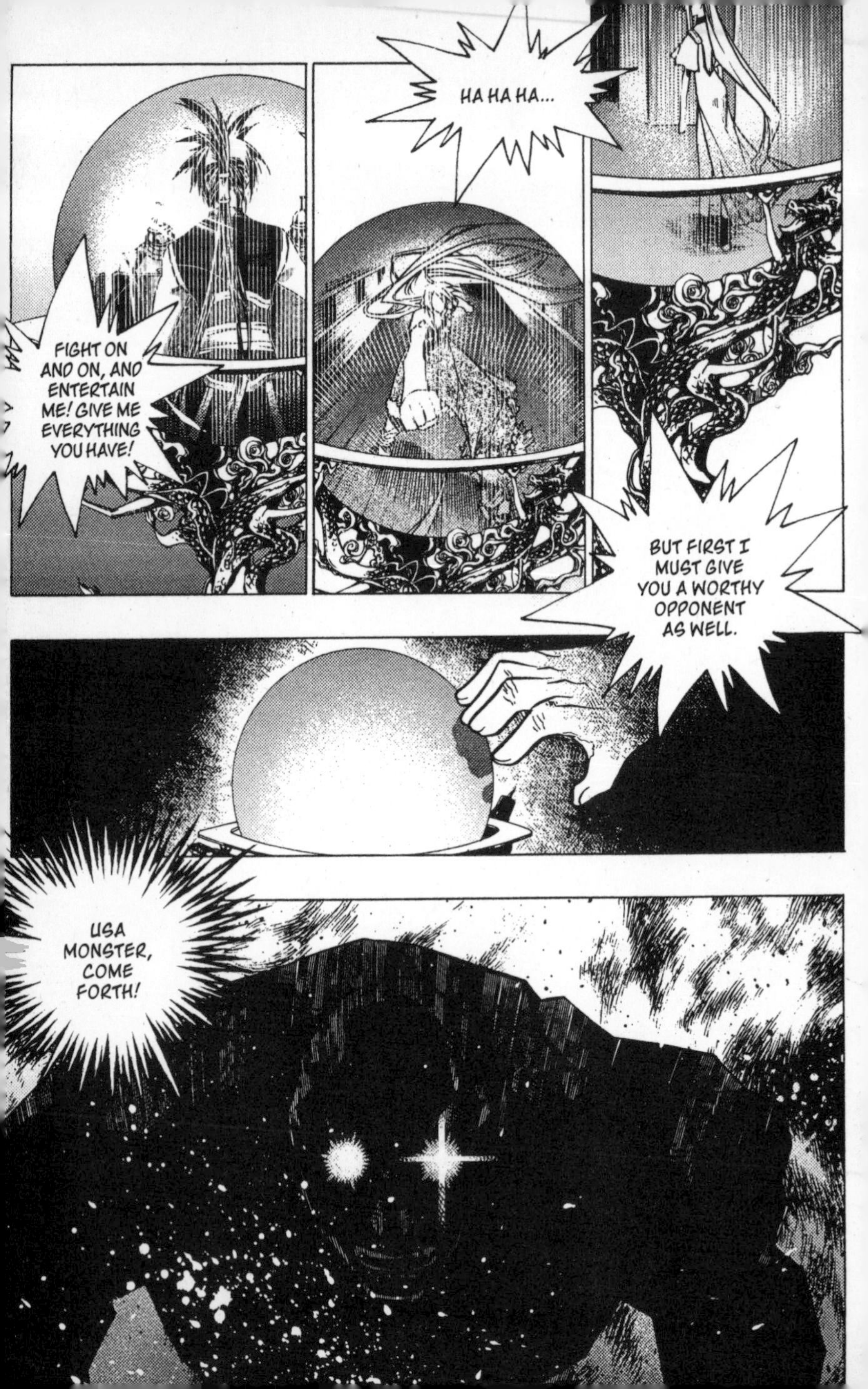
HA HA HA...
FIGHT ON AND ON, AND ENTERTAIN ME! GIVE ME EVERYTHING YOU HAVE!
BUT FIRST I MUST GIVE YOU A WORTHY OPPONENT AS WELL.
USA MONSTER, COME FORTH!

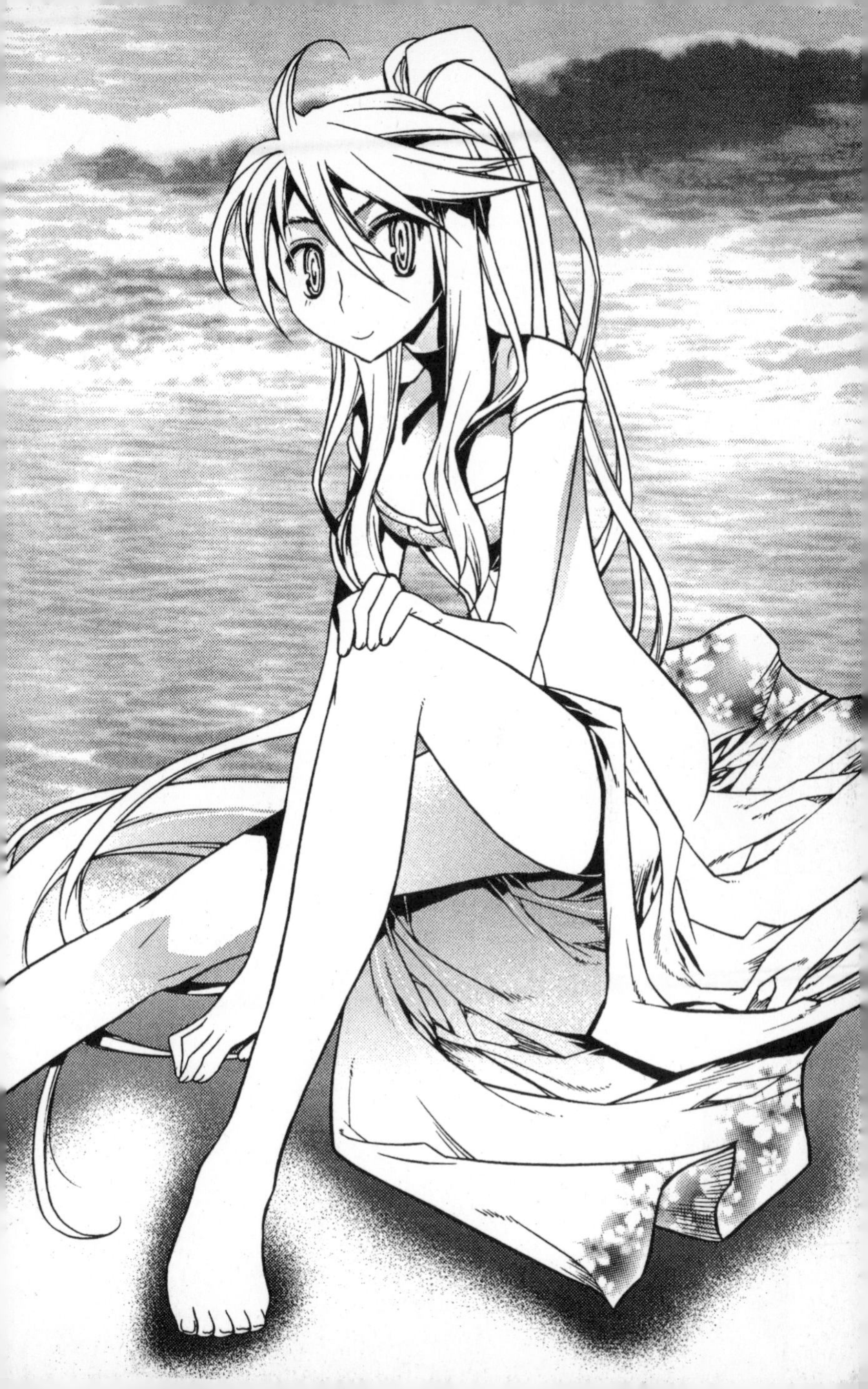

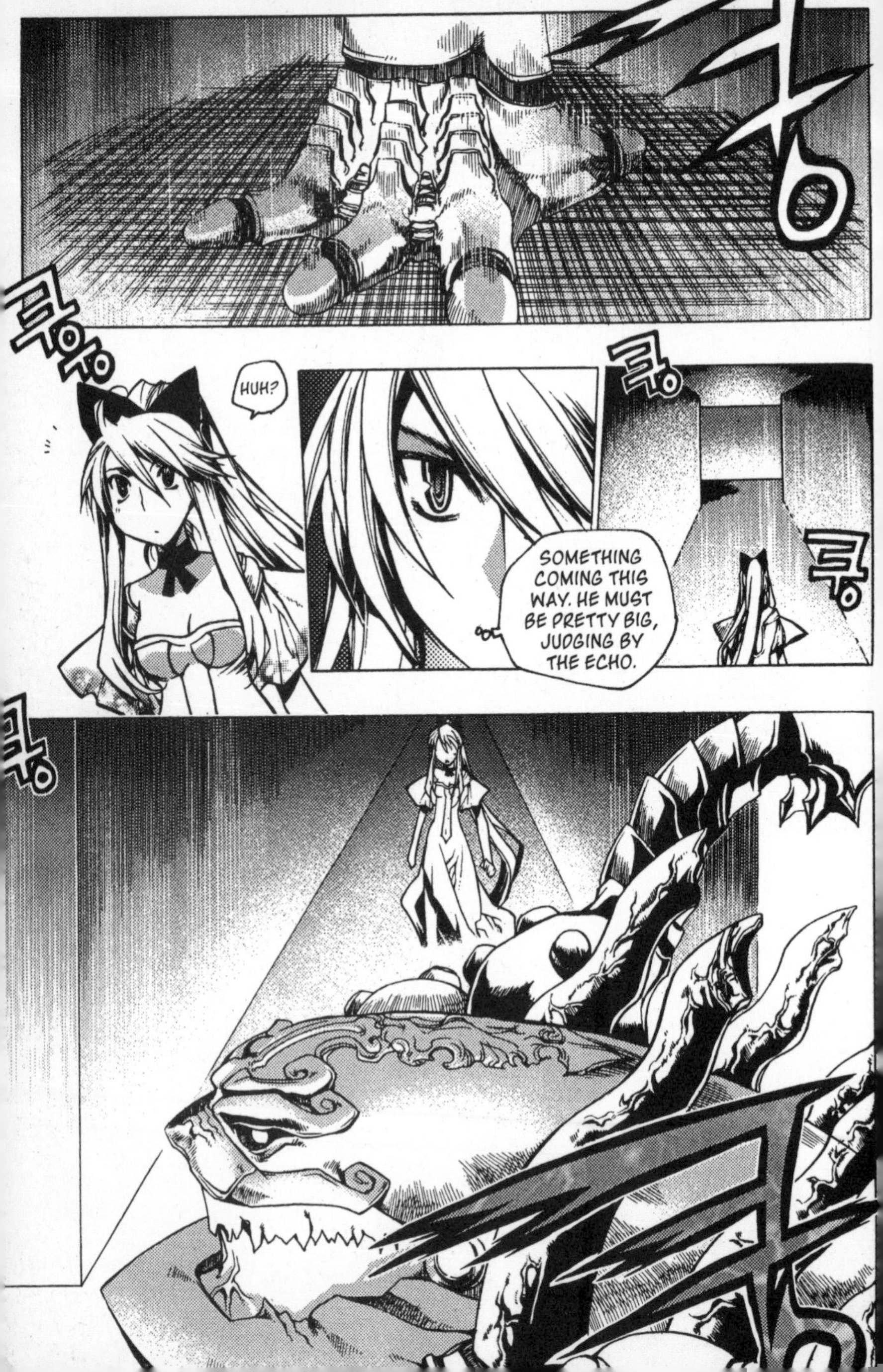

HUH?
SOMETHING COMING THIS WAY. HE MUST BE PRETTY BIG, JUDGING BY THE ECHO.

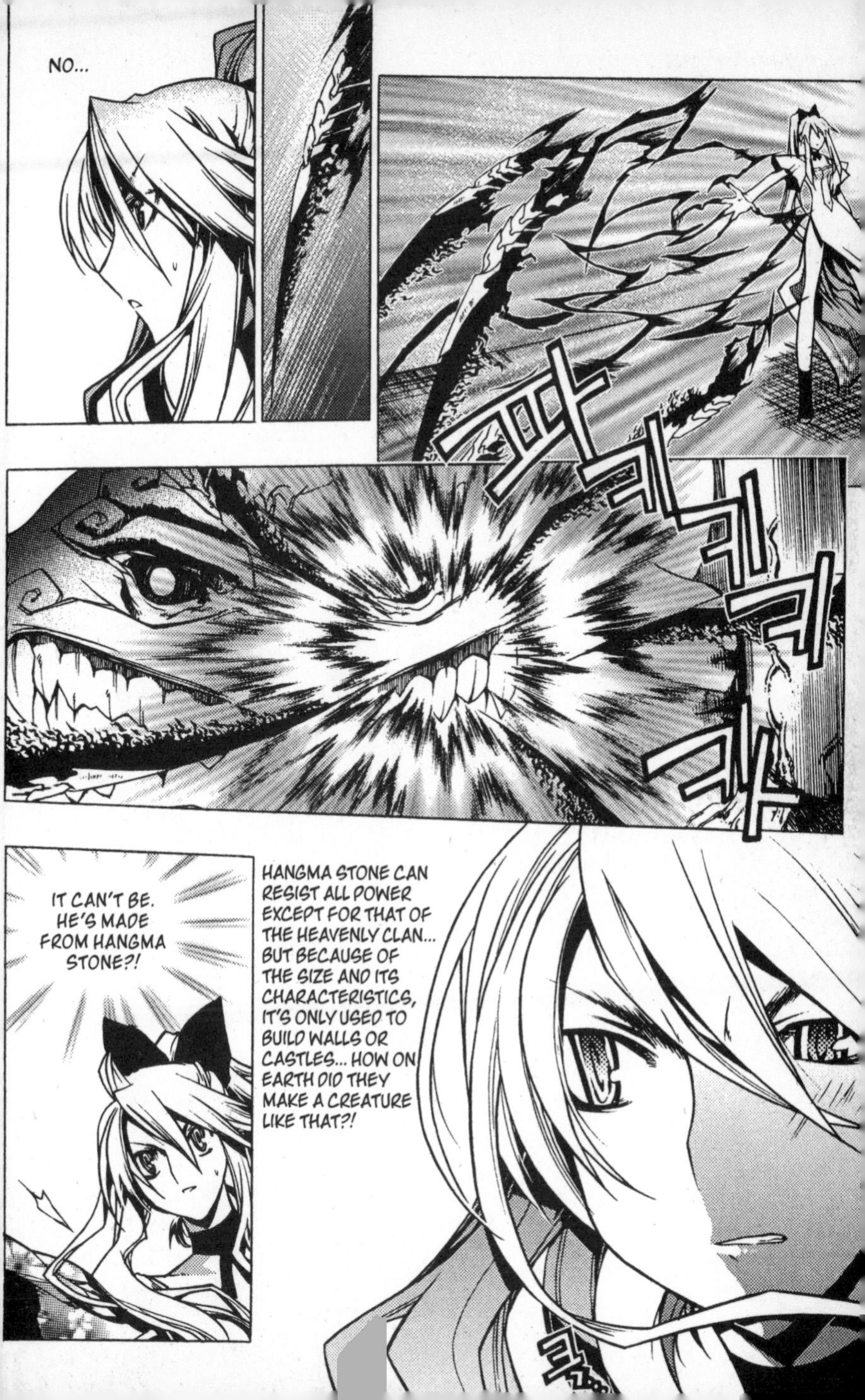
NO...
IT CAN'T BE. HE'S MADE FROM HANGMA STONE?!
HANGMA STONE CAN RESIST ALL POWER EXCEPT FOR THAT OF THE HEAVENLY CLAN... BUT BECAUSE OF THE SIZE AND ITS CHARACTERISTICS, IT'S ONLY USED TO BUILD WALLS OR CASTLES... HOW ON EARTH DID THEY MAKE A CREATURE LIKE THAT?!

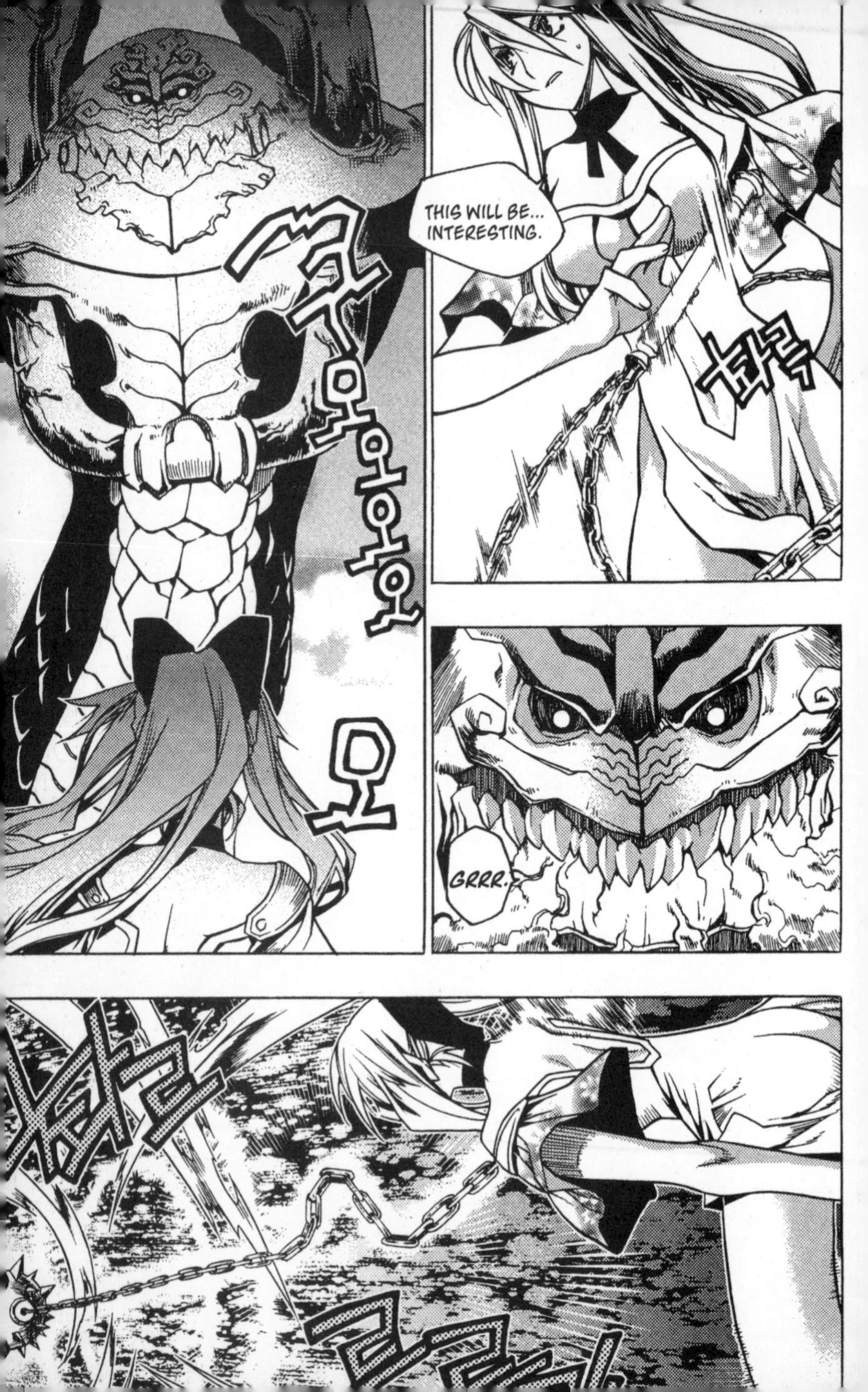
THIS WILL BE... INTERESTING.
GRRR...

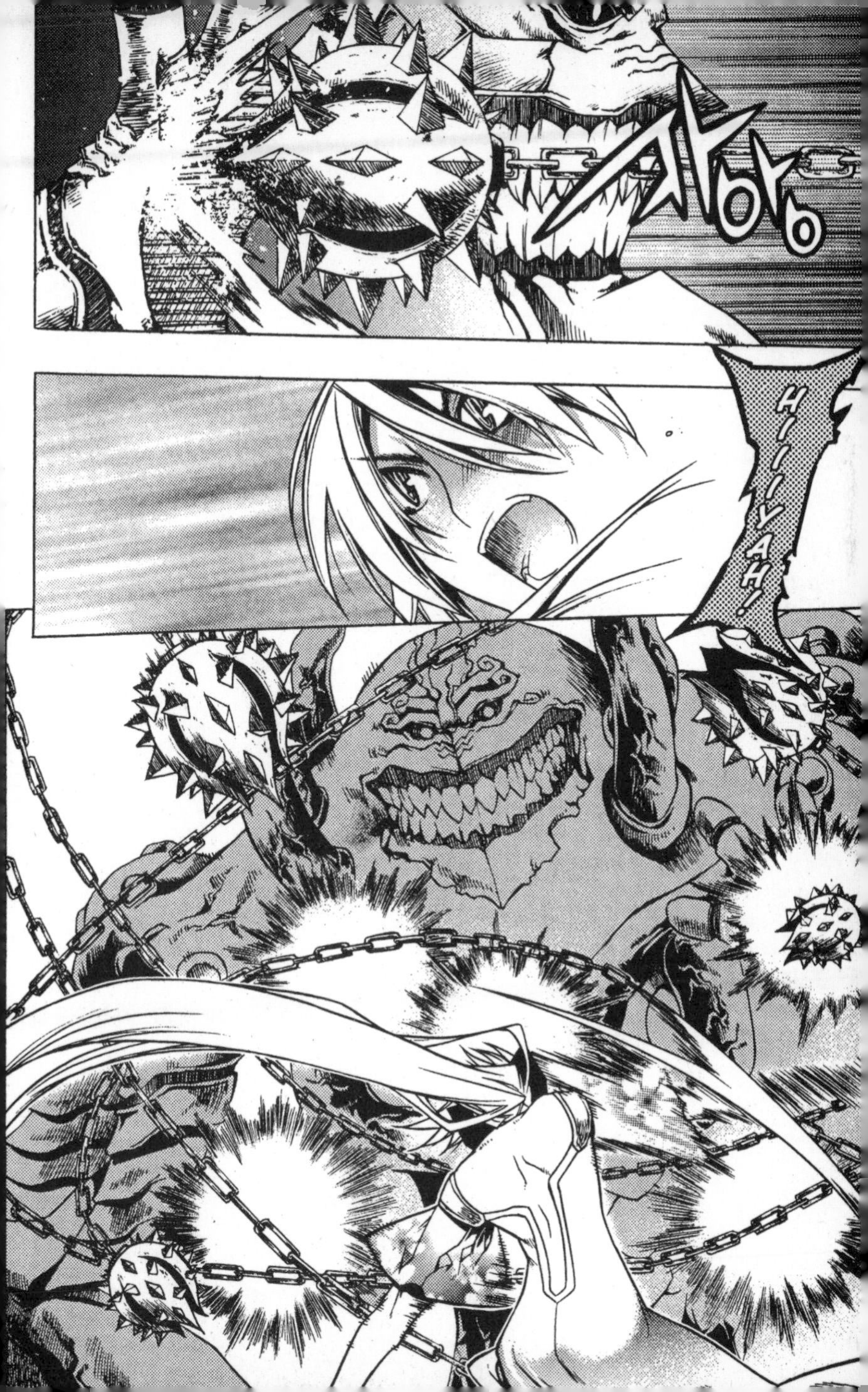
HIIIYAH!

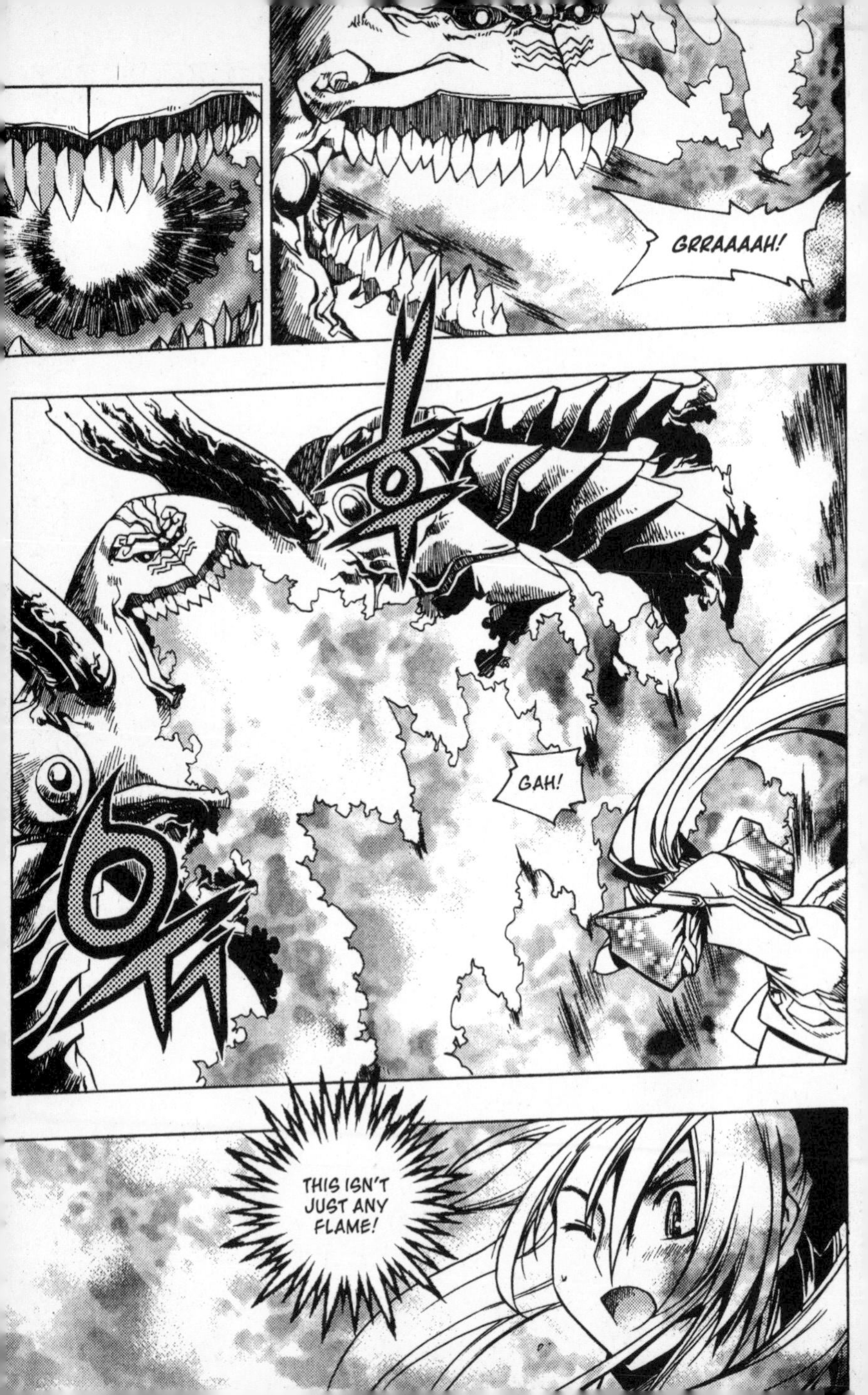
GRRAAAAH!
GAH!
THIS ISN'T JUST ANY FLAME!

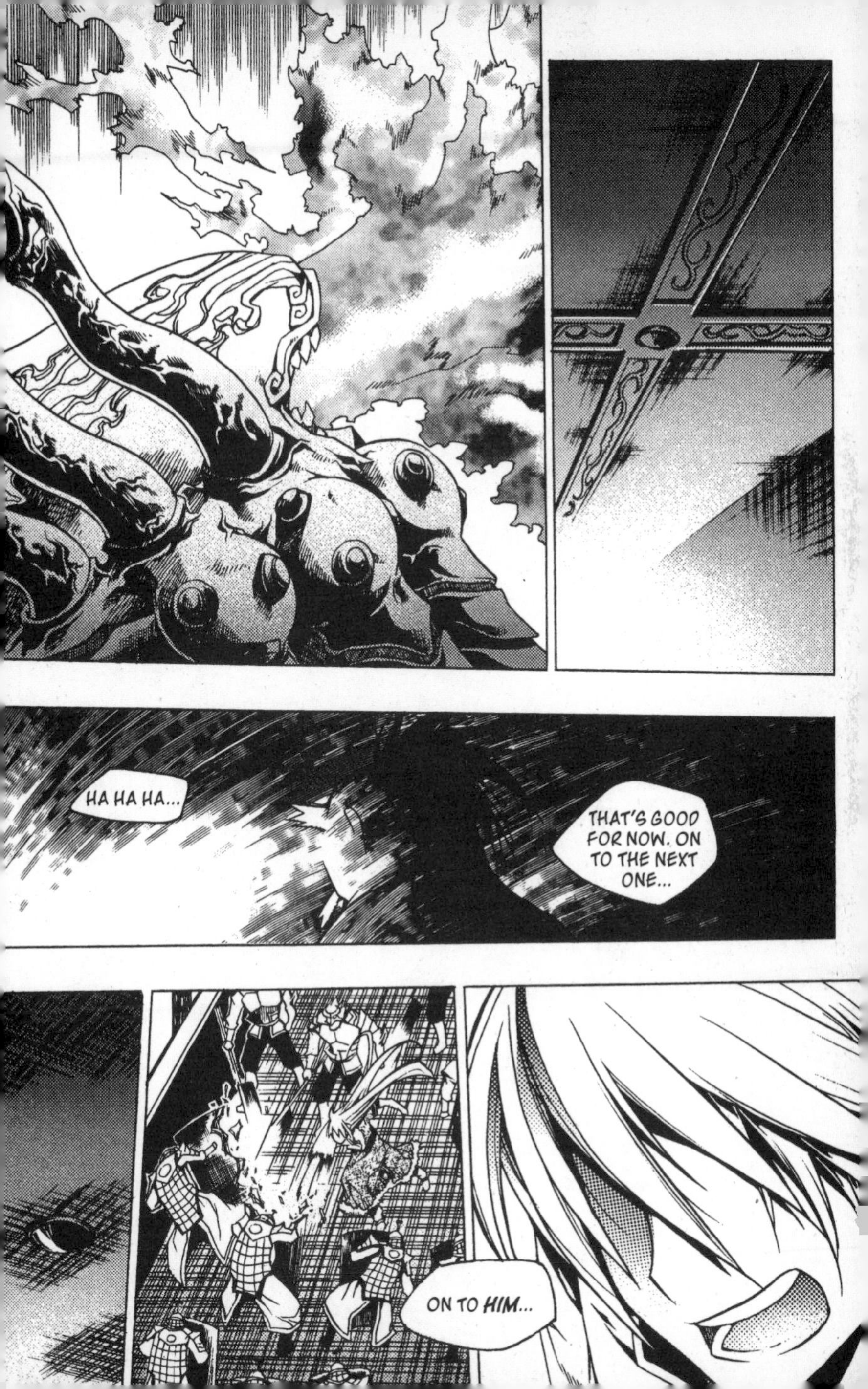
THAT'S GOOD FOR NOW. ON TO THE NEXT ONE...
HA HA HA...
ON TO HIM...

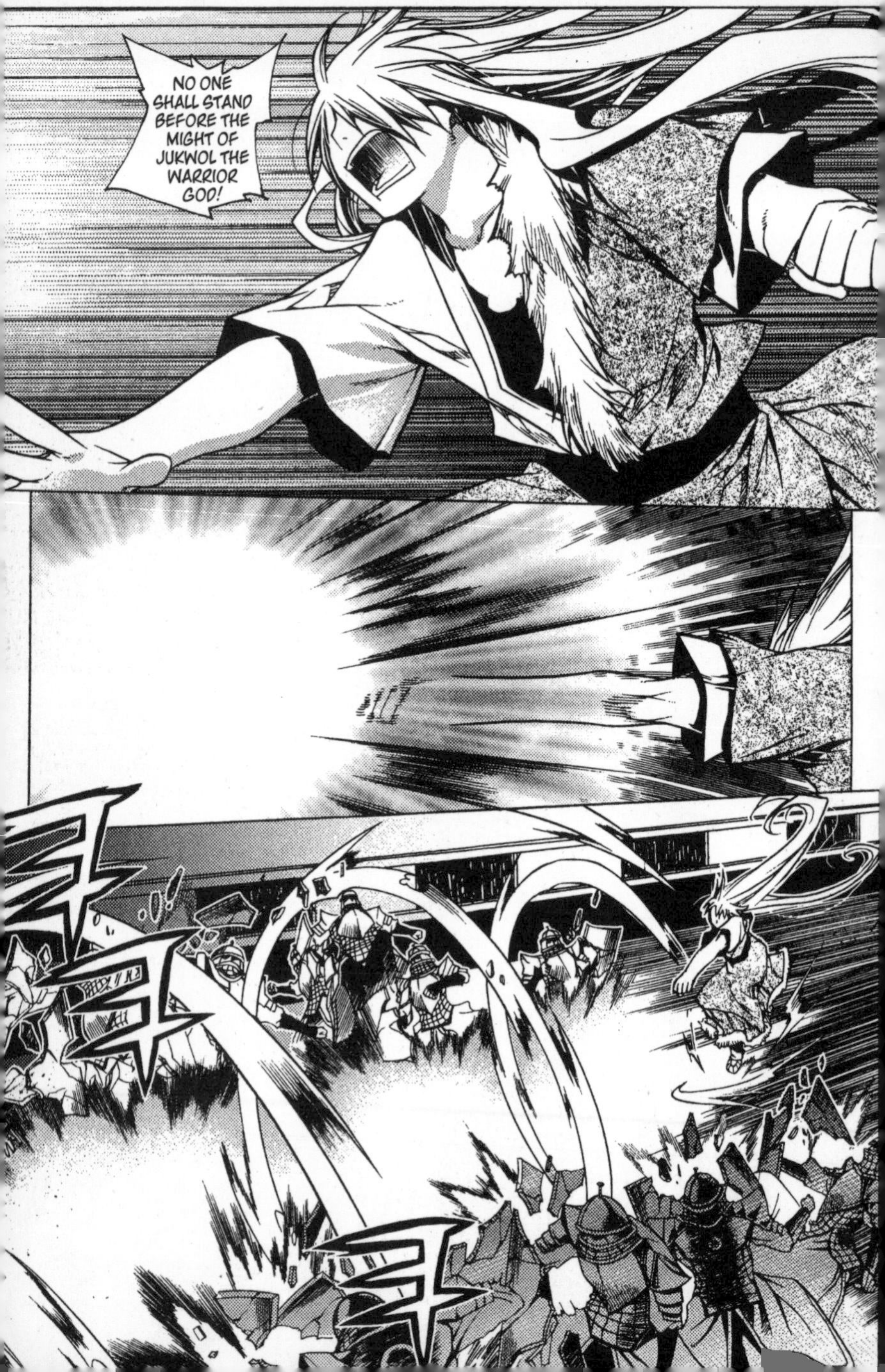
NO ONE SHALL STAND BEFORE THE MIGHT OF JUKWOL THE WARRIOR GOD!

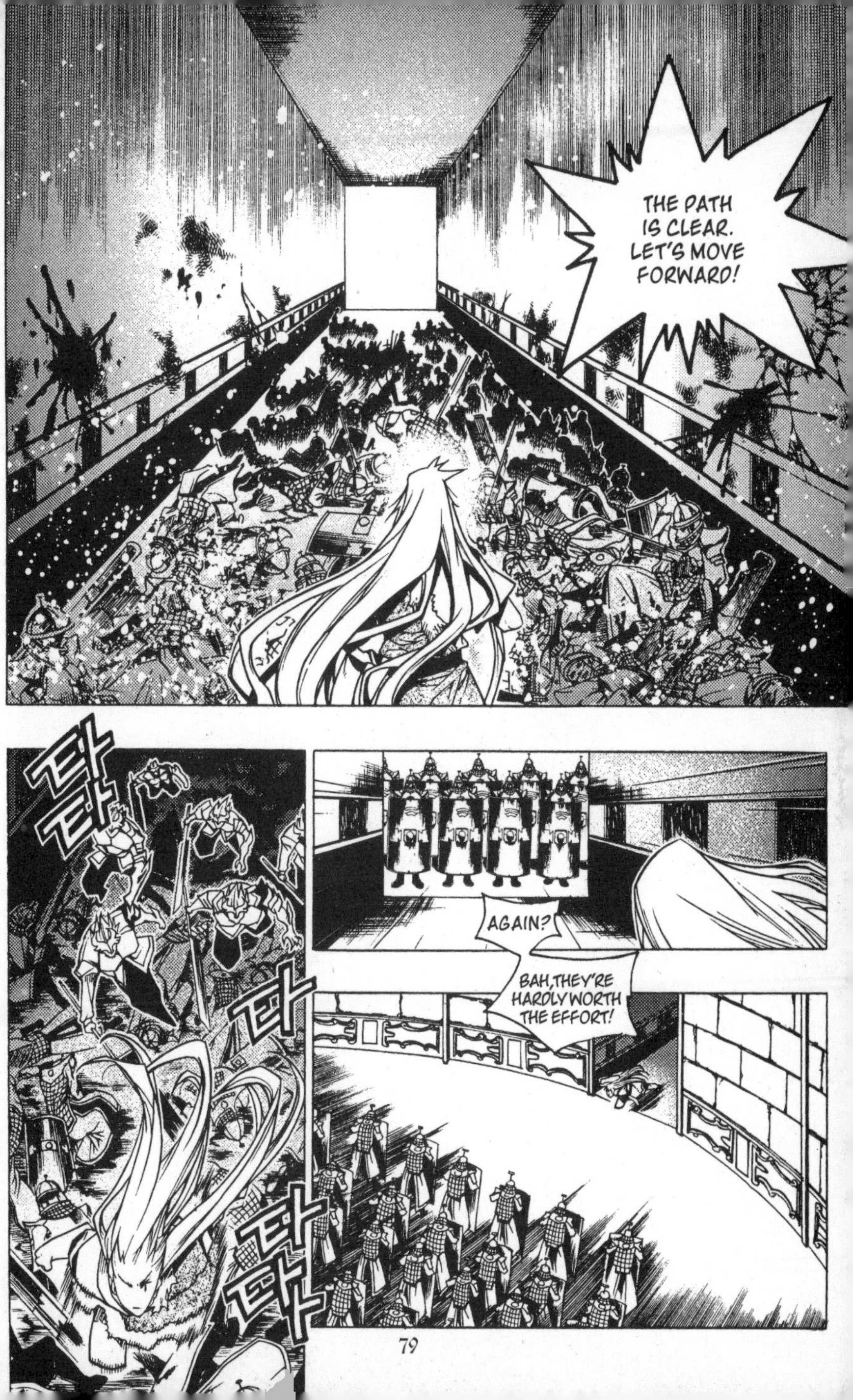
THE PATH IS CLEAR. LET'S MOVE FORWARD!
AGAIN?
BAH, THEY'RE HARDLY WORTH THE EFFORT!

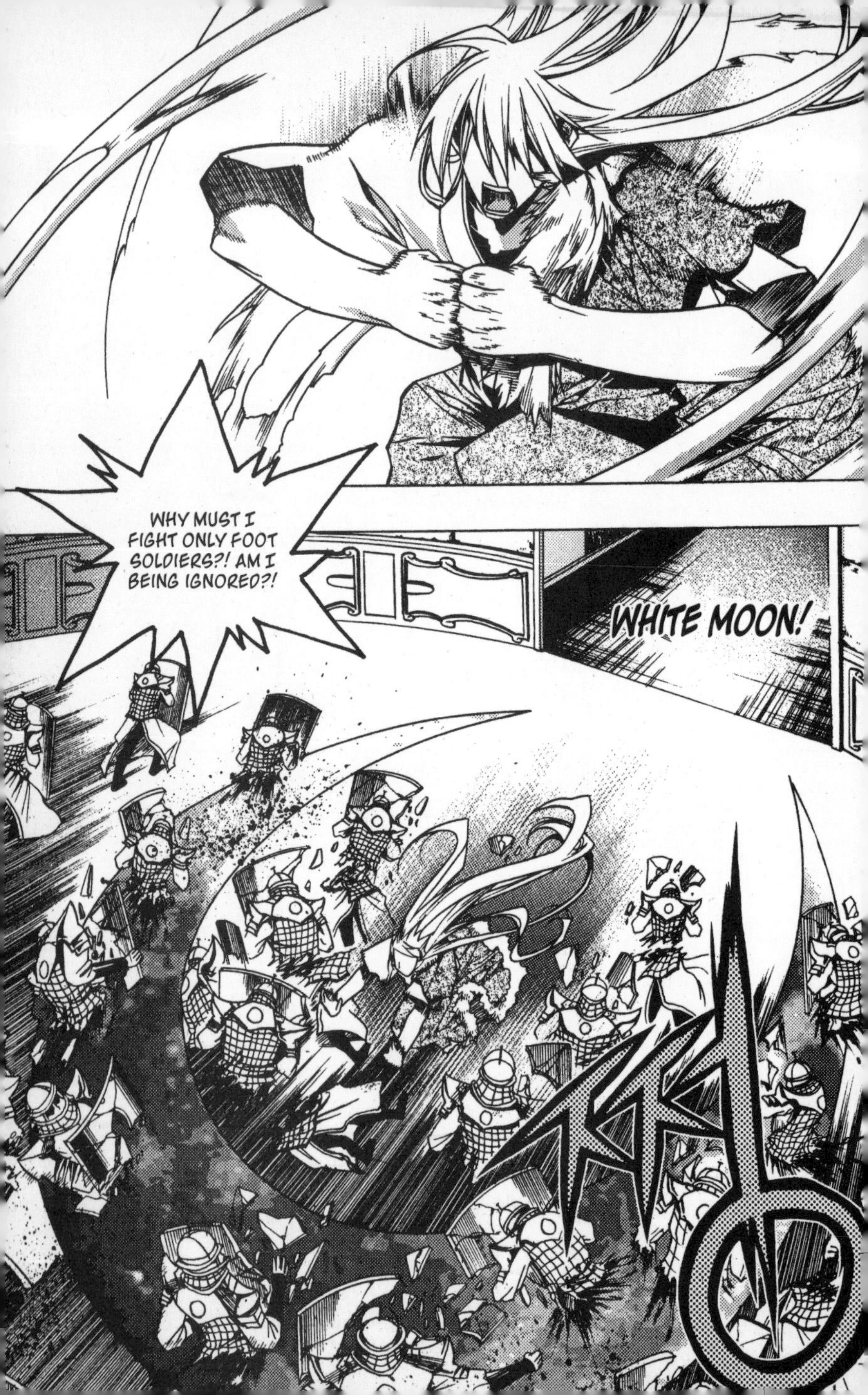
WHY MUST I FIGHT ONLY FOOT SOLDIERS?! AM I BEING IGNORED?!
WHITE MOON!

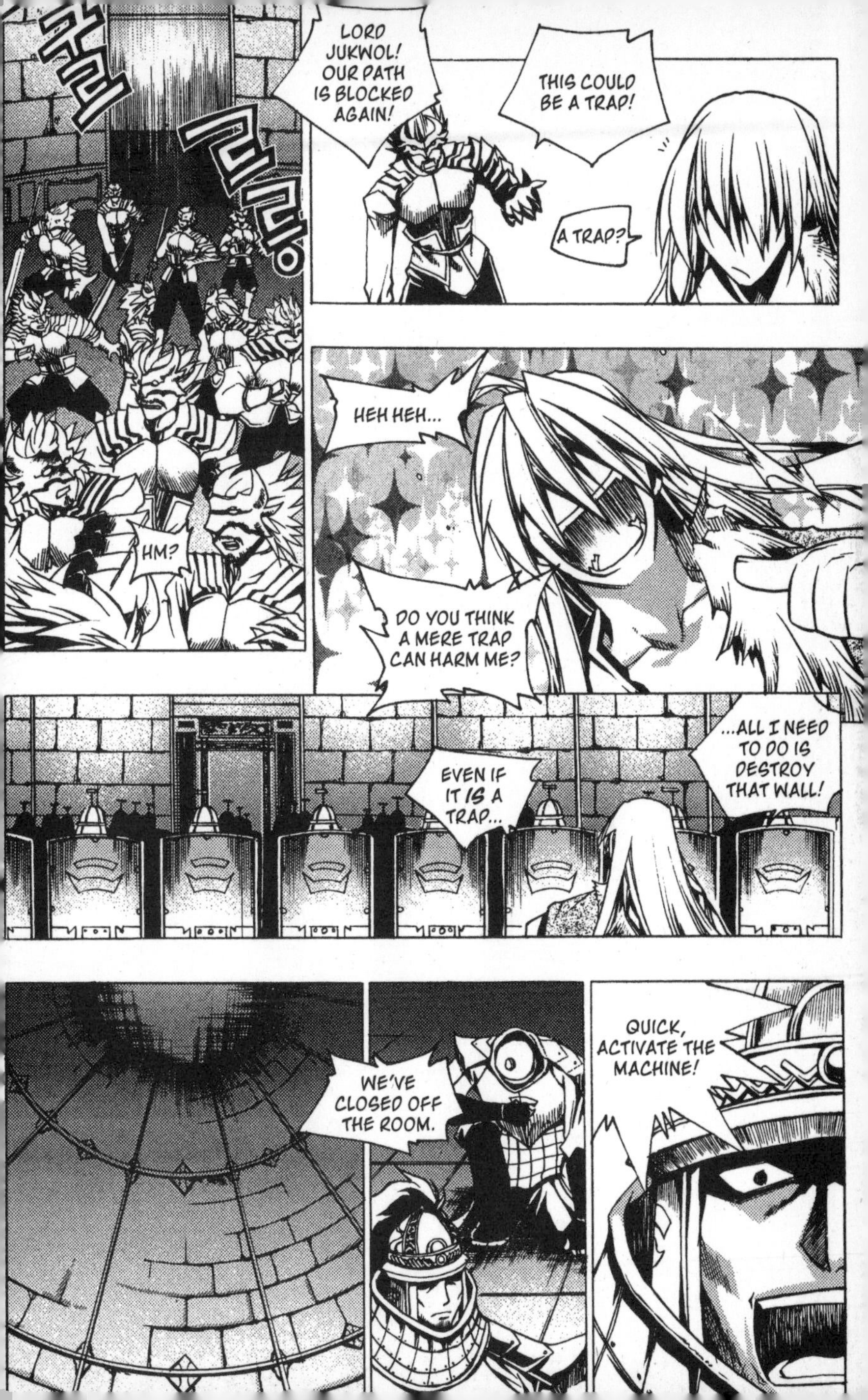
LORD JUKWOL! OUR PATH IS BLOCKED AGAIN!
THIS COULD BE A TRAP!
A TRAP?
HM?
HEH HEH...
DO YOU THINK A MERE TRAP CAN HARM ME?
EVEN IF IT IS A TRAP...
...ALL I NEED TO DO IS DESTROY THAT WALL!
WE'VE CLOSED OFF THE ROOM.
QUICK, ACTIVATE THE MACHINE!

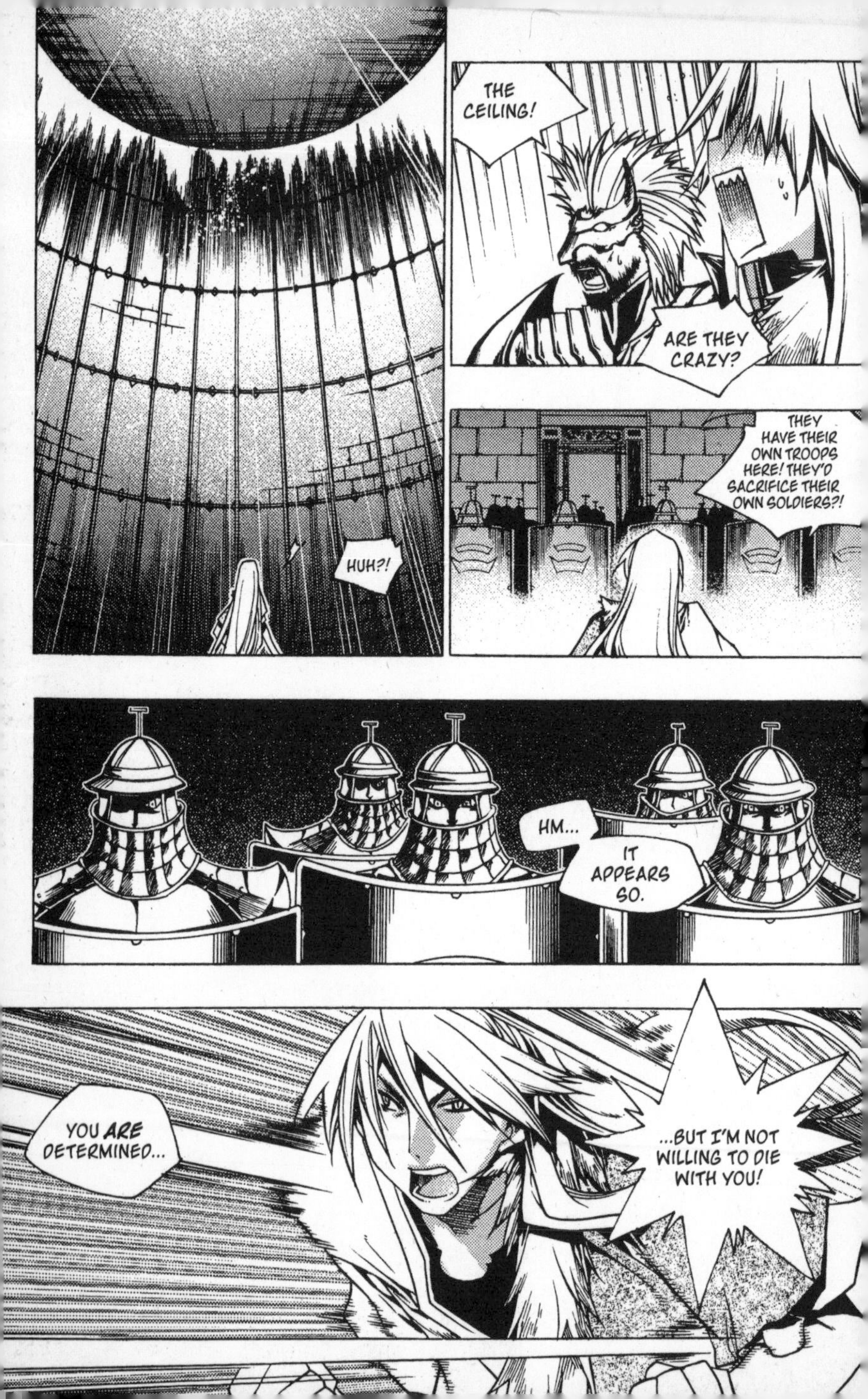
THE CEILING!
ARE THEY CRAZY?
THEY HAVE THEIR OWN TROOPS HERE! THEY'D SACRIFICE THEIR OWN SOLDIERS?!
HUH?!
HM...
IT APPEARS SO.
...BUT I'M NOT WILLING TO DIE WITH YOU!
YOU *ARE* DETERMINED...

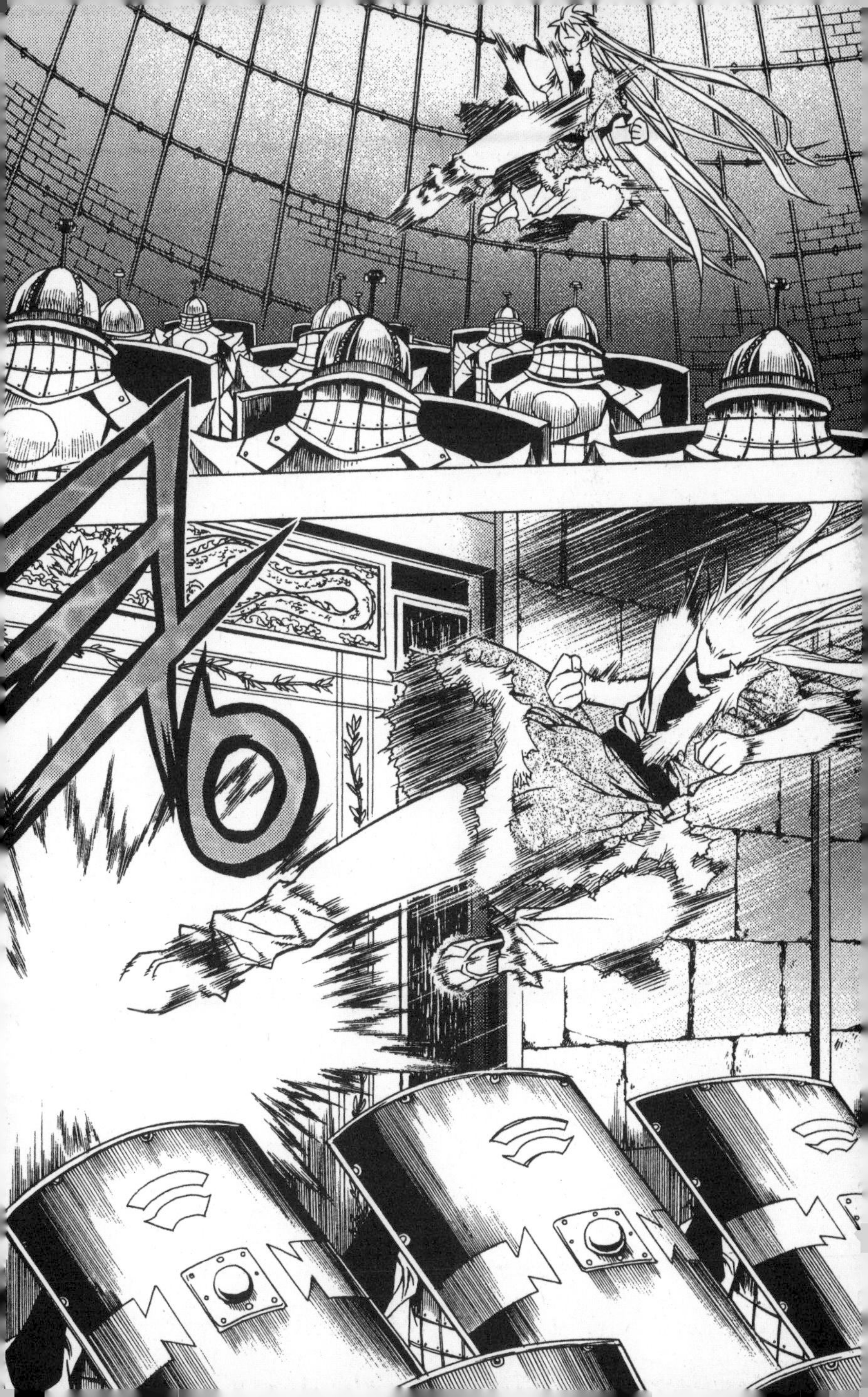

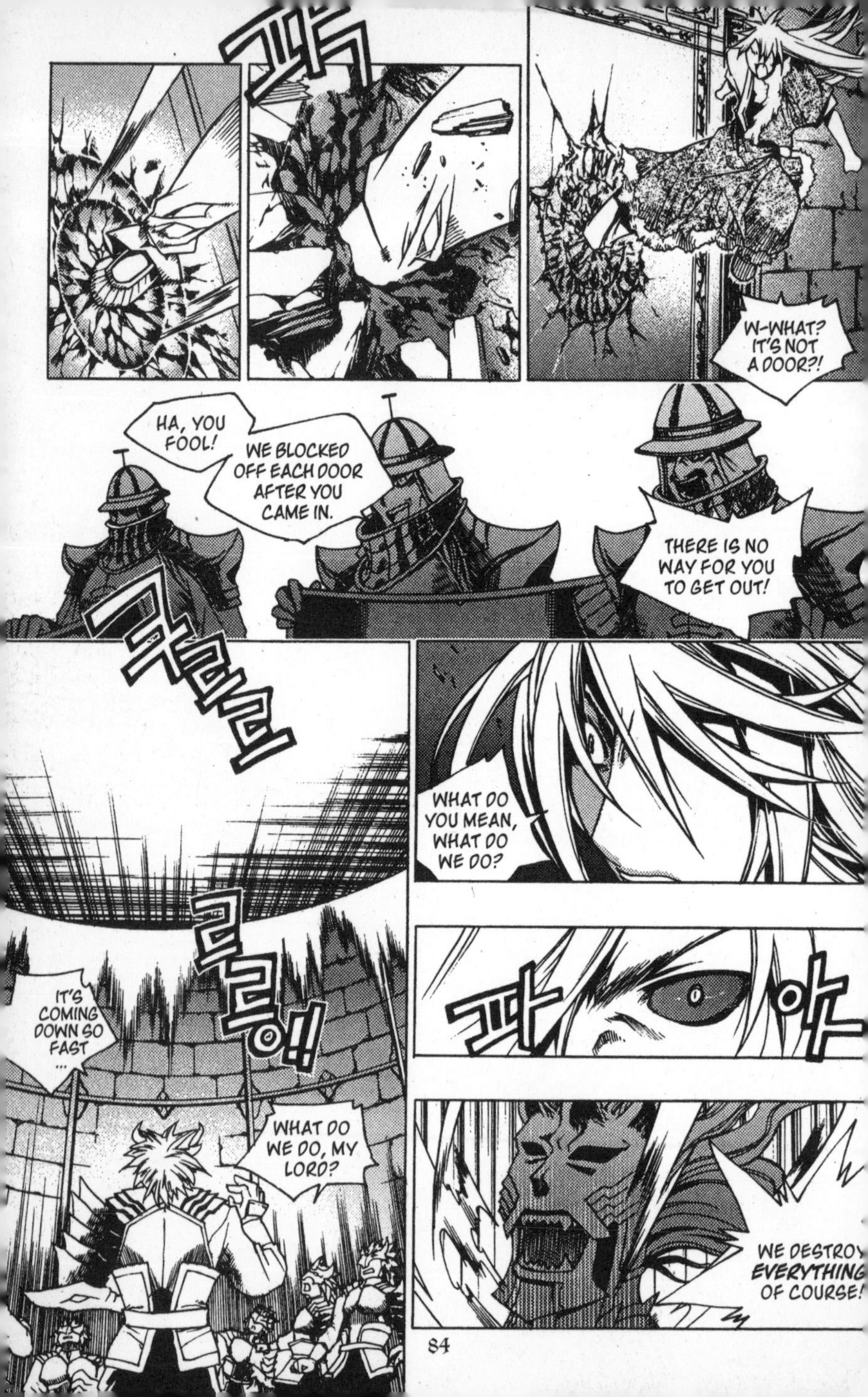
W-WHAT? IT'S NOT A DOOR?!
HA, YOU FOOL!
WE BLOCKED OFF EACH DOOR AFTER YOU CAME IN.
THERE IS NO WAY FOR YOU TO GET OUT!
IT'S COMING DOWN SO FAST ...
WHAT DO WE DO, MY LORD?
WHAT DO YOU MEAN, WHAT DO WE DO?
WE DESTROY EVERYTHING OF COURSE!

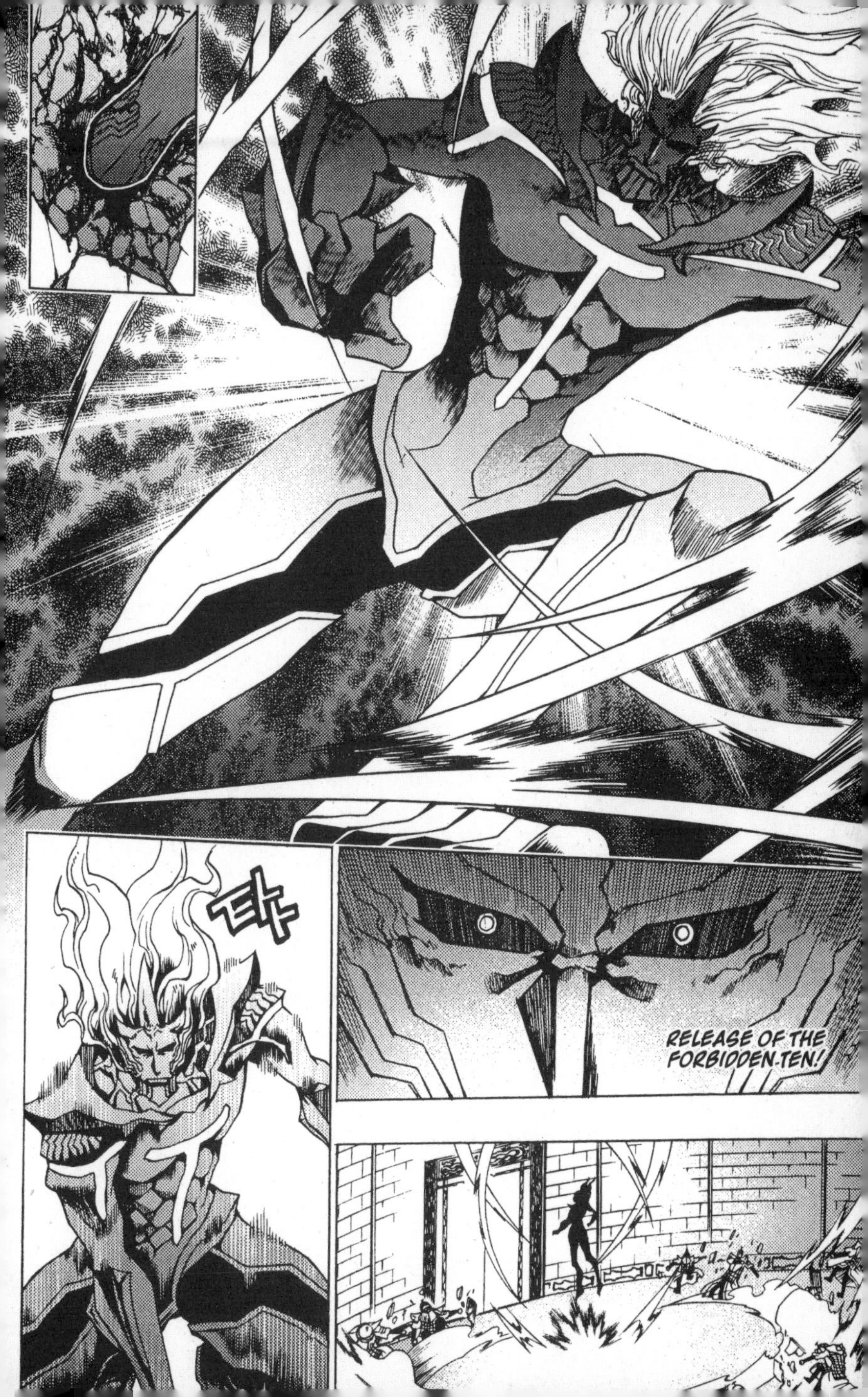
RELEASE OF THE
FORBIDDEN-TEN!
TEK

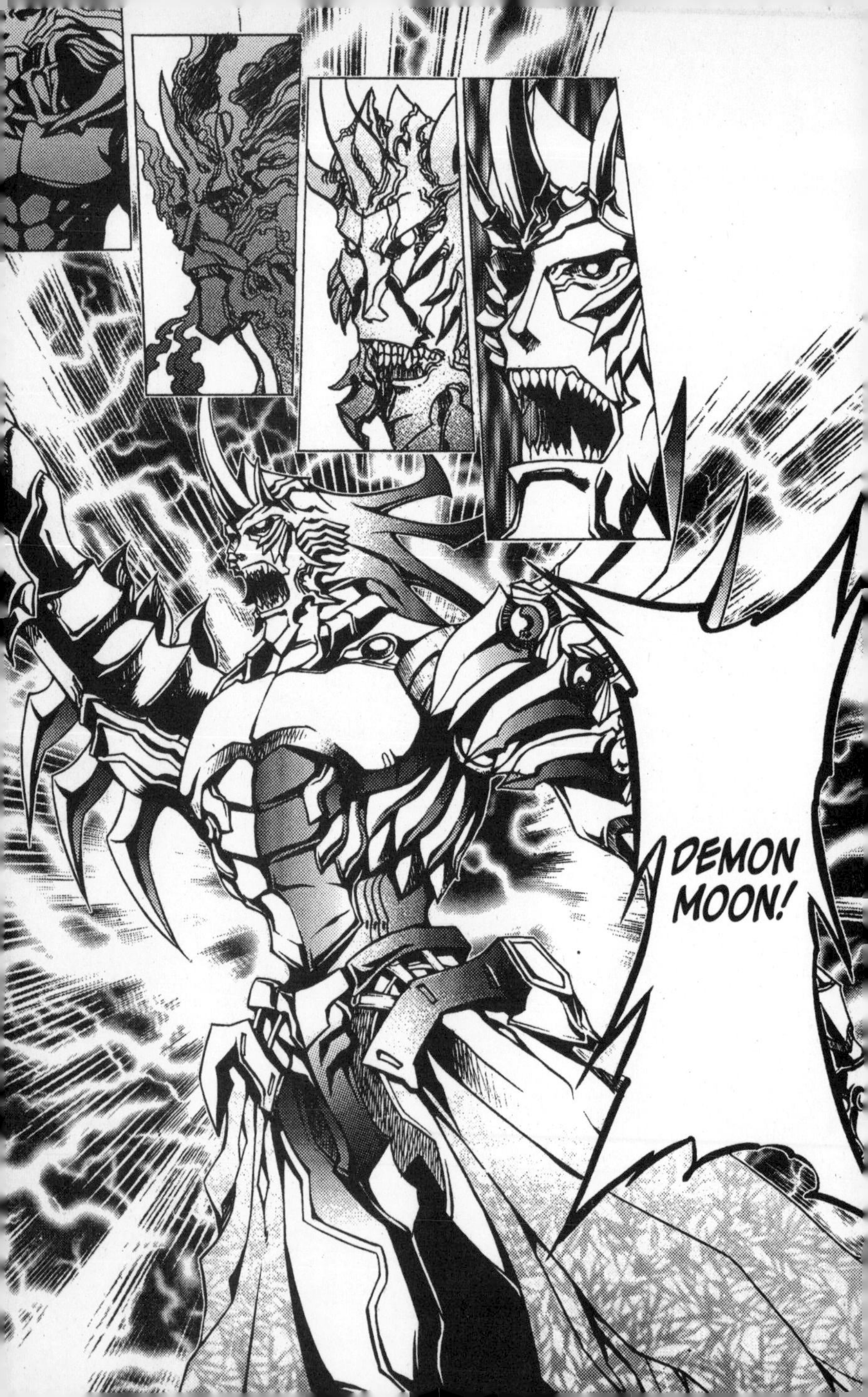
DEMON MOON!

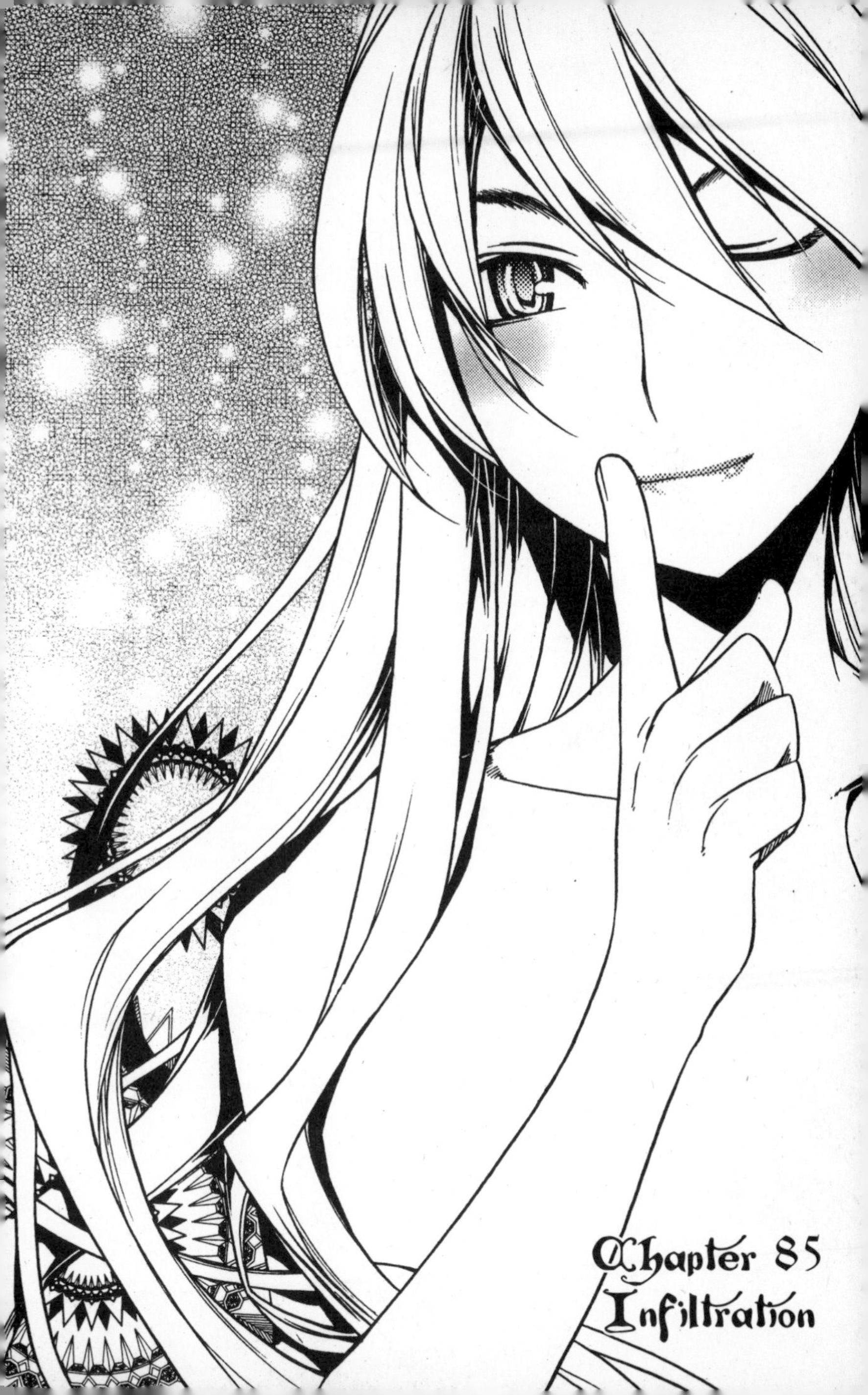

Chapter 85
Infiltration

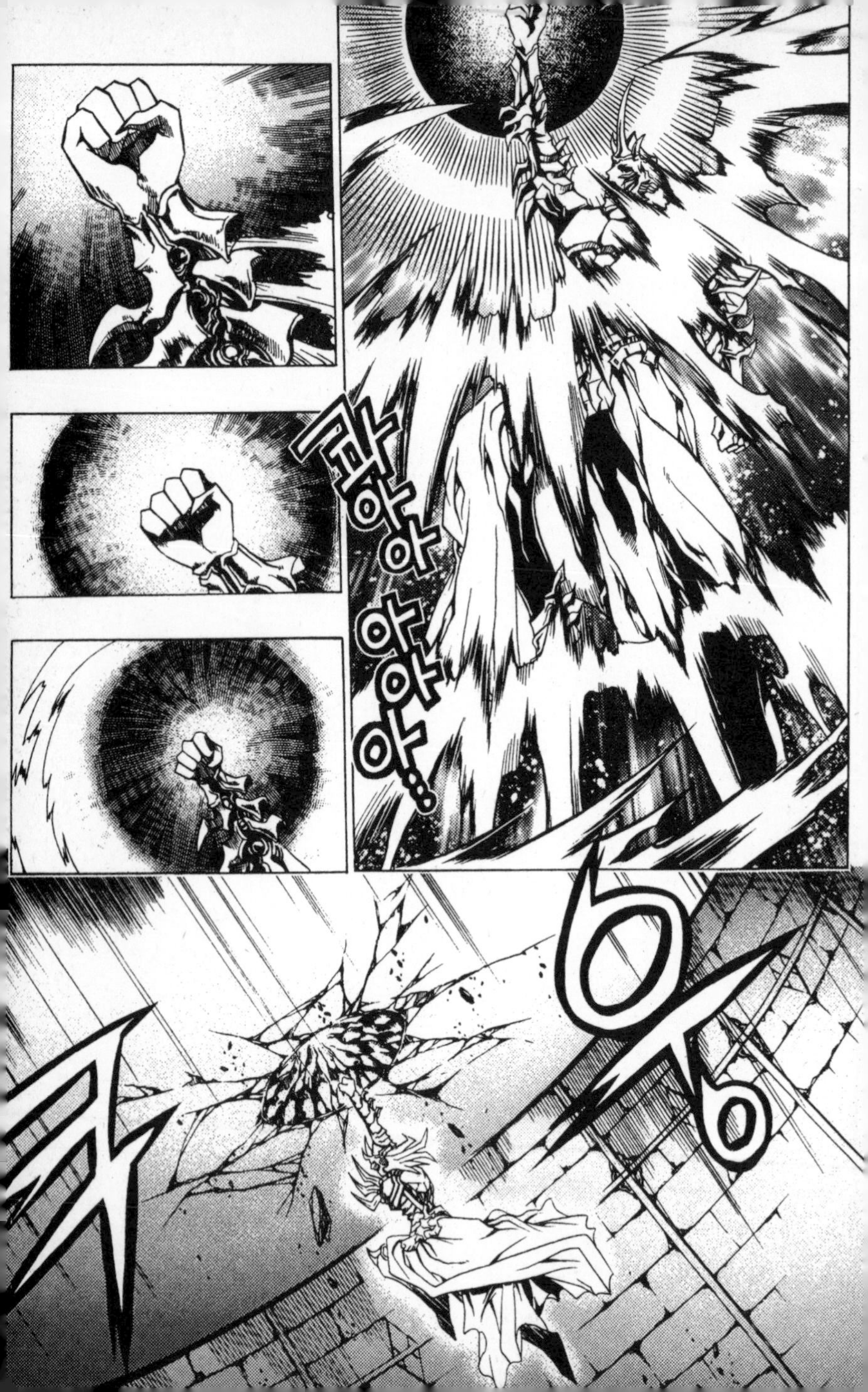
콰아아아아아...
앙

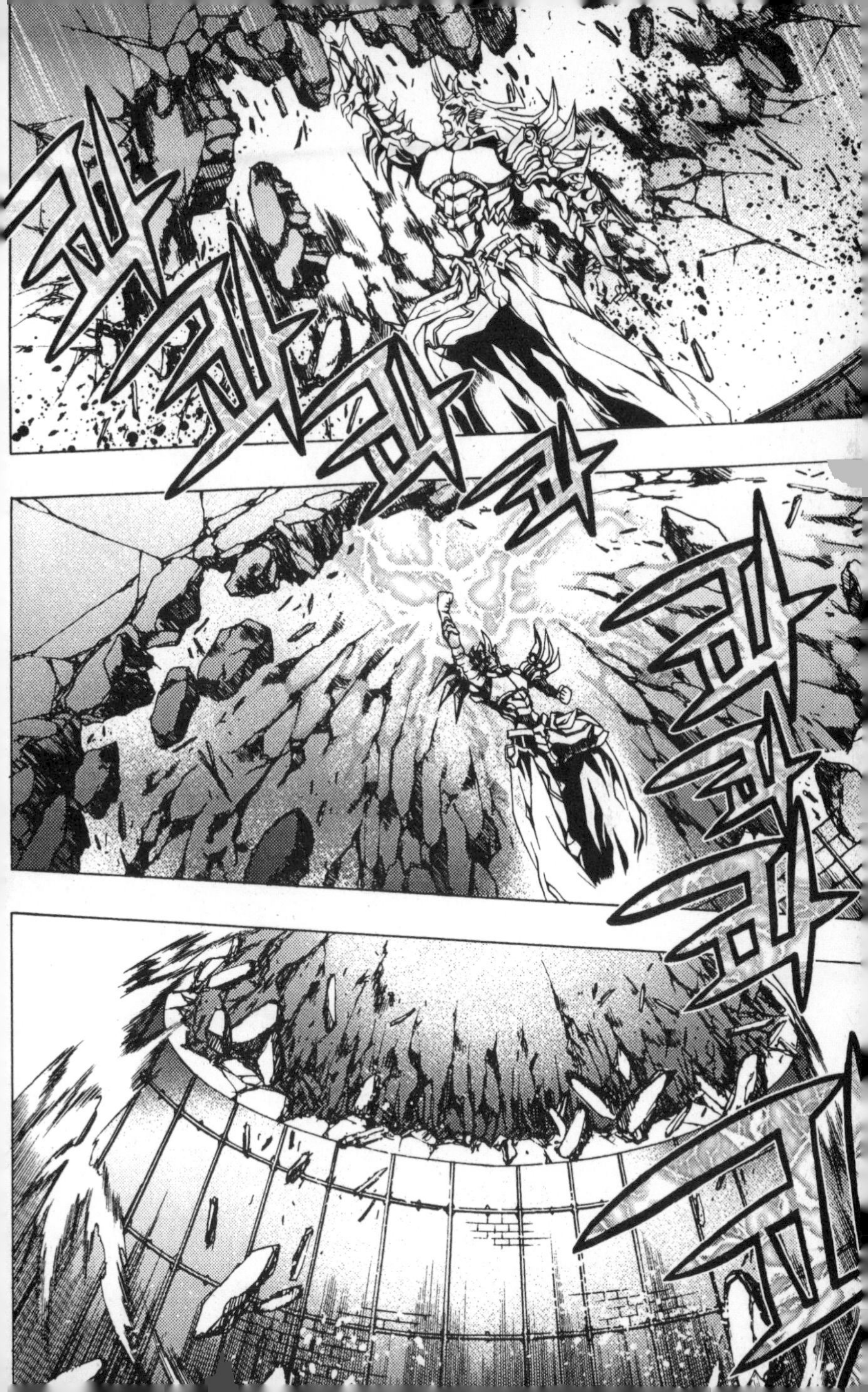

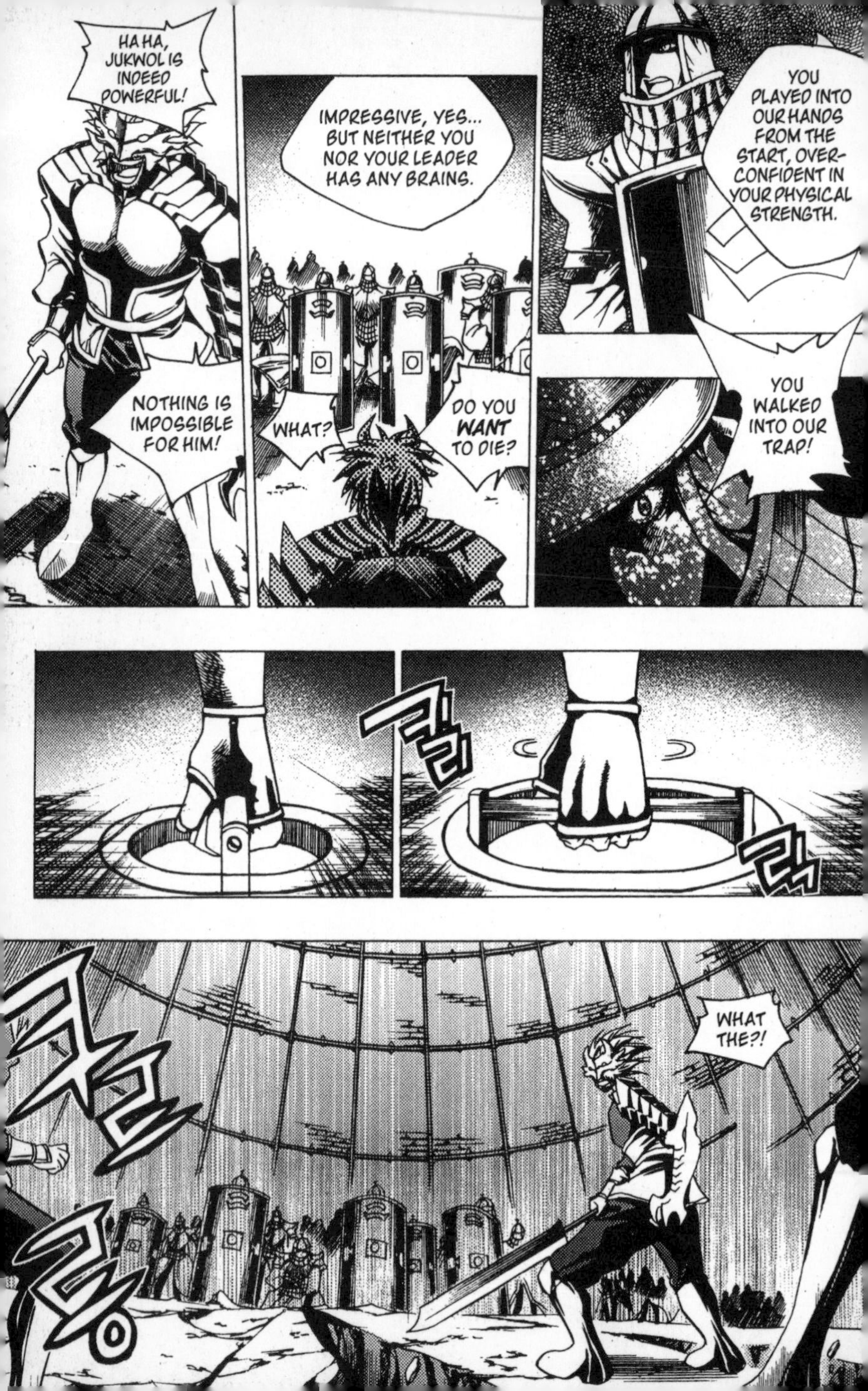
HA HA, JUKWOL IS INDEED POWERFUL!
NOTHING IS IMPOSSIBLE FOR HIM!
IMPRESSIVE, YES... BUT NEITHER YOU NOR YOUR LEADER HAS ANY BRAINS.
WHAT?
DO YOU WANT TO DIE?
YOU PLAYED INTO OUR HANDS FROM THE START, OVER-CONFIDENT IN YOUR PHYSICAL STRENGTH.
YOU WALKED INTO OUR TRAP!
WHAT THE?!

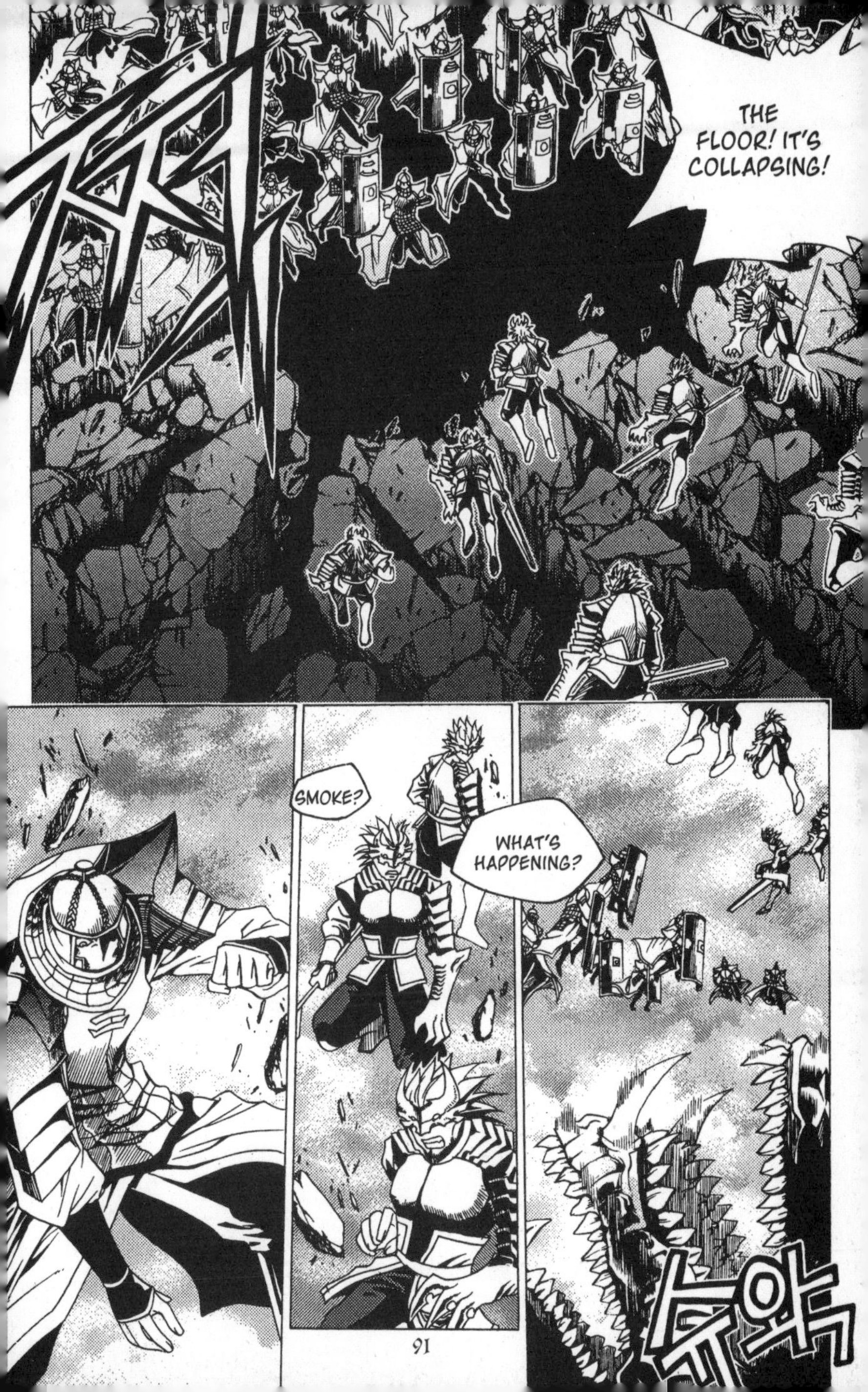
THE FLOOR! IT'S COLLAPSING!
SMOKE?
WHAT'S HAPPENING?

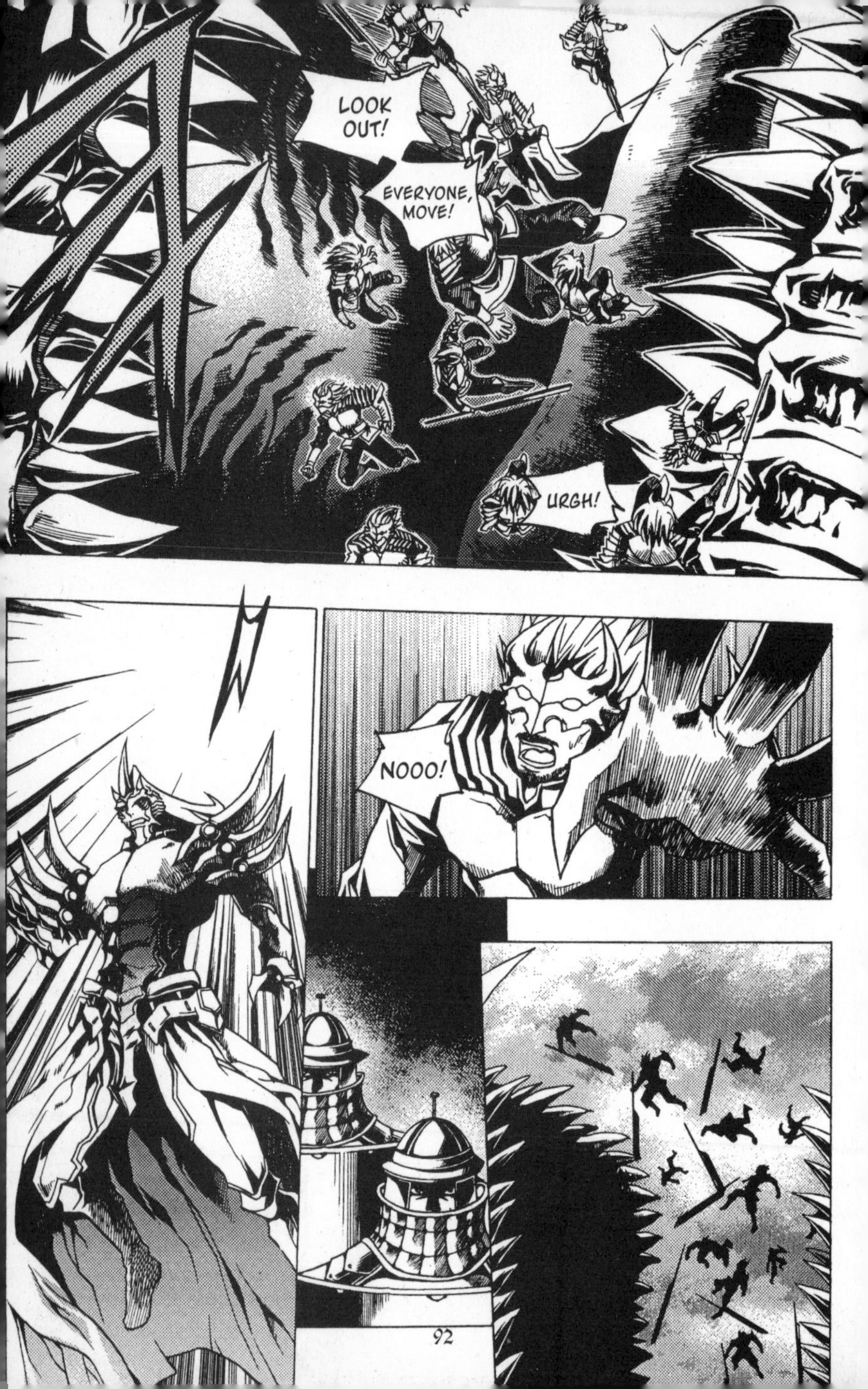
LOOK OUT!
EVERYONE, MOVE!
URGH!
NOOO!

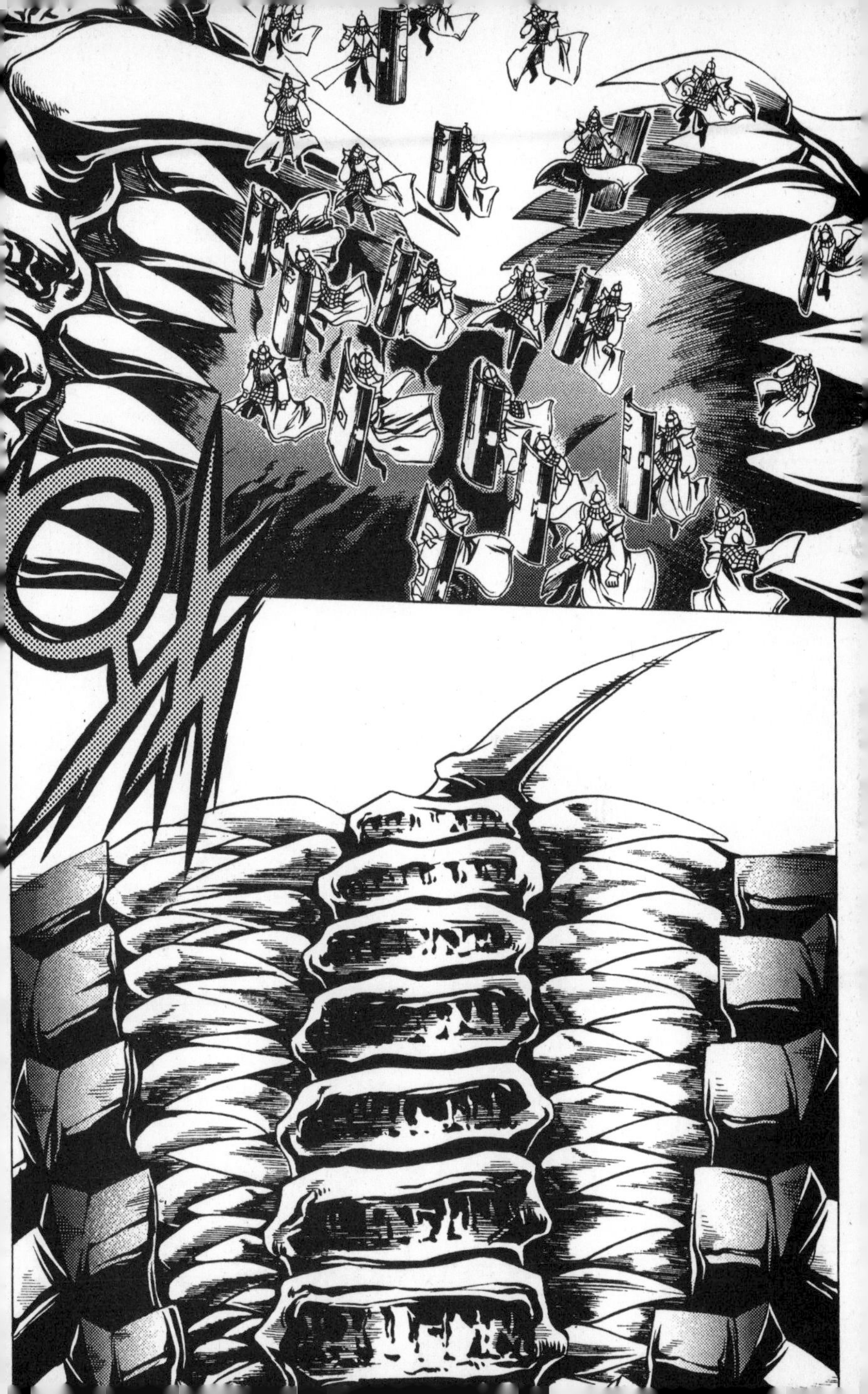

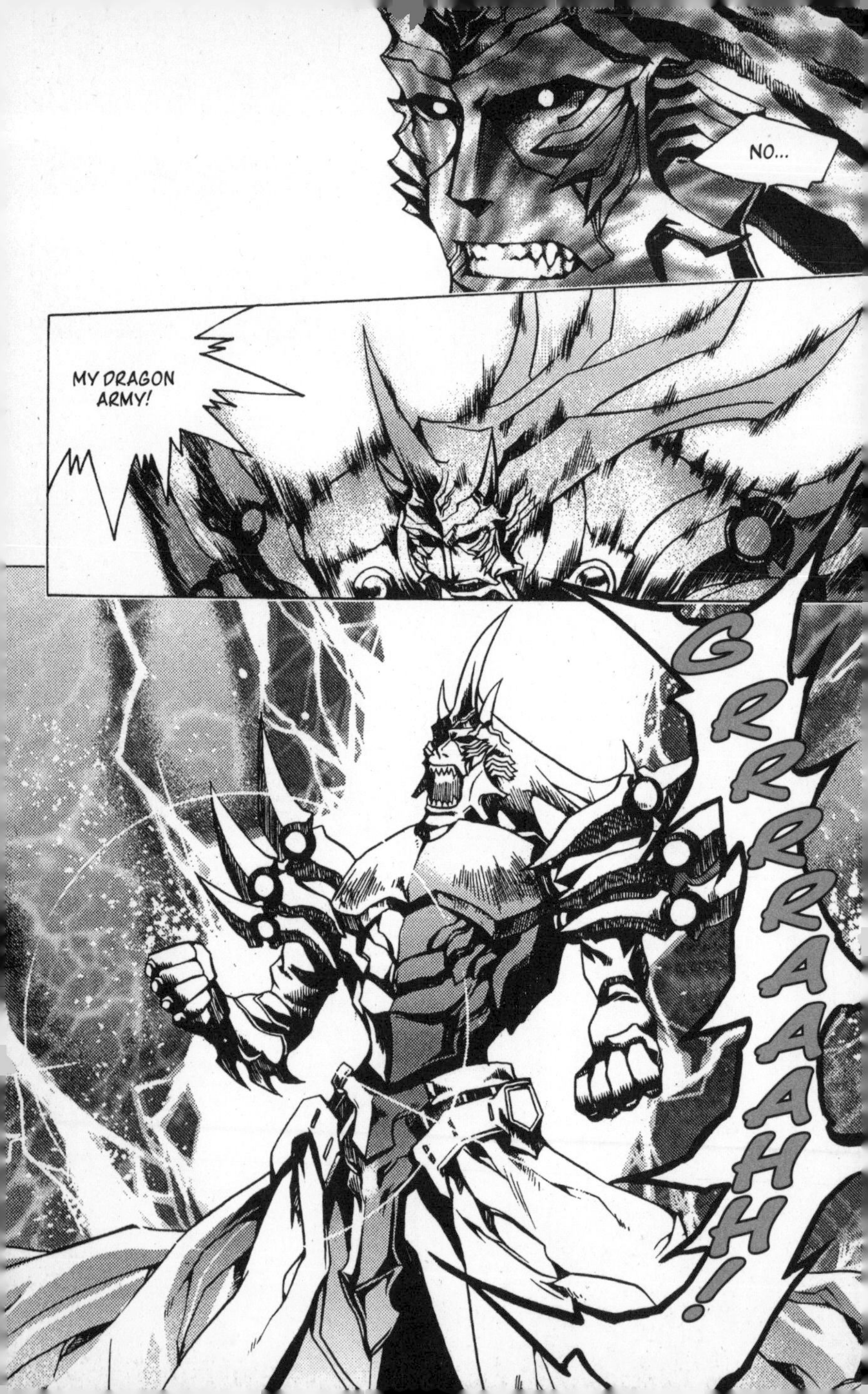
NO...
MY DRAGON ARMY!
GRRRRAAAHHH!

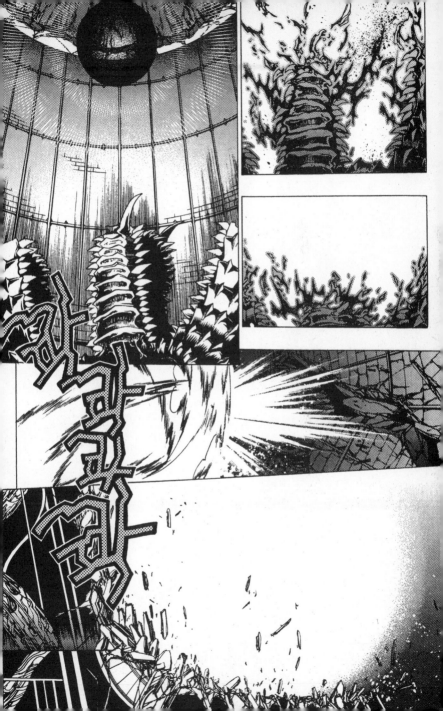

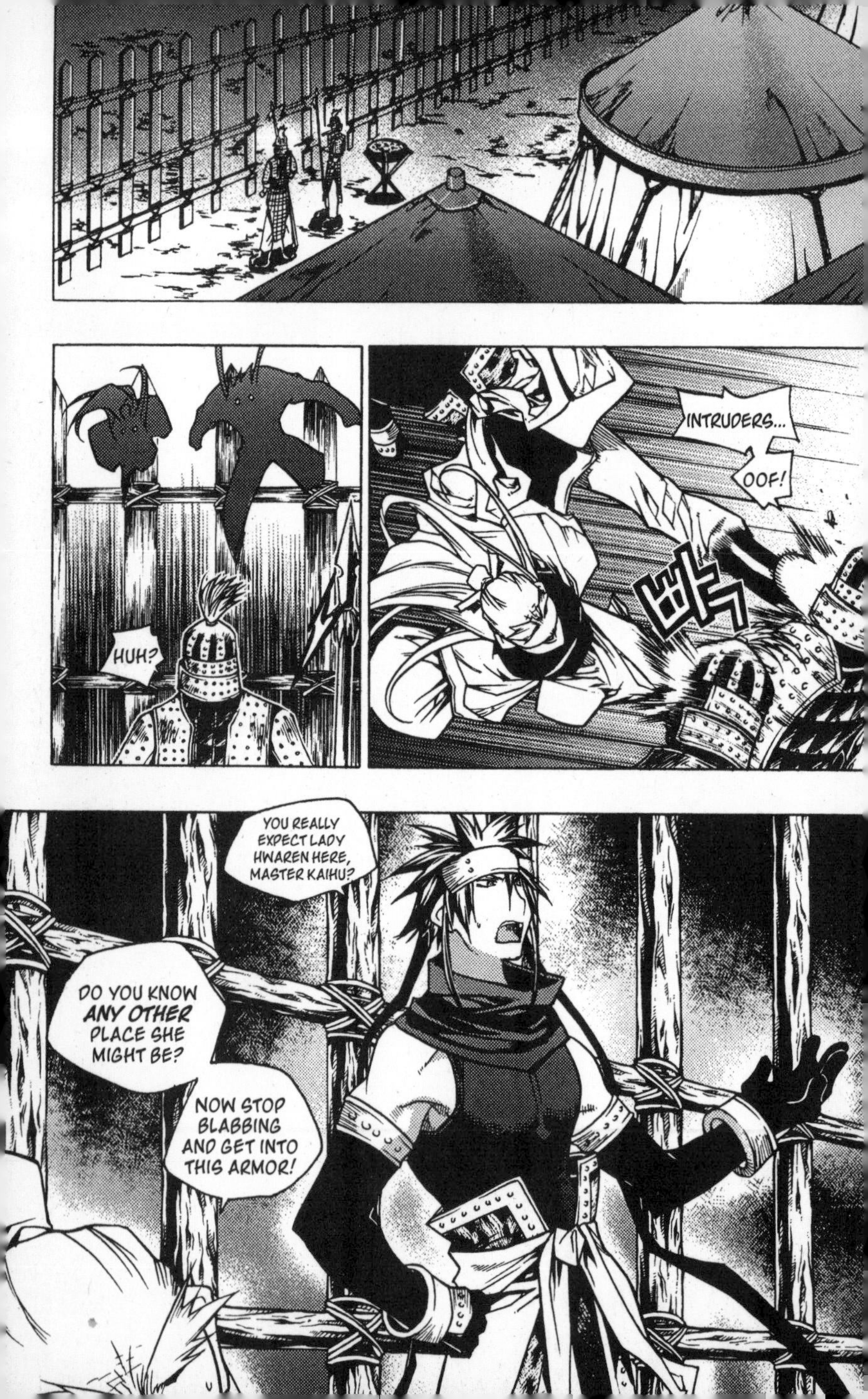
HUH?
INTRUDERS...
OOF!
YOU REALLY EXPECT LADY HWAREN HERE, MASTER KAIHU?
DO YOU KNOW ANY OTHER PLACE SHE MIGHT BE?
NOW STOP BLABBING AND GET INTO THIS ARMOR!

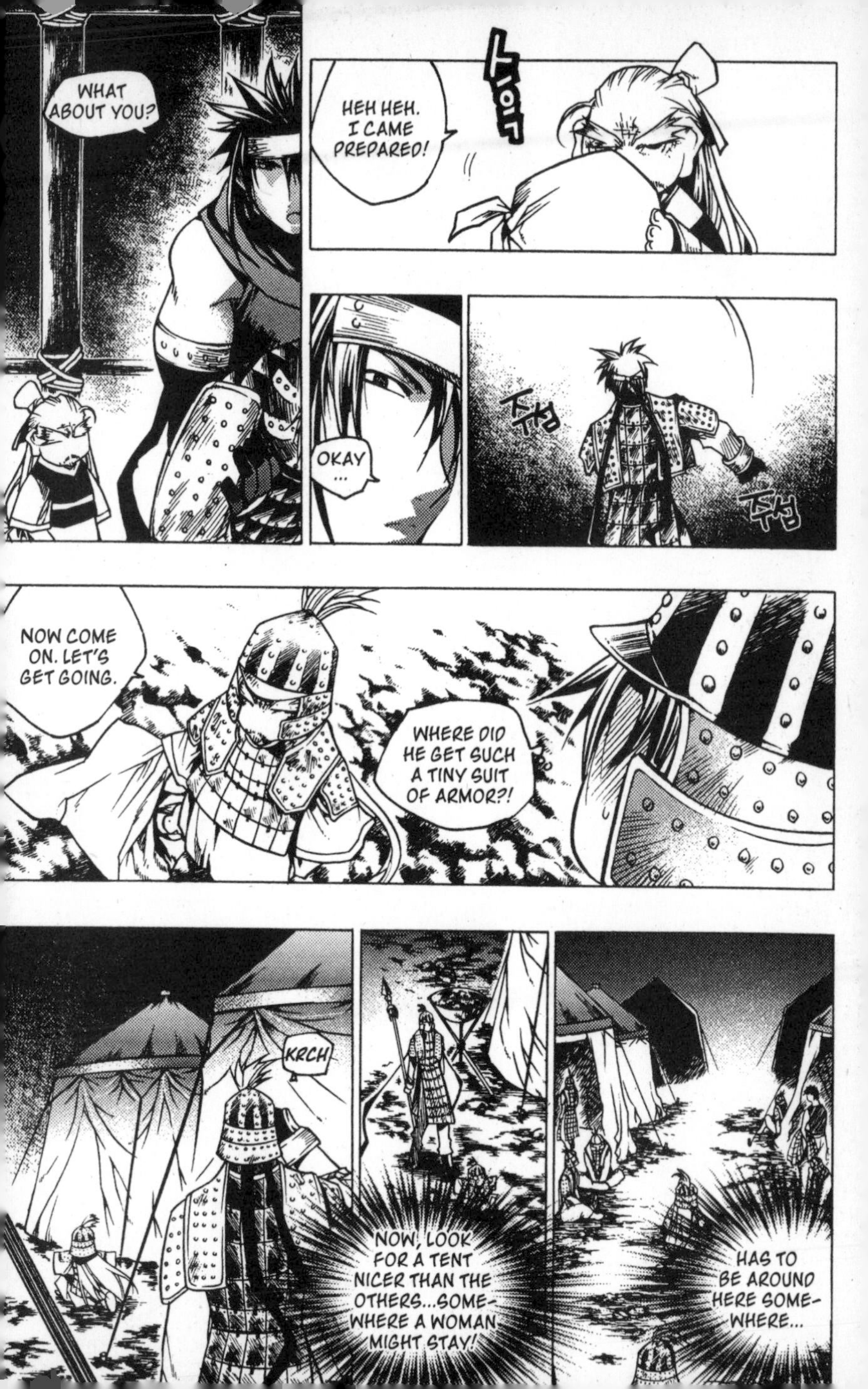
WHAT ABOUT YOU?
HEH HEH. I CAME PREPARED!
OKAY ...
NOW COME ON. LET'S GET GOING.
WHERE DID HE GET SUCH A TINY SUIT OF ARMOR?!
KRCH
NOW, LOOK FOR A TENT NICER THAN THE OTHERS...SOMEWHERE A WOMAN MIGHT STAY!
HAS TO BE AROUND HERE SOMEWHERE...

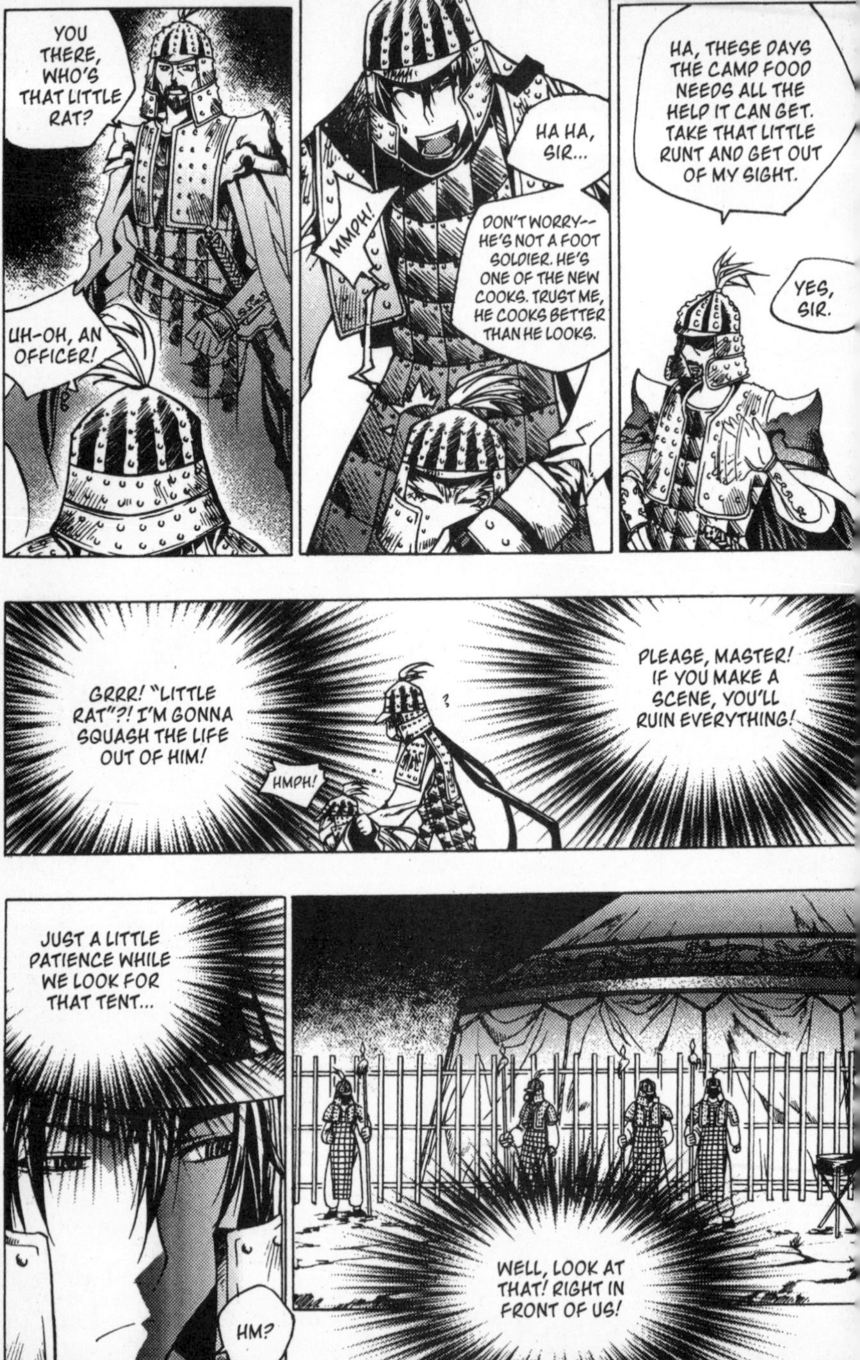
YOU THERE, WHO'S THAT LITTLE RAT?
UH-OH, AN OFFICER!
HA HA, SIR...
MMPH!
DON'T WORRY--HE'S NOT A FOOT SOLDIER. HE'S ONE OF THE NEW COOKS. TRUST ME, HE COOKS BETTER THAN HE LOOKS.
HA, THESE DAYS THE CAMP FOOD NEEDS ALL THE HELP IT CAN GET. TAKE THAT LITTLE RUNT AND GET OUT OF MY SIGHT.
YES, SIR.
GRRR! "LITTLE RAT"?! I'M GONNA SQUASH THE LIFE OUT OF HIM!
PLEASE, MASTER! IF YOU MAKE A SCENE, YOU'LL RUIN EVERYTHING!
HMPH!
JUST A LITTLE PATIENCE WHILE WE LOOK FOR THAT TENT...
HM?
WELL, LOOK AT THAT! RIGHT IN FRONT OF US!

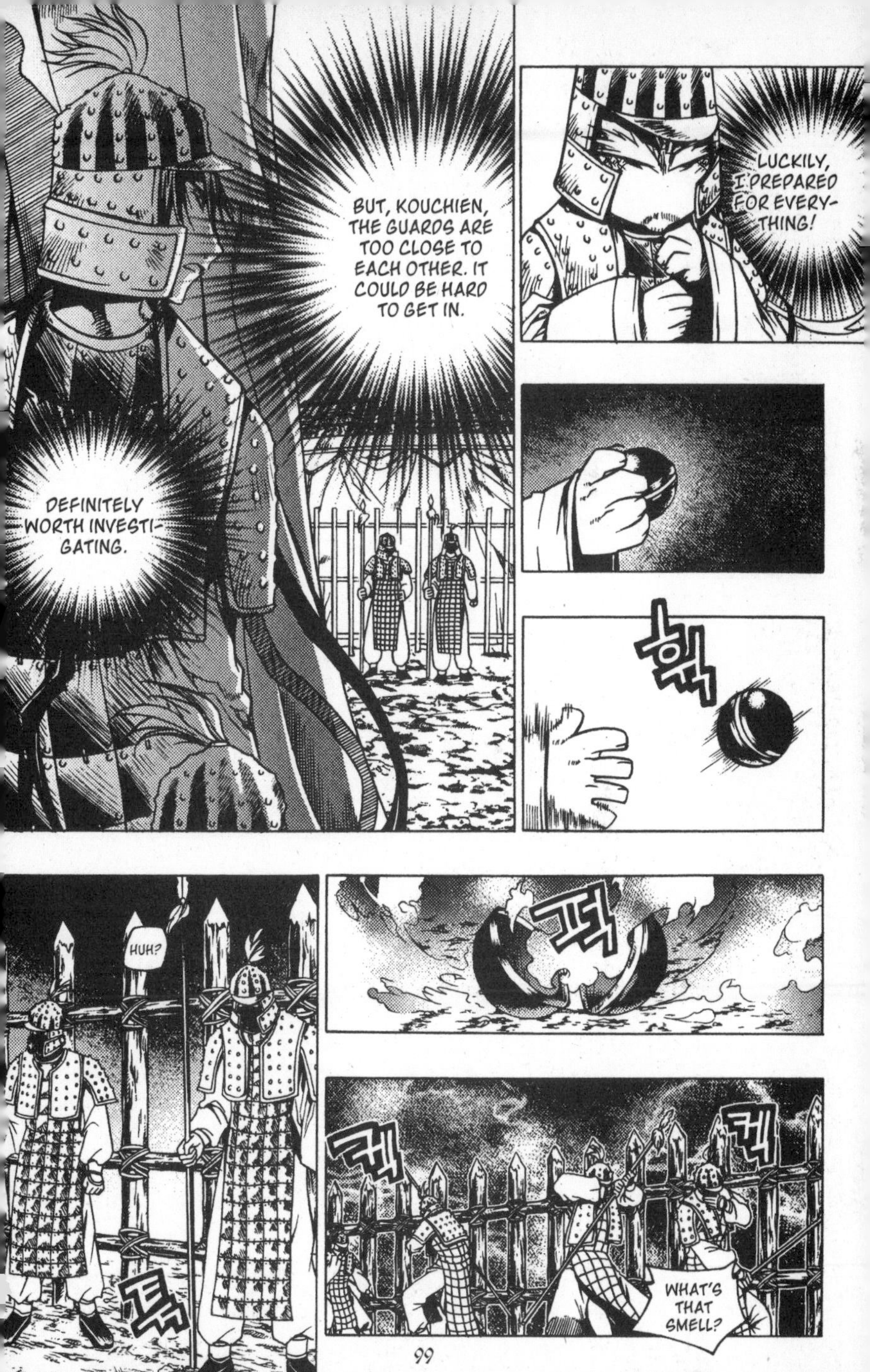
DEFINITELY WORTH INVESTI-GATING.
BUT, KOUCHIEN, THE GUARDS ARE TOO CLOSE TO EACH OTHER. IT COULD BE HARD TO GET IN.
LUCKILY, I PREPARED FOR EVERY-THING!
휙
HUH?
켁
켁
WHAT'S THAT SMELL?

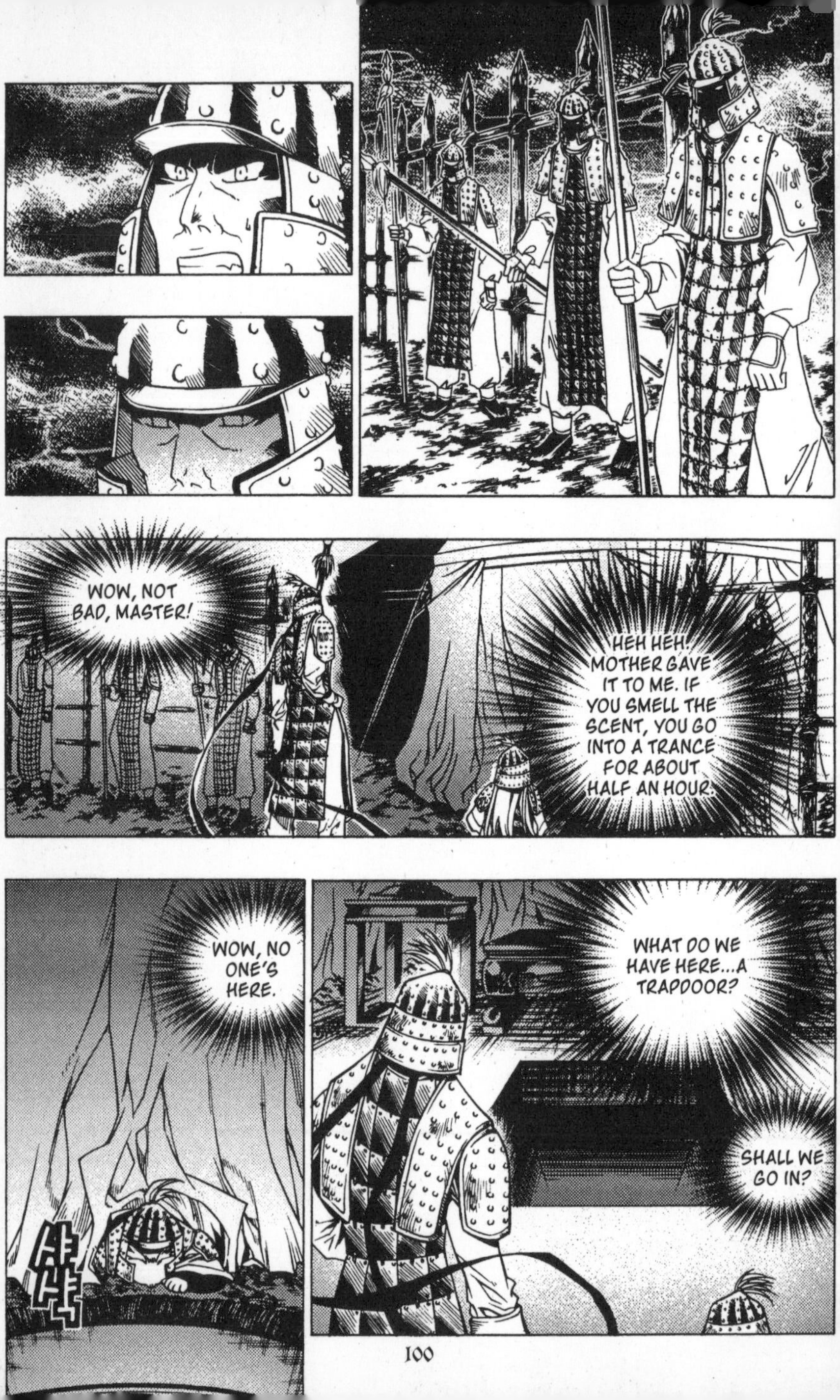
WOW, NOT BAD, MASTER!
HEH HEH. MOTHER GAVE IT TO ME. IF YOU SMELL THE SCENT, YOU GO INTO A TRANCE FOR ABOUT HALF AN HOUR.
WOW, NO ONE'S HERE.
WHAT DO WE HAVE HERE...A TRAPDOOR?
SHALL WE GO IN?

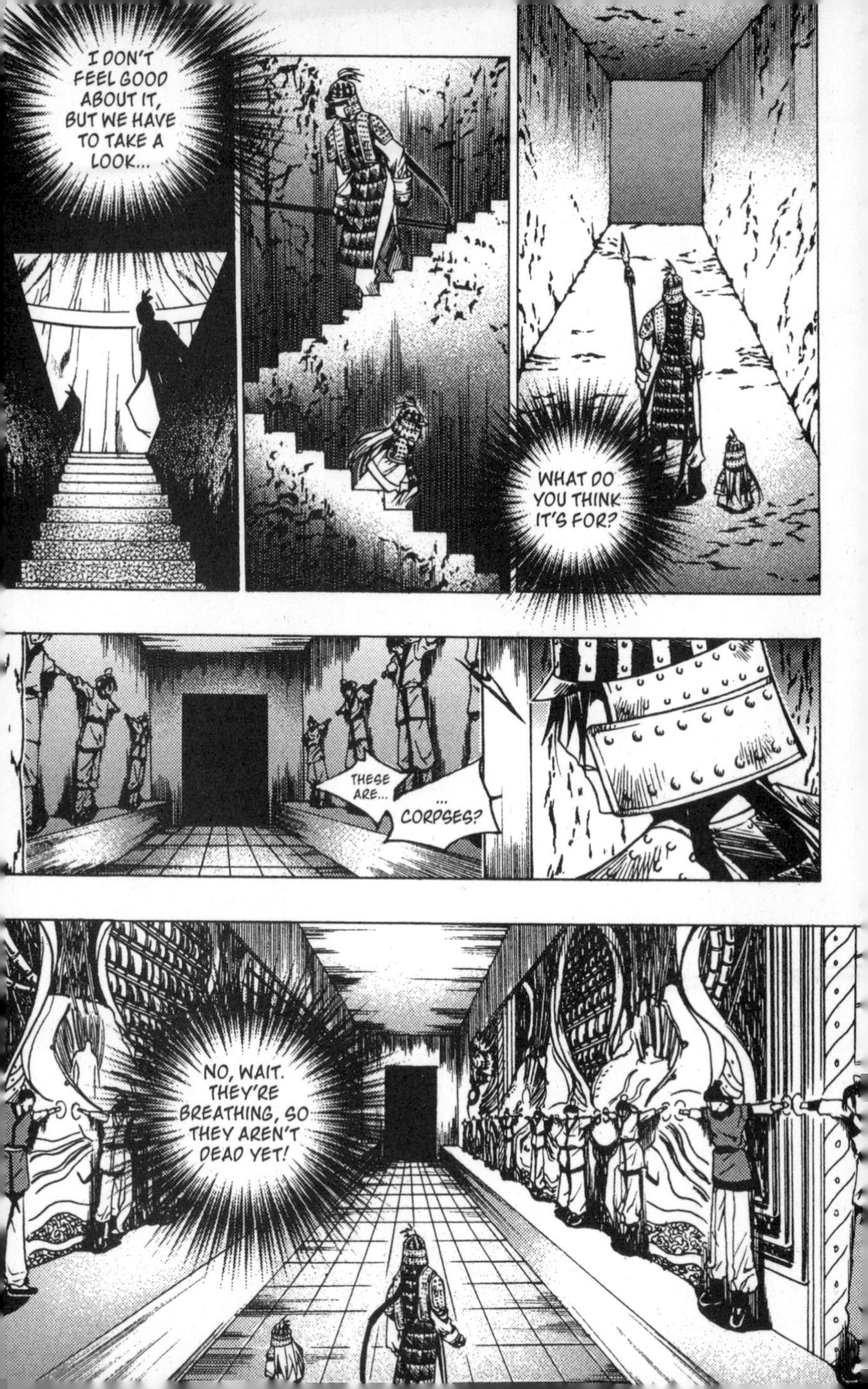
I DON'T FEEL GOOD ABOUT IT, BUT WE HAVE TO TAKE A LOOK...
WHAT DO YOU THINK IT'S FOR?
THESE ARE...
...CORPSES?
NO, WAIT. THEY'RE BREATHING, SO THEY AREN'T DEAD YET!

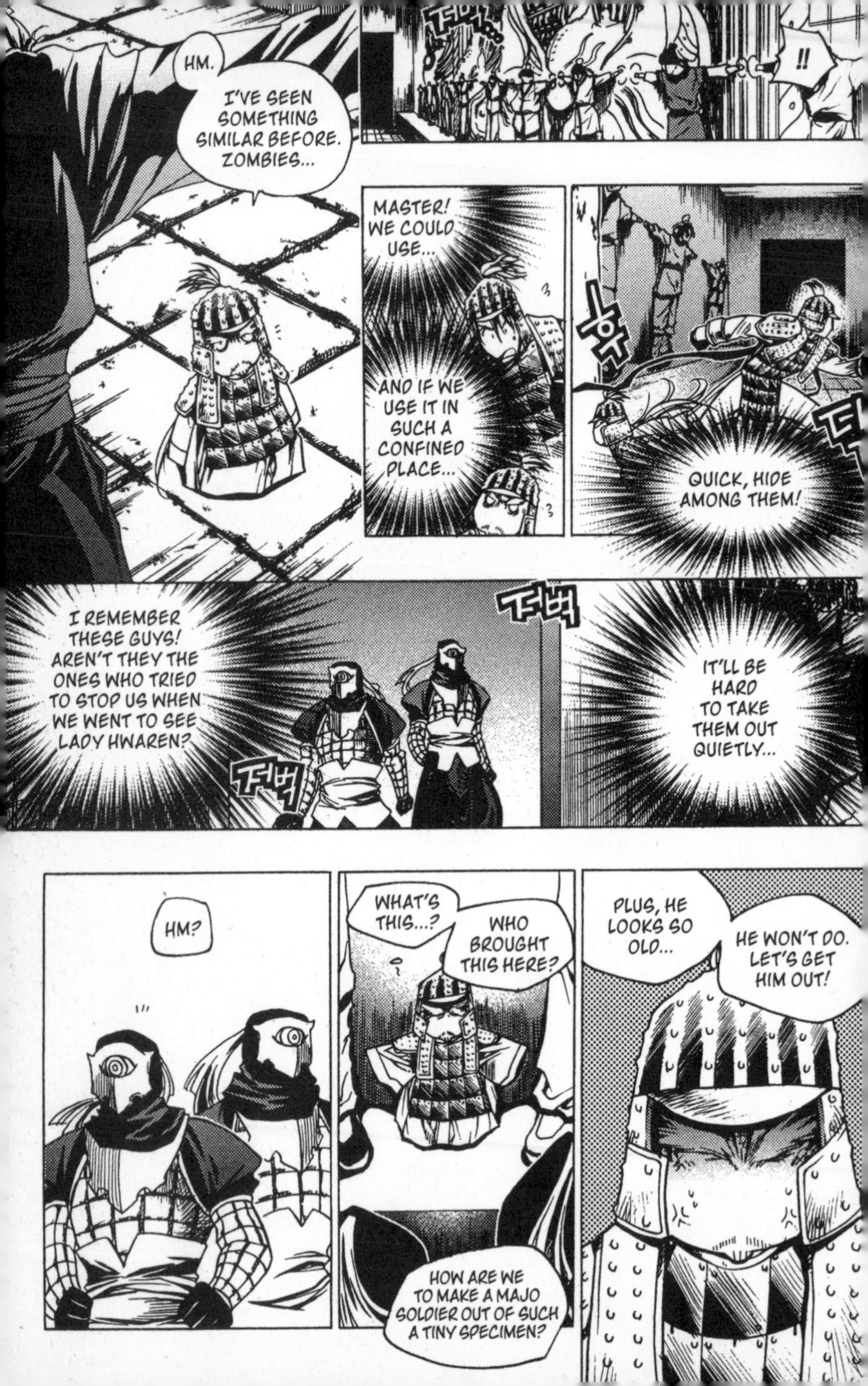
HM.
I'VE SEEN SOMETHING SIMILAR BEFORE. ZOMBIES...
!!
MASTER! WE COULD USE...
AND IF WE USE IT IN SUCH A CONFINED PLACE...
QUICK, HIDE AMONG THEM!
I REMEMBER THESE GUYS! AREN'T THEY THE ONES WHO TRIED TO STOP US WHEN WE WENT TO SEE LADY HWAREN?
저벅
저벅
IT'LL BE HARD TO TAKE THEM OUT QUIETLY...
HM?
WHAT'S THIS...?
WHO BROUGHT THIS HERE?
HOW ARE WE TO MAKE A MAJO SOLDIER OUT OF SUCH A TINY SPECIMEN?
PLUS, HE LOOKS SO OLD...
HE WON'T DO. LET'S GET HIM OUT!

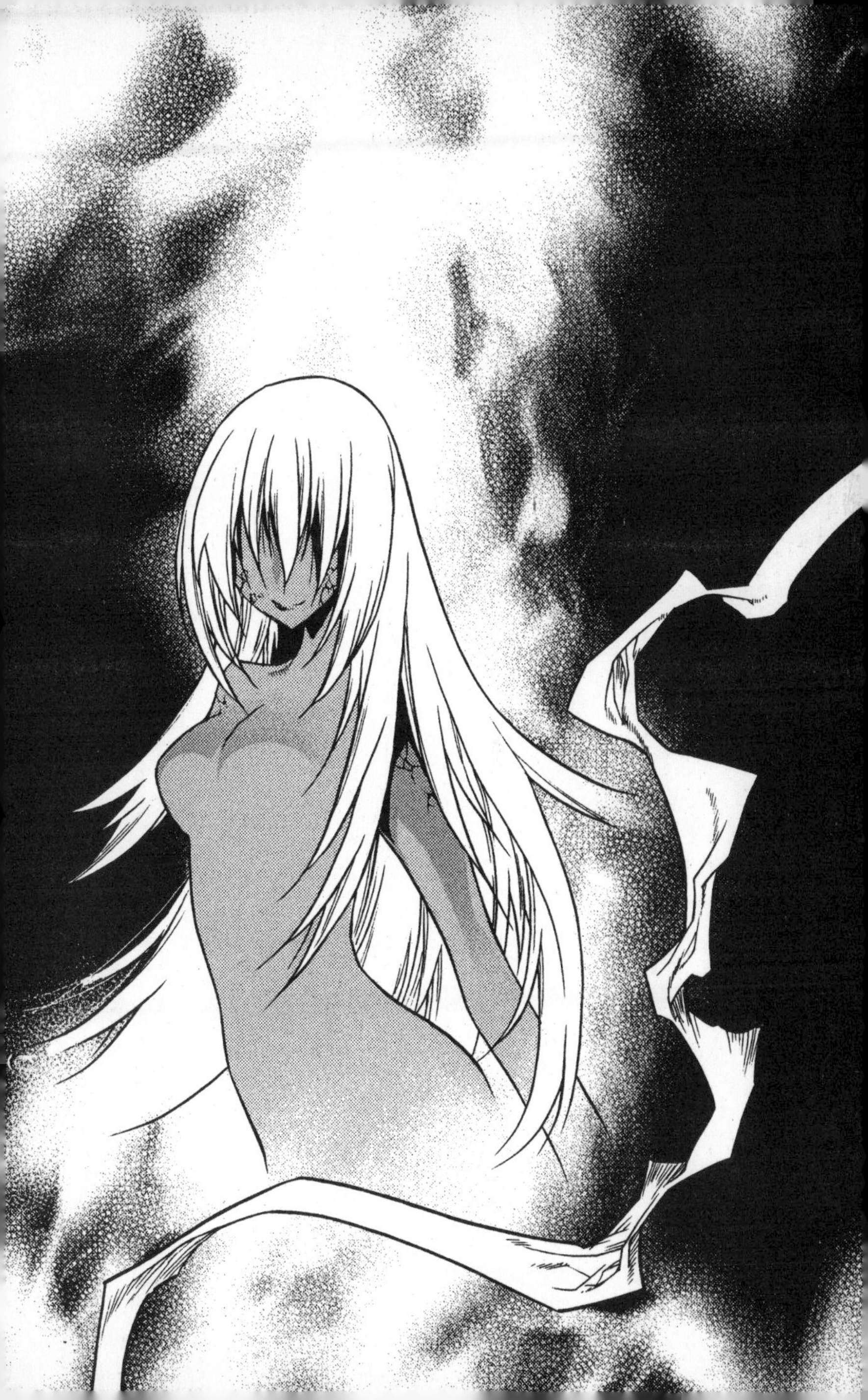

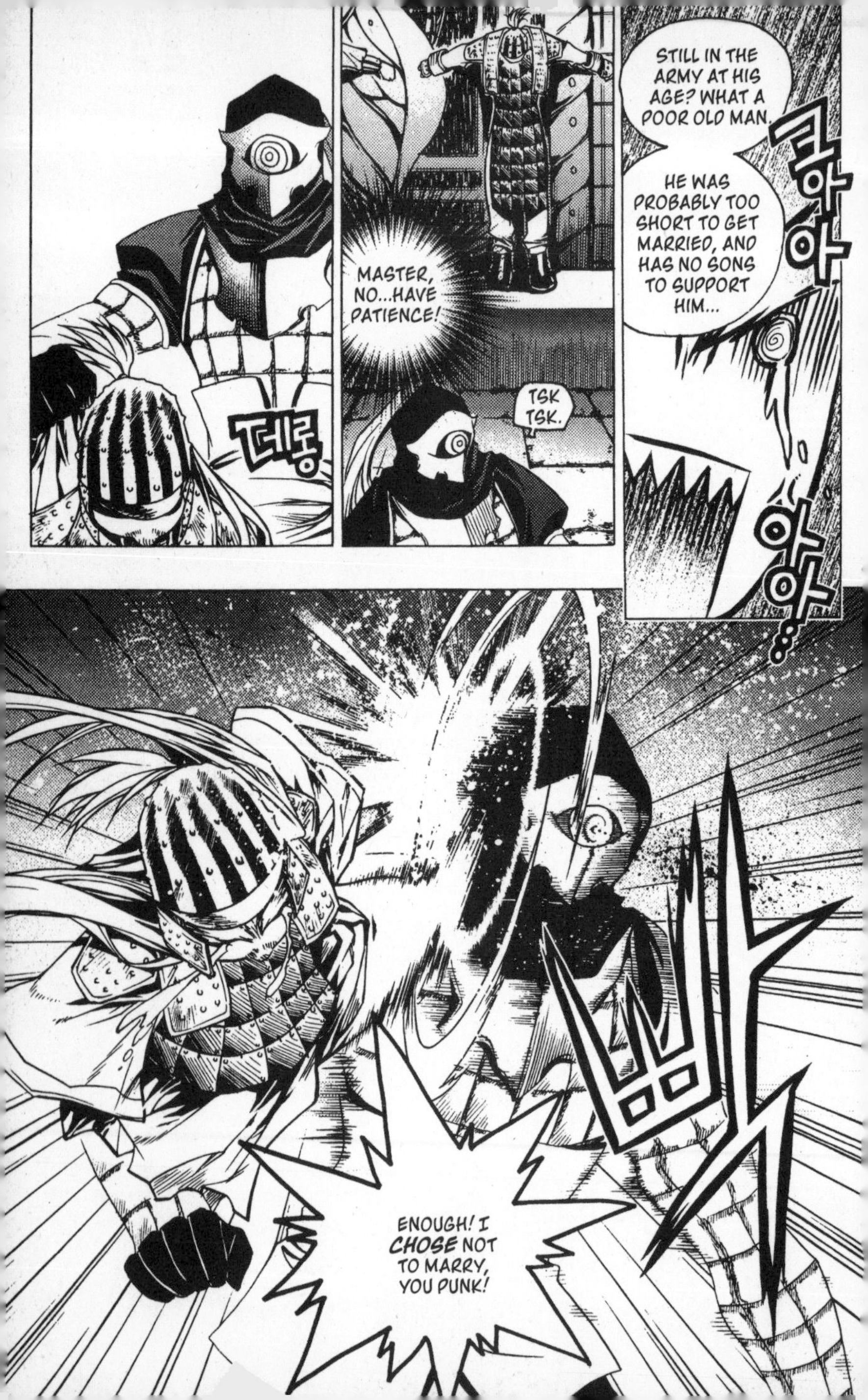
메롱
MASTER, NO...HAVE PATIENCE!
TSK TSK.
STILL IN THE ARMY AT HIS AGE? WHAT A POOR OLD MAN.
HE WAS PROBABLY TOO SHORT TO GET MARRIED, AND HAS NO SONS TO SUPPORT HIM...
ENOUGH! I **CHOSE** NOT TO MARRY, YOU PUNK!

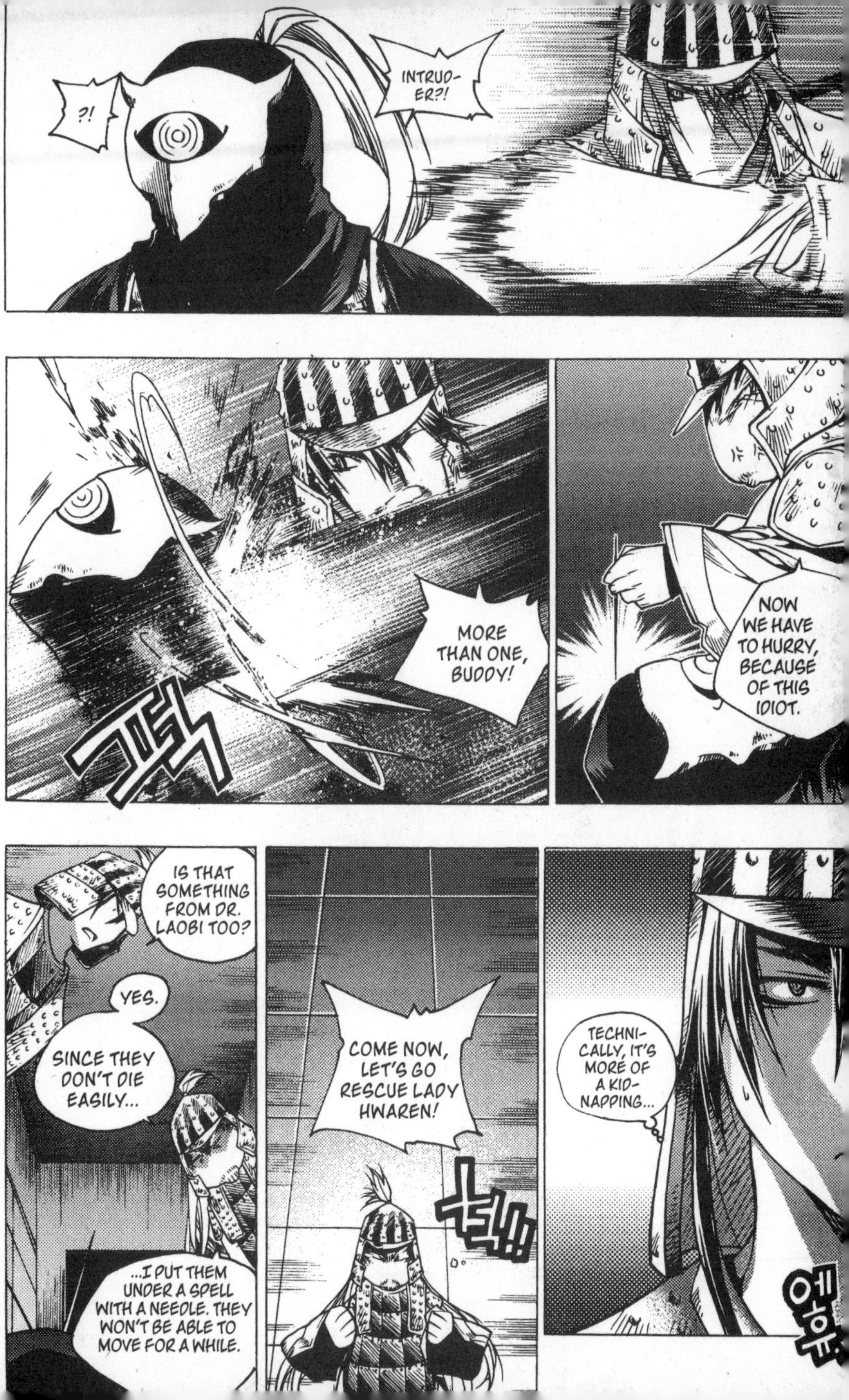
?!
INTRUDER?!
MORE THAN ONE, BUDDY!
NOW WE HAVE TO HURRY, BECAUSE OF THIS IDIOT.
IS THAT SOMETHING FROM DR. LAOBI TOO?
YES.
SINCE THEY DON'T DIE EASILY...
...I PUT THEM UNDER A SPELL WITH A NEEDLE. THEY WON'T BE ABLE TO MOVE FOR A WHILE.
COME NOW, LET'S GO RESCUE LADY HWAREN!
TECHNICALLY, IT'S MORE OF A KIDNAPPING...

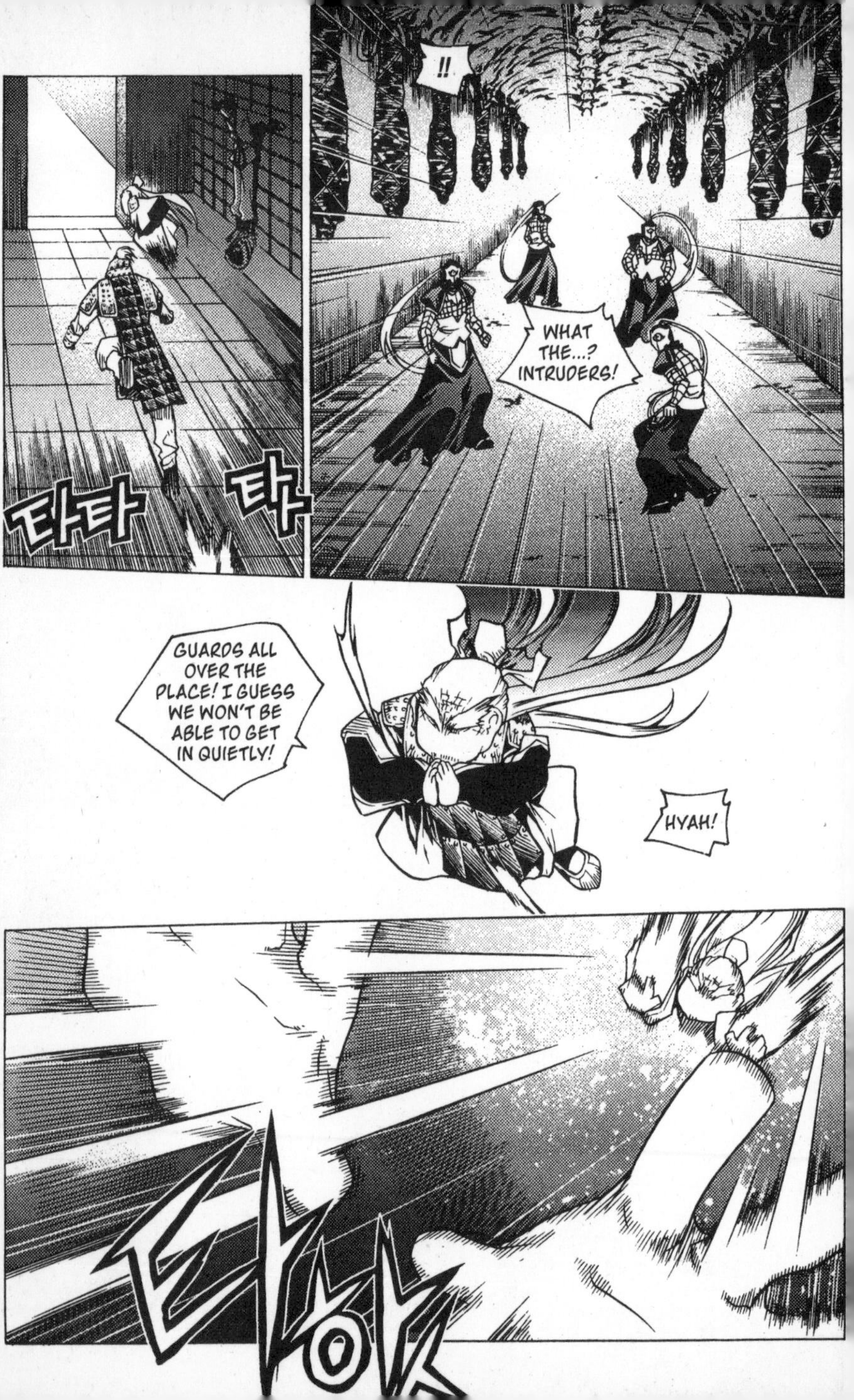
!!
WHAT THE...? INTRUDERS!
GUARDS ALL OVER THE PLACE! I GUESS WE WON'T BE ABLE TO GET IN QUIETLY!
HYAH!

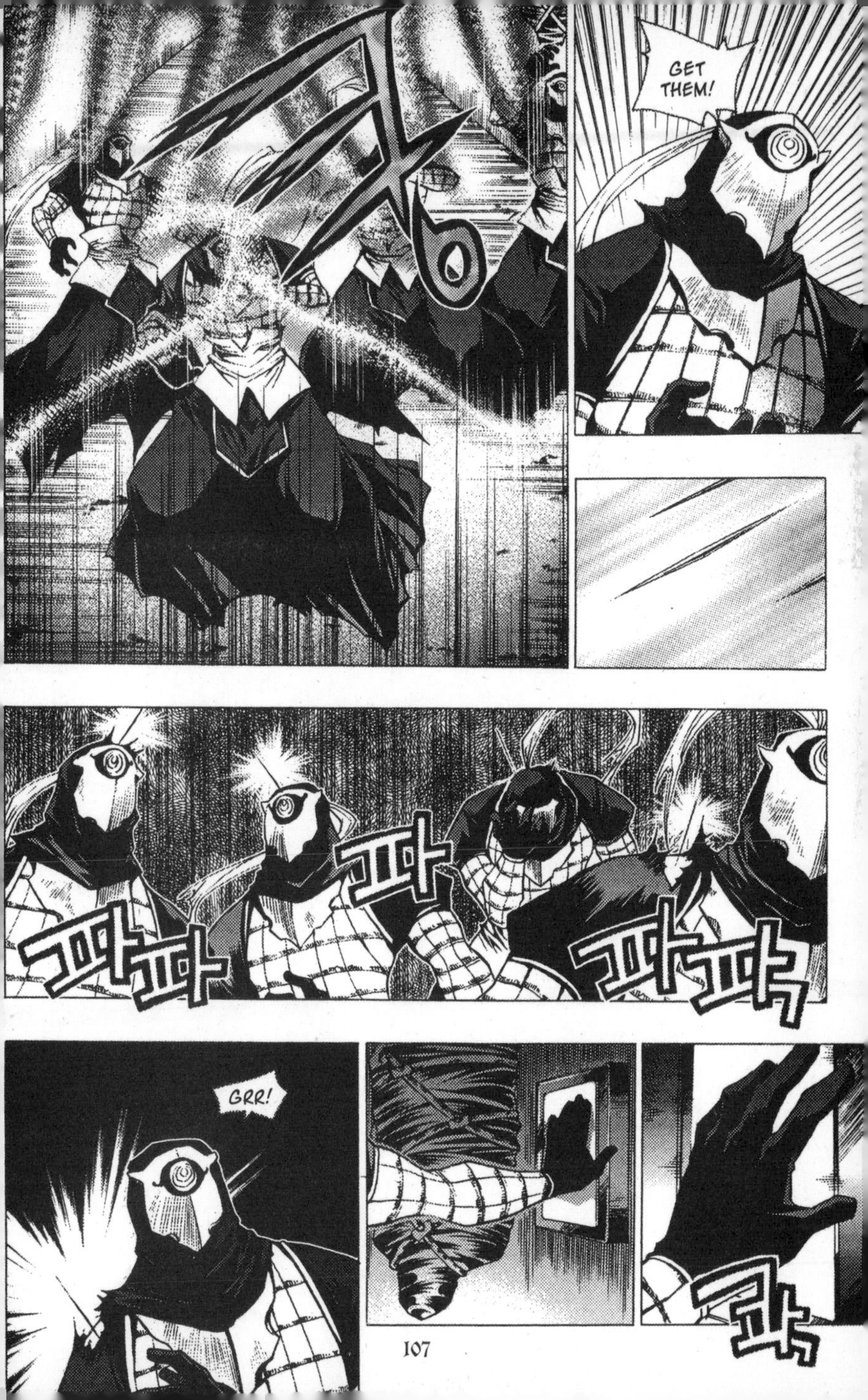
GET THEM!
GRR!

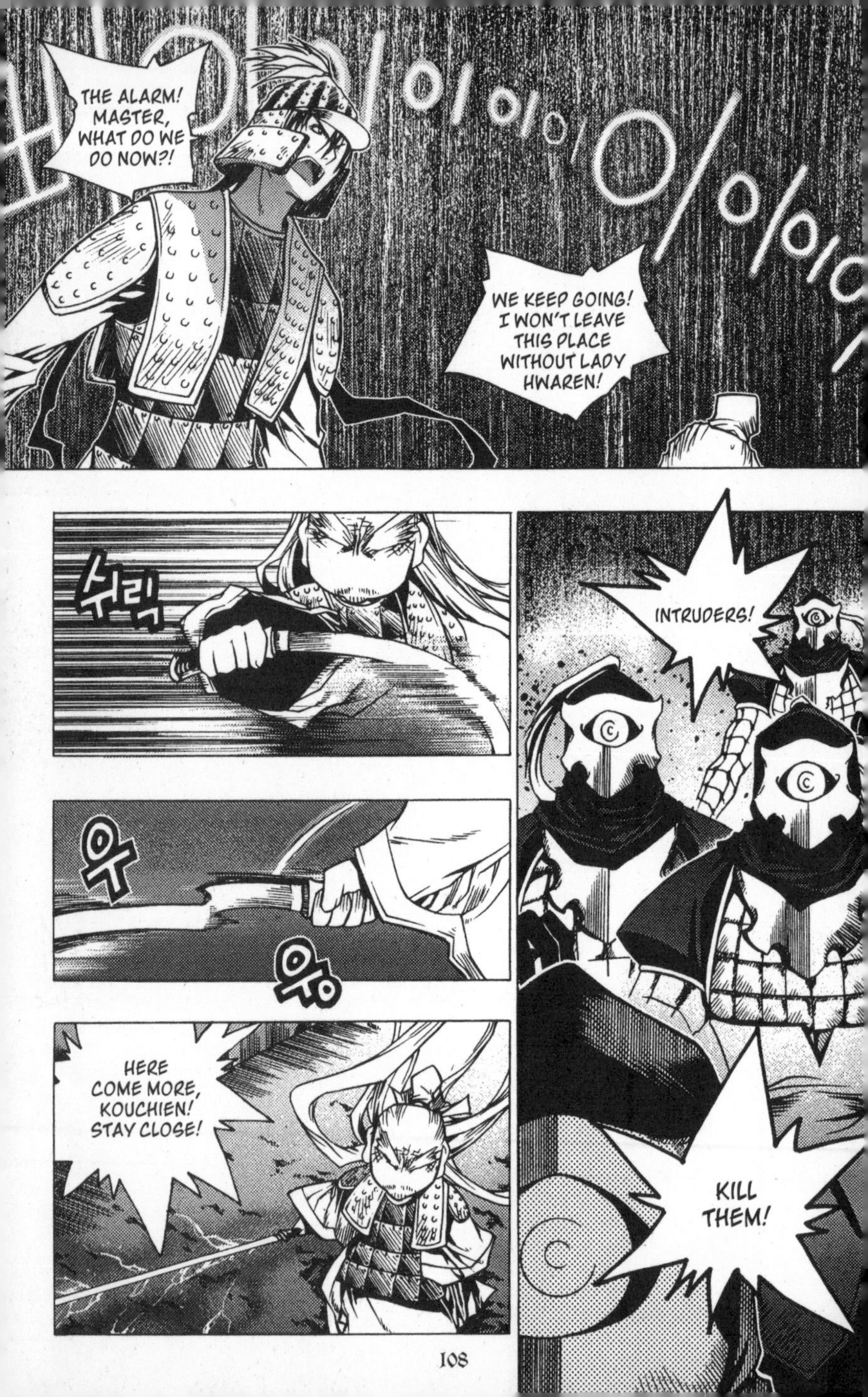
THE ALARM! MASTER, WHAT DO WE DO NOW?!
WE KEEP GOING! I WON'T LEAVE THIS PLACE WITHOUT LADY HWAREN!
쉬릭
우
웅
HERE COME MORE, KOUCHIEN! STAY CLOSE!
INTRUDERS!
KILL THEM!

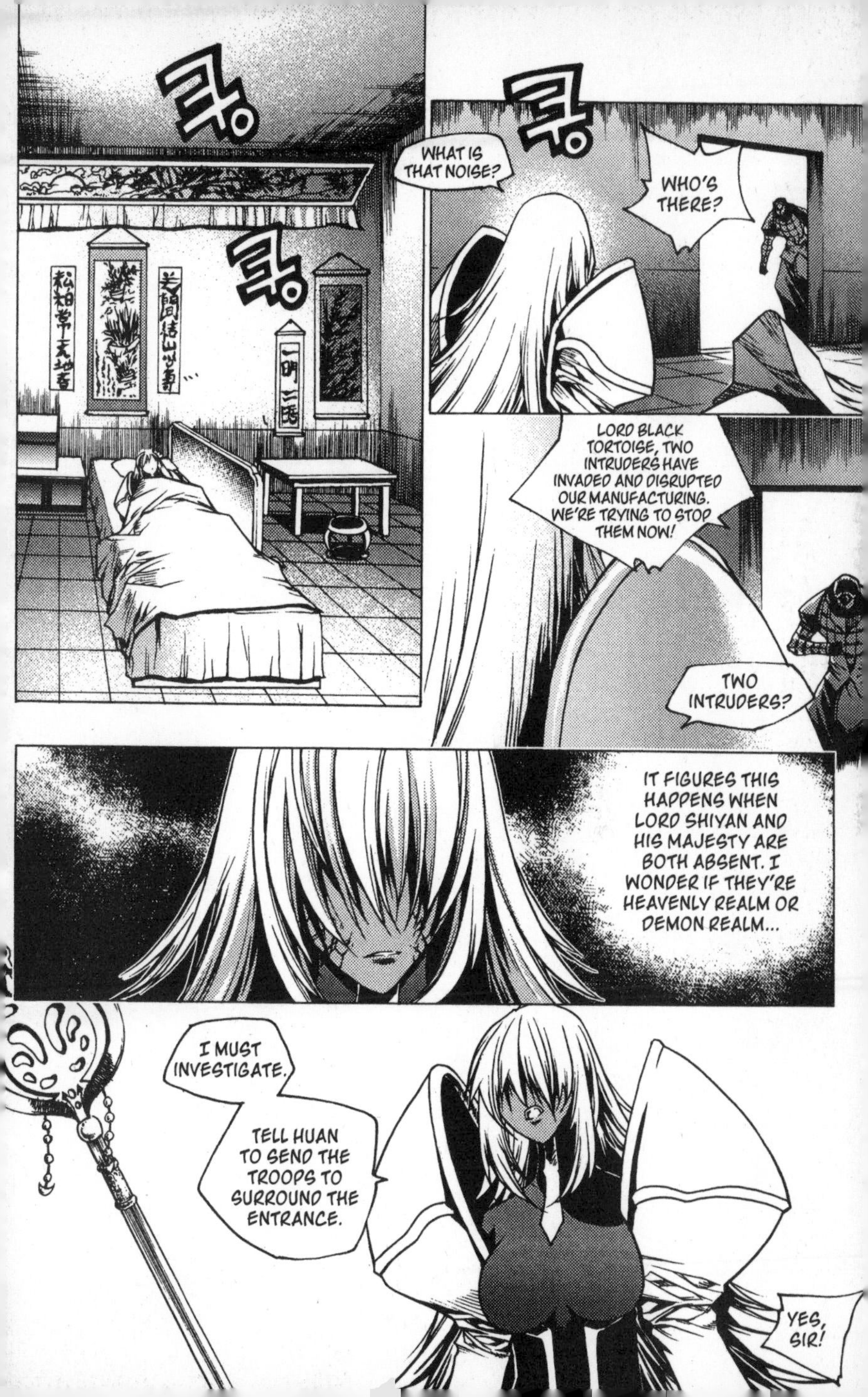

쿵
쿵
...
쿵
WHAT IS THAT NOISE?
WHO'S THERE?
LORD BLACK TORTOISE, TWO INTRUDERS HAVE INVADED AND DISRUPTED OUR MANUFACTURING. WE'RE TRYING TO STOP THEM NOW!
TWO INTRUDERS?
IT FIGURES THIS HAPPENS WHEN LORD SHIYAN AND HIS MAJESTY ARE BOTH ABSENT. I WONDER IF THEY'RE HEAVENLY REALM OR DEMON REALM...
I MUST INVESTIGATE.
TELL HUAN TO SEND THE TROOPS TO SURROUND THE ENTRANCE.
YES, SIR!

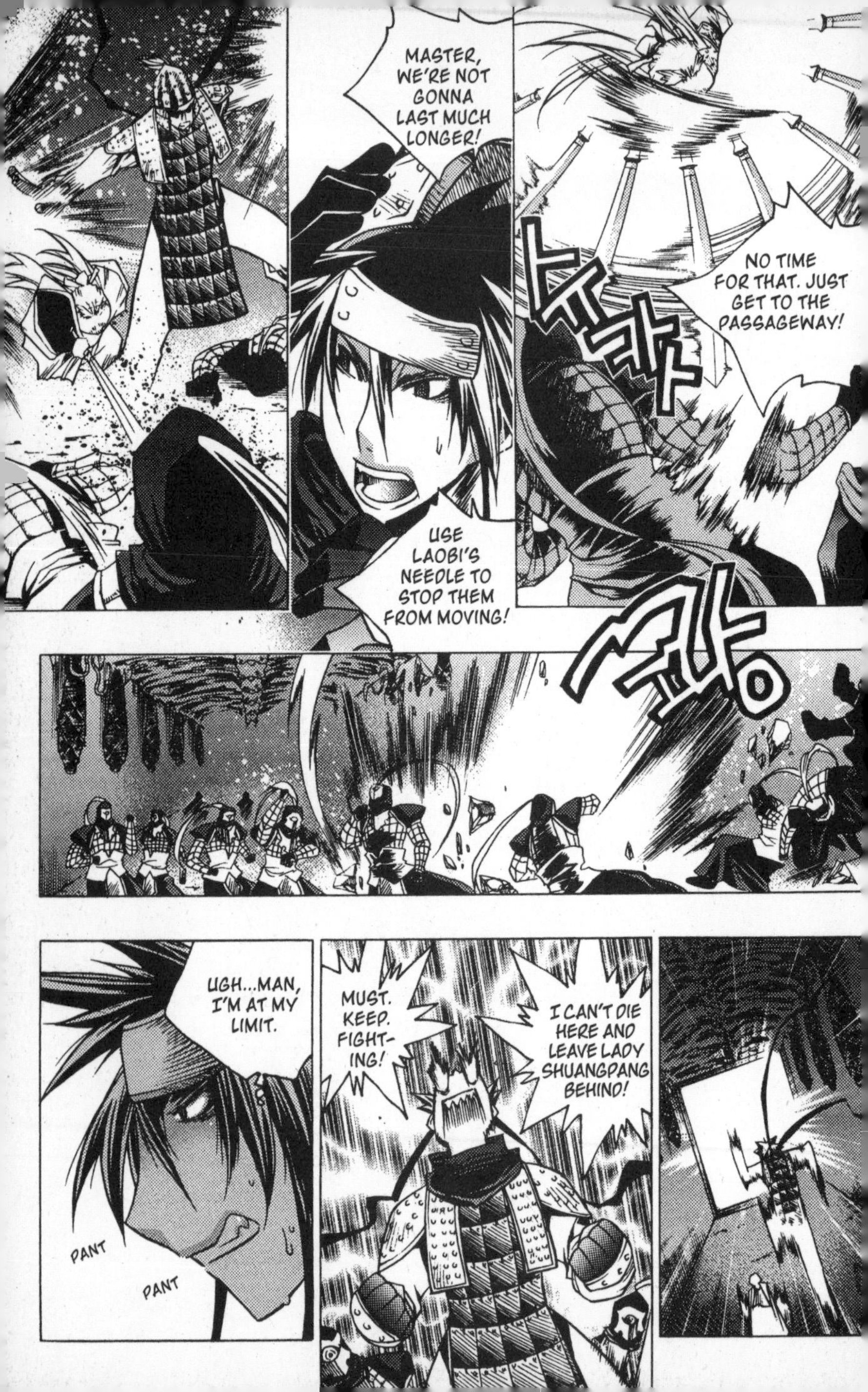
MASTER, WE'RE NOT GONNA LAST MUCH LONGER!
USE LAOBI'S NEEDLE TO STOP THEM FROM MOVING!
NO TIME FOR THAT. JUST GET TO THE PASSAGEWAY!
UGH...MAN, I'M AT MY LIMIT.
PANT
PANT
MUST. KEEP. FIGHT-ING!
I CAN'T DIE HERE AND LEAVE LADY SHUANGPANG BEHIND!

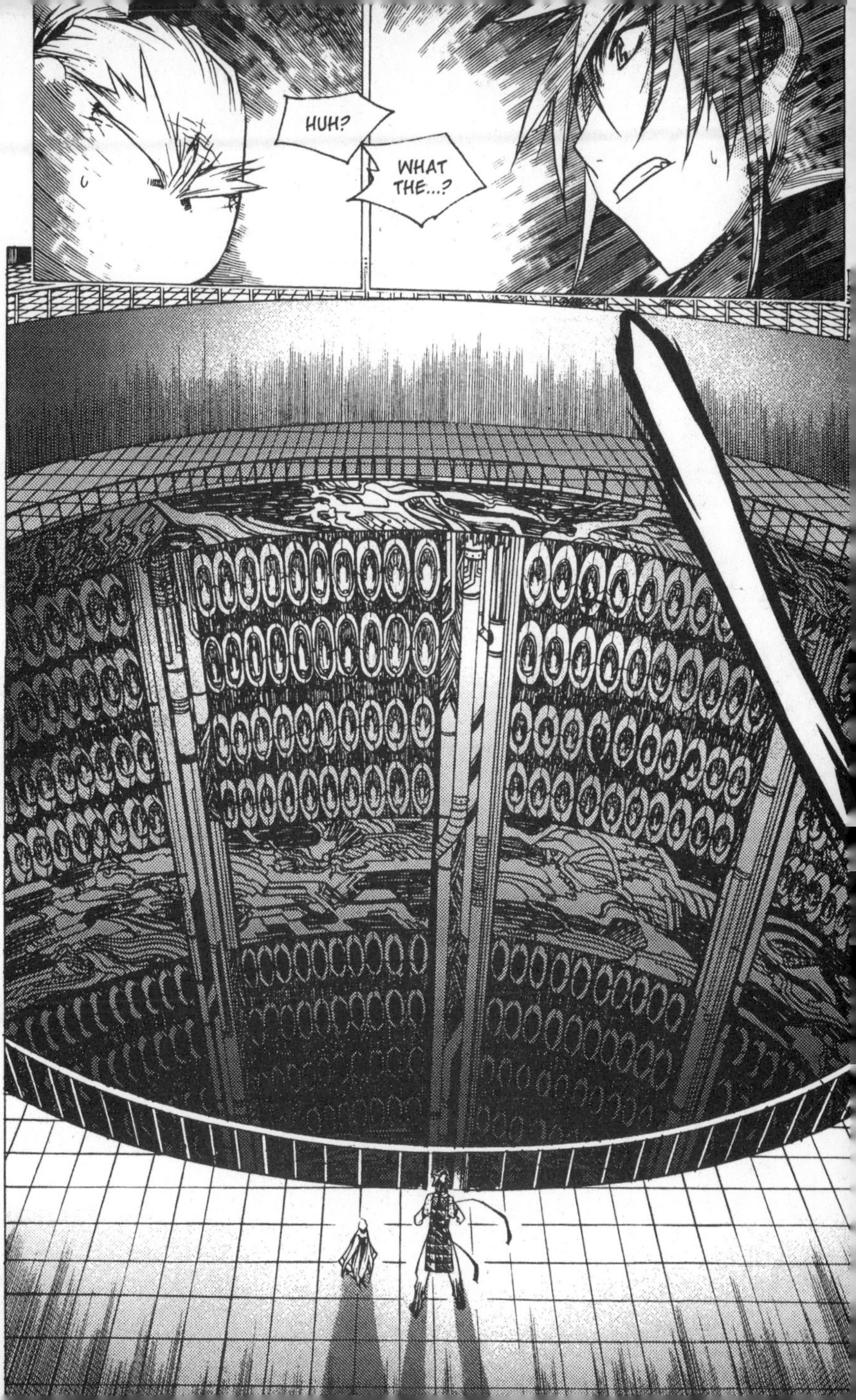
HUH?
WHAT THE...?

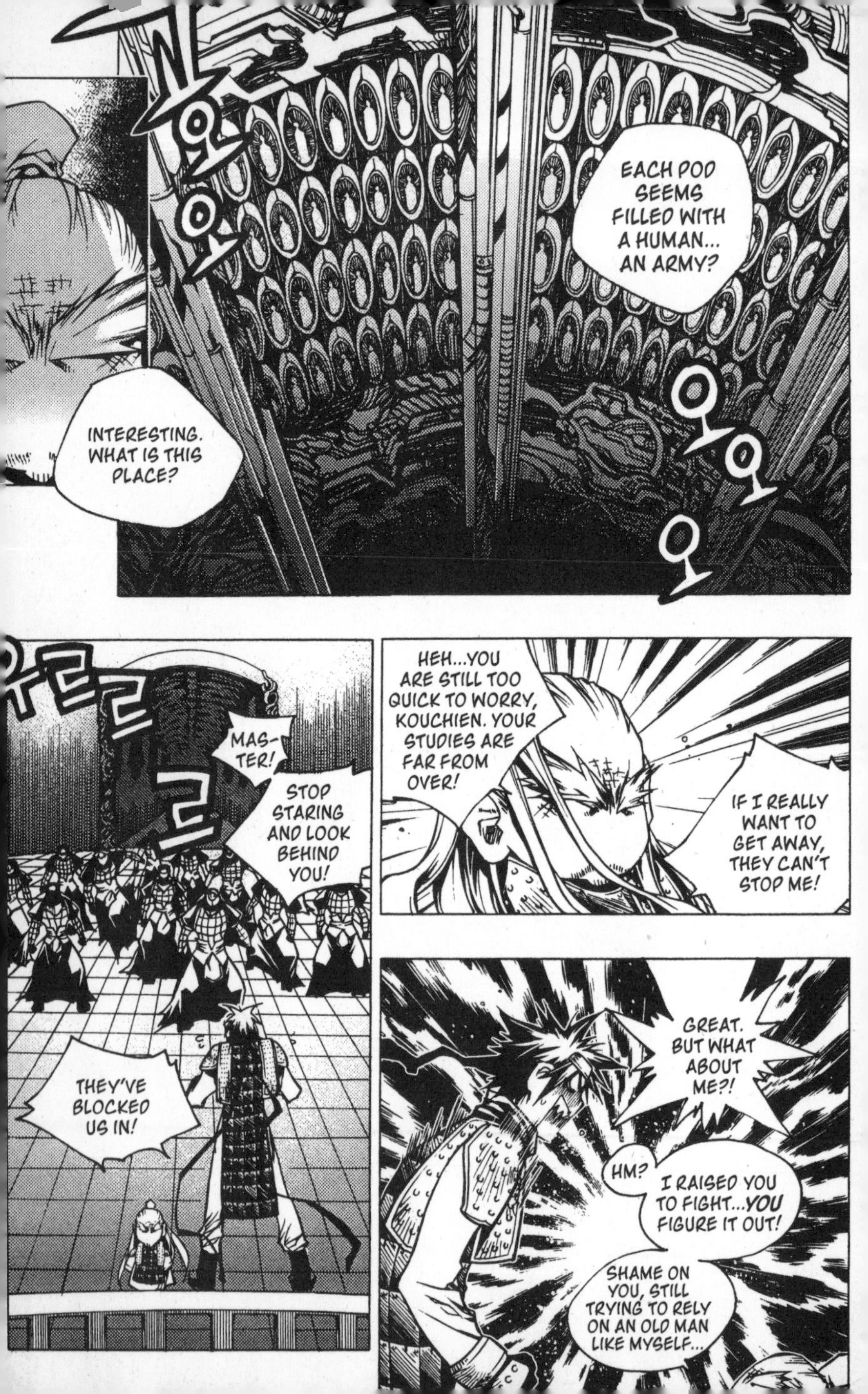
INTERESTING. WHAT IS THIS PLACE?
EACH POD SEEMS FILLED WITH A HUMAN... AN ARMY?
MAS-TER!
STOP STARING AND LOOK BEHIND YOU!
THEY'VE BLOCKED US IN!
HEH...YOU ARE STILL TOO QUICK TO WORRY, KOUCHIEN. YOUR STUDIES ARE FAR FROM OVER!
IF I REALLY WANT TO GET AWAY, THEY CAN'T STOP ME!
GREAT. BUT WHAT ABOUT ME?!
HM?
I RAISED YOU TO FIGHT...*YOU* FIGURE IT OUT!
SHAME ON YOU, STILL TRYING TO RELY ON AN OLD MAN LIKE MYSELF...

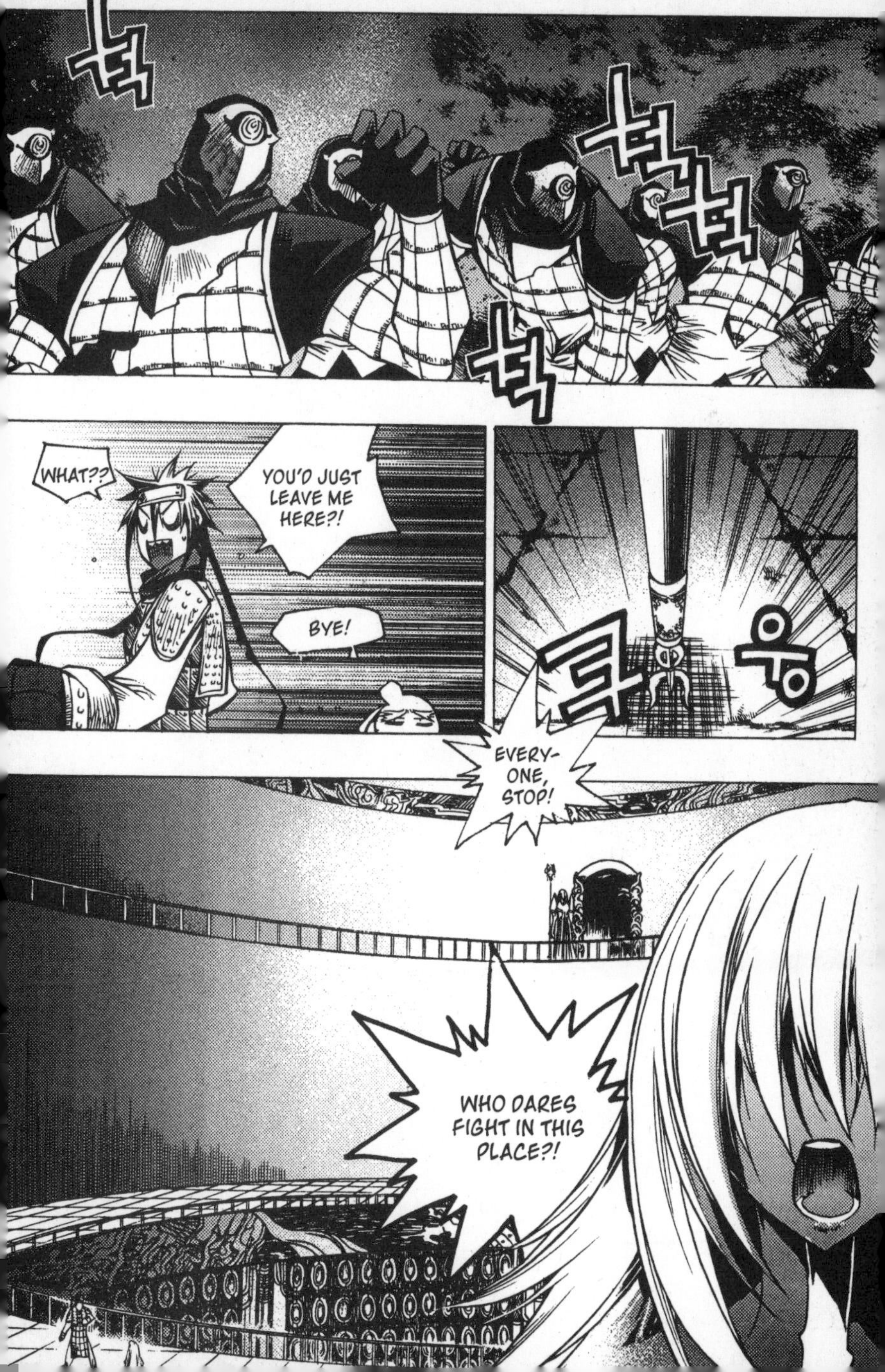
척
척
척
척
WHAT??
YOU'D JUST LEAVE ME HERE?!
BYE!
쿵
EVERY-ONE, STOP!
WHO DARES FIGHT IN THIS PLACE?!

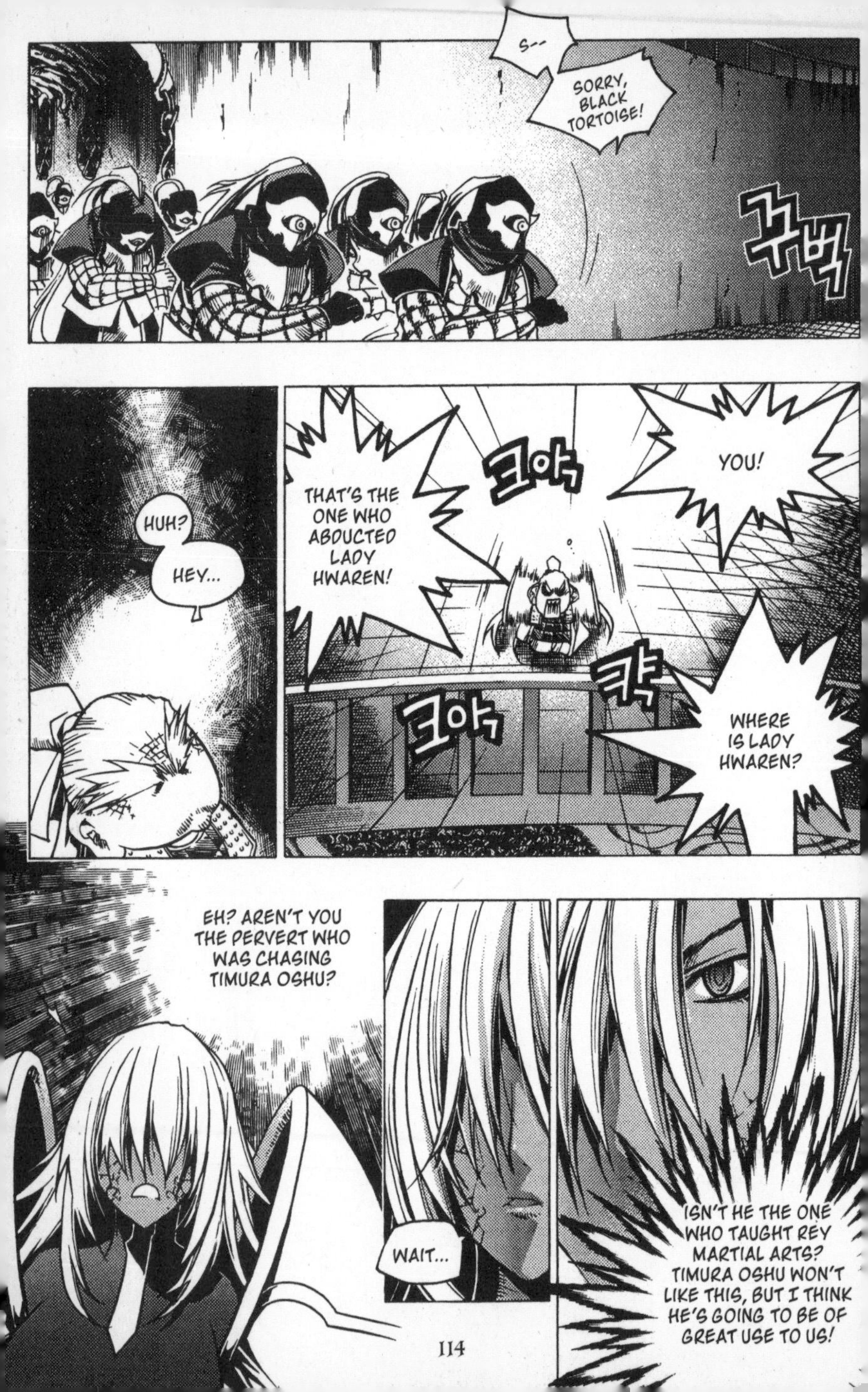
S--
SORRY, BLACK TORTOISE!
꾸벅
HUH?
HEY...
YOU!
THAT'S THE ONE WHO ABDUCTED LADY HWAREN!
크아
캬
크아
WHERE IS LADY HWAREN?
EH? AREN'T YOU THE PERVERT WHO WAS CHASING TIMURA OSHU?
WAIT...
ISN'T HE THE ONE WHO TAUGHT REY MARTIAL ARTS? TIMURA OSHU WON'T LIKE THIS, BUT I THINK HE'S GOING TO BE OF GREAT USE TO US!

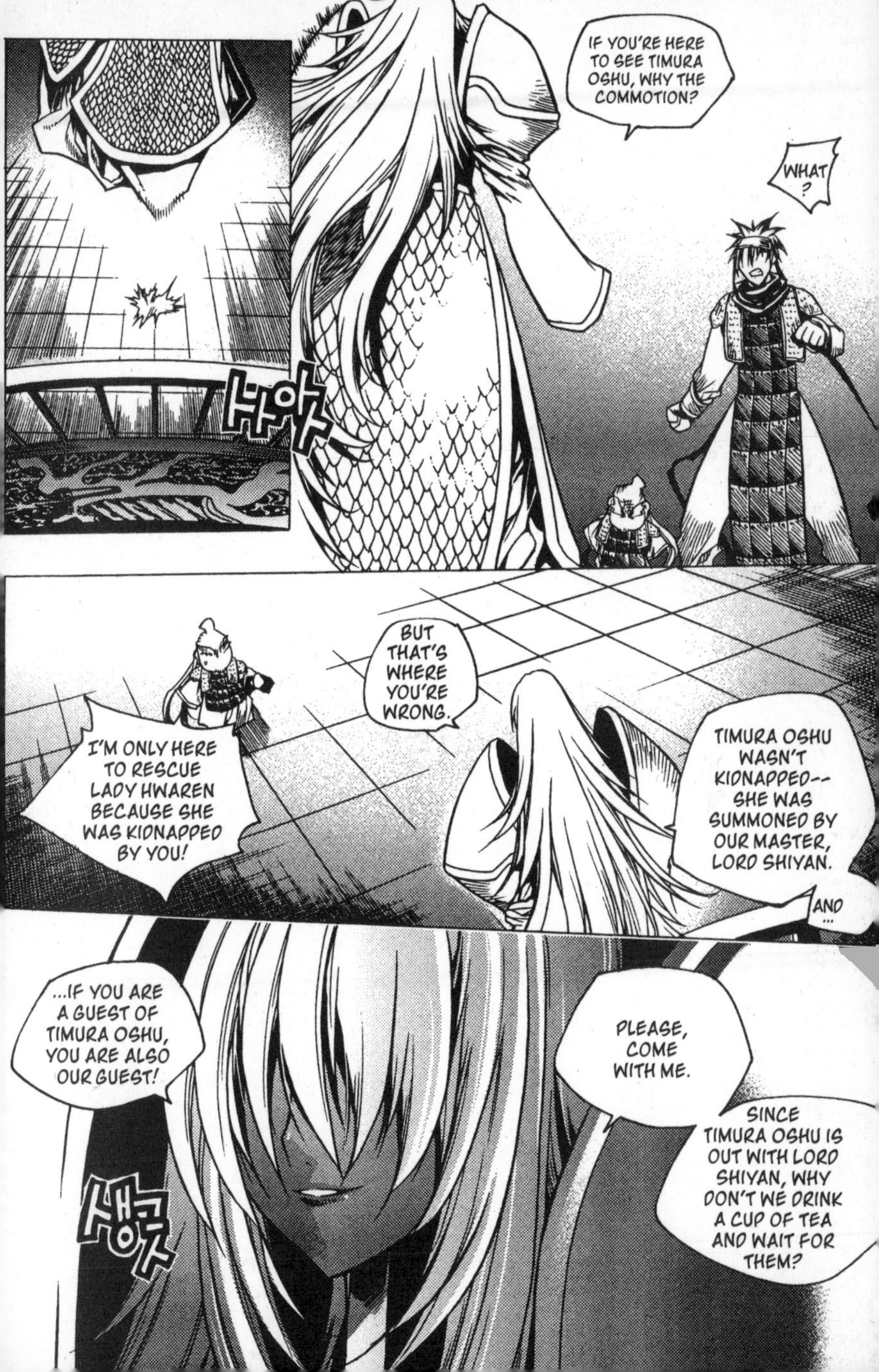
IF YOU'RE HERE TO SEE TIMURA OSHU, WHY THE COMMOTION?
WHAT?
I'M ONLY HERE TO RESCUE LADY HWAREN BECAUSE SHE WAS KIDNAPPED BY YOU!
BUT THAT'S WHERE YOU'RE WRONG.
TIMURA OSHU WASN'T KIDNAPPED-- SHE WAS SUMMONED BY OUR MASTER, LORD SHIYAN.
AND ...
...IF YOU ARE A GUEST OF TIMURA OSHU, YOU ARE ALSO OUR GUEST!
PLEASE, COME WITH ME.
SINCE TIMURA OSHU IS OUT WITH LORD SHIYAN, WHY DON'T WE DRINK A CUP OF TEA AND WAIT FOR THEM?

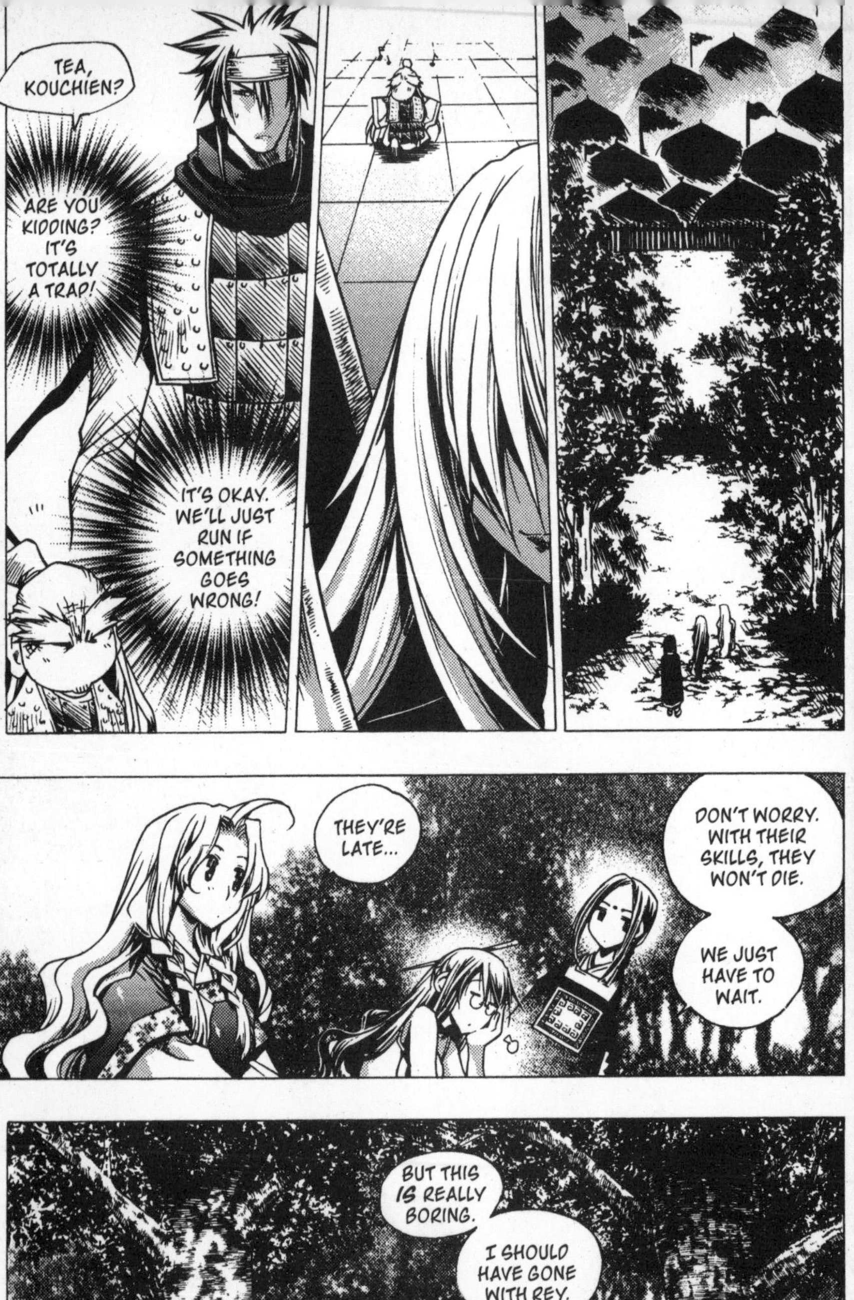
TEA, KOUCHIEN?
ARE YOU KIDDING? IT'S TOTALLY A TRAP!
IT'S OKAY. WE'LL JUST RUN IF SOMETHING GOES WRONG!
THEY'RE LATE...
DON'T WORRY. WITH THEIR SKILLS, THEY WON'T DIE.
WE JUST HAVE TO WAIT.
BUT THIS *IS* REALLY BORING.
I SHOULD HAVE GONE WITH REY.

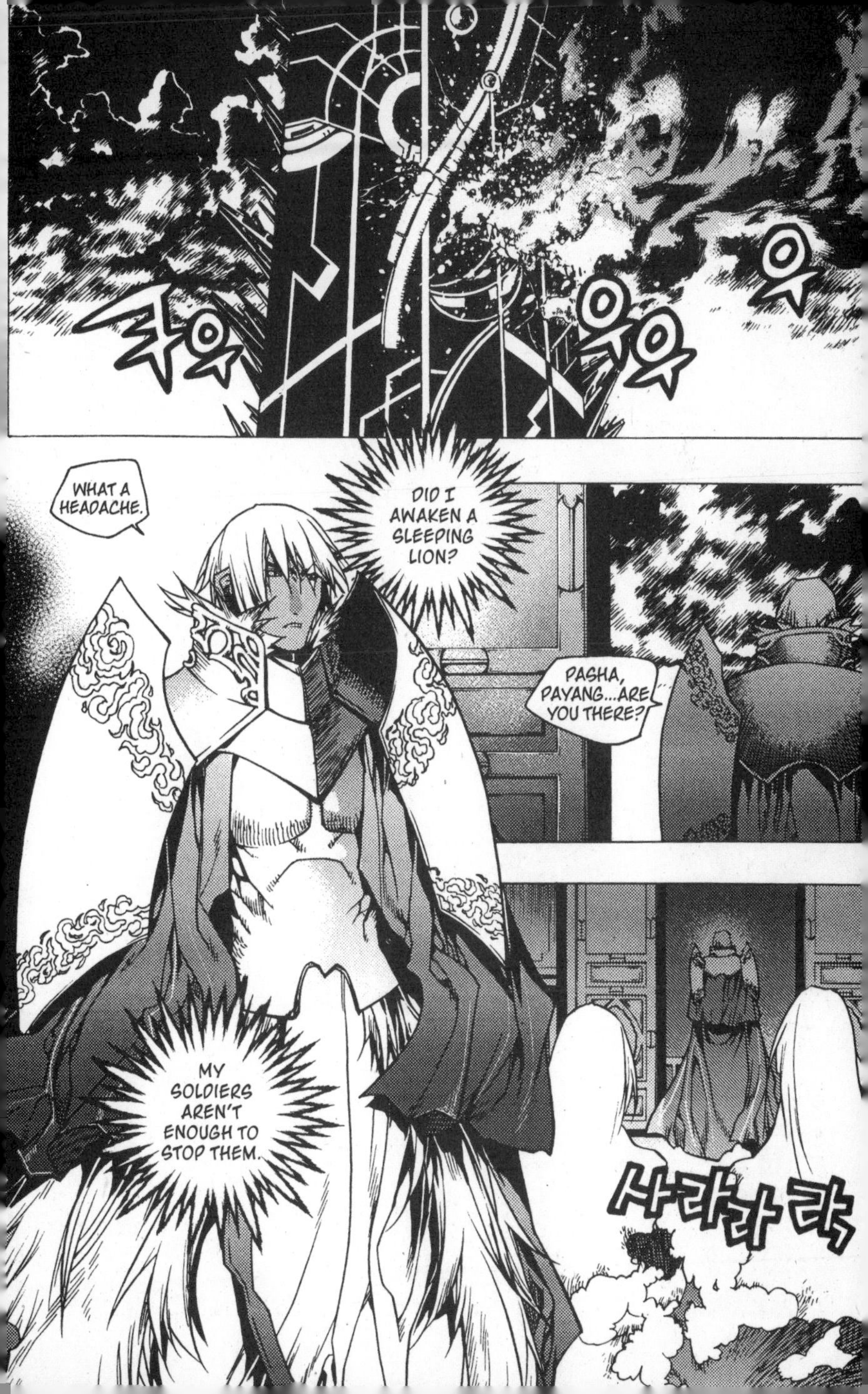
WHAT A HEADACHE.
DID I AWAKEN A SLEEPING LION?
PASHA, PAYANG...ARE YOU THERE?
MY SOLDIERS AREN'T ENOUGH TO STOP THEM.
사라라락

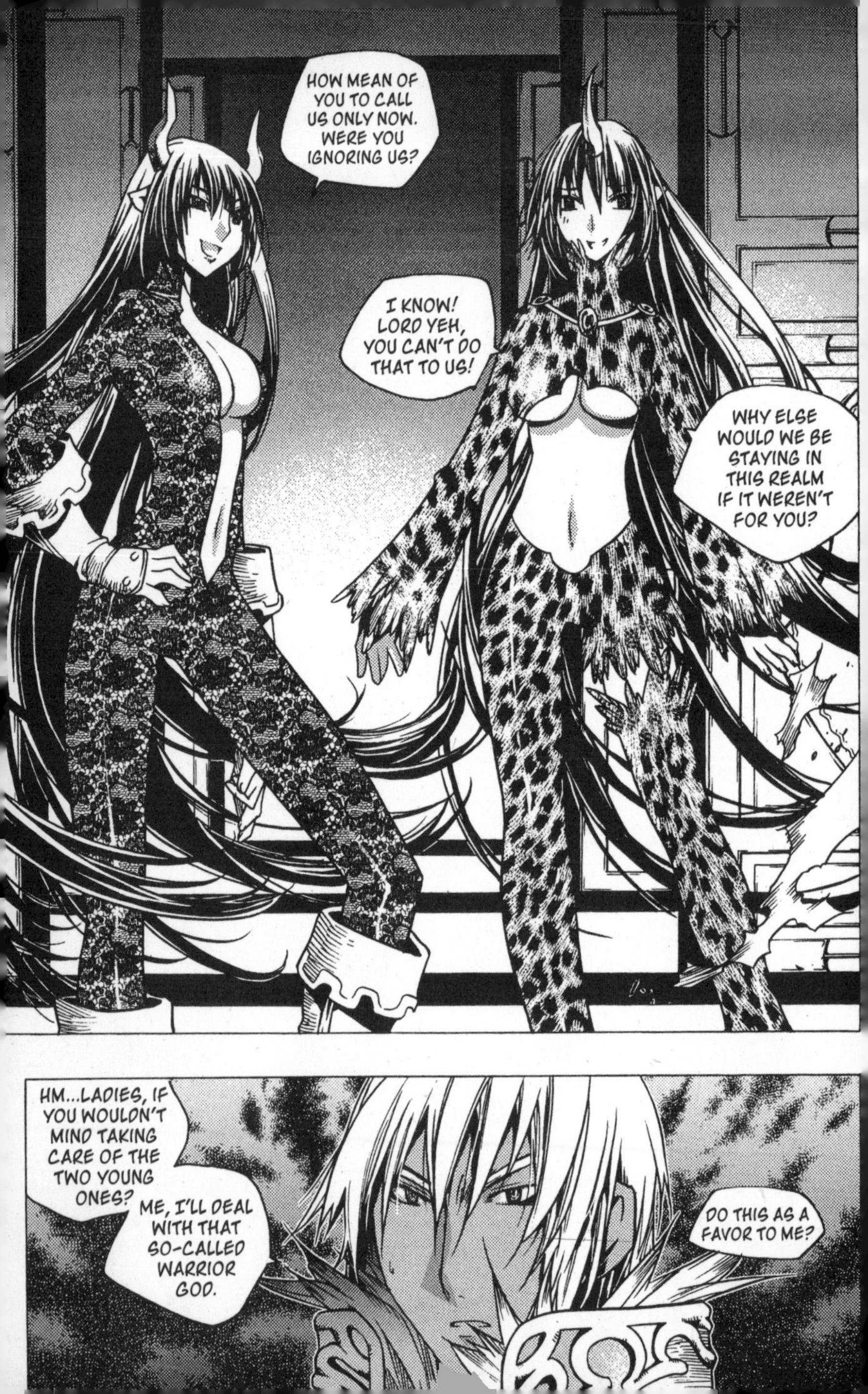
HOW MEAN OF YOU TO CALL US ONLY NOW. WERE YOU IGNORING US?
I KNOW! LORD YEH, YOU CAN'T DO THAT TO US!
WHY ELSE WOULD WE BE STAYING IN THIS REALM IF IT WEREN'T FOR YOU?
HM...LADIES, IF YOU WOULDN'T MIND TAKING CARE OF THE TWO YOUNG ONES?
ME, I'LL DEAL WITH THAT SO-CALLED WARRIOR GOD.
DO THIS AS A FAVOR TO ME?

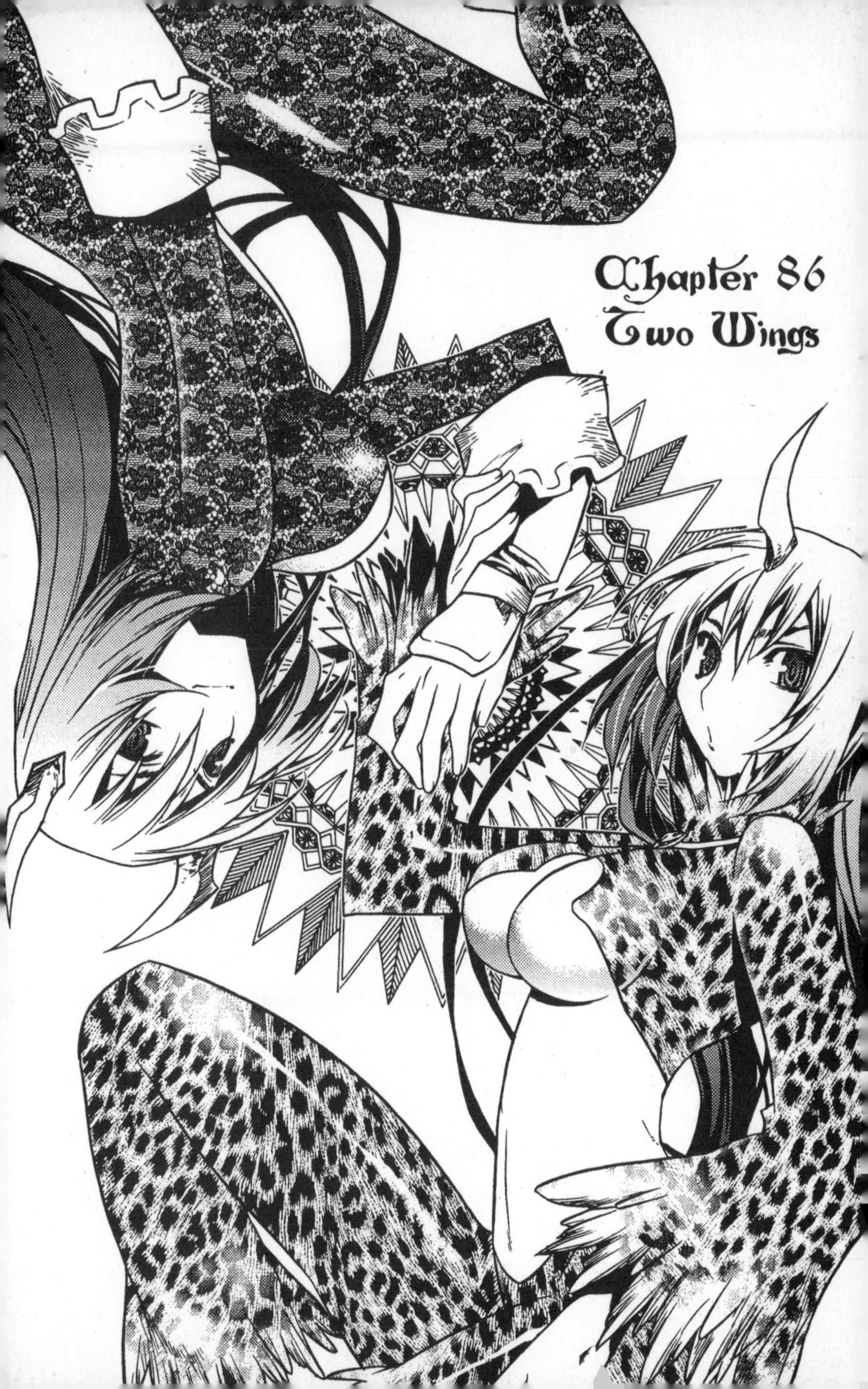
Chapter 86
Two Wings

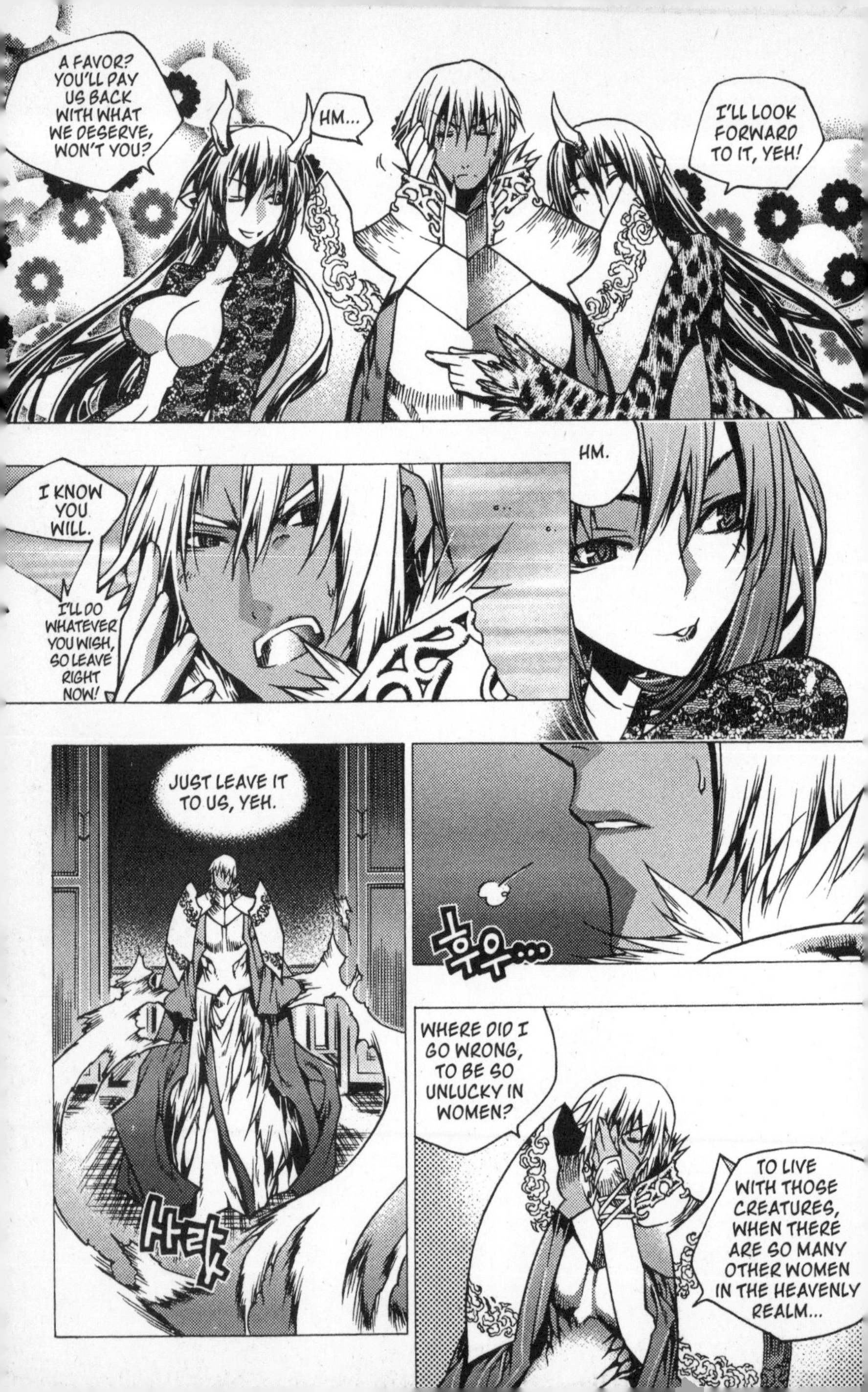
A FAVOR? YOU'LL PAY US BACK WITH WHAT WE DESERVE, WON'T YOU?
HM...
I'LL LOOK FORWARD TO IT, YEH!
I KNOW YOU WILL.
I'LL DO WHATEVER YOU WISH, SO LEAVE RIGHT NOW!
HM.
JUST LEAVE IT TO US, YEH.
후우...
WHERE DID I GO WRONG, TO BE SO UNLUCKY IN WOMEN?
TO LIVE WITH THOSE CREATURES, WHEN THERE ARE SO MANY OTHER WOMEN IN THE HEAVENLY REALM...

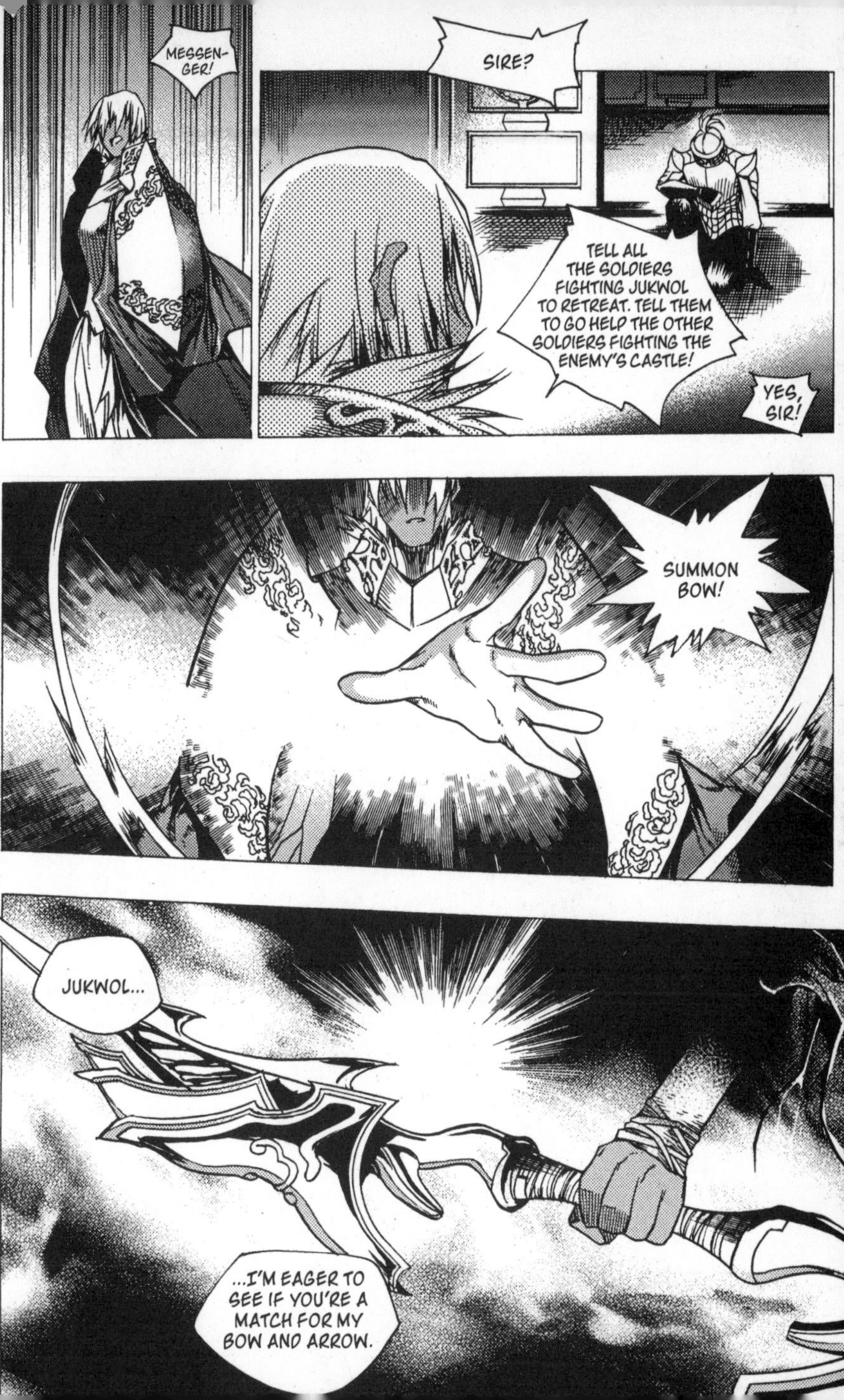
MESSEN-GER!
SIRE?
TELL ALL THE SOLDIERS FIGHTING JUKWOL TO RETREAT. TELL THEM TO GO HELP THE OTHER SOLDIERS FIGHTING THE ENEMY'S CASTLE!
YES, SIR!
SUMMON BOW!
JUKWOL...
...I'M EAGER TO SEE IF YOU'RE A MATCH FOR MY BOW AND ARROW.

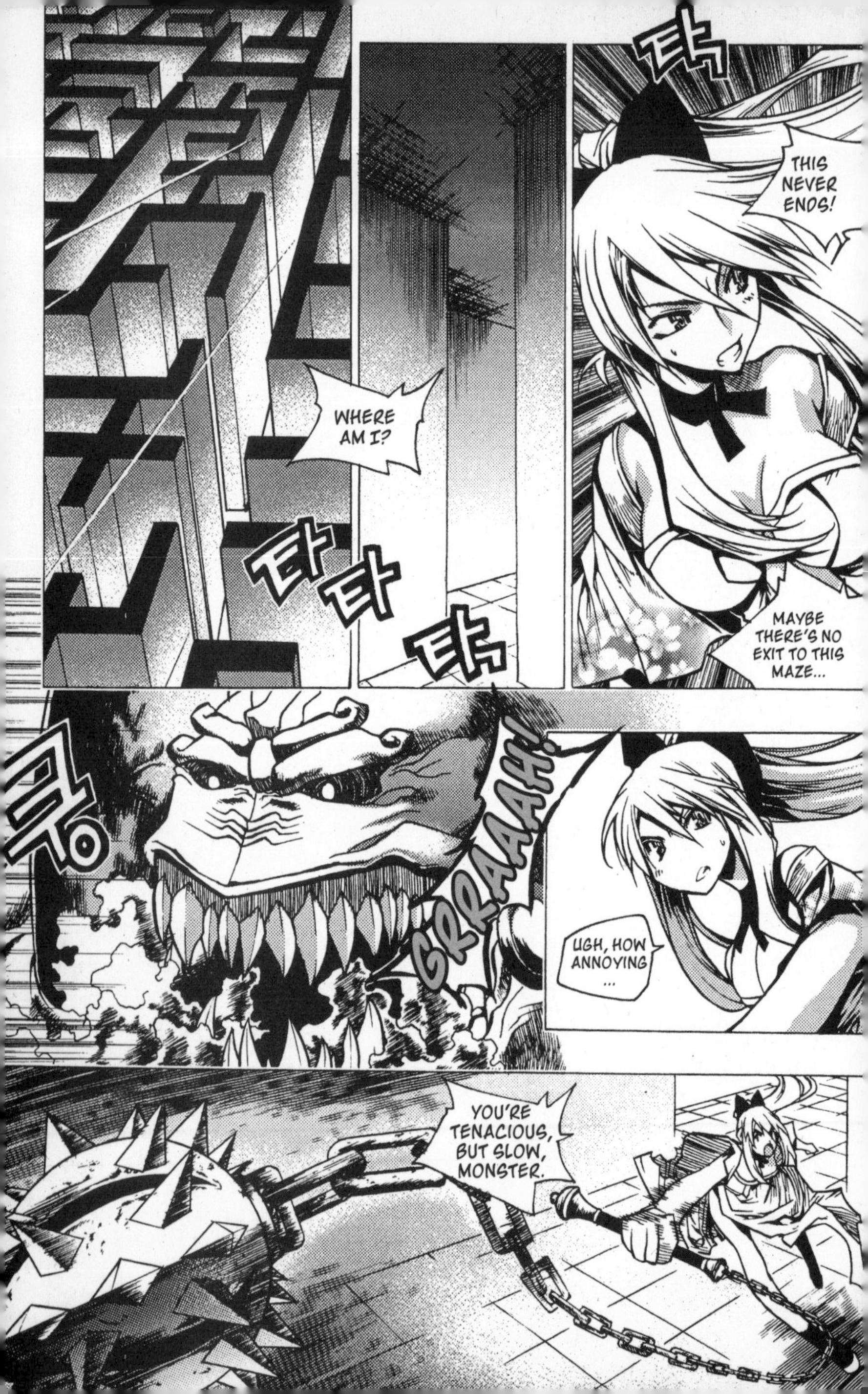
WHERE AM I?
타 타 탁
탁
THIS NEVER ENDS!
MAYBE THERE'S NO EXIT TO THIS MAZE...
GRRAAAH!
UGH, HOW ANNOYING ...
YOU'RE TENACIOUS, BUT SLOW, MONSTER.

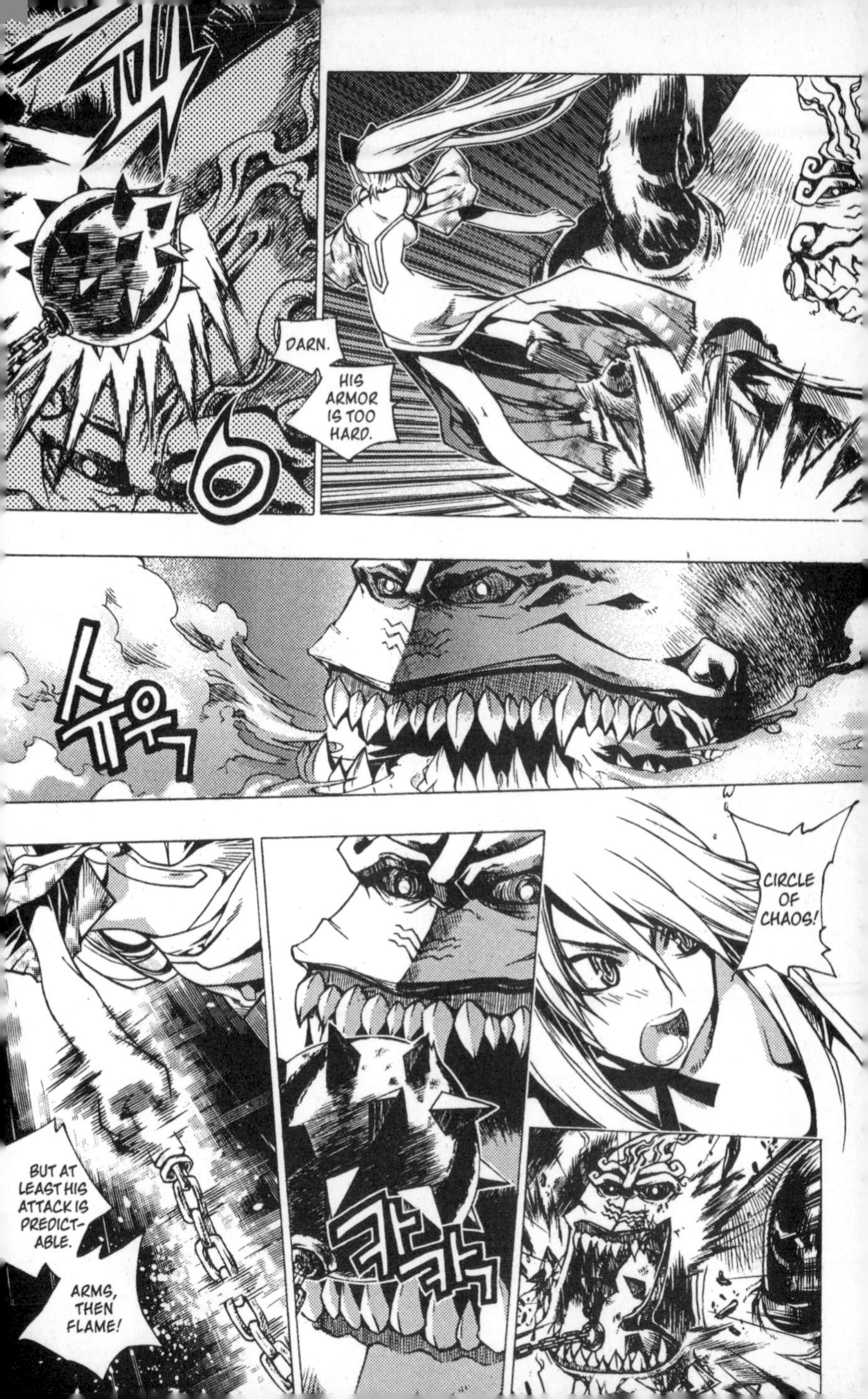
DARN.
HIS ARMOR IS TOO HARD.
BUT AT LEAST HIS ATTACK IS PREDICTABLE.
ARMS, THEN FLAME!
CIRCLE OF CHAOS!

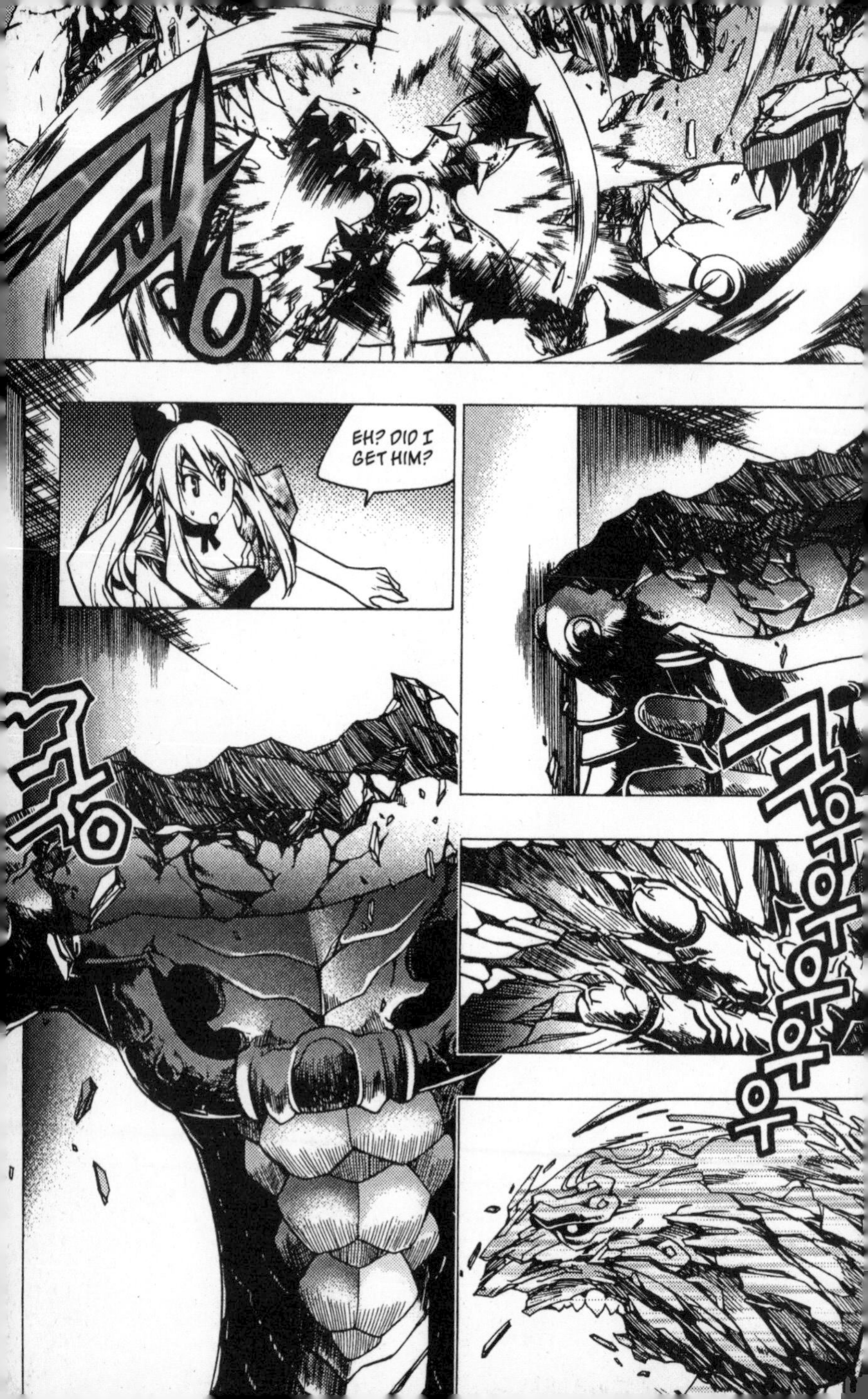
EH? DID I GET HIM?

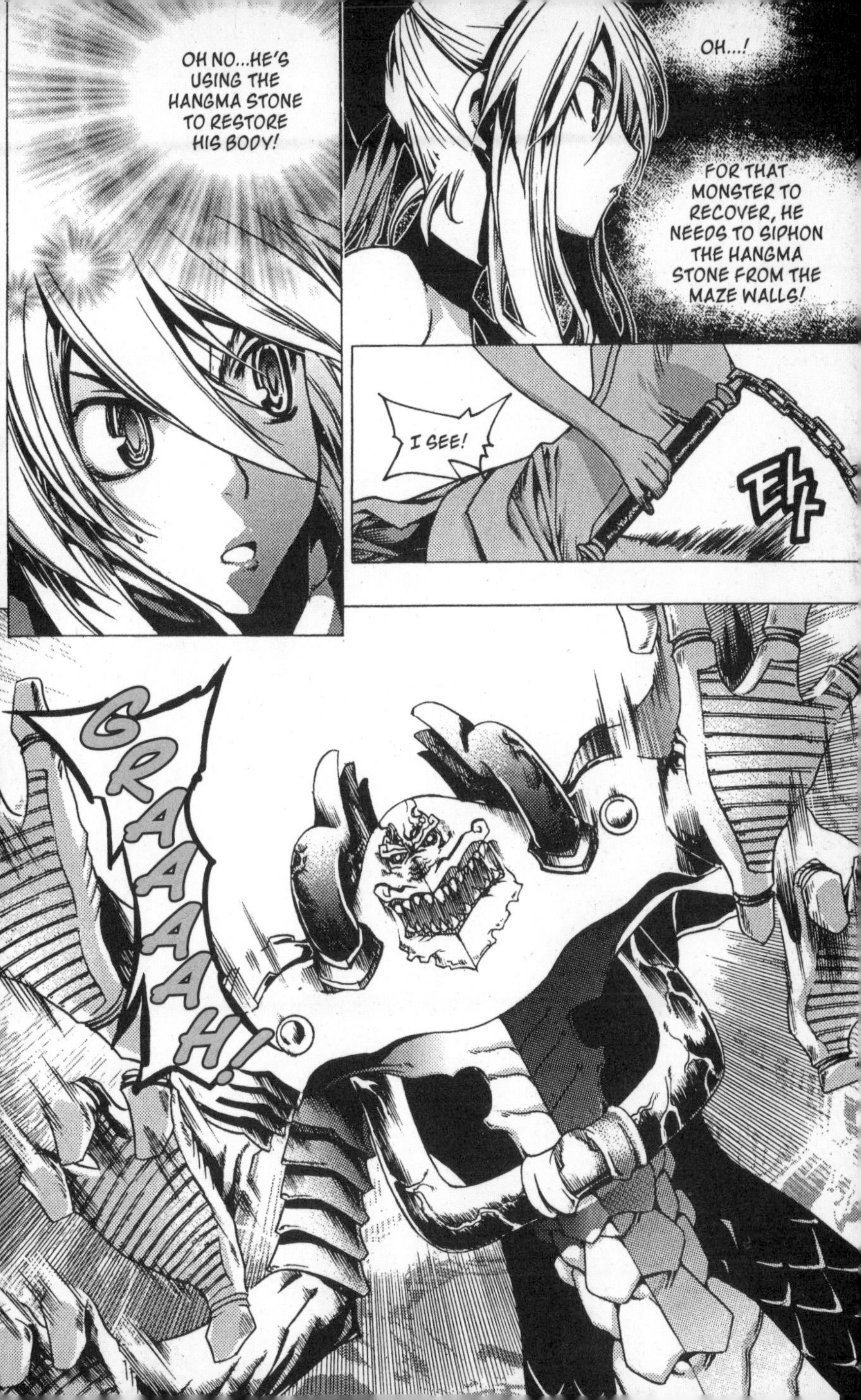
OH NO...HE'S USING THE HANGMA STONE TO RESTORE HIS BODY!
OH...!
FOR THAT MONSTER TO RECOVER, HE NEEDS TO SIPHON THE HANGMA STONE FROM THE MAZE WALLS!
I SEE!
탁
GRAAAAAH!

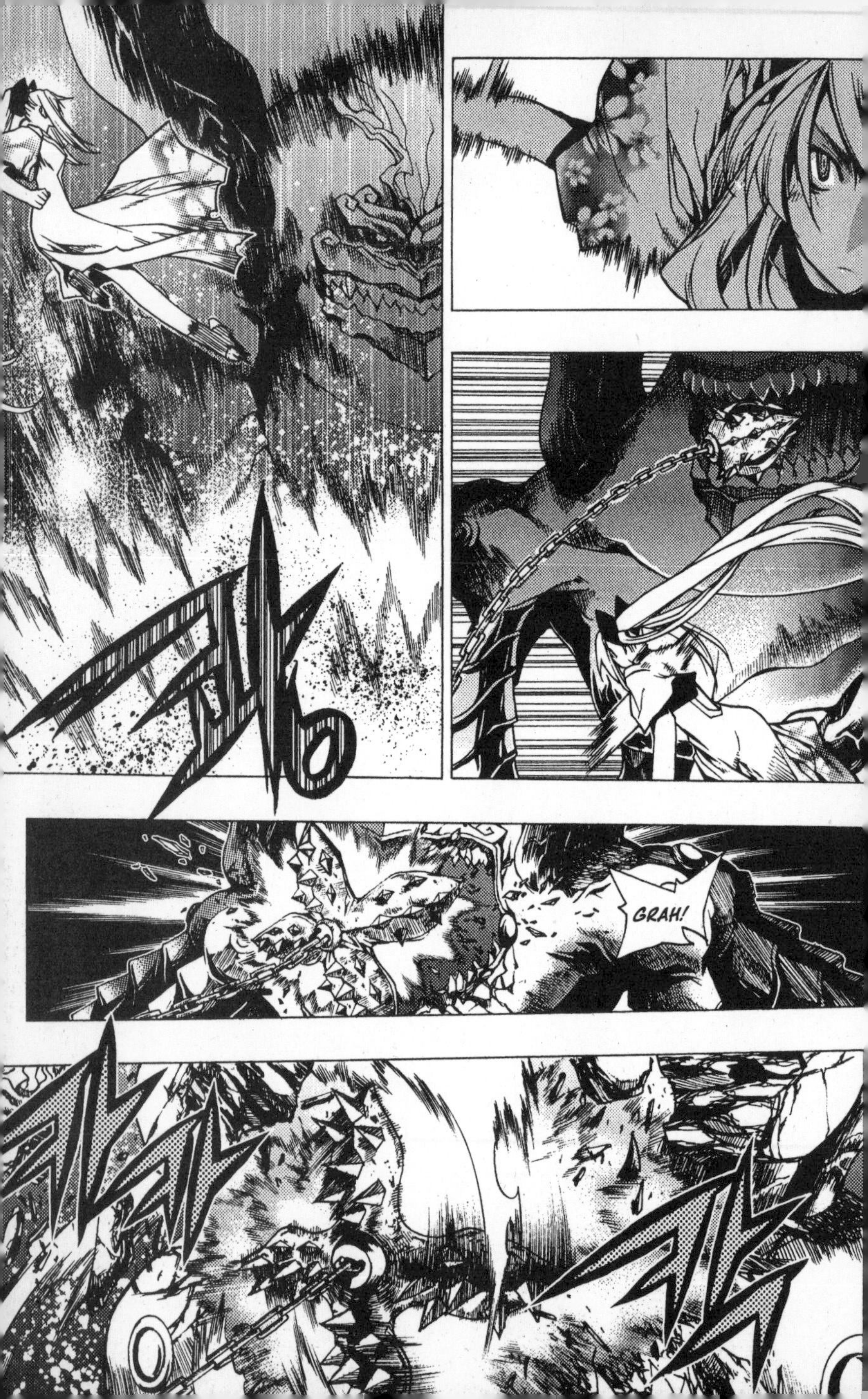
GRAH!

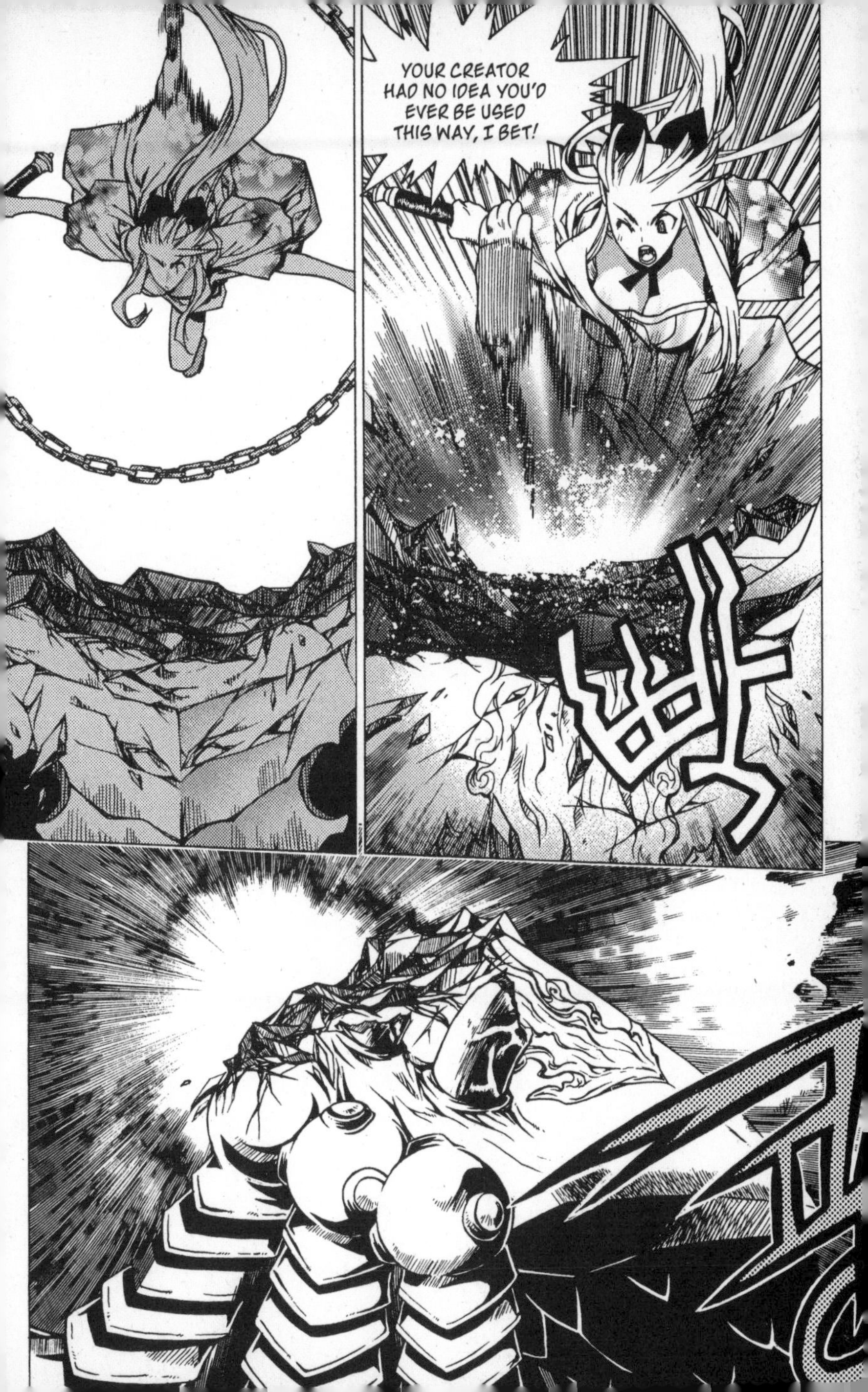
YOUR CREATOR HAD NO IDEA YOU'D EVER BE USED THIS WAY, I BET!

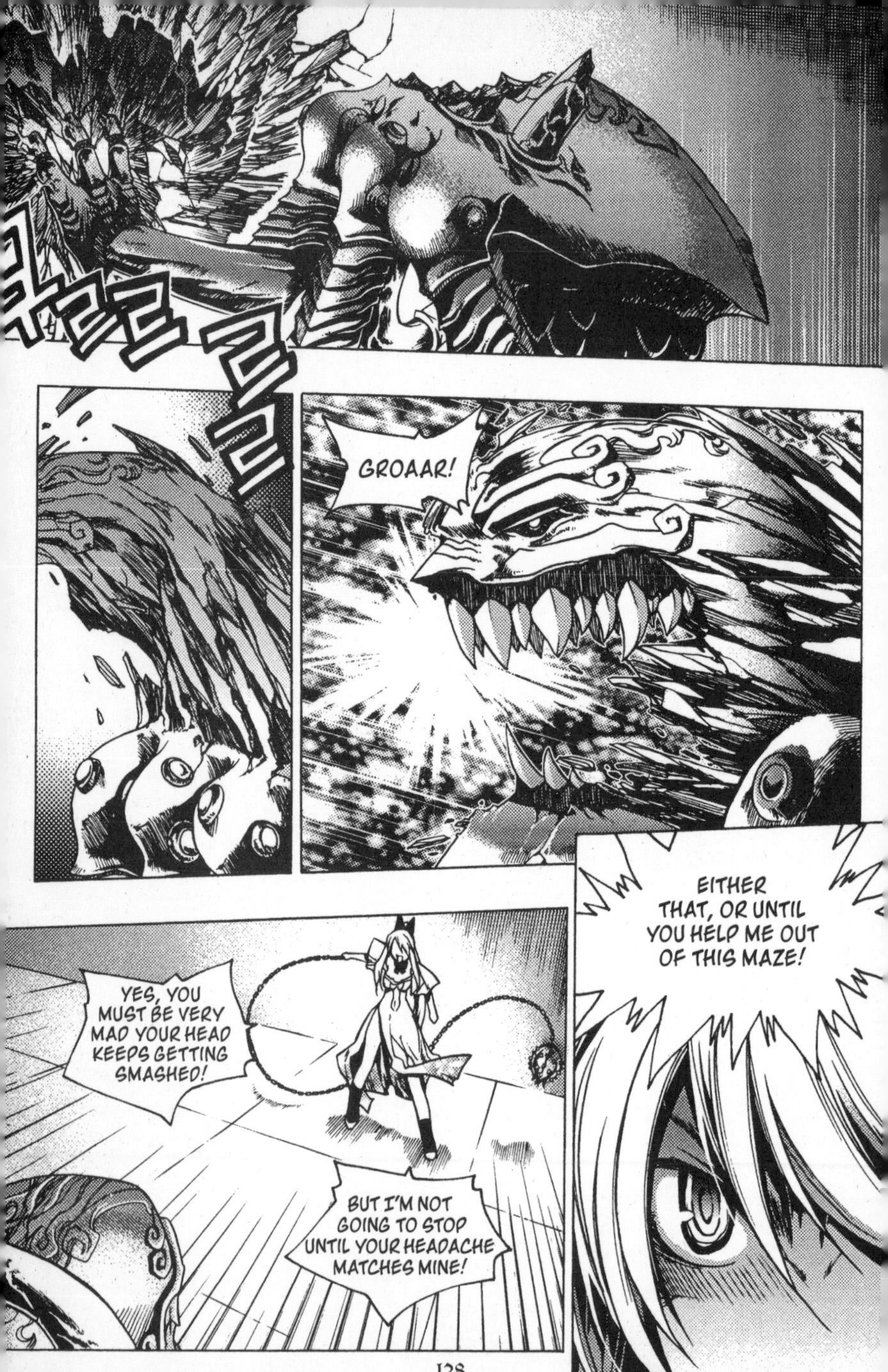
GROAAR!
YES, YOU MUST BE VERY MAD YOUR HEAD KEEPS GETTING SMASHED!
BUT I'M NOT GOING TO STOP UNTIL YOUR HEADACHE MATCHES MINE!
EITHER THAT, OR UNTIL YOU HELP ME OUT OF THIS MAZE!

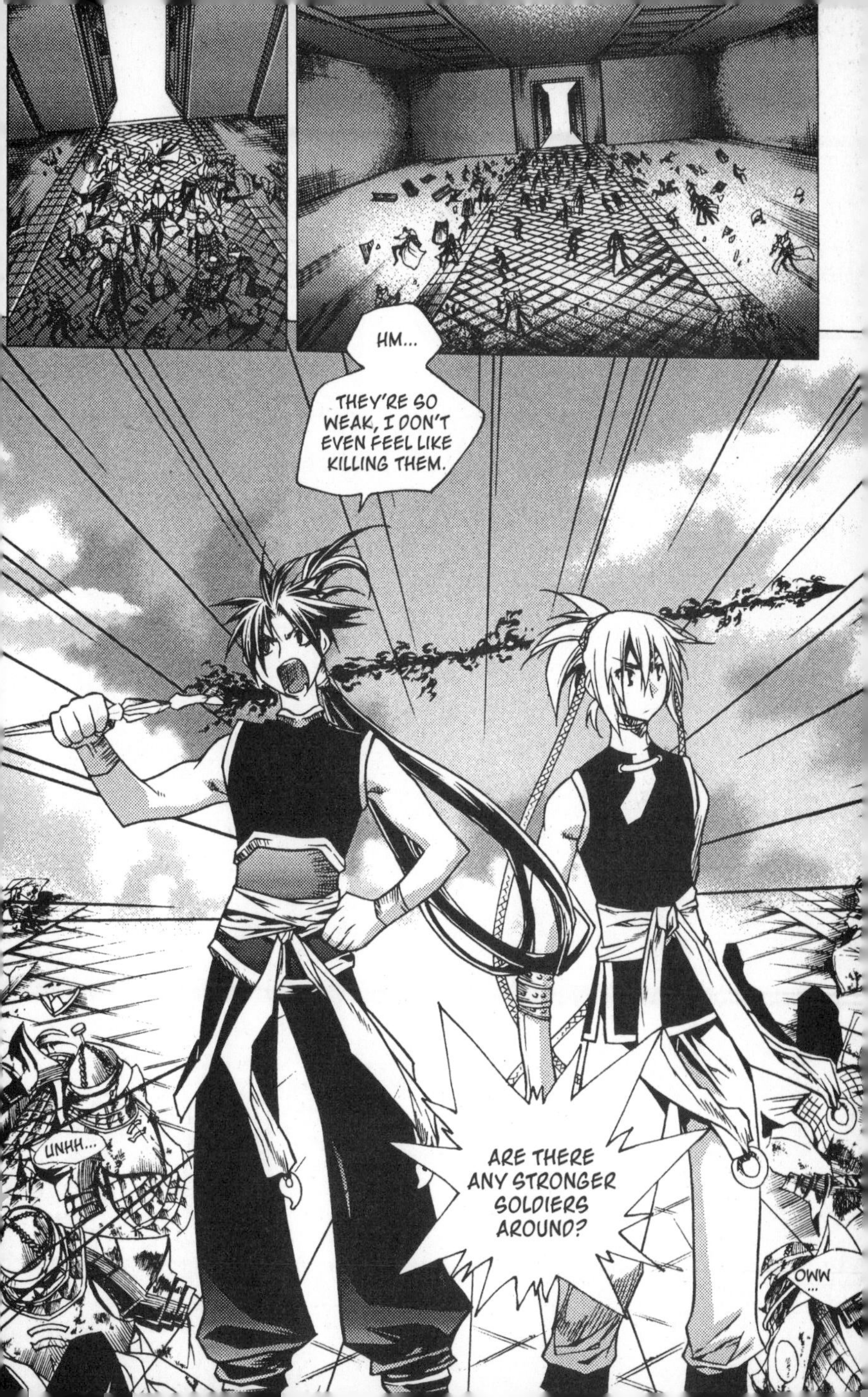
HM...
THEY'RE SO WEAK, I DON'T EVEN FEEL LIKE KILLING THEM.
ARE THERE ANY STRONGER SOLDIERS AROUND?
OWW...
UNHH...

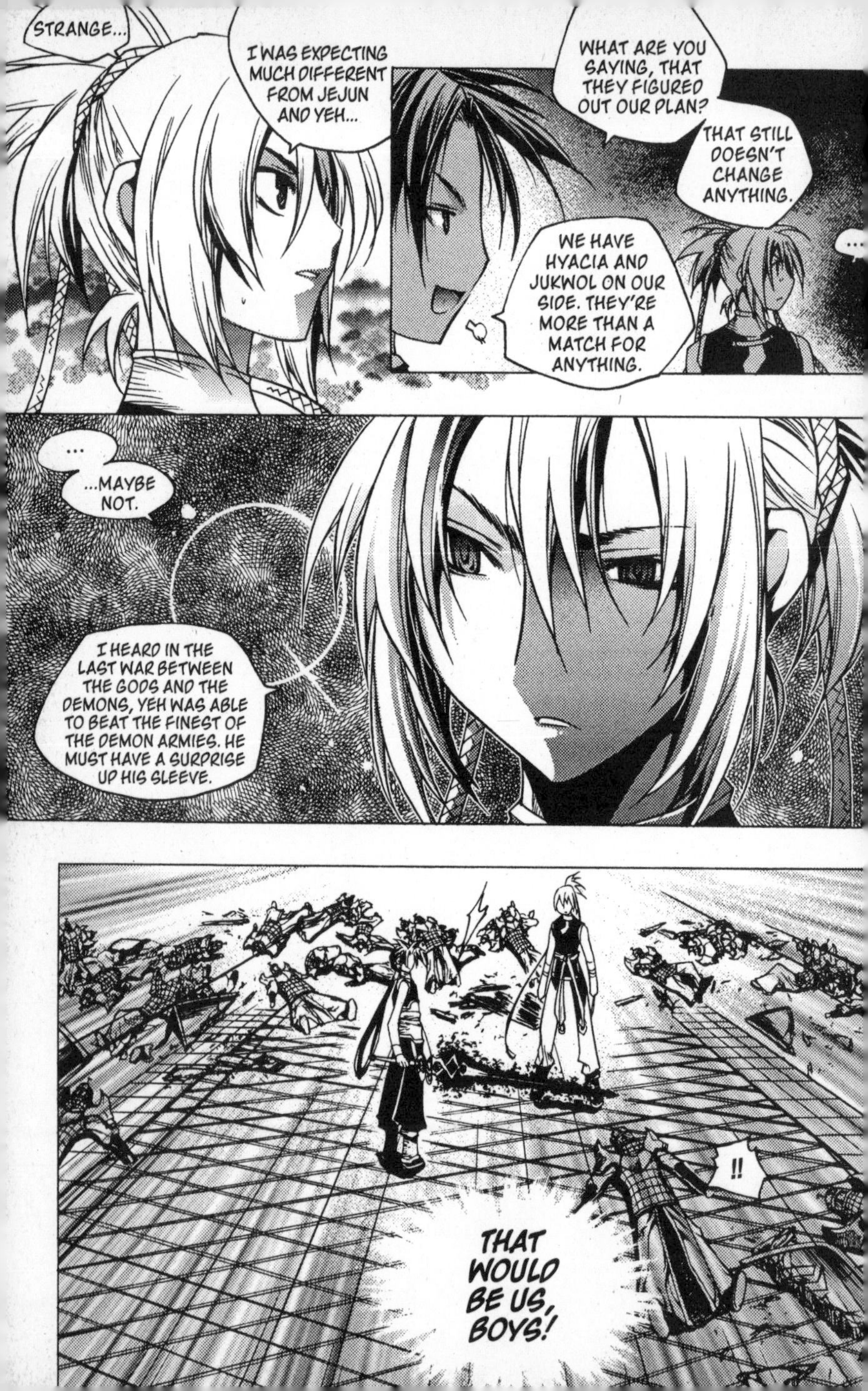
STRANGE...
I WAS EXPECTING MUCH DIFFERENT FROM JEJUN AND YEH...
WHAT ARE YOU SAYING, THAT THEY FIGURED OUT OUR PLAN?
THAT STILL DOESN'T CHANGE ANYTHING.
WE HAVE HYACIA AND JUKWOL ON OUR SIDE. THEY'RE MORE THAN A MATCH FOR ANYTHING.
...
...
...MAYBE NOT.
I HEARD IN THE LAST WAR BETWEEN THE GODS AND THE DEMONS, YEH WAS ABLE TO BEAT THE FINEST OF THE DEMON ARMIES. HE MUST HAVE A SURPRISE UP HIS SLEEVE.
!!
THAT WOULD BE US, BOYS!

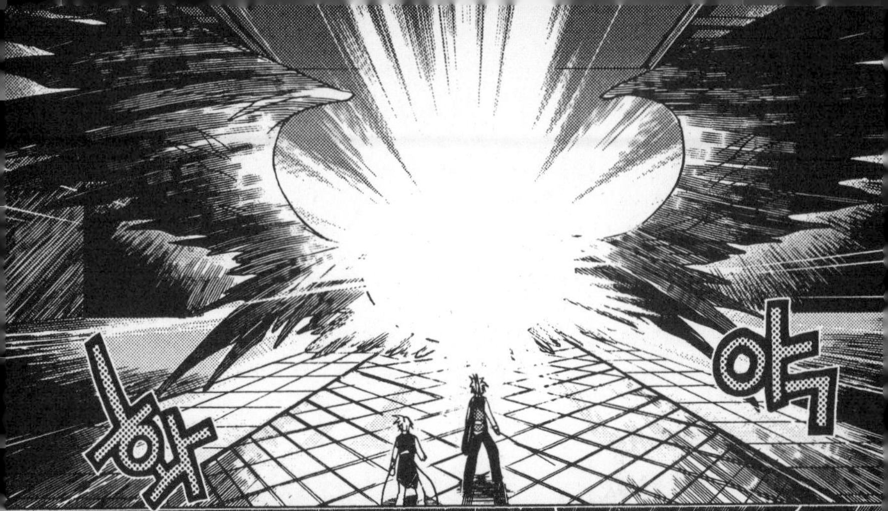
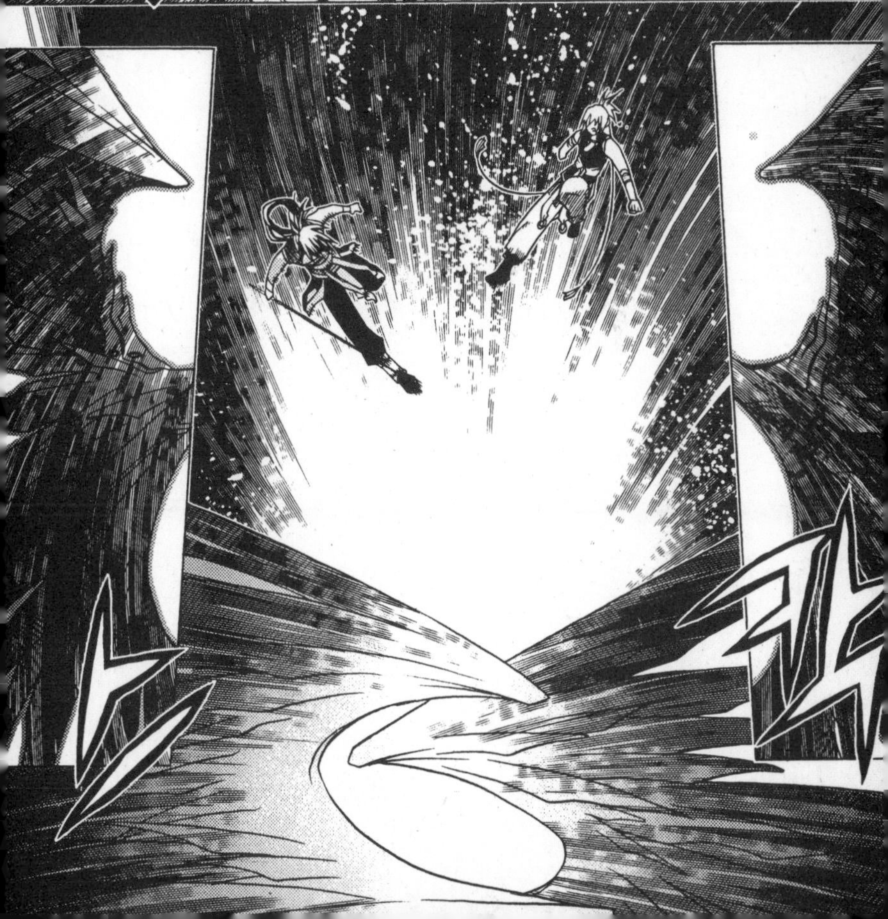

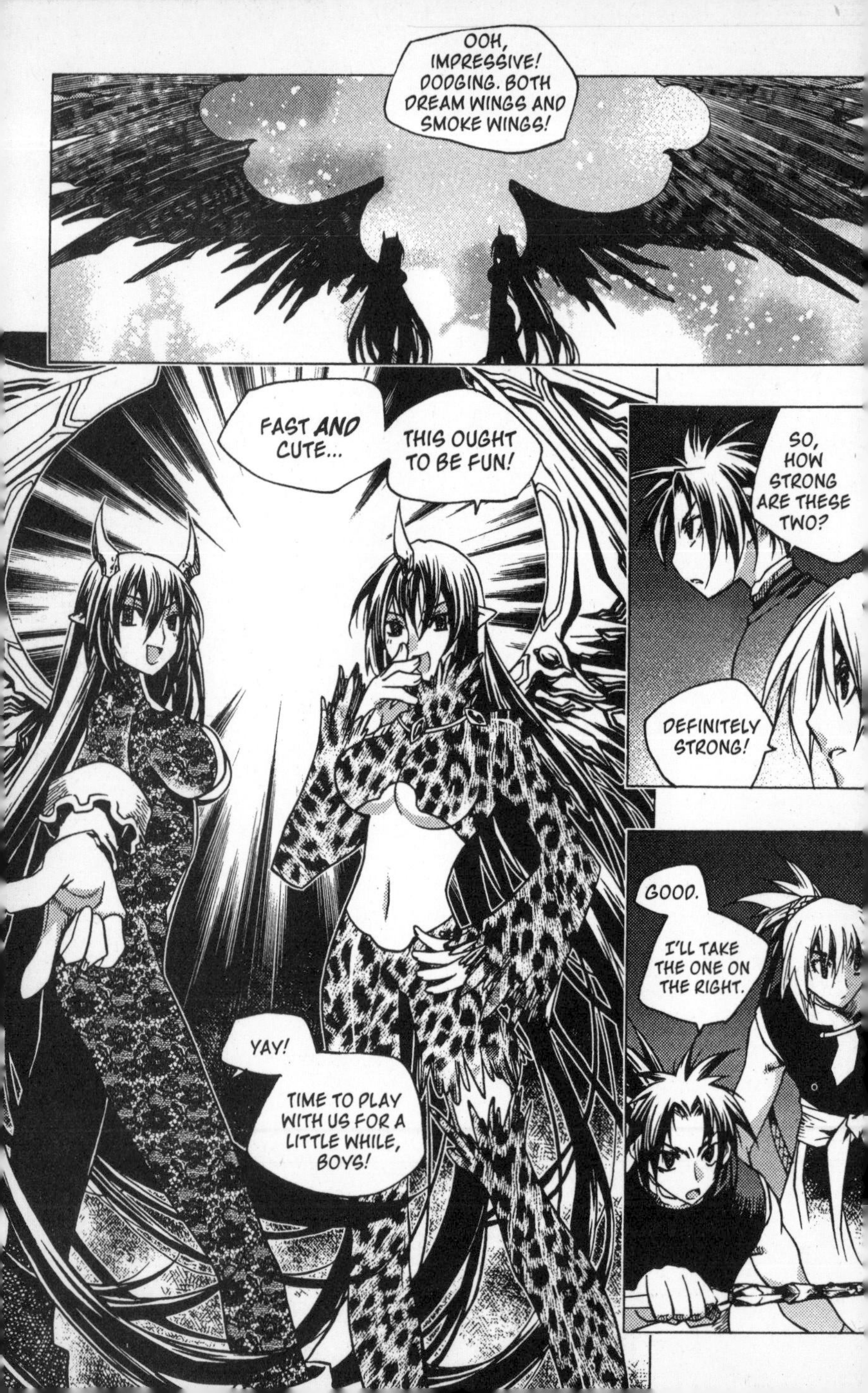
OOH, IMPRESSIVE! DODGING. BOTH DREAM WINGS AND SMOKE WINGS!
SO, HOW STRONG ARE THESE TWO?
DEFINITELY STRONG!
GOOD.
I'LL TAKE THE ONE ON THE RIGHT.
THIS OUGHT TO BE FUN!
FAST **AND** CUTE...
YAY!
TIME TO PLAY WITH US FOR A LITTLE WHILE, BOYS!

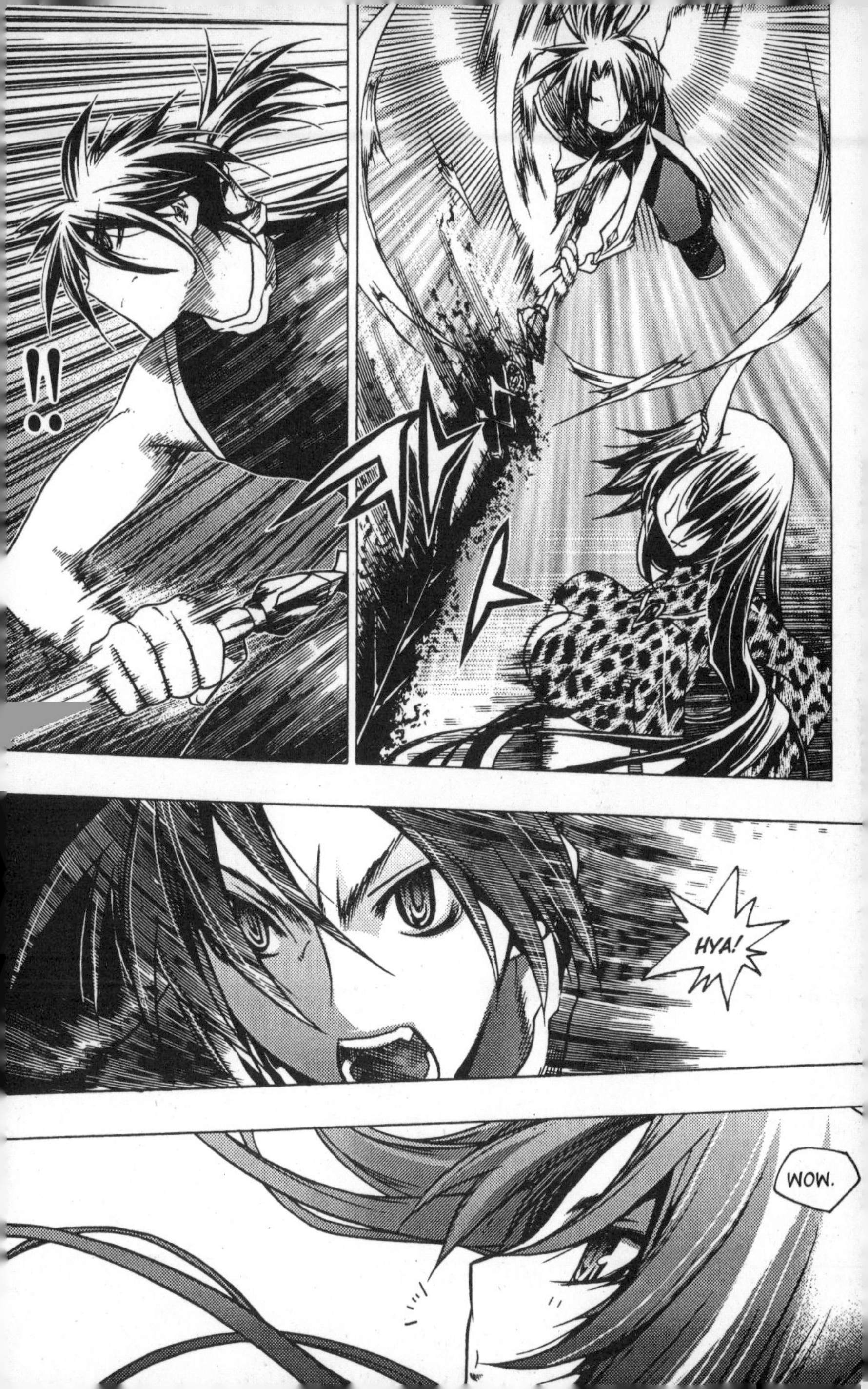
!!
HYA!
WOW.

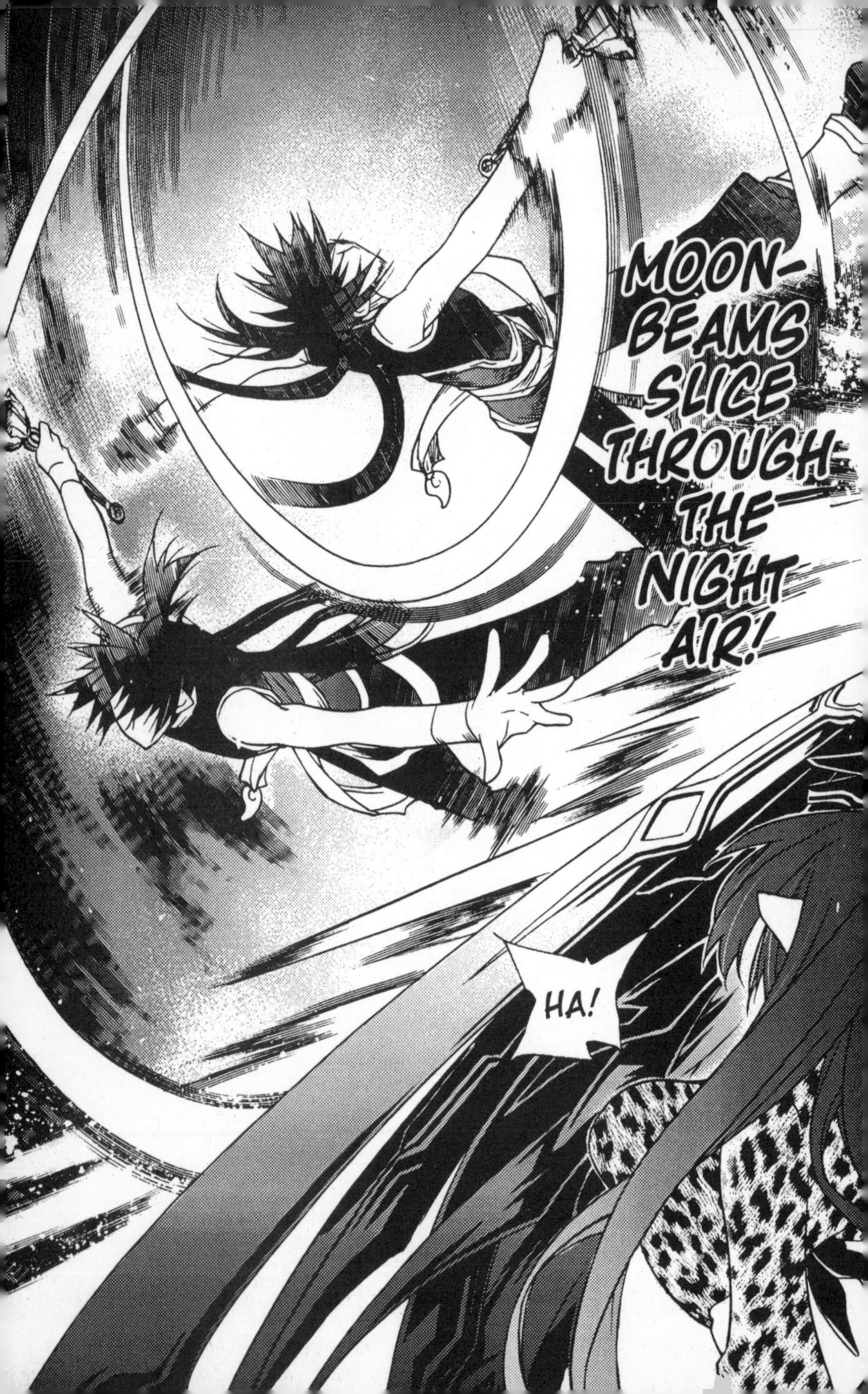
MOON-BEAMS SLICE THROUGH THE NIGHT AIR!
HA!

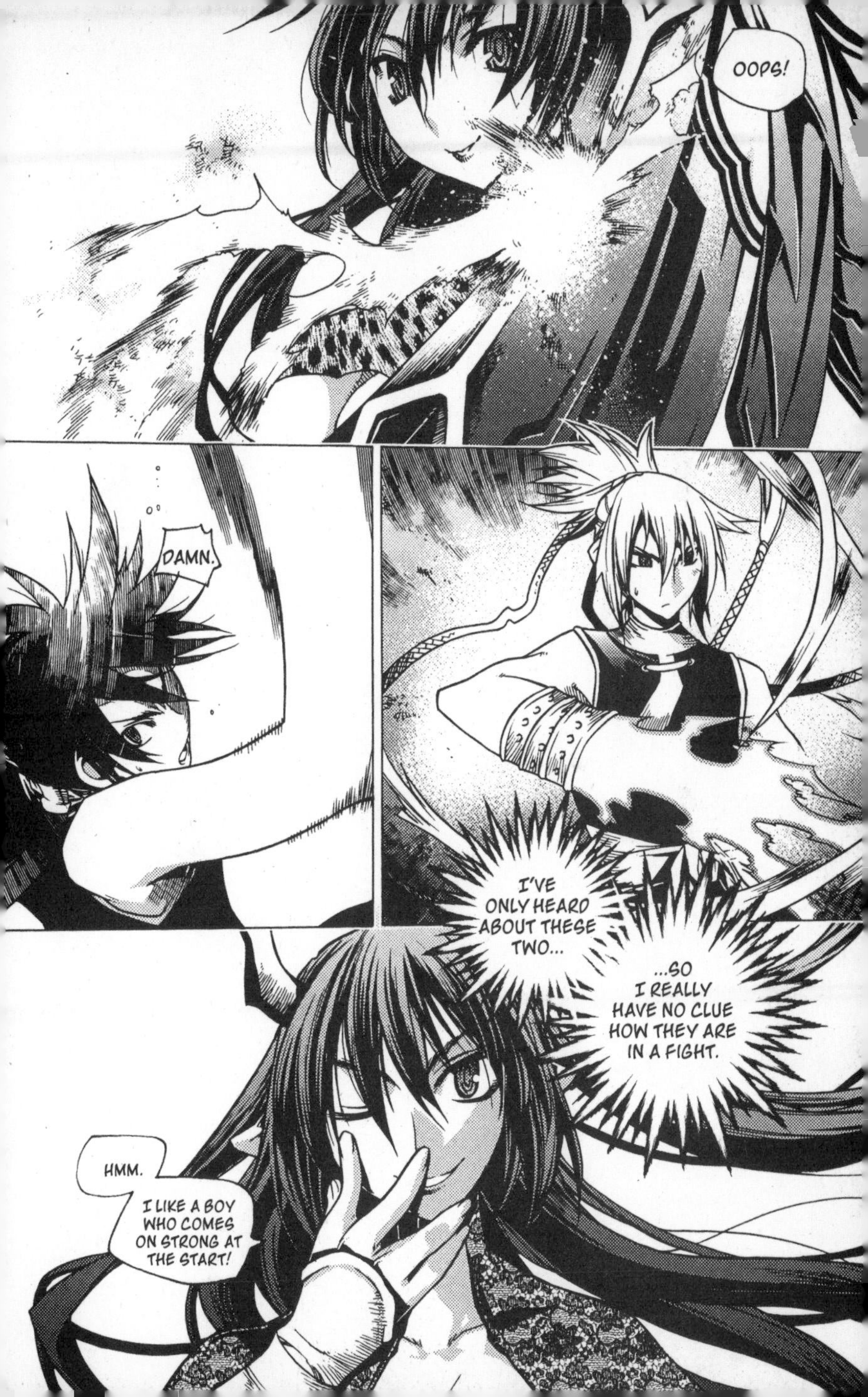
OOPS!
DAMN.
I'VE ONLY HEARD ABOUT THESE TWO...
...SO I REALLY HAVE NO CLUE HOW THEY ARE IN A FIGHT.
HMM.
I LIKE A BOY WHO COMES ON STRONG AT THE START!

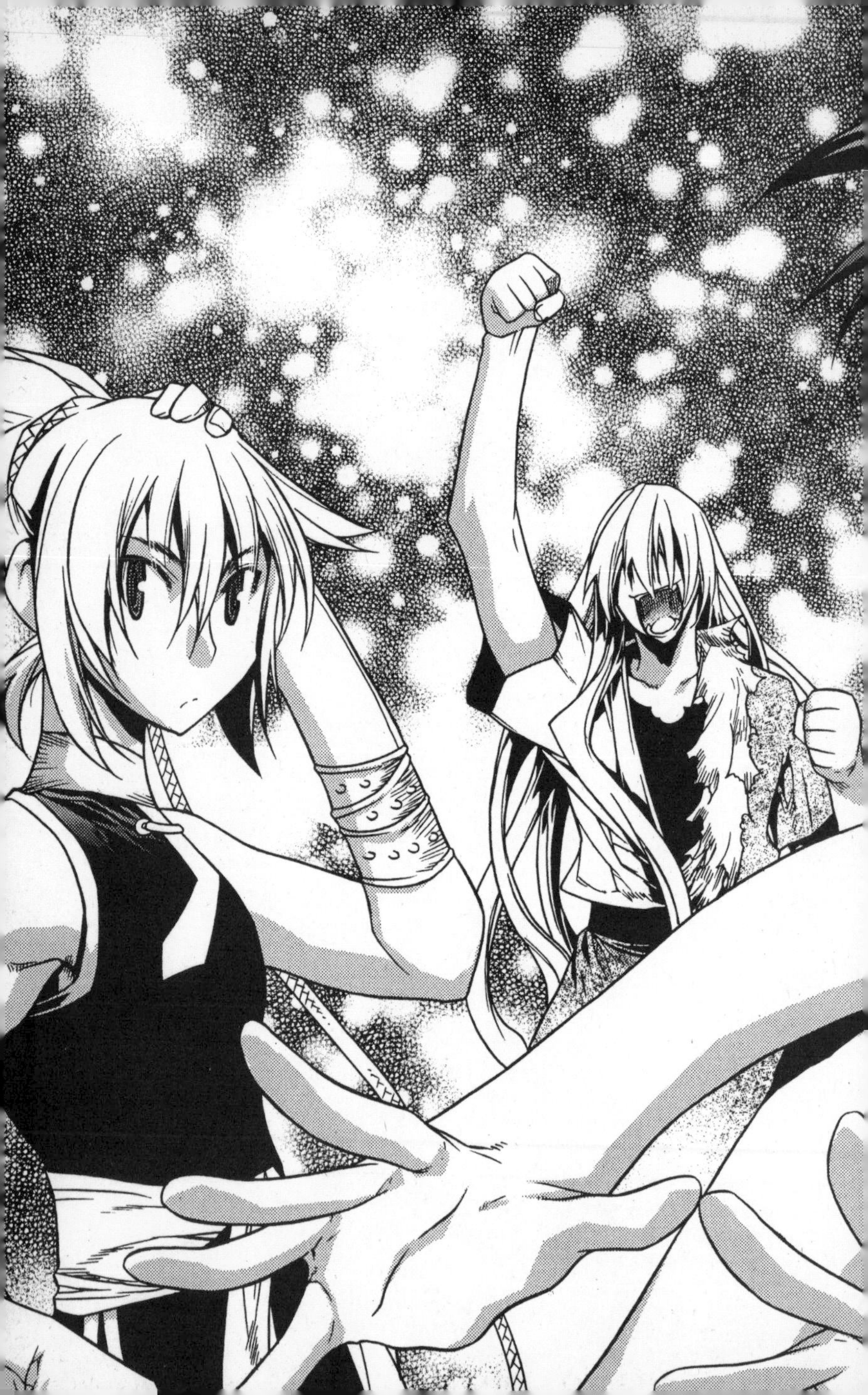

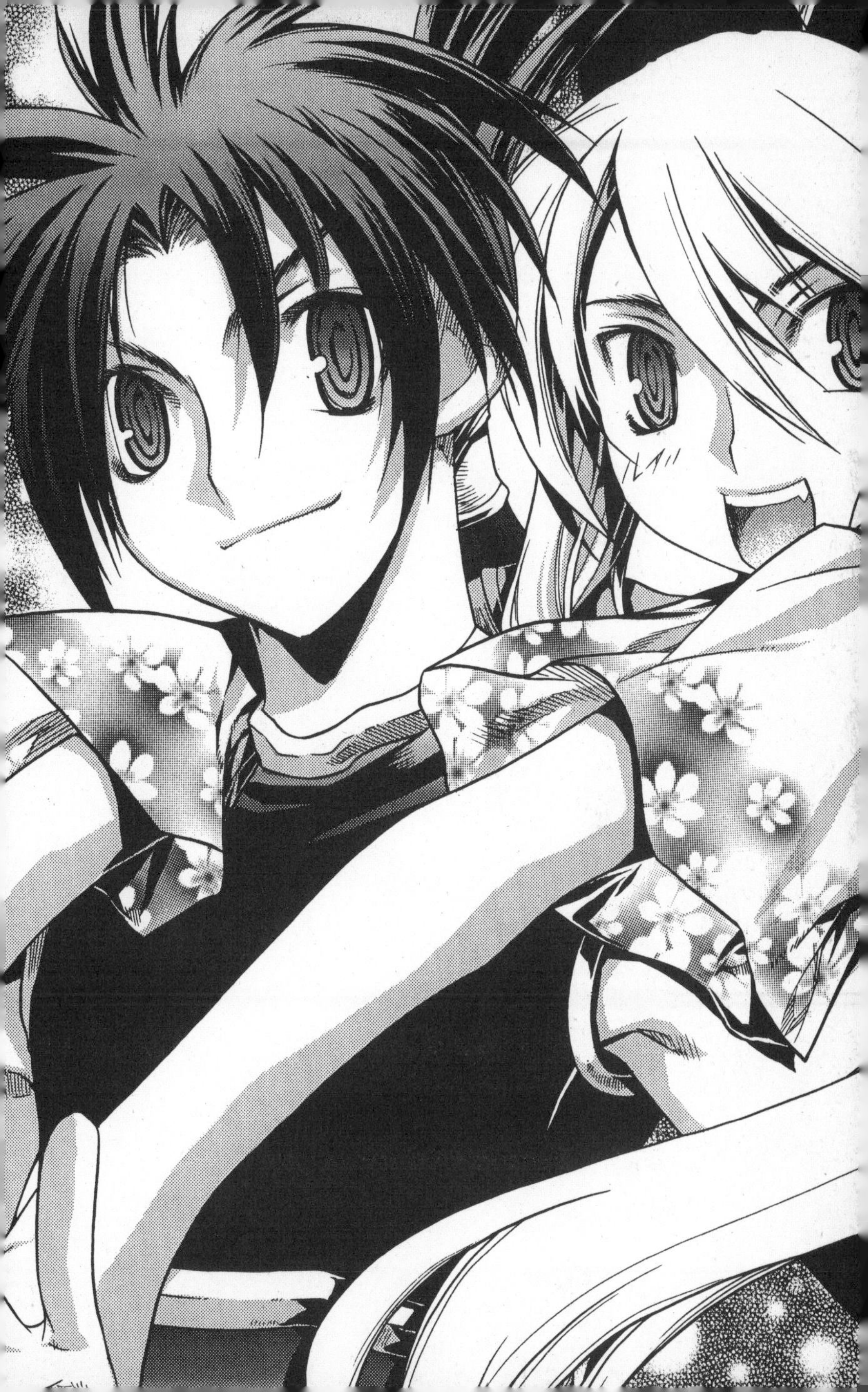

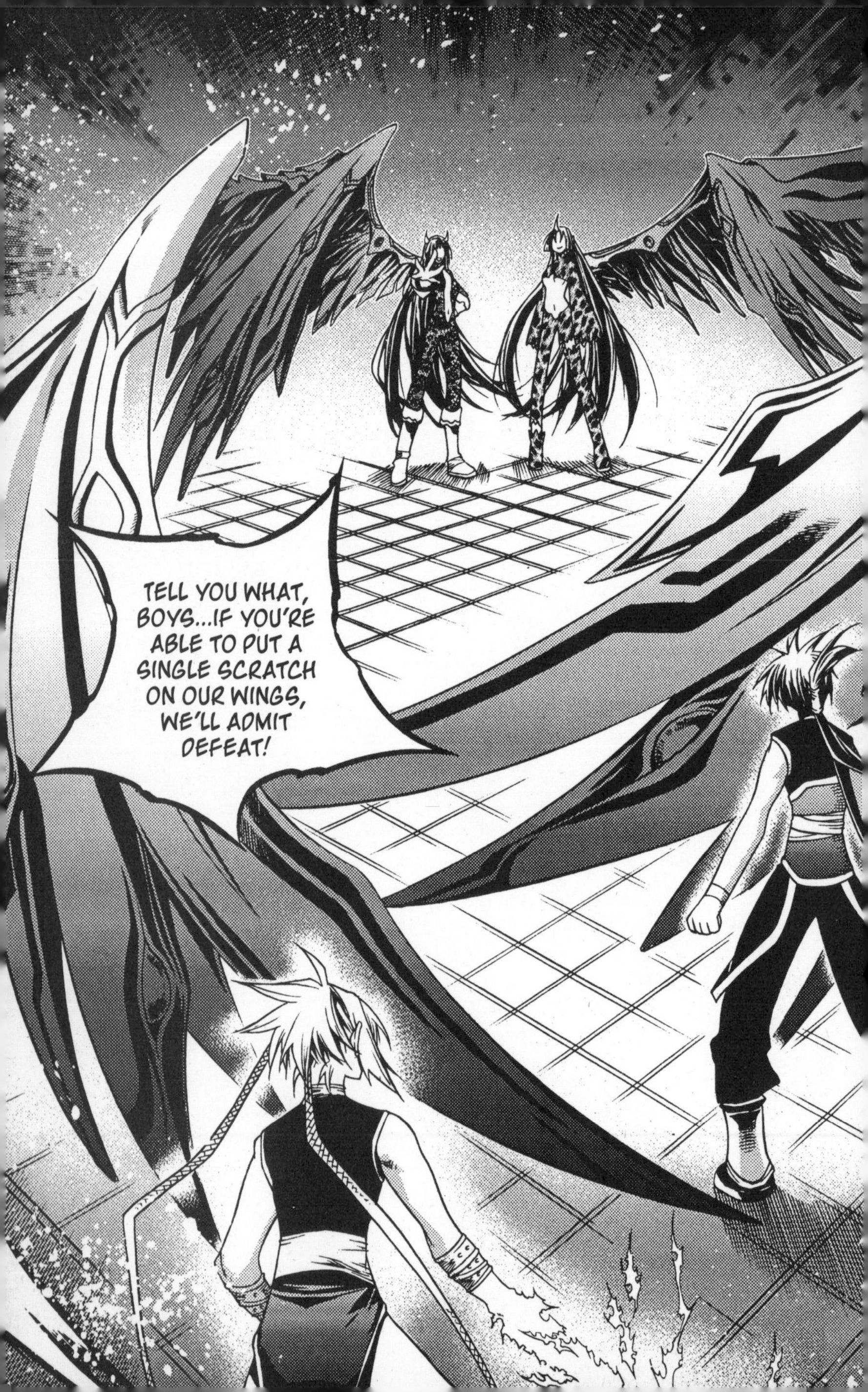
TELL YOU WHAT, BOYS...IF YOU'RE ABLE TO PUT A SINGLE SCRATCH ON OUR WINGS, WE'LL ADMIT DEFEAT!

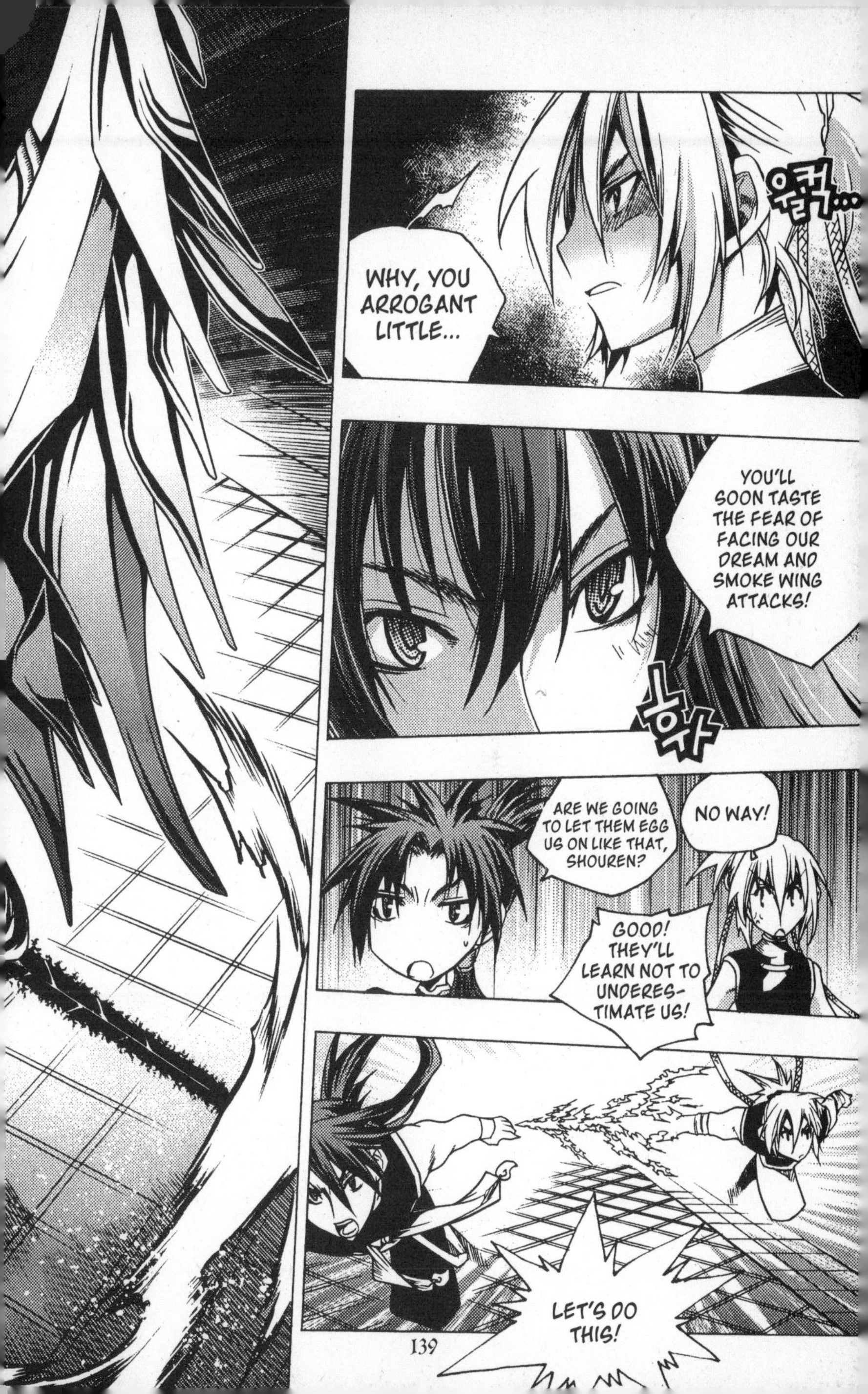
WHY, YOU ARROGANT LITTLE...
YOU'LL SOON TASTE THE FEAR OF FACING OUR DREAM AND SMOKE WING ATTACKS!
ARE WE GOING TO LET THEM EGG US ON LIKE THAT, SHOUREN?
NO WAY!
GOOD! THEY'LL LEARN NOT TO UNDERES-TIMATE US!
LET'S DO THIS!

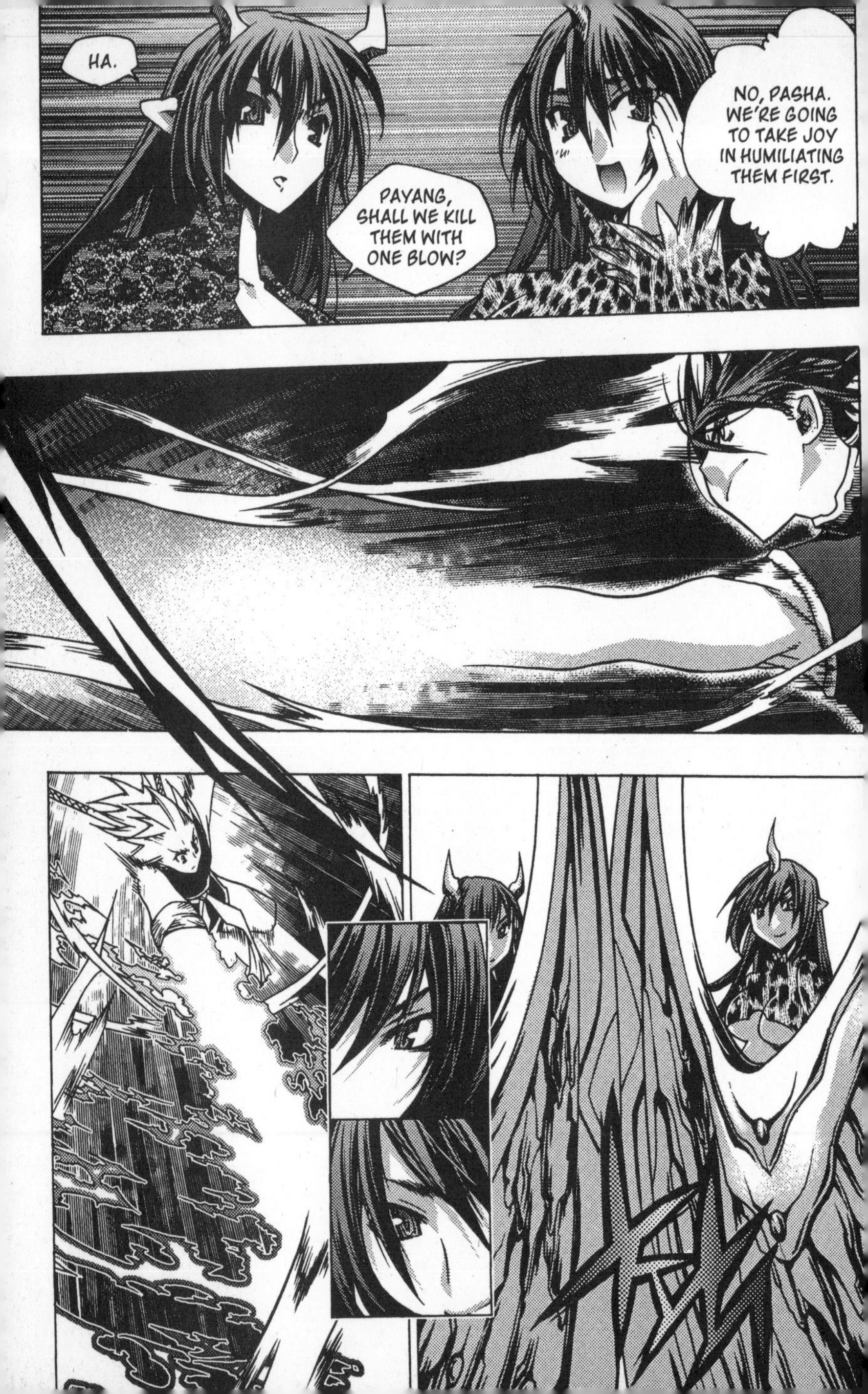
NO, PASHA. WE'RE GOING TO TAKE JOY IN HUMILIATING THEM FIRST.
PAYANG, SHALL WE KILL THEM WITH ONE BLOW?
HA.

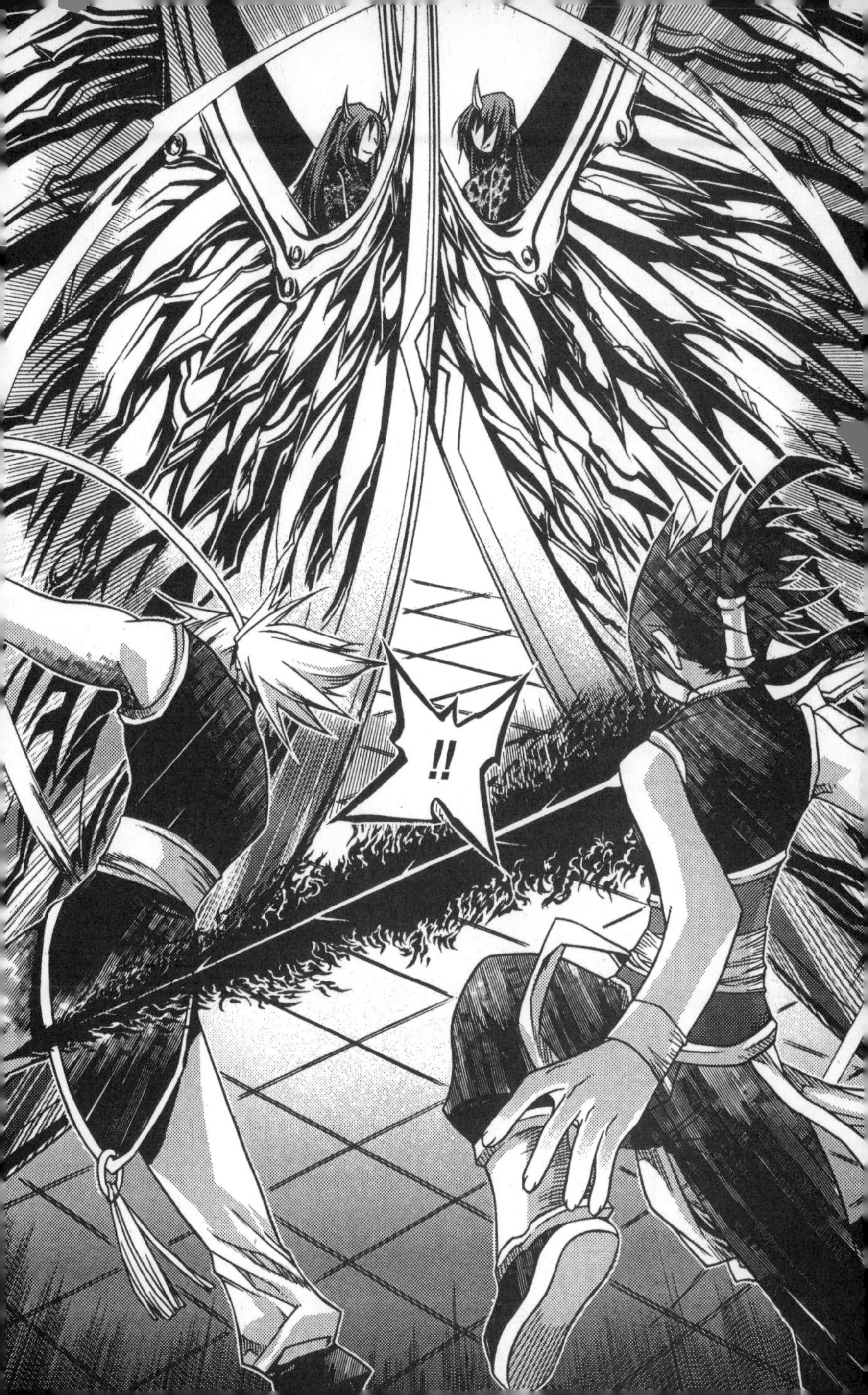
!!

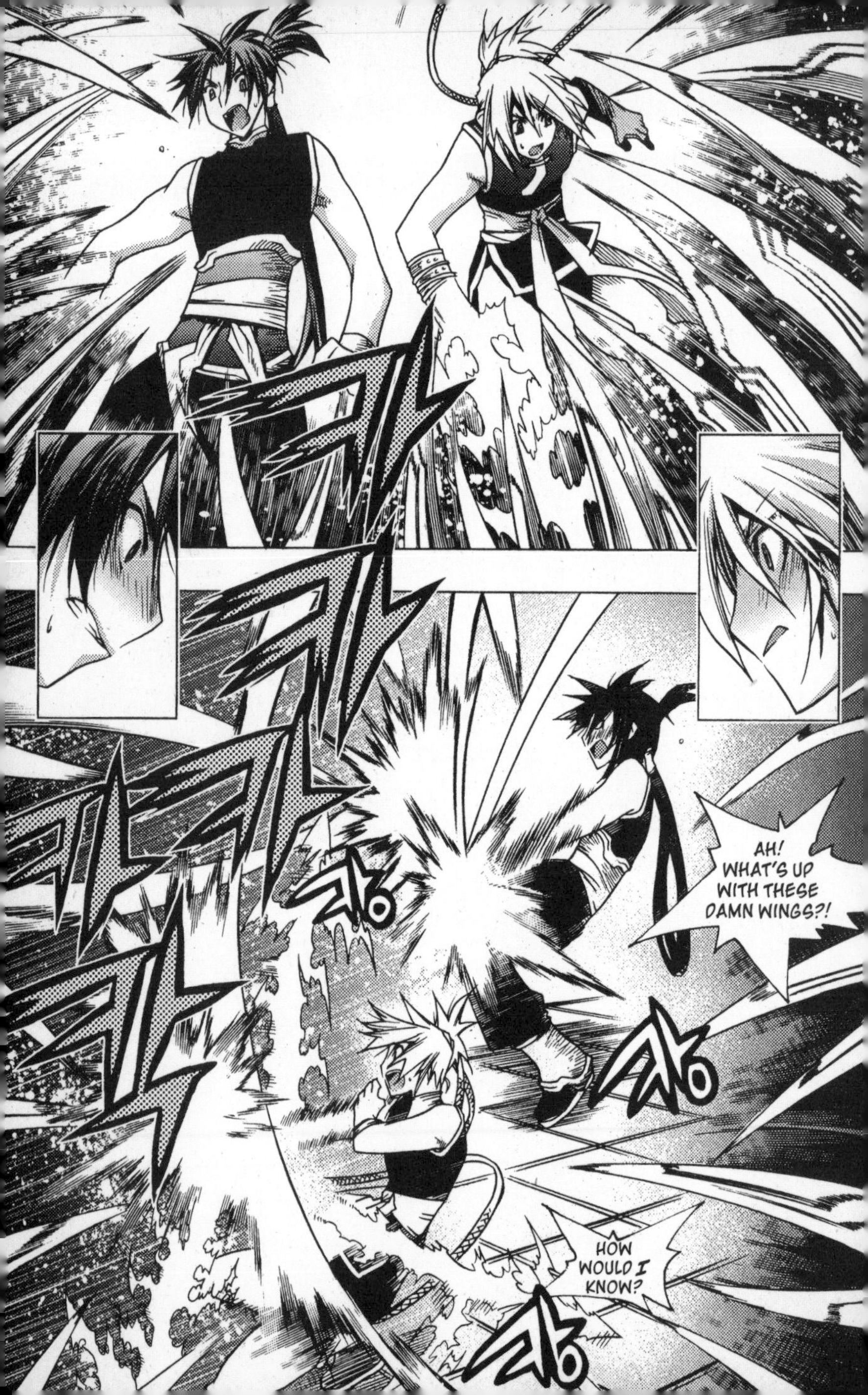
AH! WHAT'S UP WITH THESE DAMN WINGS?!
HOW WOULD I KNOW?

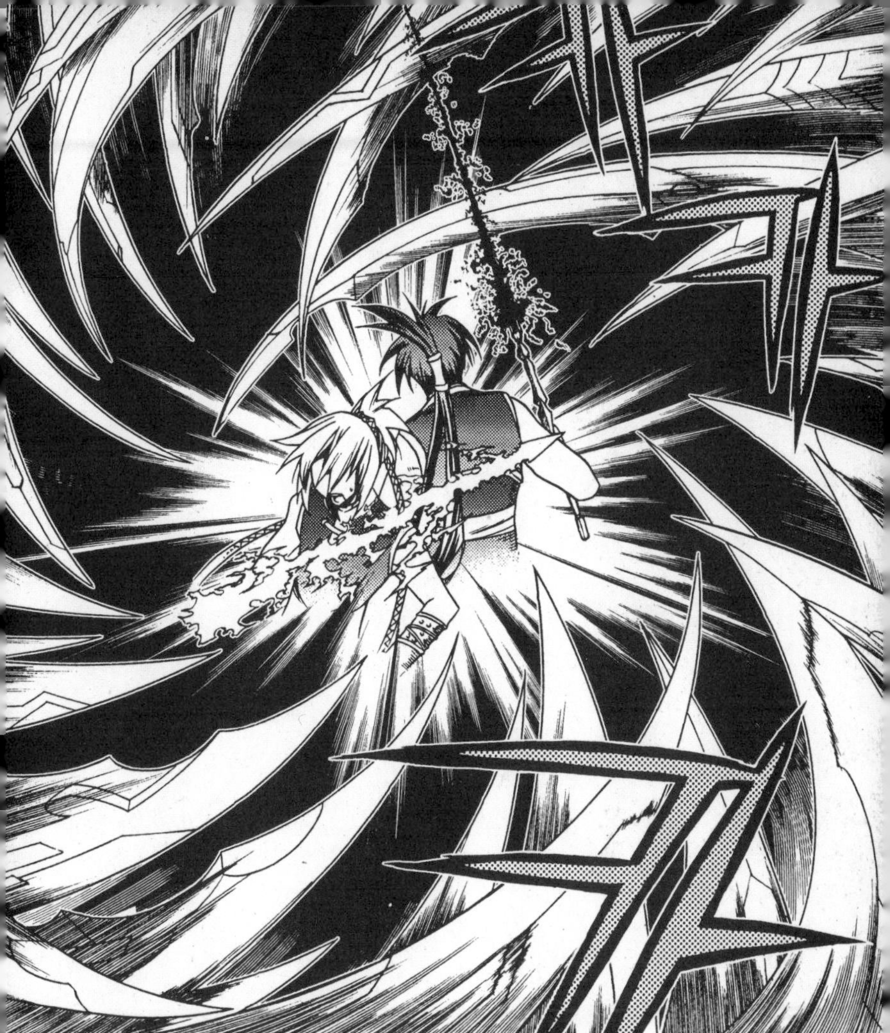

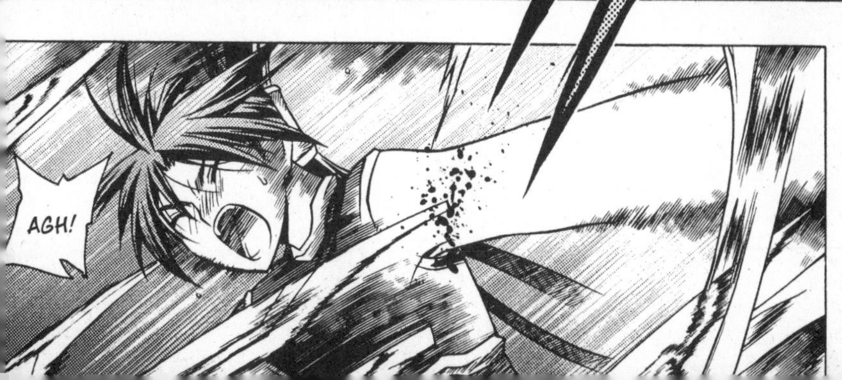
AGH!

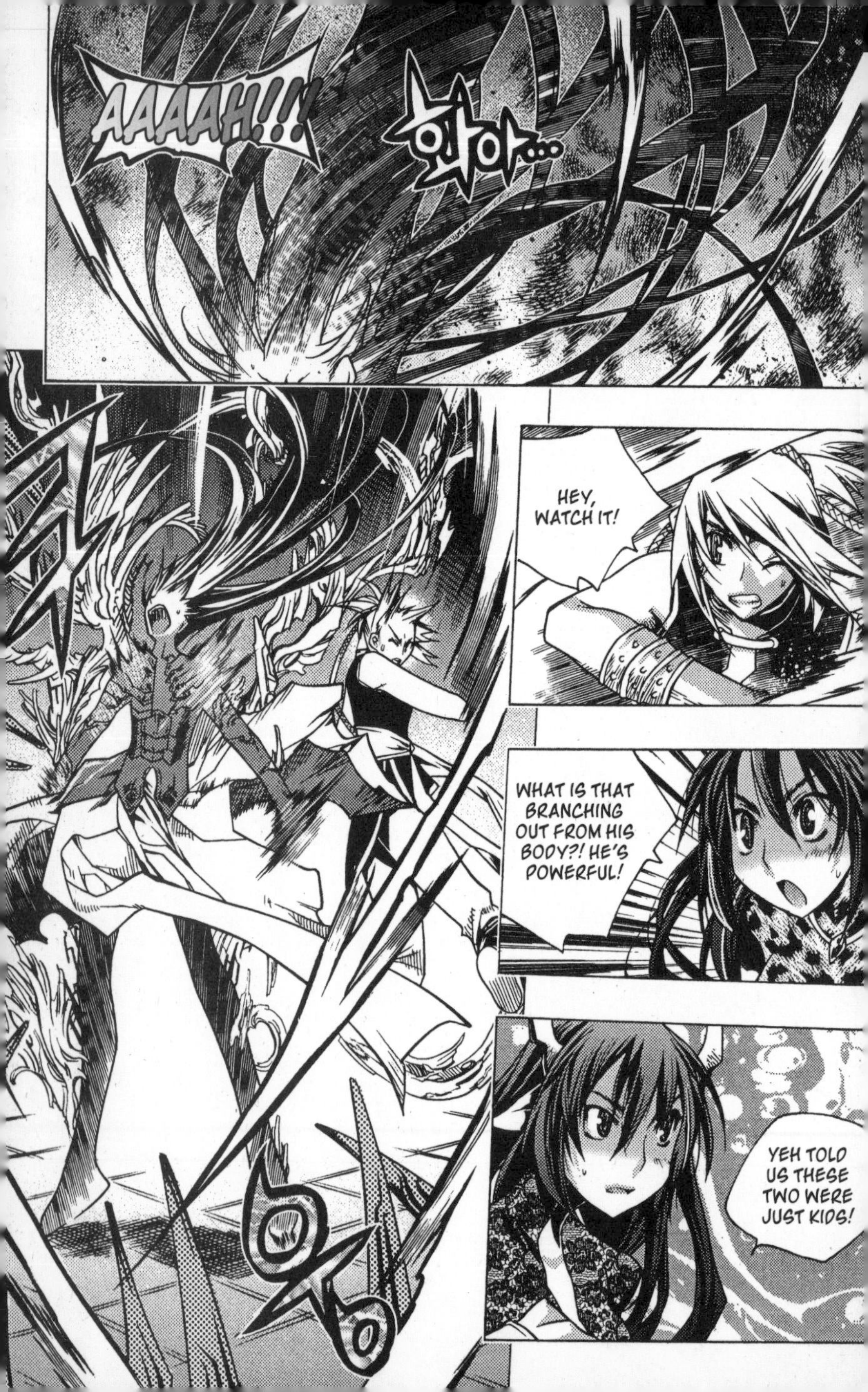
AAAAH!!!
HEY, WATCH IT!
WHAT IS THAT BRANCHING OUT FROM HIS BODY?! HE'S POWERFUL!
YEH TOLD US THESE TWO WERE JUST KIDS!

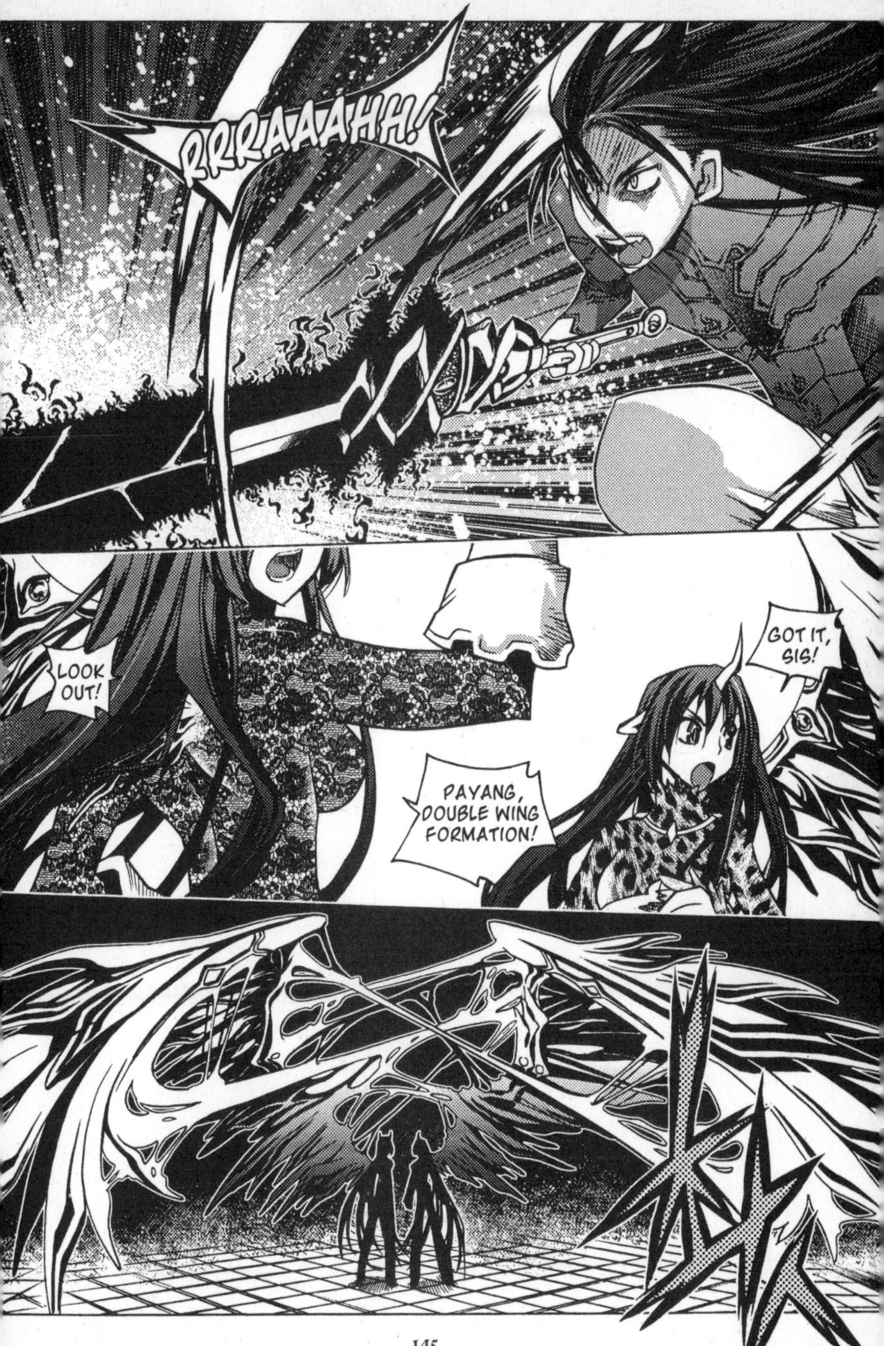
RRRAAAHH!
GOT IT, SIS!
PAYANG, DOUBLE WING FORMATION!
LOOK OUT!

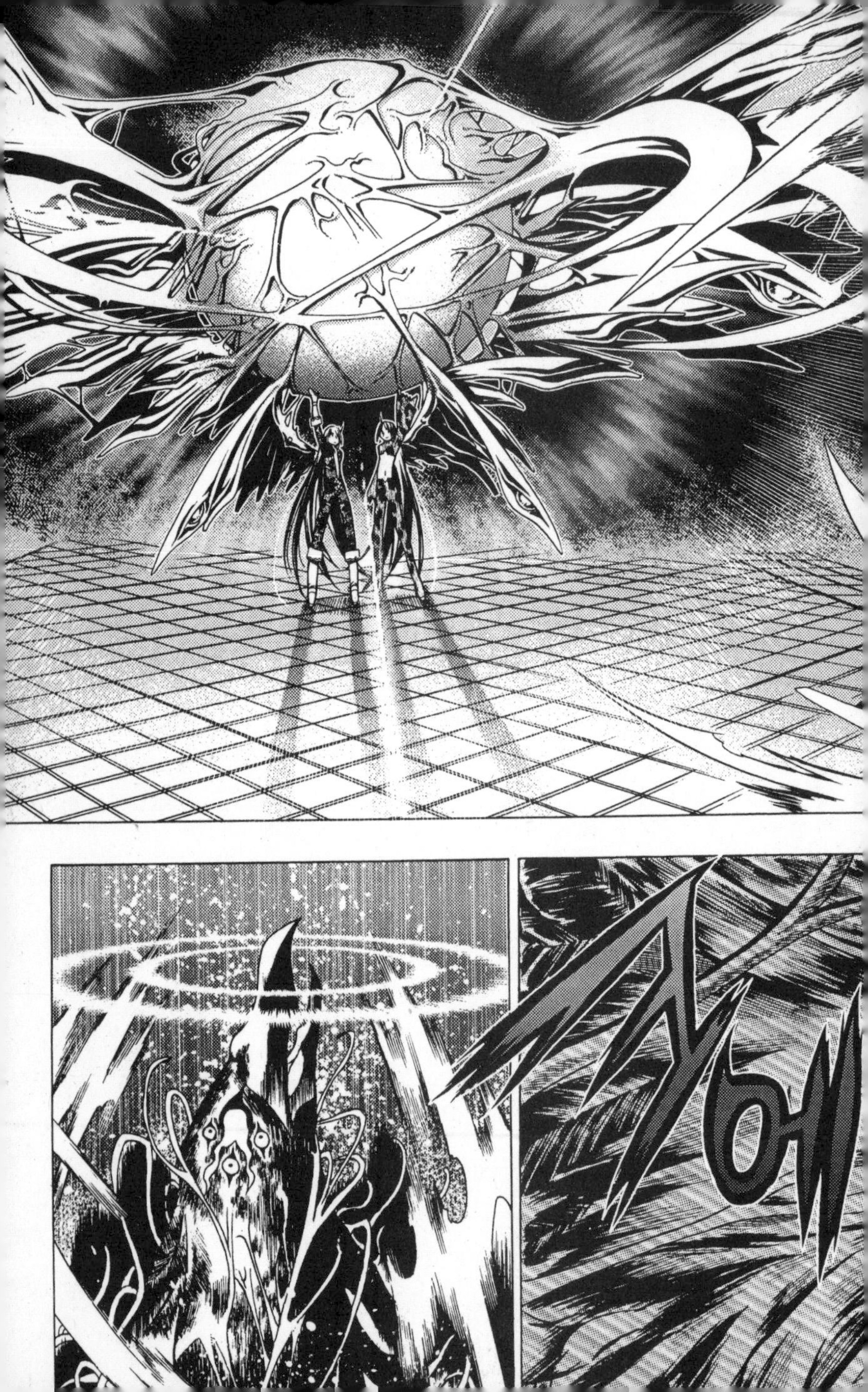

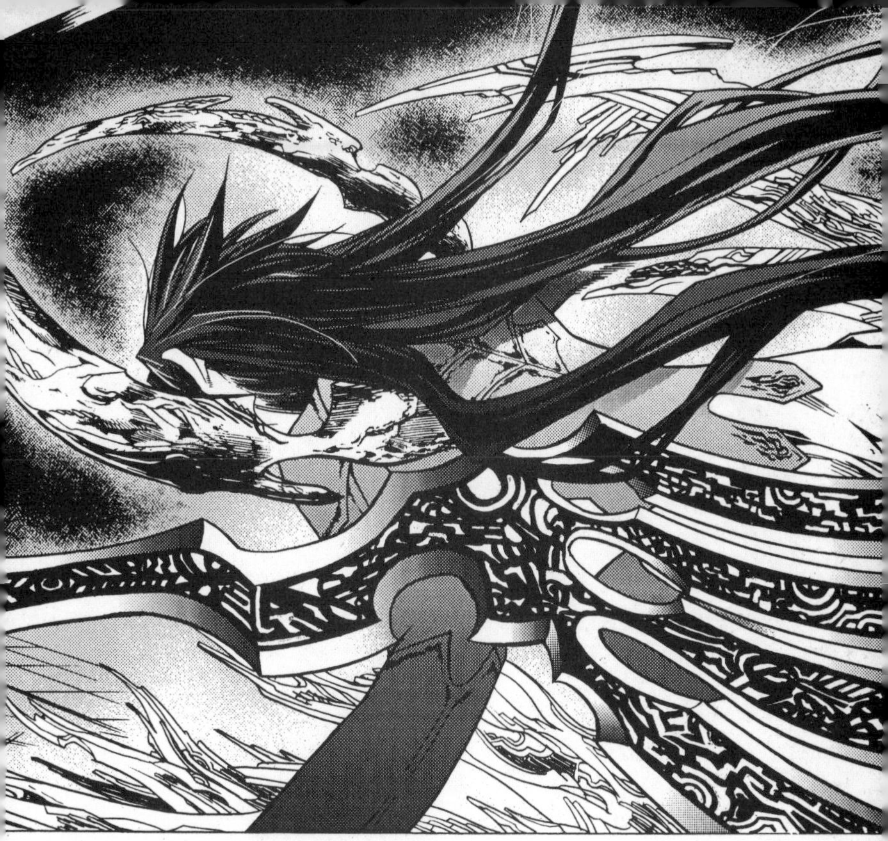
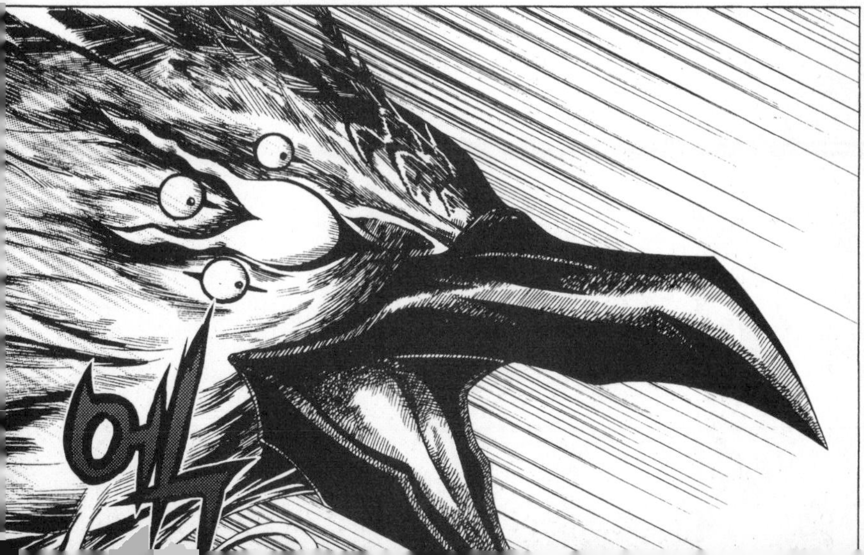

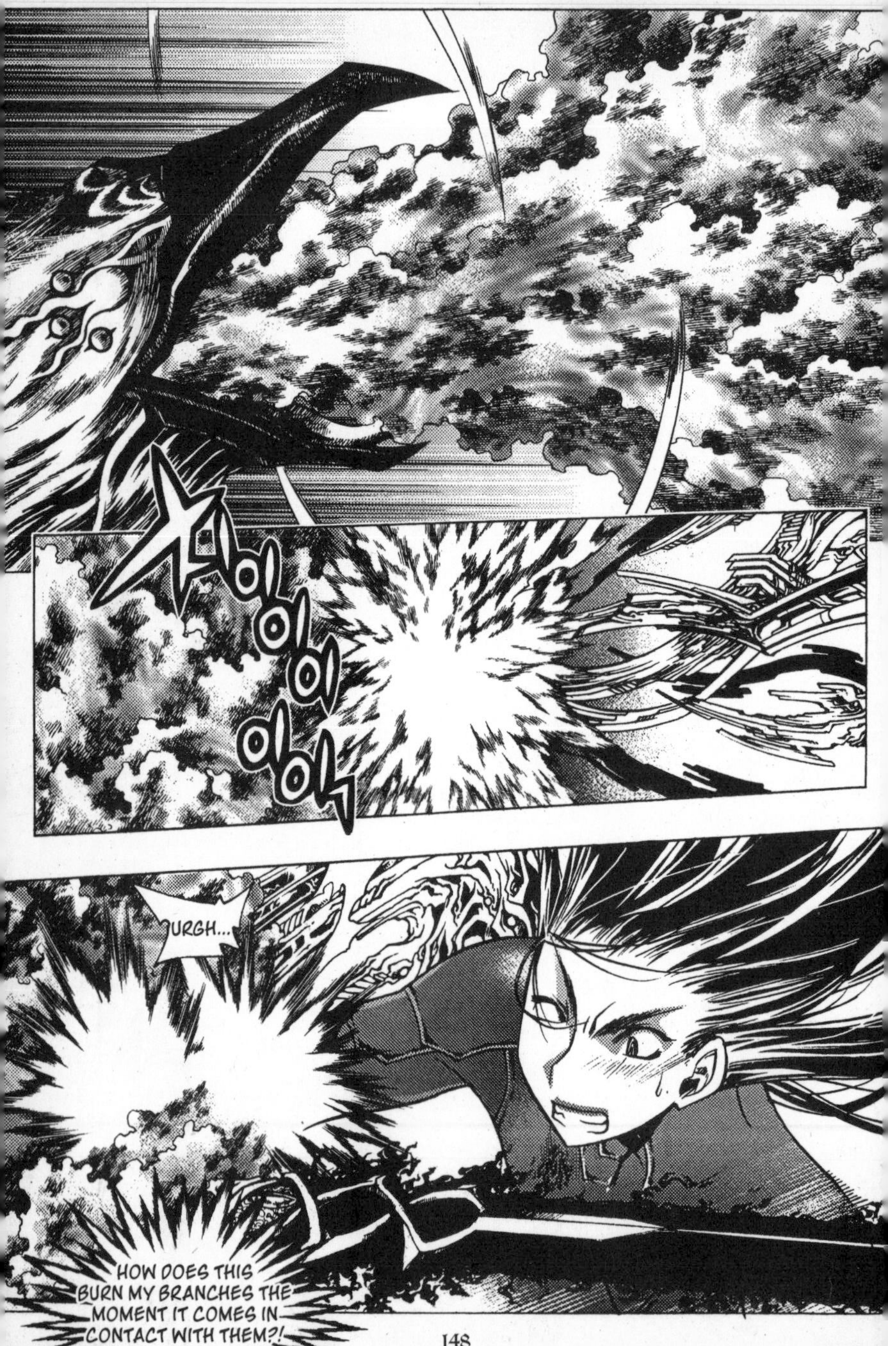

ZOOOOOOM
URGH...
HOW DOES THIS BURN MY BRANCHES THE MOMENT IT COMES IN CONTACT WITH THEM?!

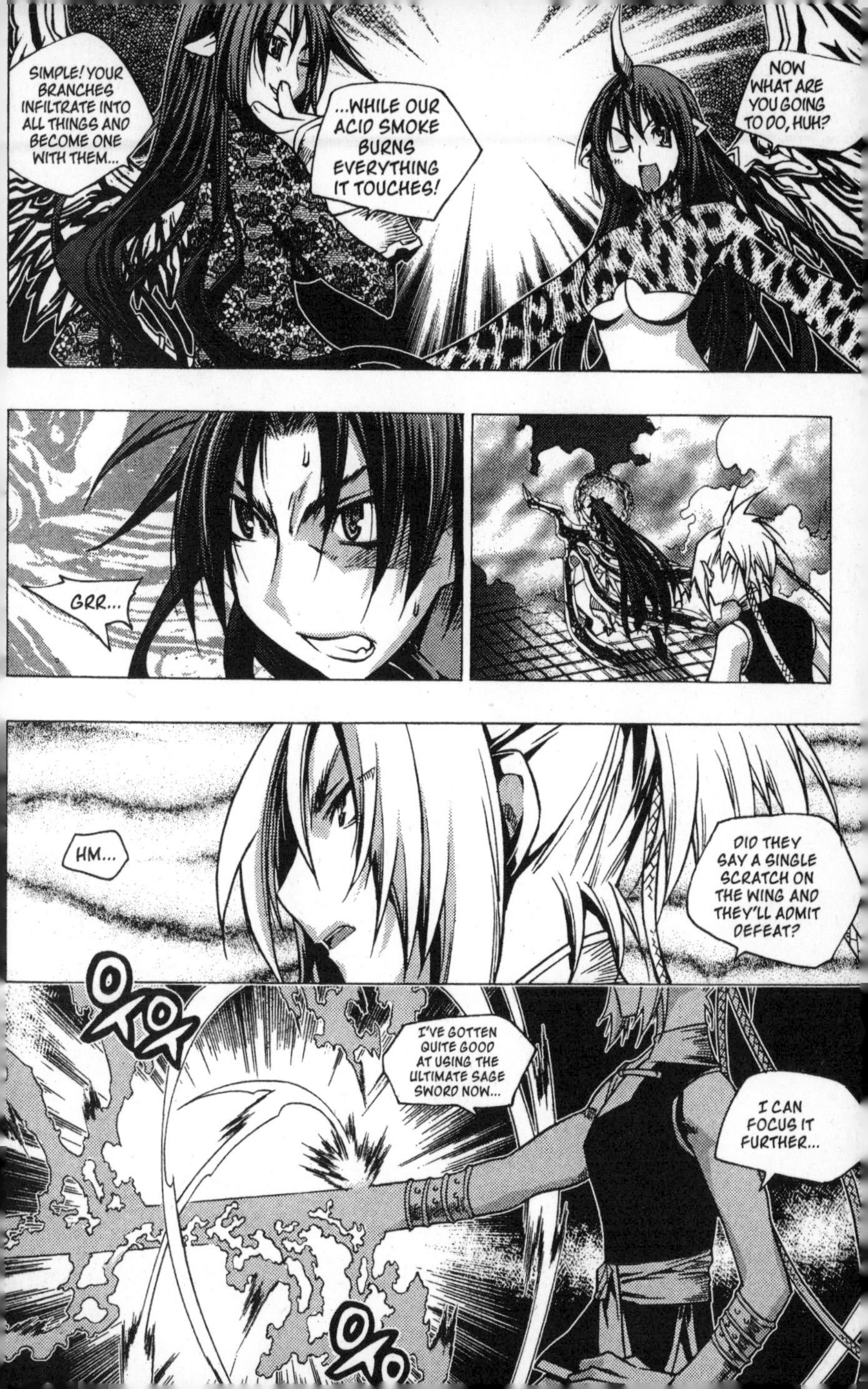
SIMPLE! YOUR BRANCHES INFILTRATE INTO ALL THINGS AND BECOME ONE WITH THEM...
...WHILE OUR ACID SMOKE BURNS EVERYTHING IT TOUCHES!
NOW WHAT ARE YOU GOING TO DO, HUH?
GRR...
HM...
DID THEY SAY A SINGLE SCRATCH ON THE WING AND THEY'LL ADMIT DEFEAT?
I'VE GOTTEN QUITE GOOD AT USING THE ULTIMATE SAGE SWORD NOW...
I CAN FOCUS IT FURTHER...

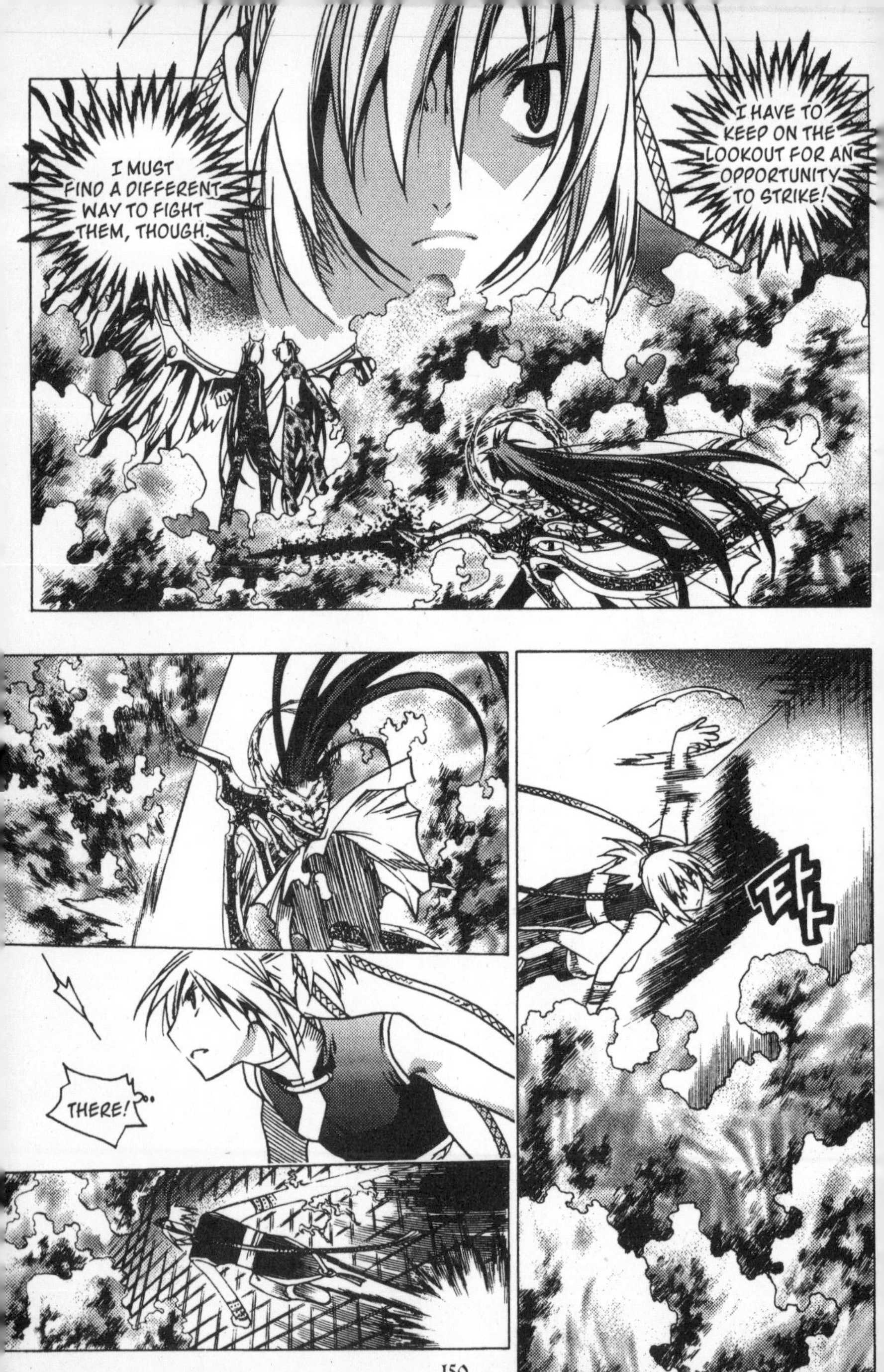
I HAVE TO KEEP ON THE LOOKOUT FOR AN OPPORTUNITY TO STRIKE!
I MUST FIND A DIFFERENT WAY TO FIGHT THEM, THOUGH.
THERE!

Chapter 87
Ice Arrows

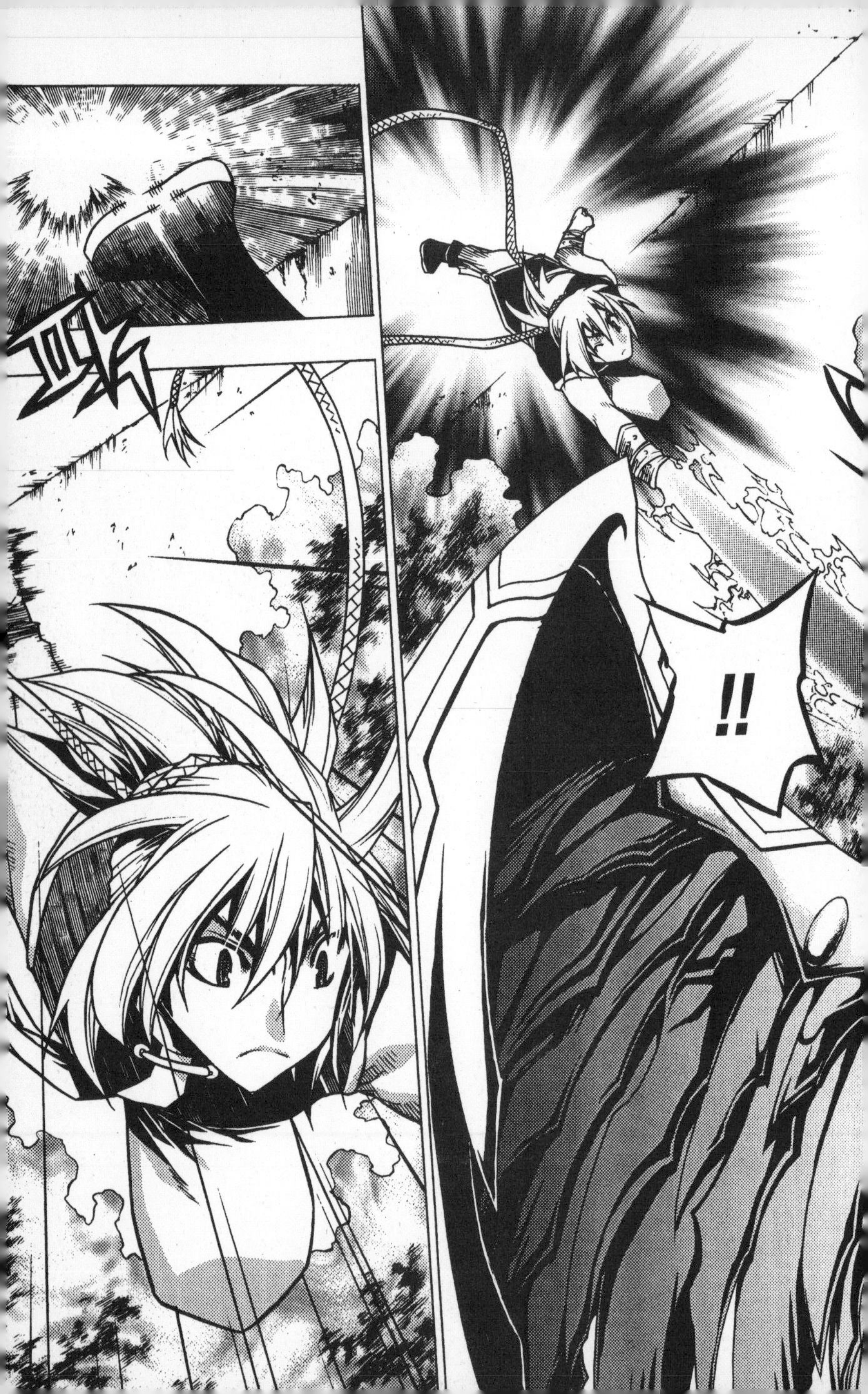
!!

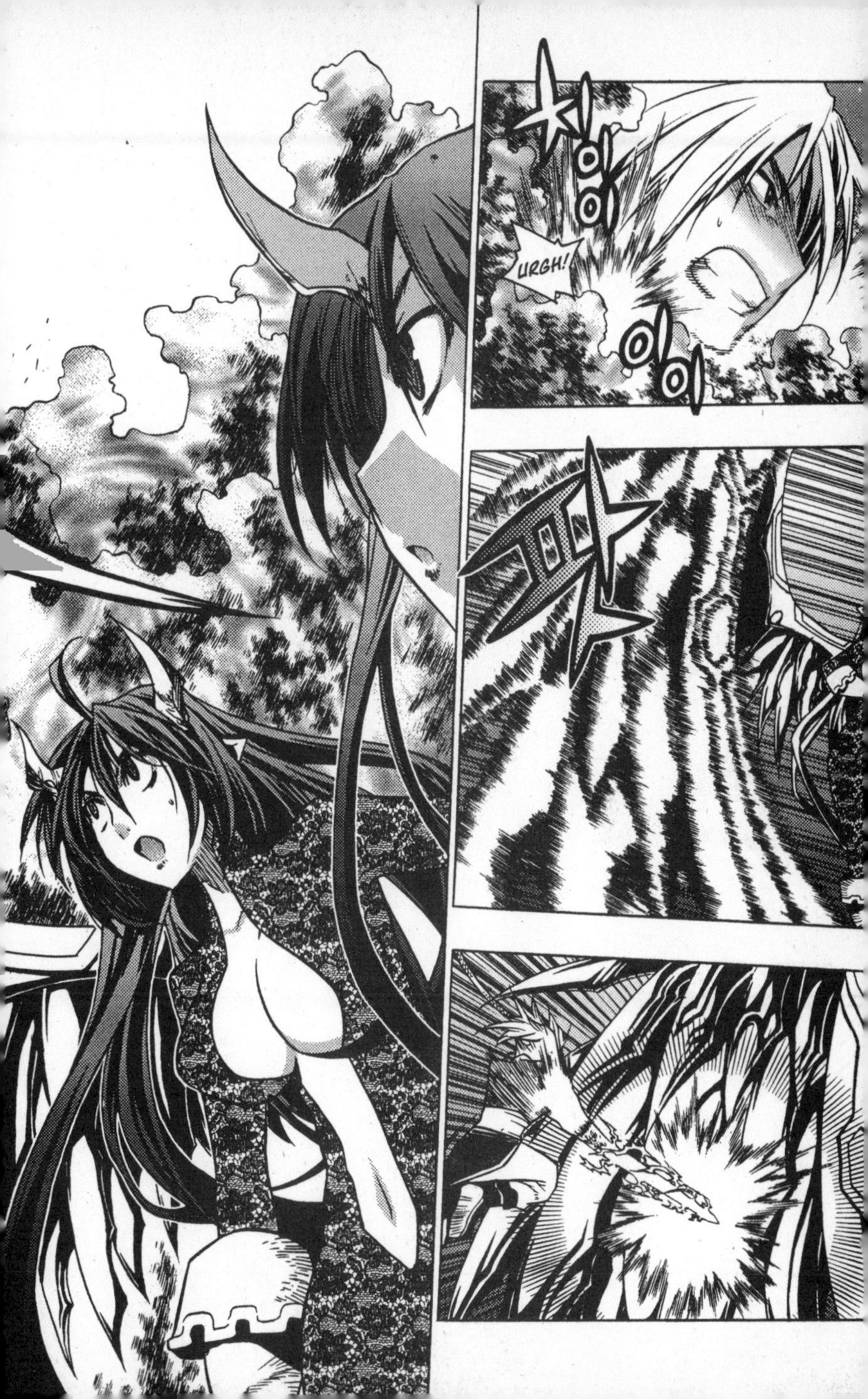
URGH!

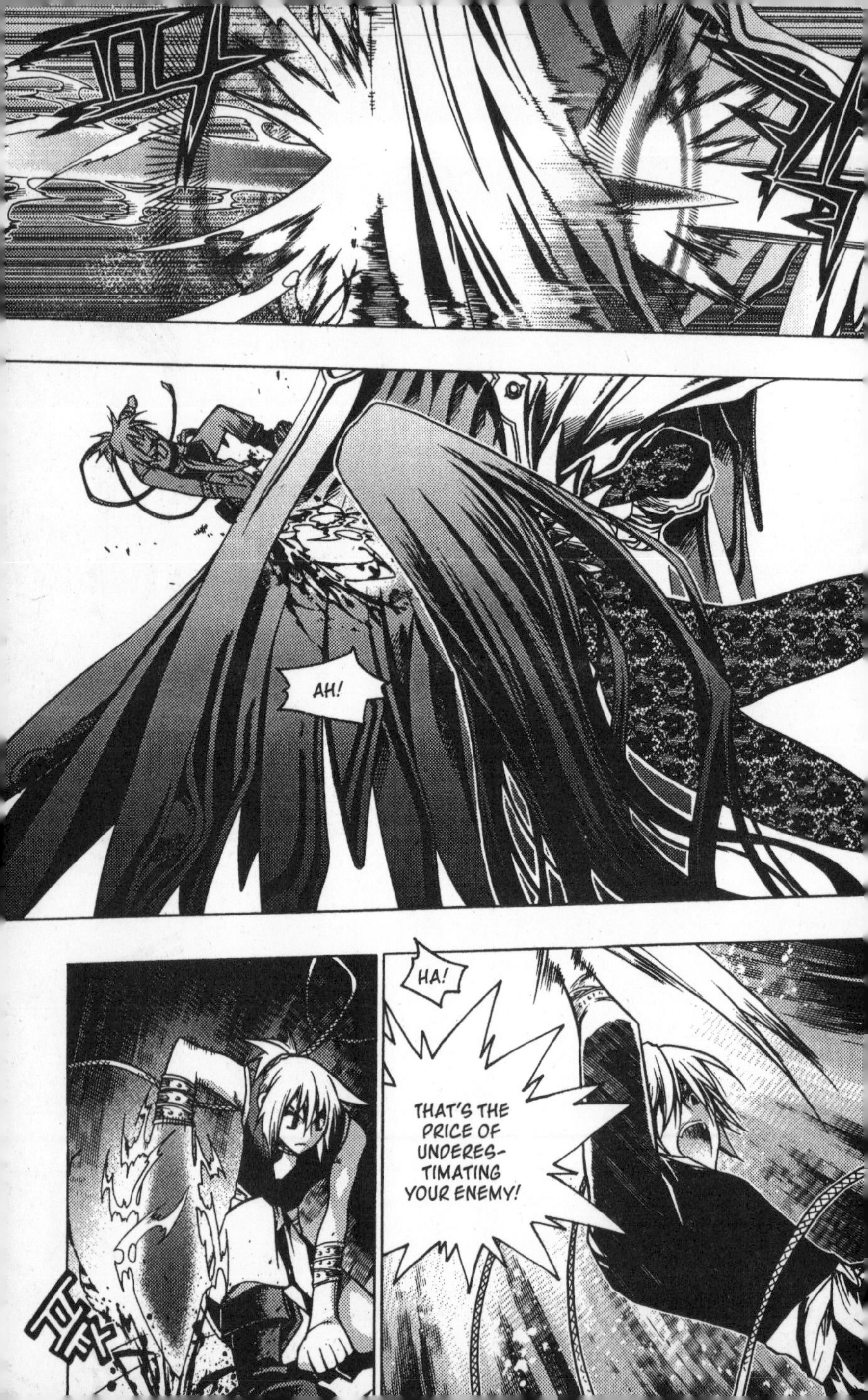
AH!
HA!
THAT'S THE PRICE OF UNDERES-TIMATING YOUR ENEMY!

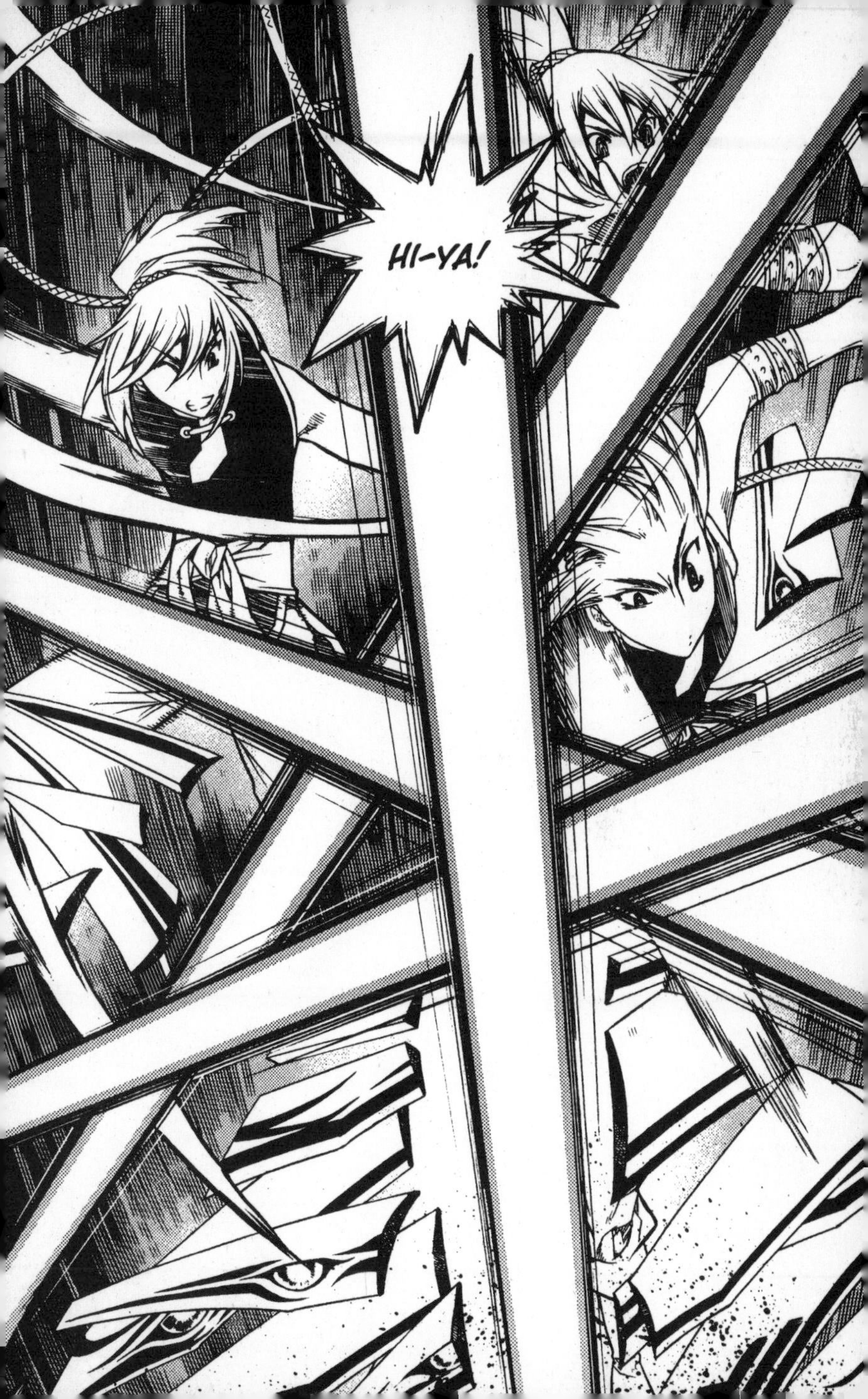
HI-YA!

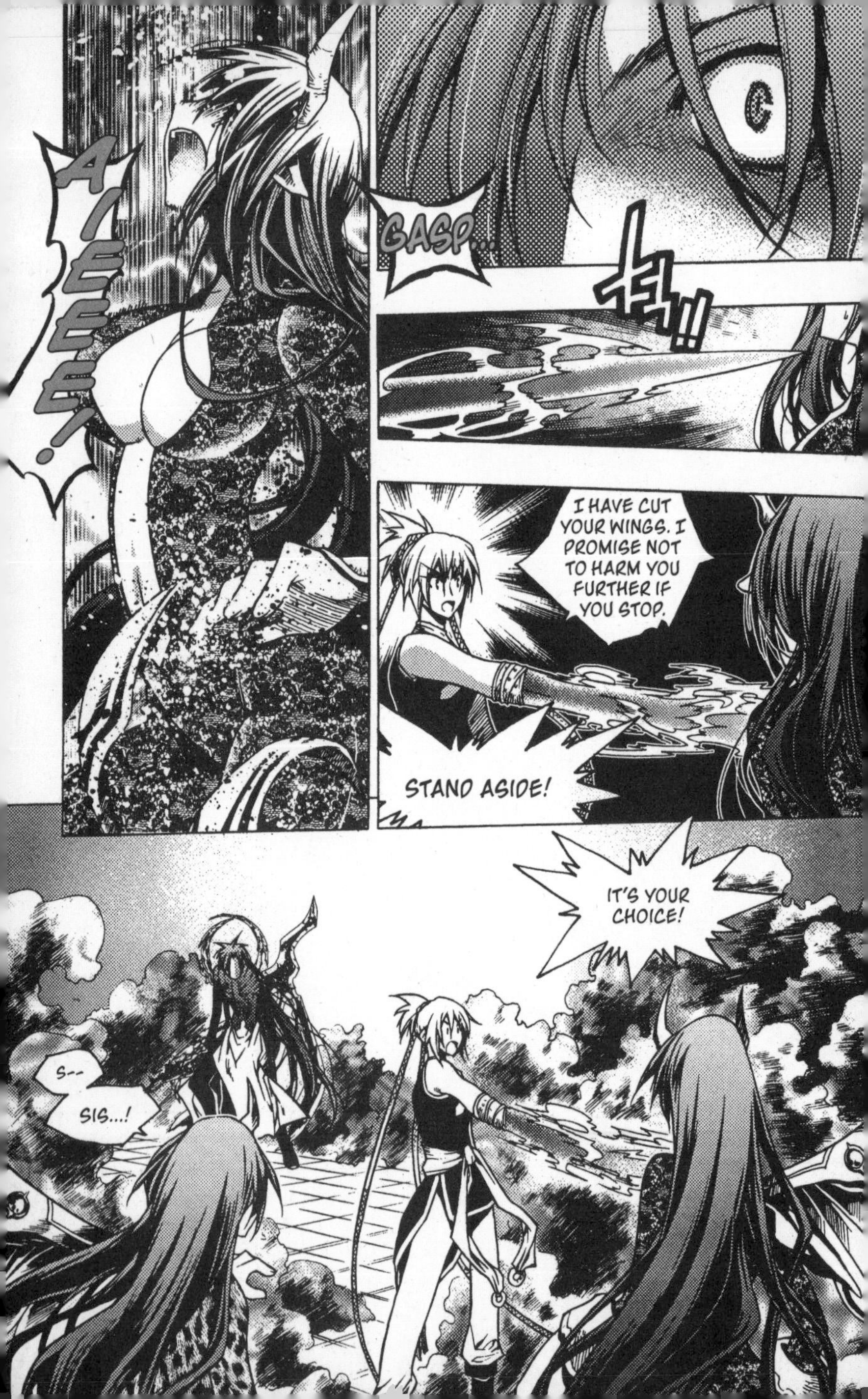
GASP...
I HAVE CUT YOUR WINGS. I PROMISE NOT TO HARM YOU FURTHER IF YOU STOP.
STAND ASIDE!
AIEEEE!!
IT'S YOUR CHOICE!
S-- SIS...!

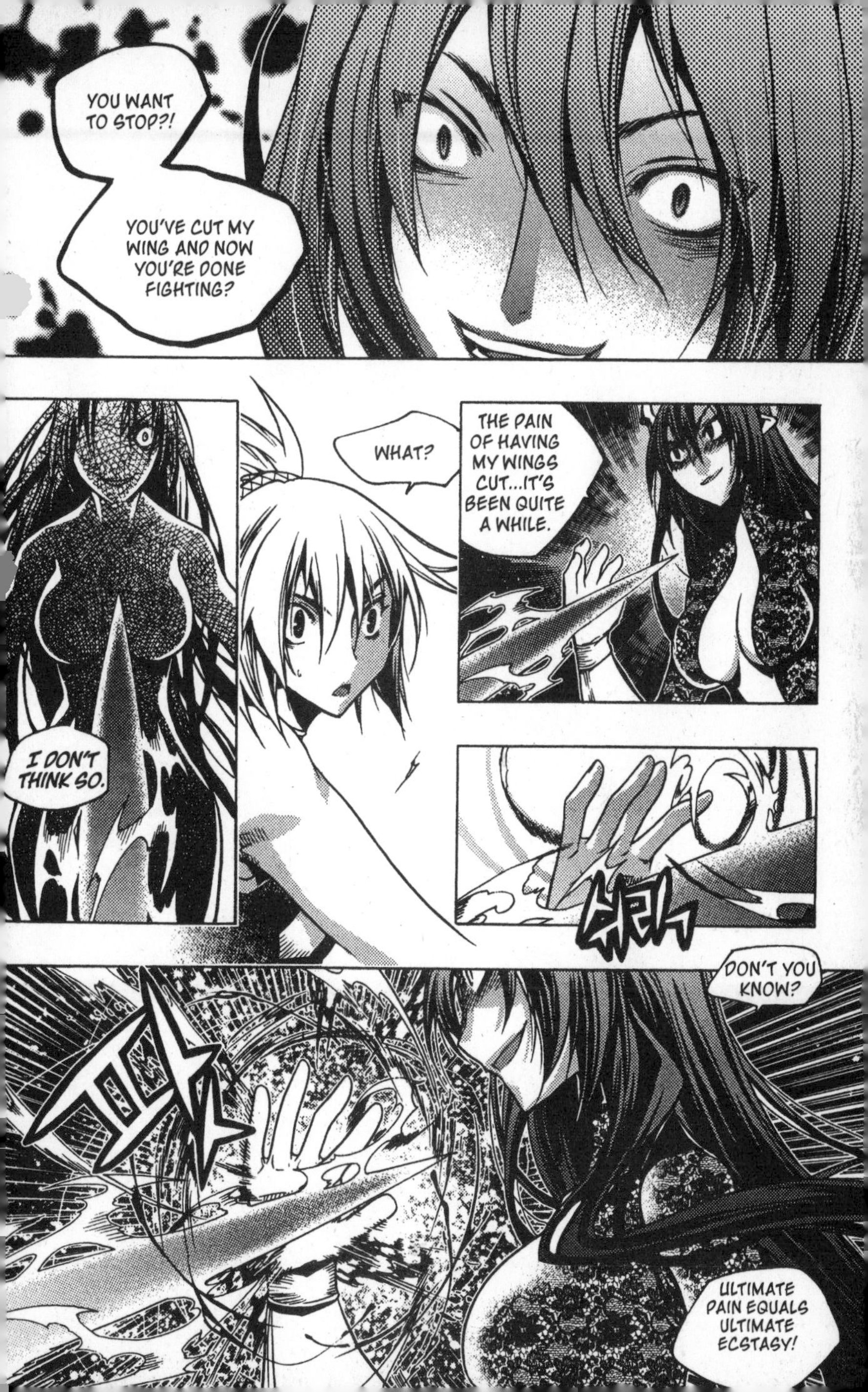
YOU WANT TO STOP?!
YOU'VE CUT MY WING AND NOW YOU'RE DONE FIGHTING?
THE PAIN OF HAVING MY WINGS CUT...IT'S BEEN QUITE A WHILE.
WHAT?
I DON'T THINK SO.
DON'T YOU KNOW?
ULTIMATE PAIN EQUALS ULTIMATE ECSTASY!

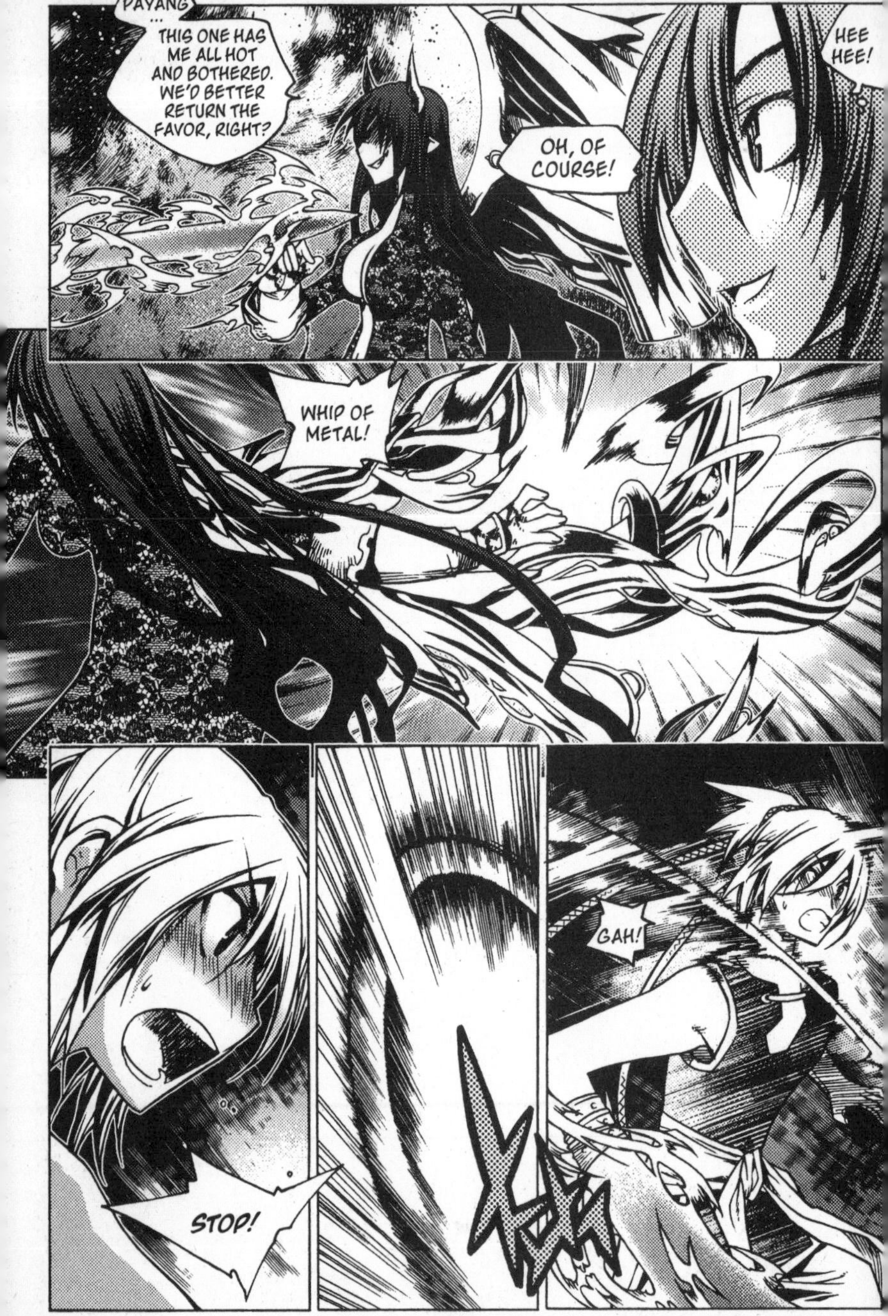
HEE HEE!
PAYANG ... THIS ONE HAS ME ALL HOT AND BOTHERED. WE'D BETTER RETURN THE FAVOR, RIGHT?
OH, OF COURSE!
WHIP OF METAL!
GAH!
STOP!

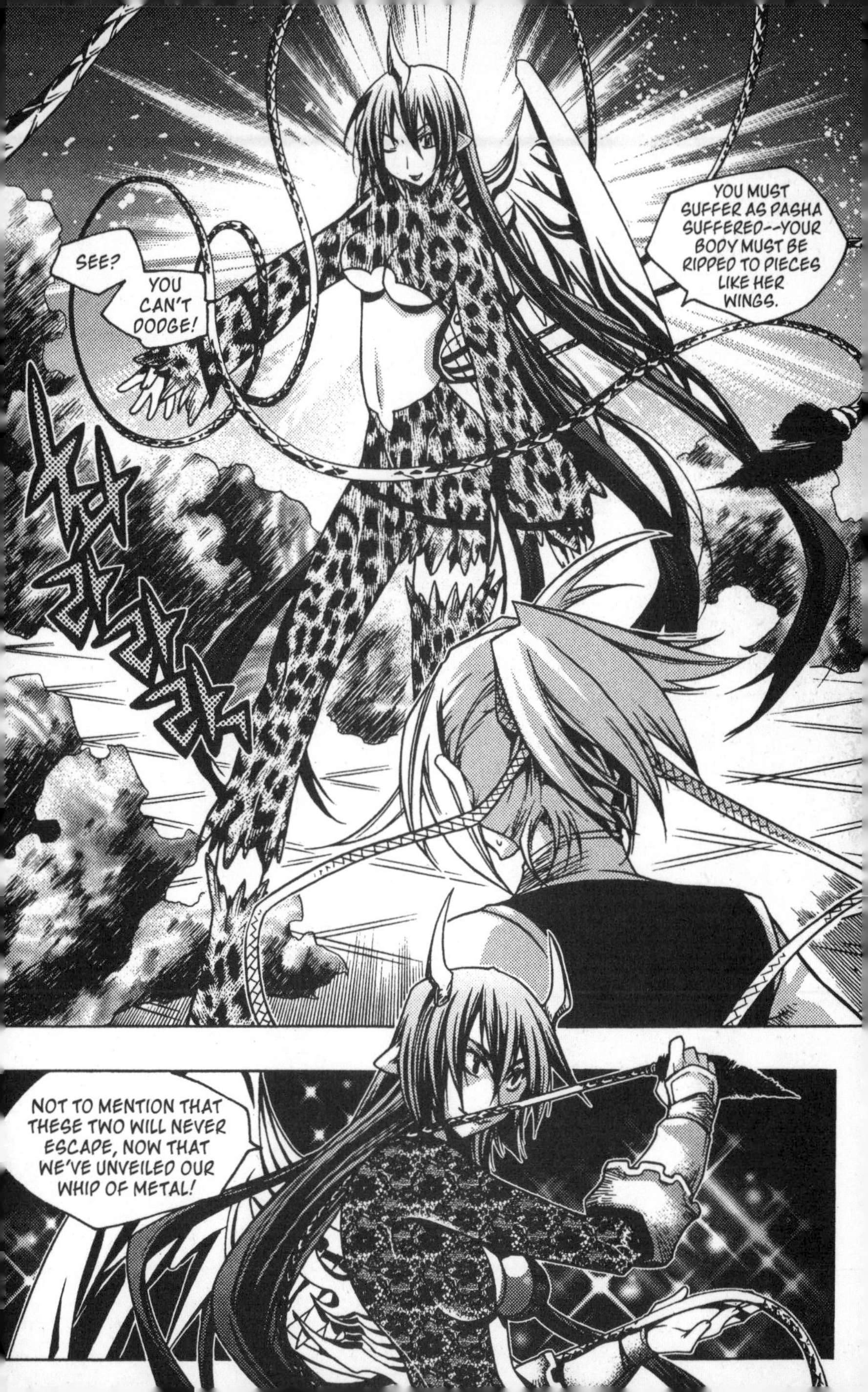
YOU MUST SUFFER AS PASHA SUFFERED--YOUR BODY MUST BE RIPPED TO PIECES LIKE HER WINGS.
SEE?
YOU CAN'T DODGE!
NOT TO MENTION THAT THESE TWO WILL NEVER ESCAPE, NOW THAT WE'VE UNVEILED OUR WHIP OF METAL!

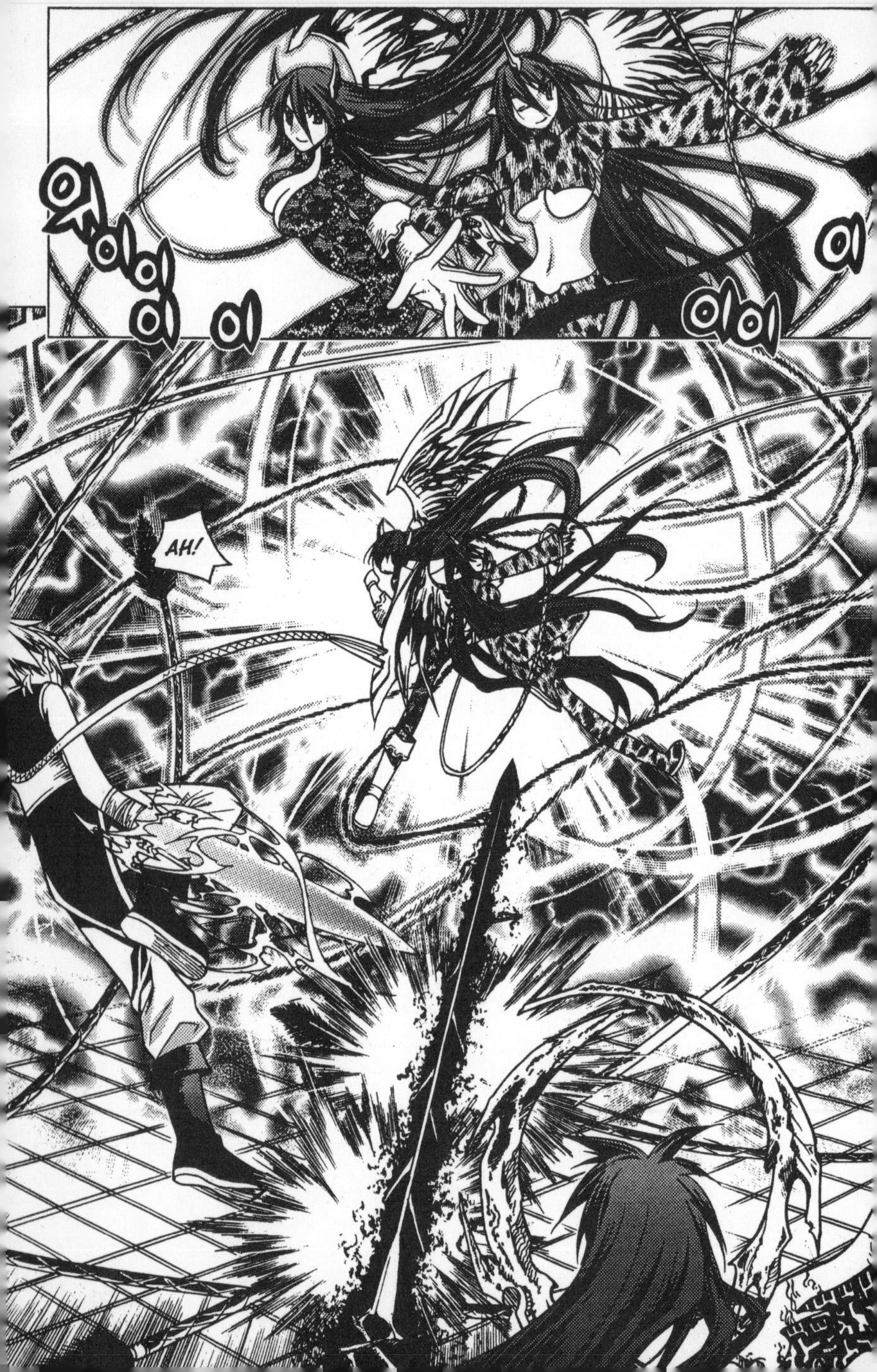
AH!

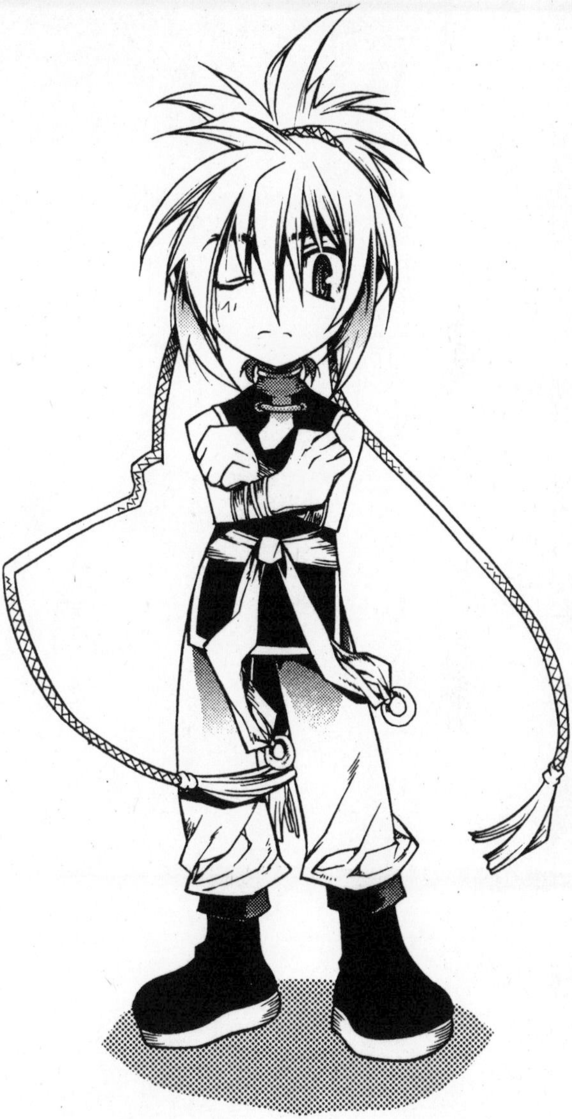

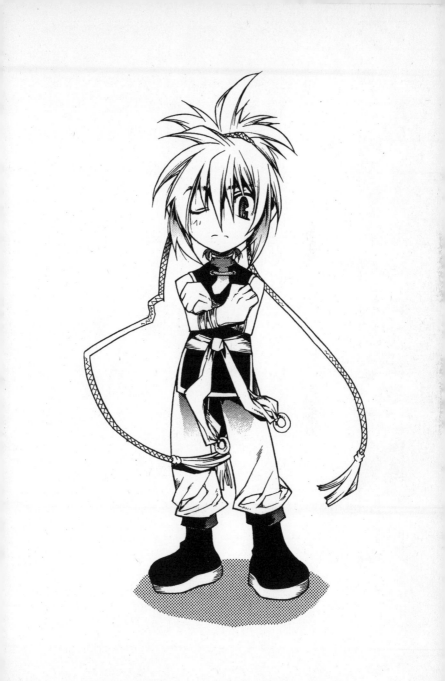

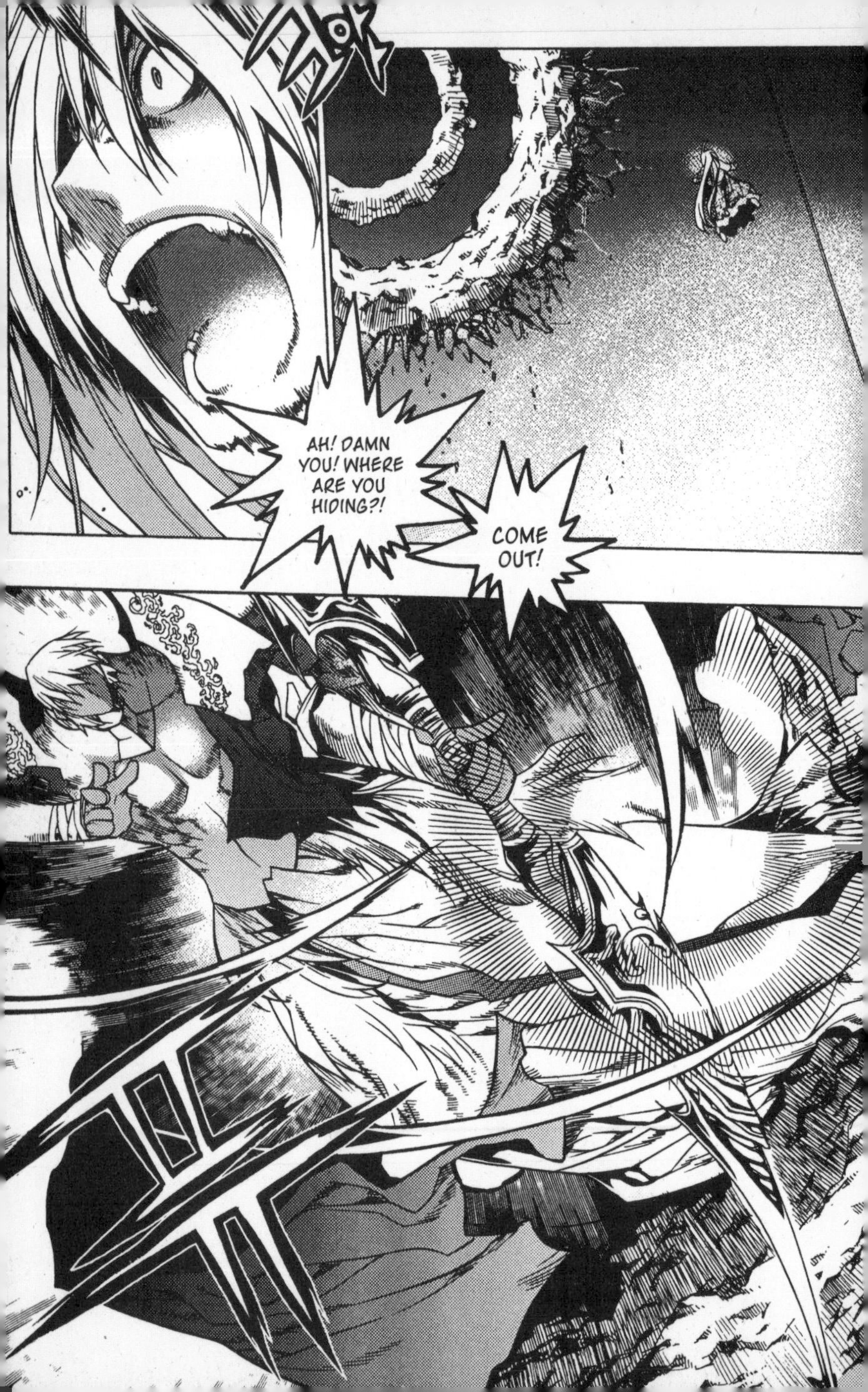
AH! DAMN YOU! WHERE ARE YOU HIDING?!
COME OUT!

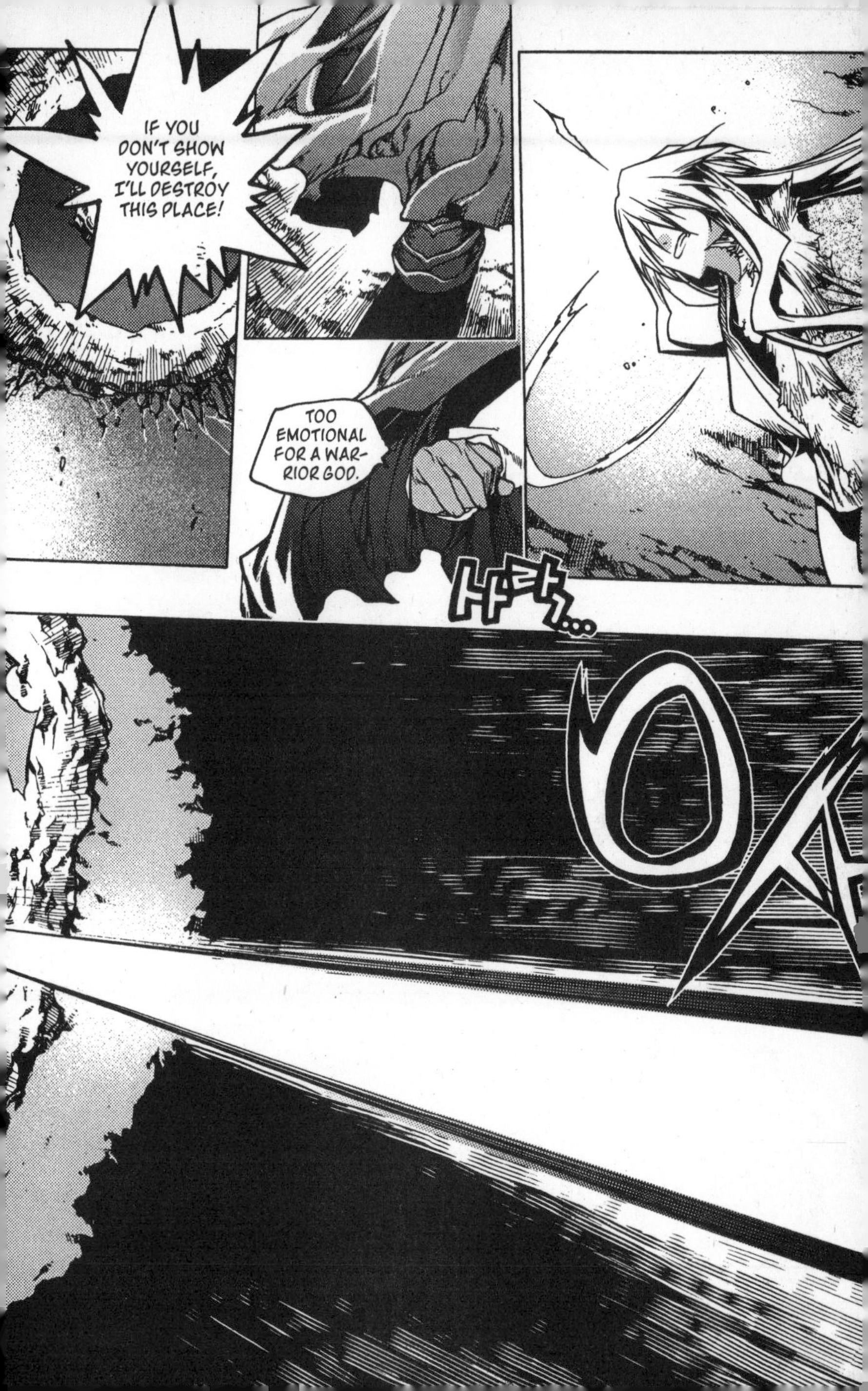
IF YOU DON'T SHOW YOURSELF, I'LL DESTROY THIS PLACE!
TOO EMOTIONAL FOR A WARRIOR GOD.

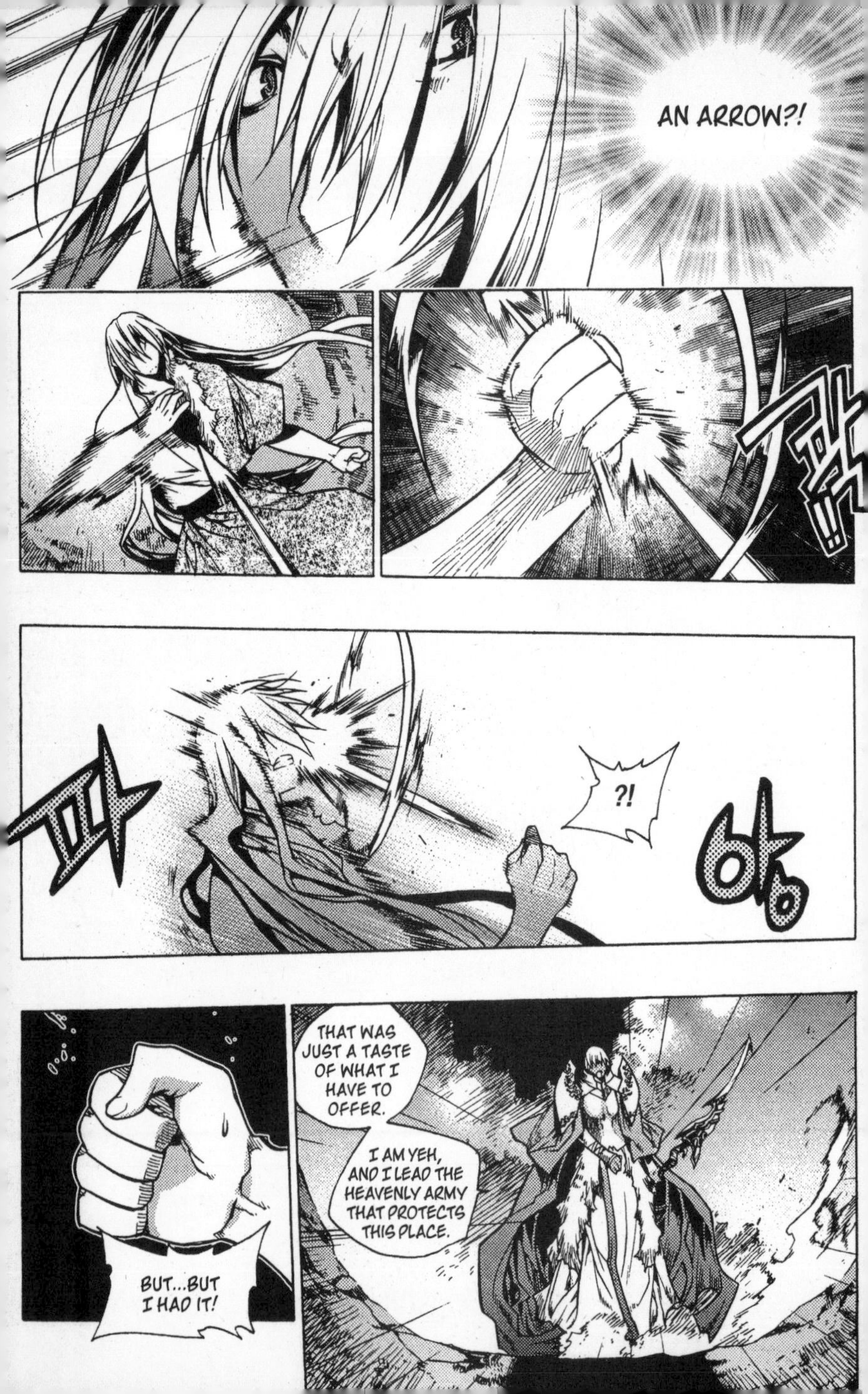
AN ARROW?!
?!
BUT...BUT I HAD IT!
THAT WAS JUST A TASTE OF WHAT I HAVE TO OFFER.
I AM YEH, AND I LEAD THE HEAVENLY ARMY THAT PROTECTS THIS PLACE.

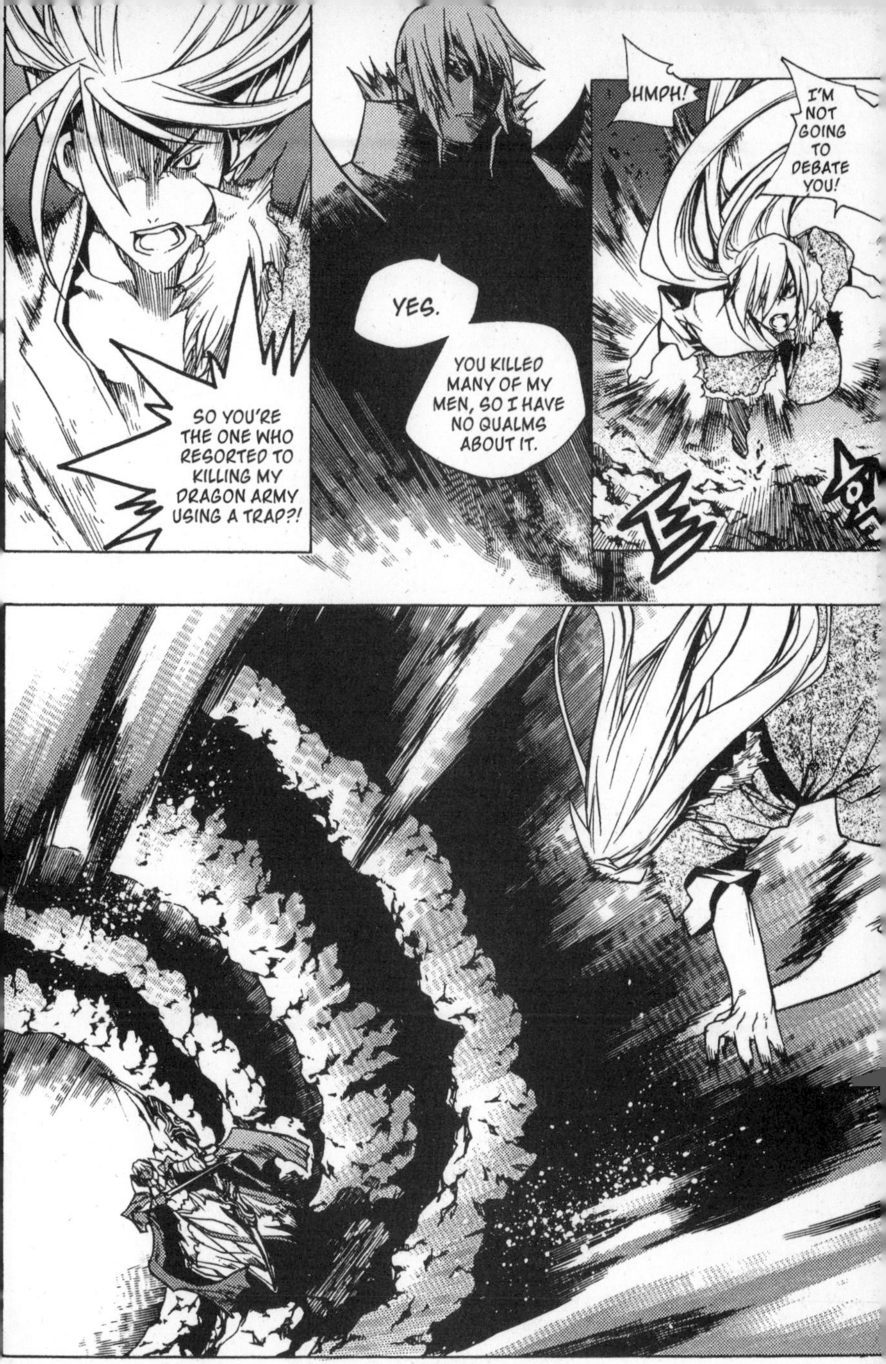
SO YOU'RE THE ONE WHO RESORTED TO KILLING MY DRAGON ARMY USING A TRAP?!
YES.
YOU KILLED MANY OF MY MEN, SO I HAVE NO QUALMS ABOUT IT.
HMPH!
I'M NOT GOING TO DEBATE YOU!

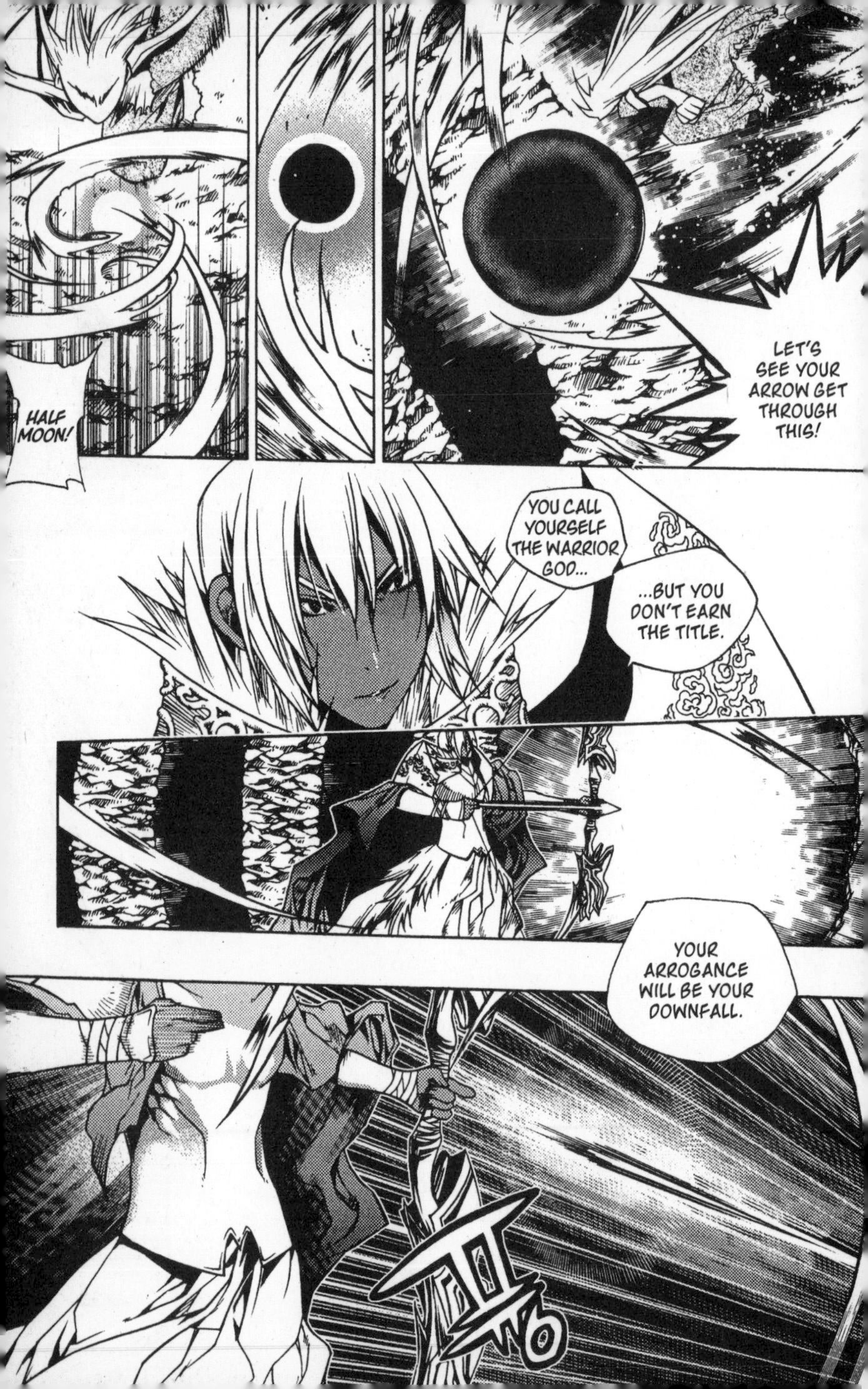
LET'S SEE YOUR ARROW GET THROUGH THIS!
HALF MOON!
YOU CALL YOURSELF THE WARRIOR GOD...
...BUT YOU DON'T EARN THE TITLE.
YOUR ARROGANCE WILL BE YOUR DOWNFALL.

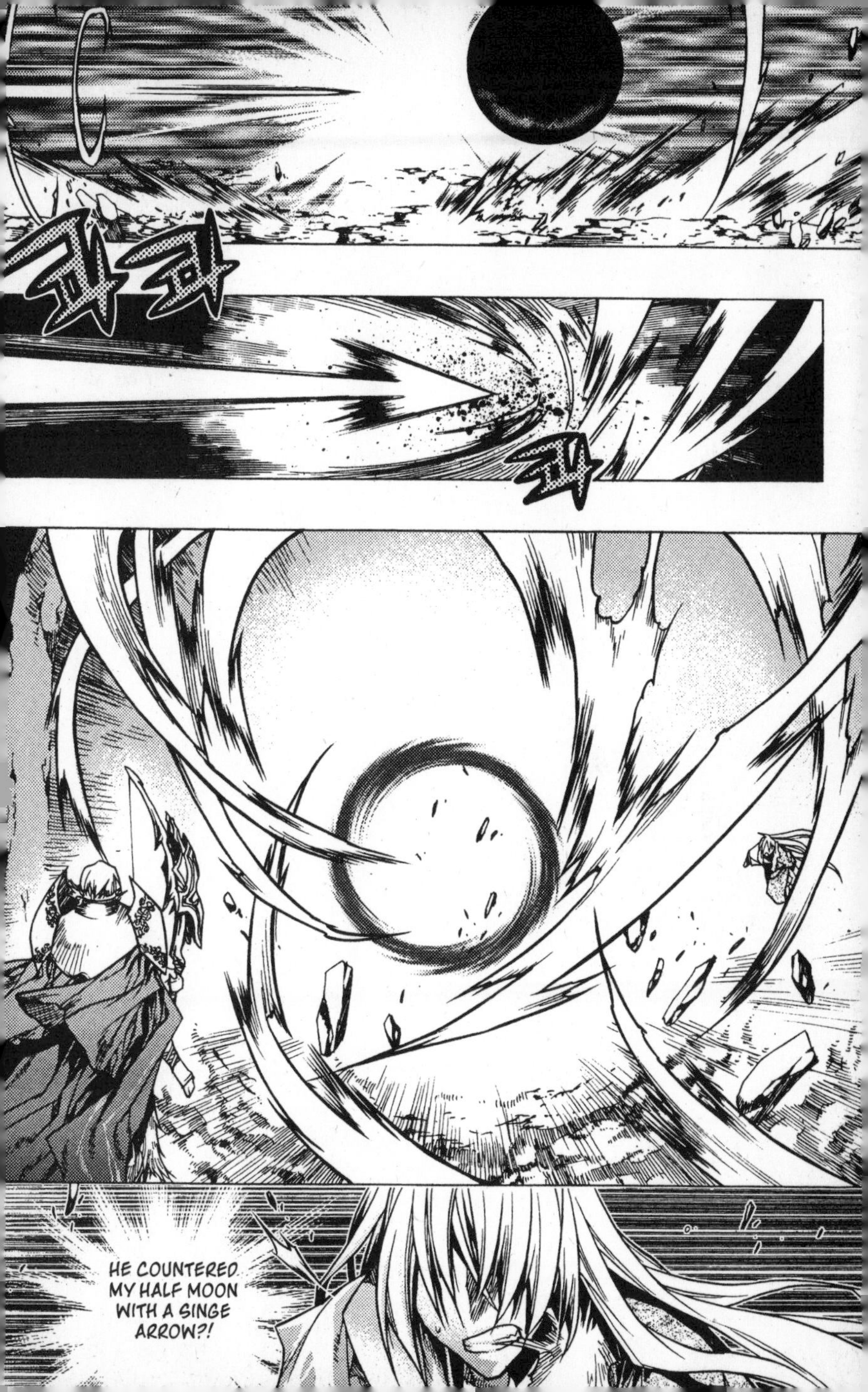
HE COUNTERED MY HALF MOON WITH A SINGE ARROW?!

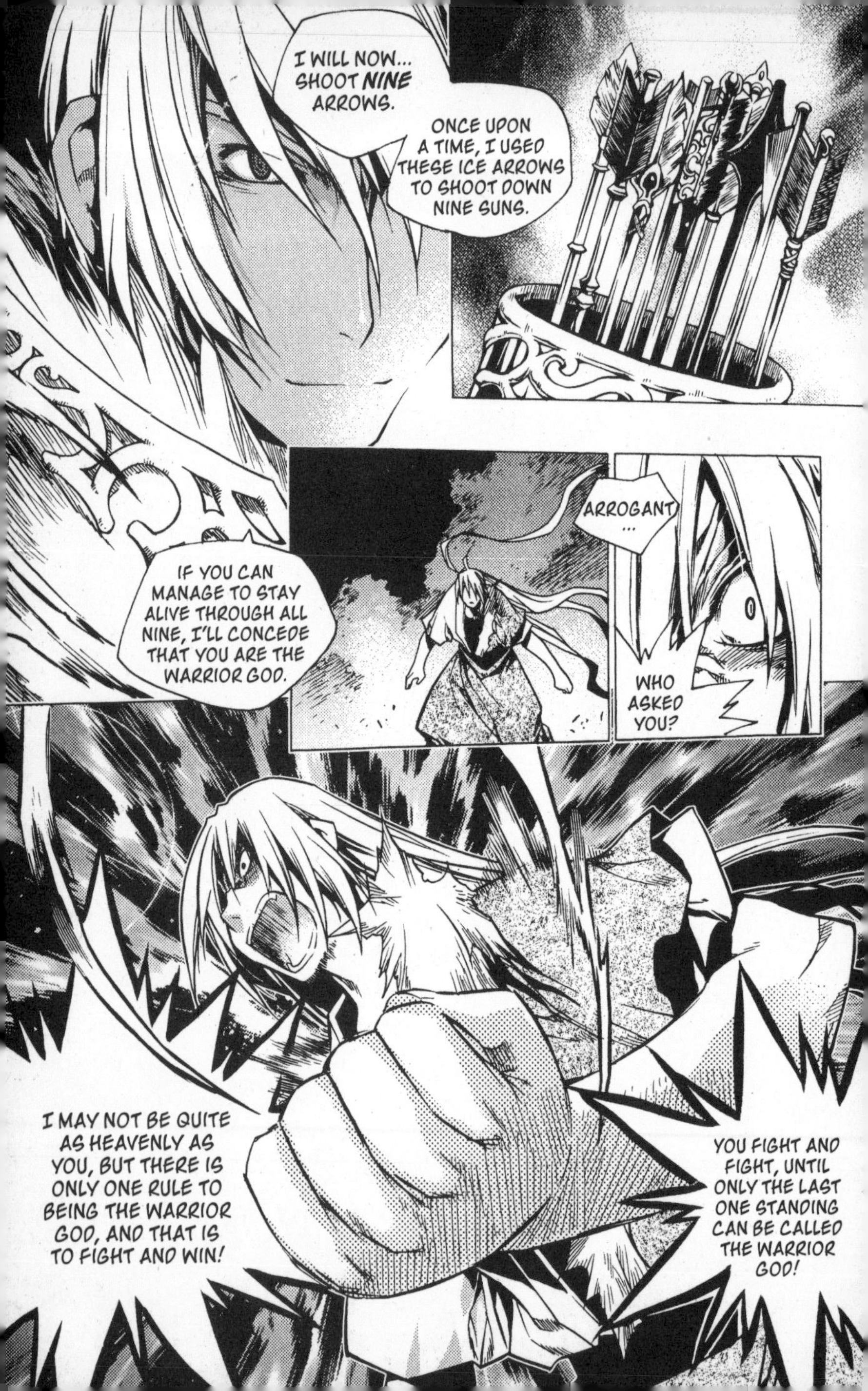
I WILL NOW... SHOOT NINE ARROWS.
ONCE UPON A TIME, I USED THESE ICE ARROWS TO SHOOT DOWN NINE SUNS.
IF YOU CAN MANAGE TO STAY ALIVE THROUGH ALL NINE, I'LL CONCEDE THAT YOU ARE THE WARRIOR GOD.
ARROGANT...
WHO ASKED YOU?
I MAY NOT BE QUITE AS HEAVENLY AS YOU, BUT THERE IS ONLY ONE RULE TO BEING THE WARRIOR GOD, AND THAT IS TO FIGHT AND WIN!
YOU FIGHT AND FIGHT, UNTIL ONLY THE LAST ONE STANDING CAN BE CALLED THE WARRIOR GOD!

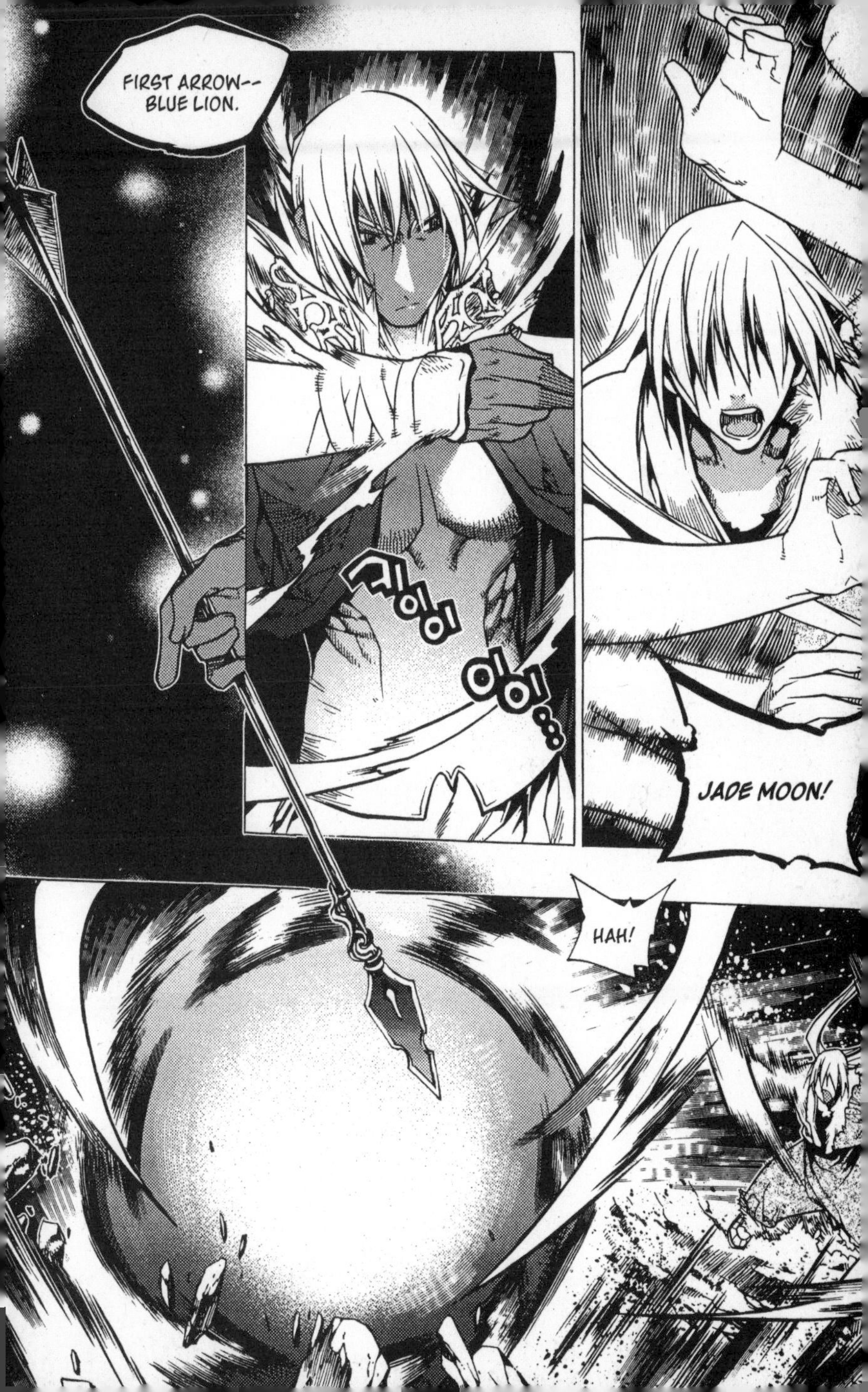
FIRST ARROW--
BLUE LION.
JADE MOON!
HAH!

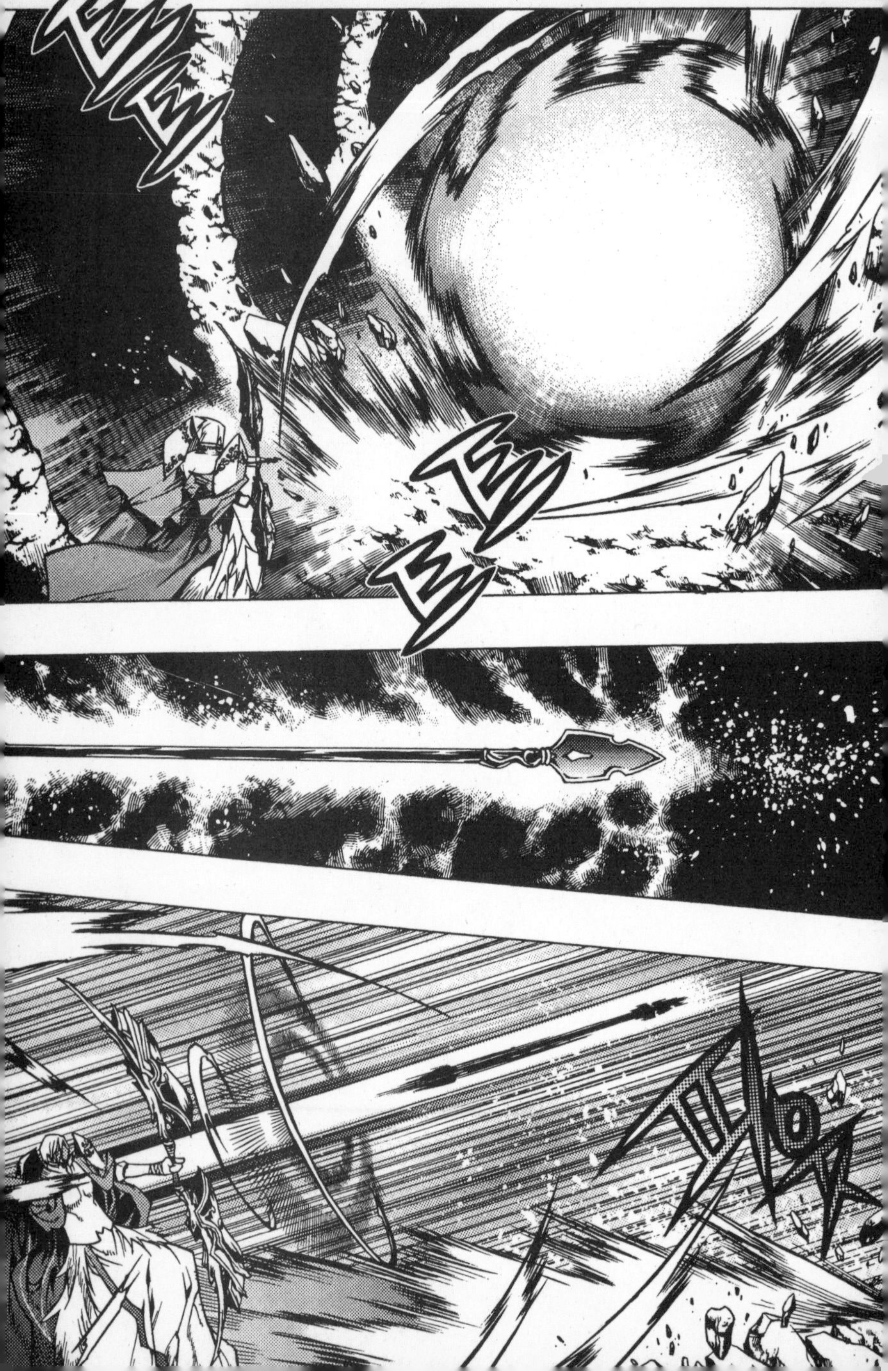

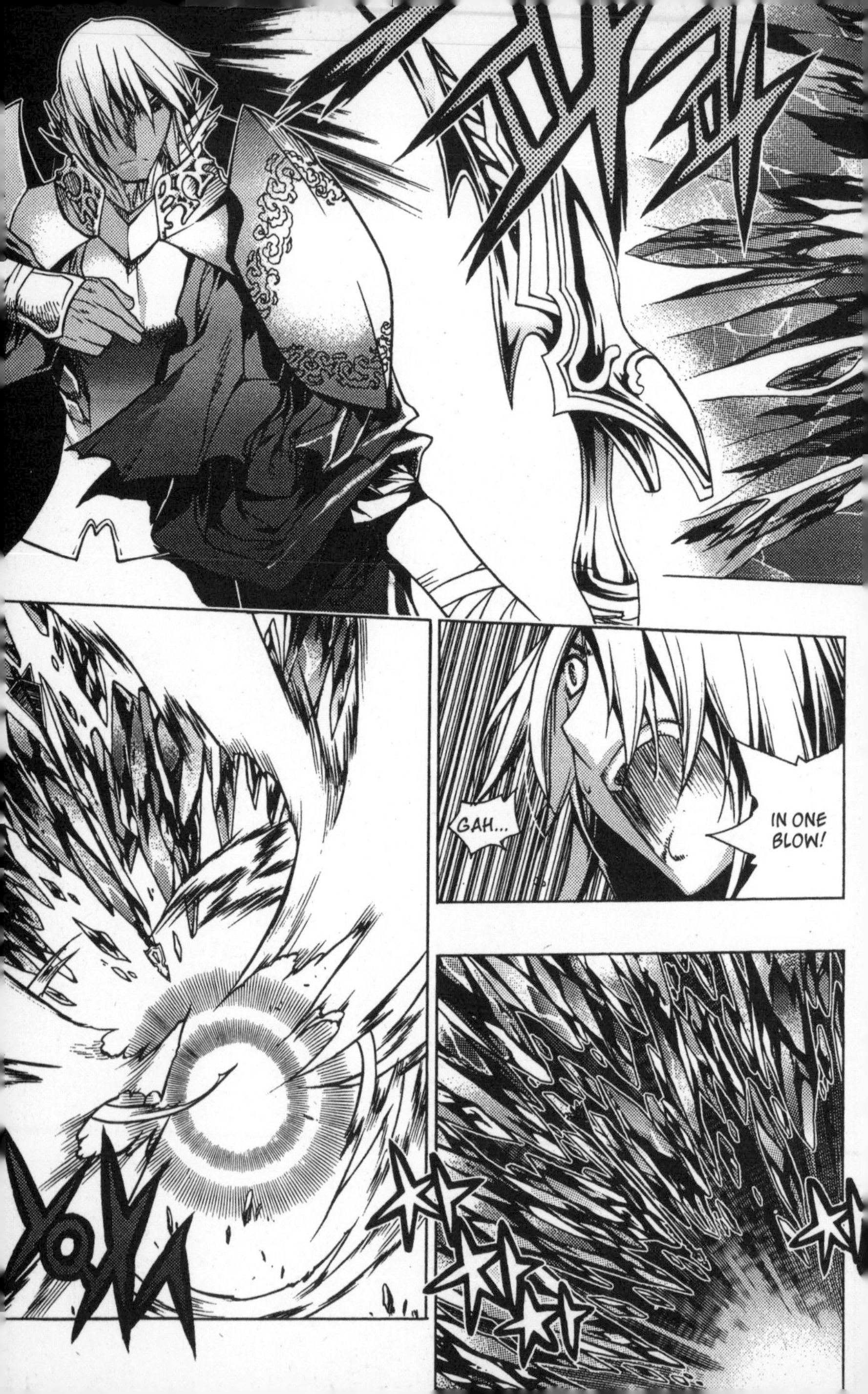
IN ONE BLOW!
GAH...

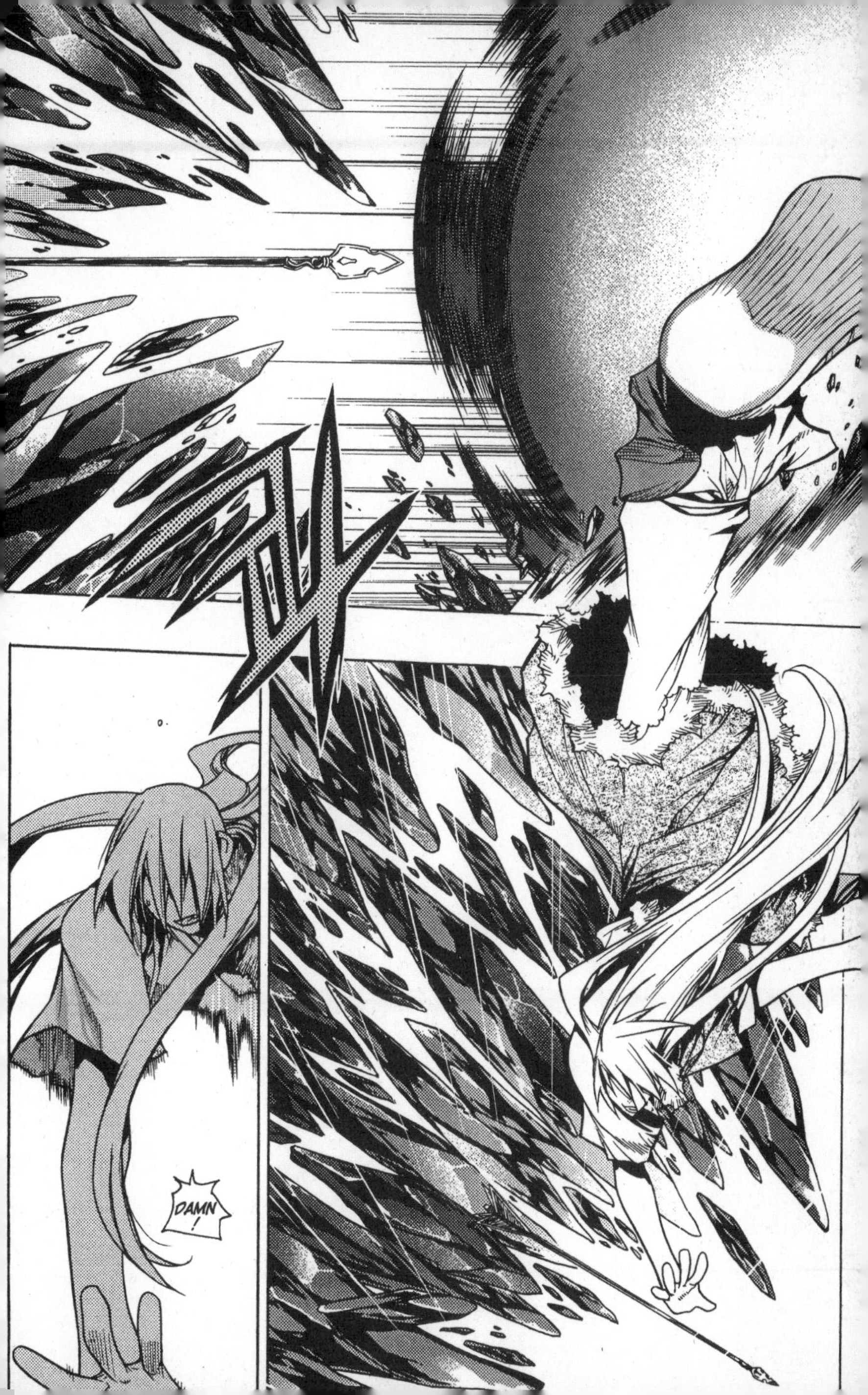
DAMN!

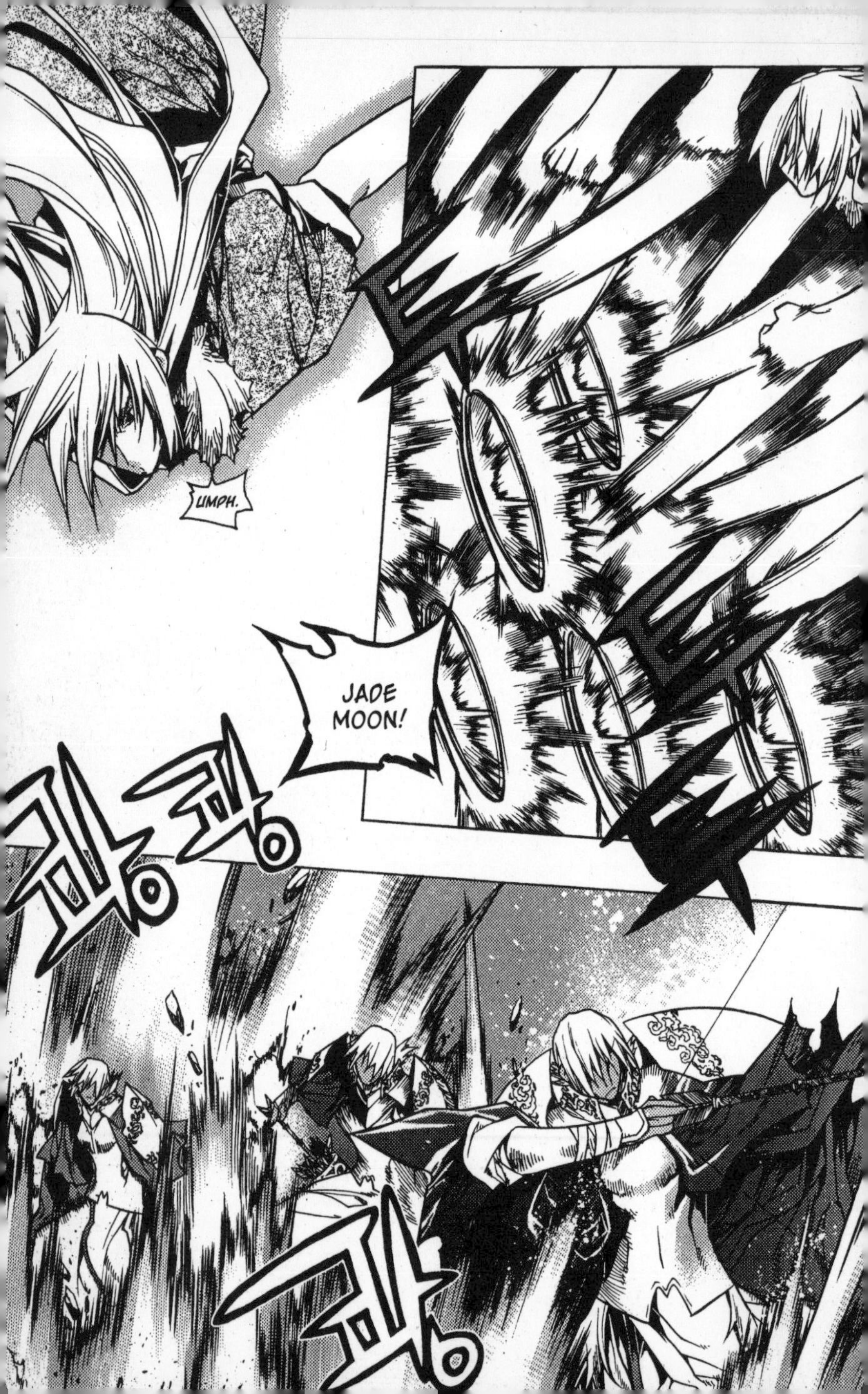
UMPH.
JADE
MOON!

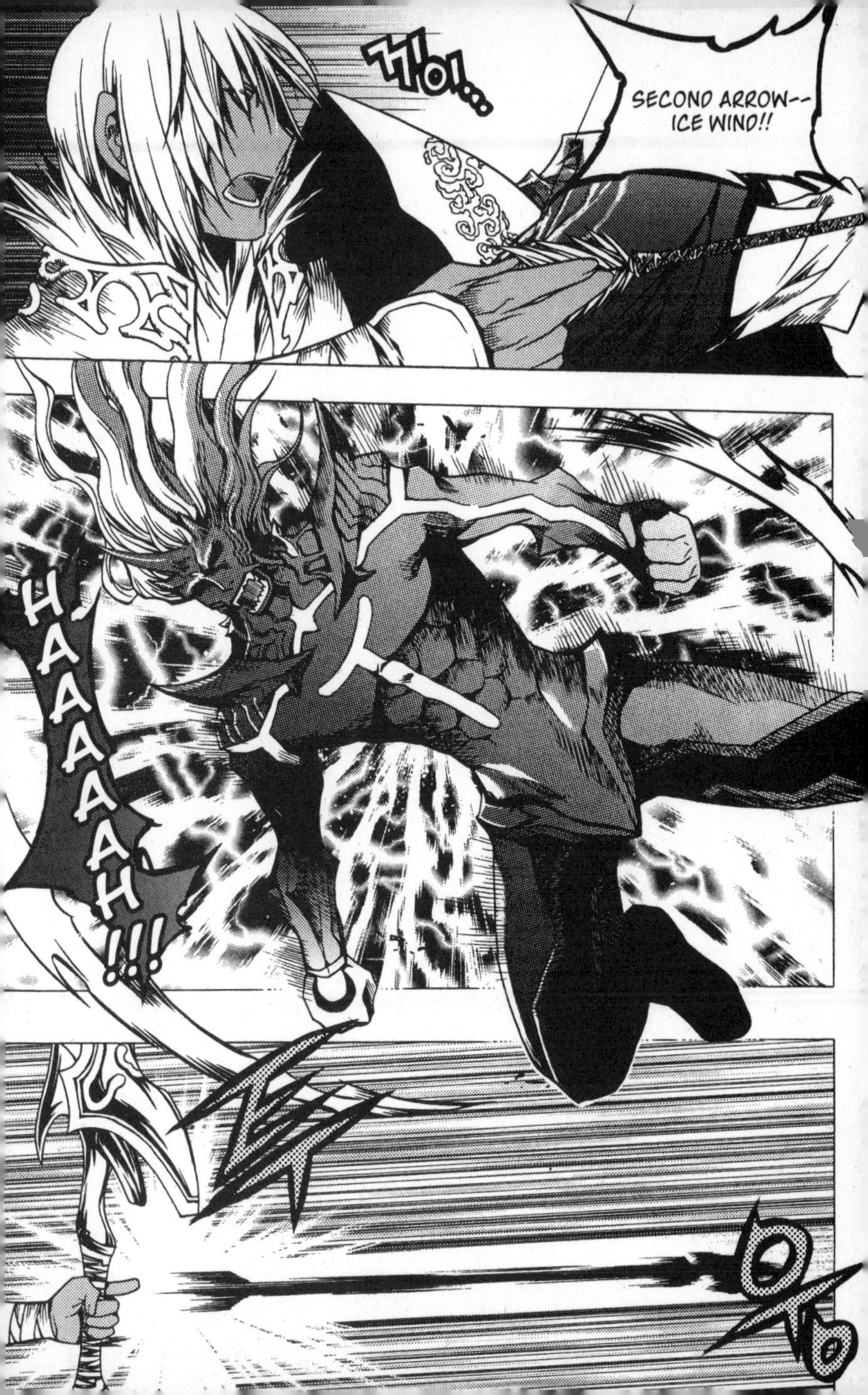
SECOND ARROW--
ICE WIND!!
GYA!...
HAAAAAAH!!!

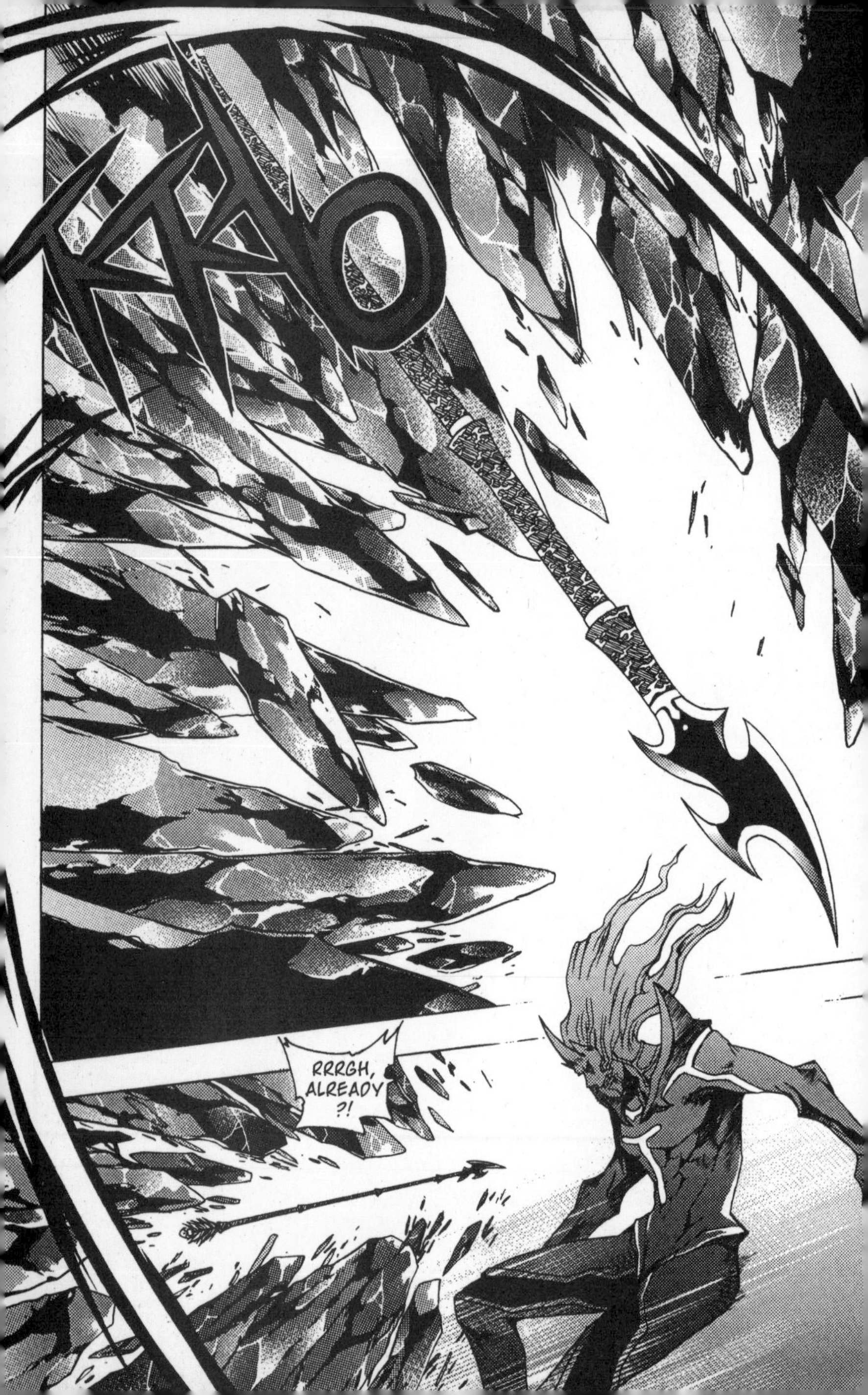
KRAK
RRRGH,
ALREADY
?!

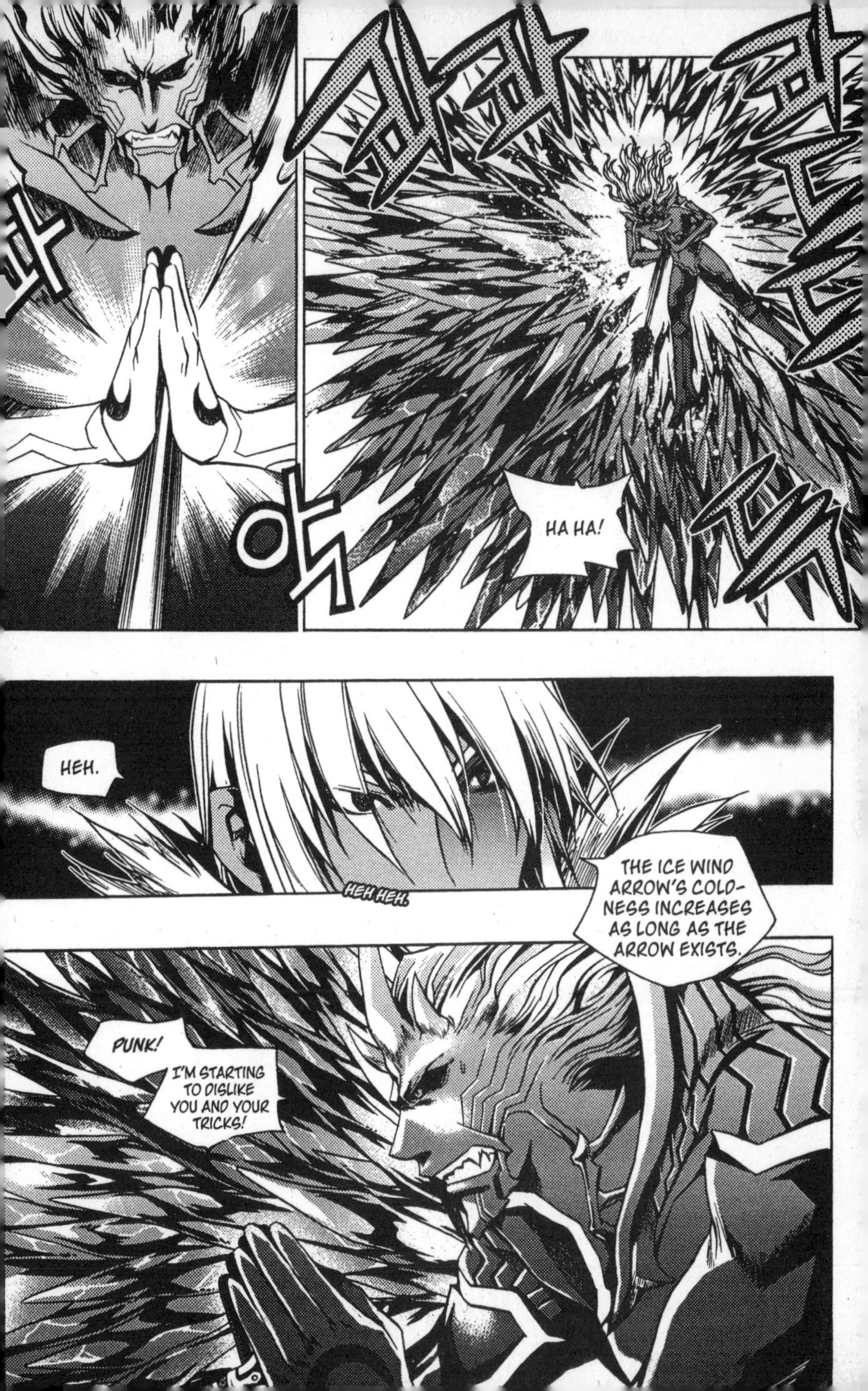
HA HA!
HEH.
HEH HEH.
THE ICE WIND ARROW'S COLD-NESS INCREASES AS LONG AS THE ARROW EXISTS.
PUNK!
I'M STARTING TO DISLIKE YOU AND YOUR TRICKS!

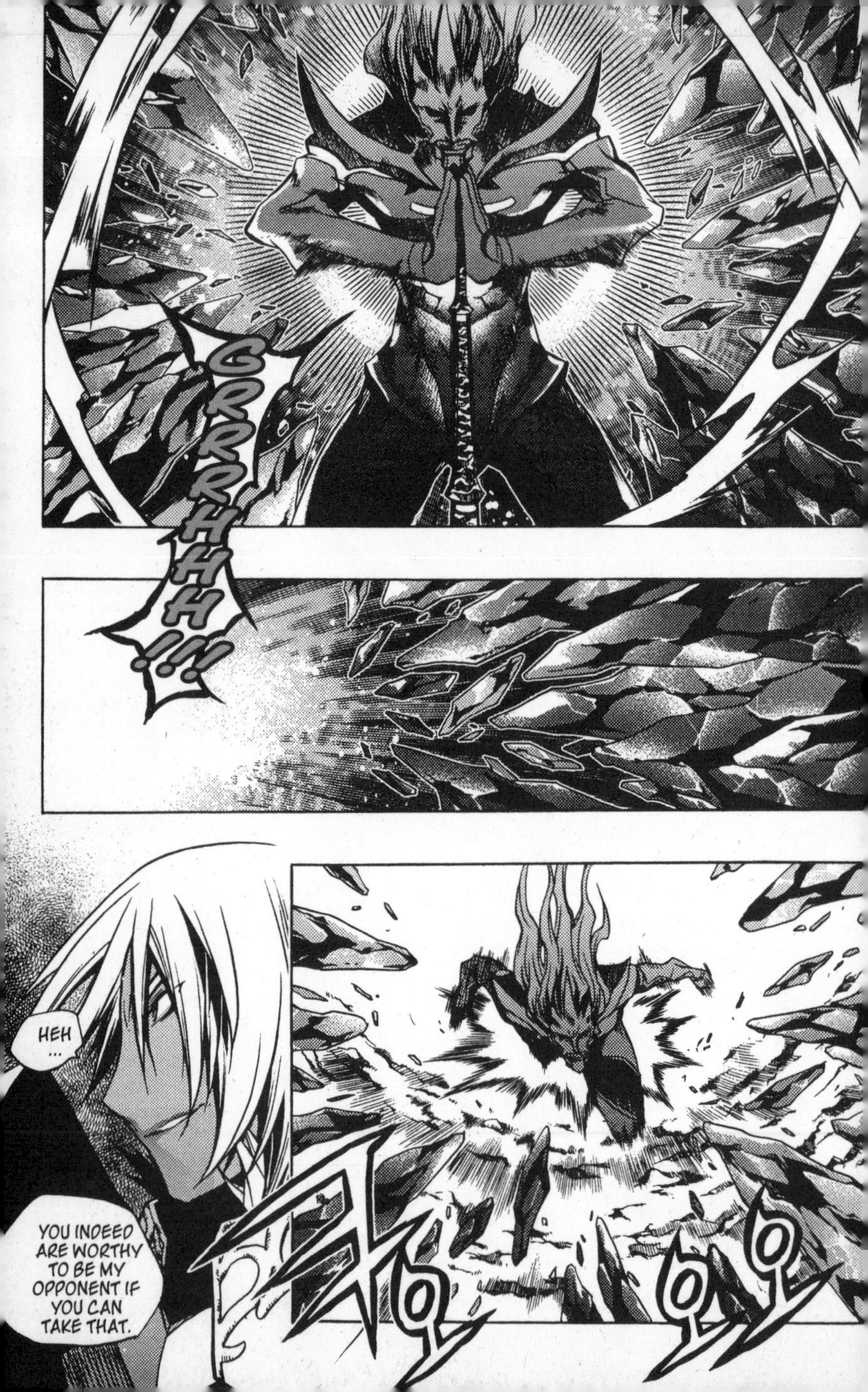
GRRRHHH!!!
HEH ...
YOU INDEED ARE WORTHY TO BE MY OPPONENT IF YOU CAN TAKE THAT.

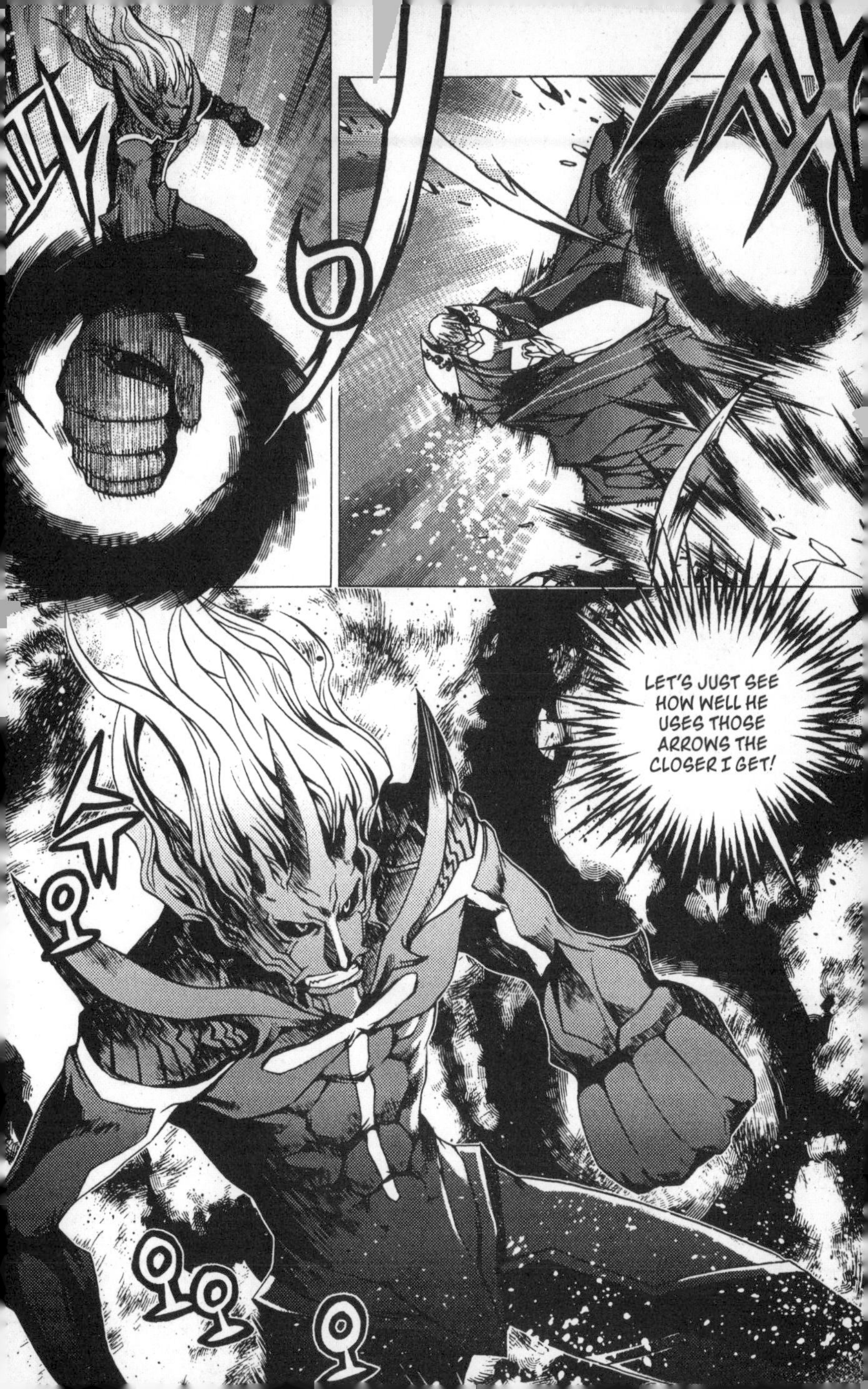
LET'S JUST SEE HOW WELL HE USES THOSE ARROWS THE CLOSER I GET!

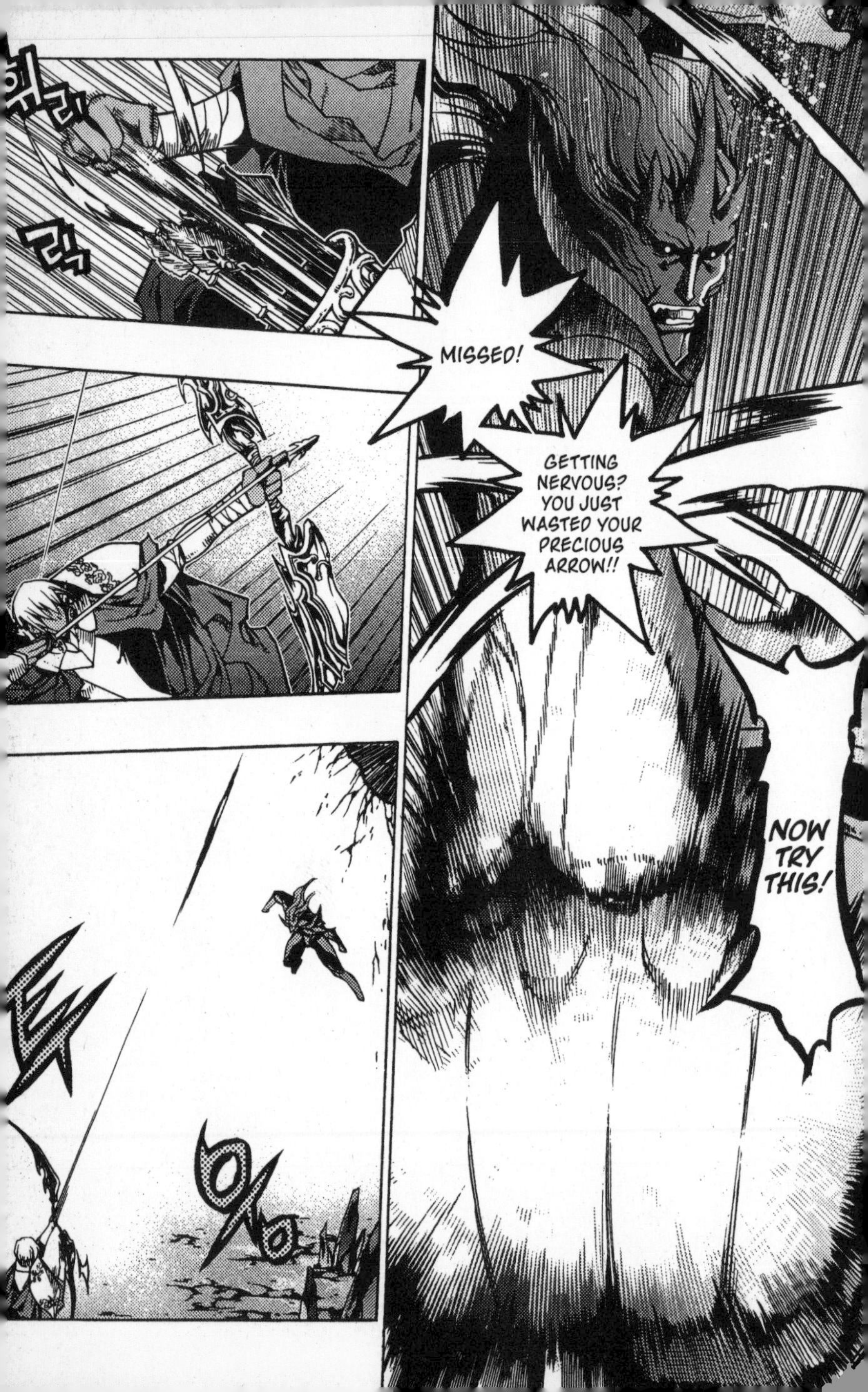
MISSED!
GETTING NERVOUS? YOU JUST WASTED YOUR PRECIOUS ARROW!!
NOW TRY THIS!

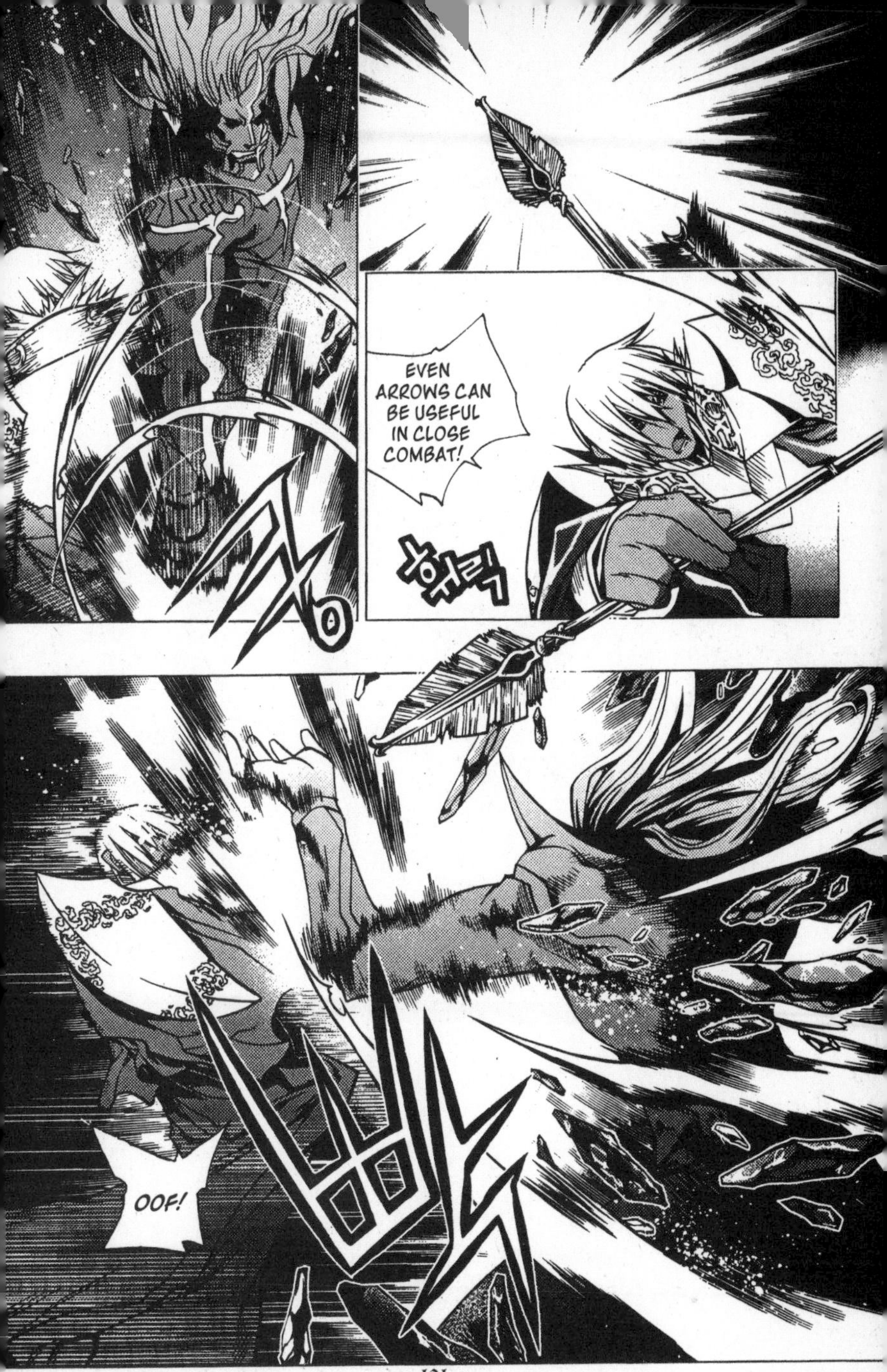
EVEN ARROWS CAN BE USEFUL IN CLOSE COMBAT!
휘릭
OOF!

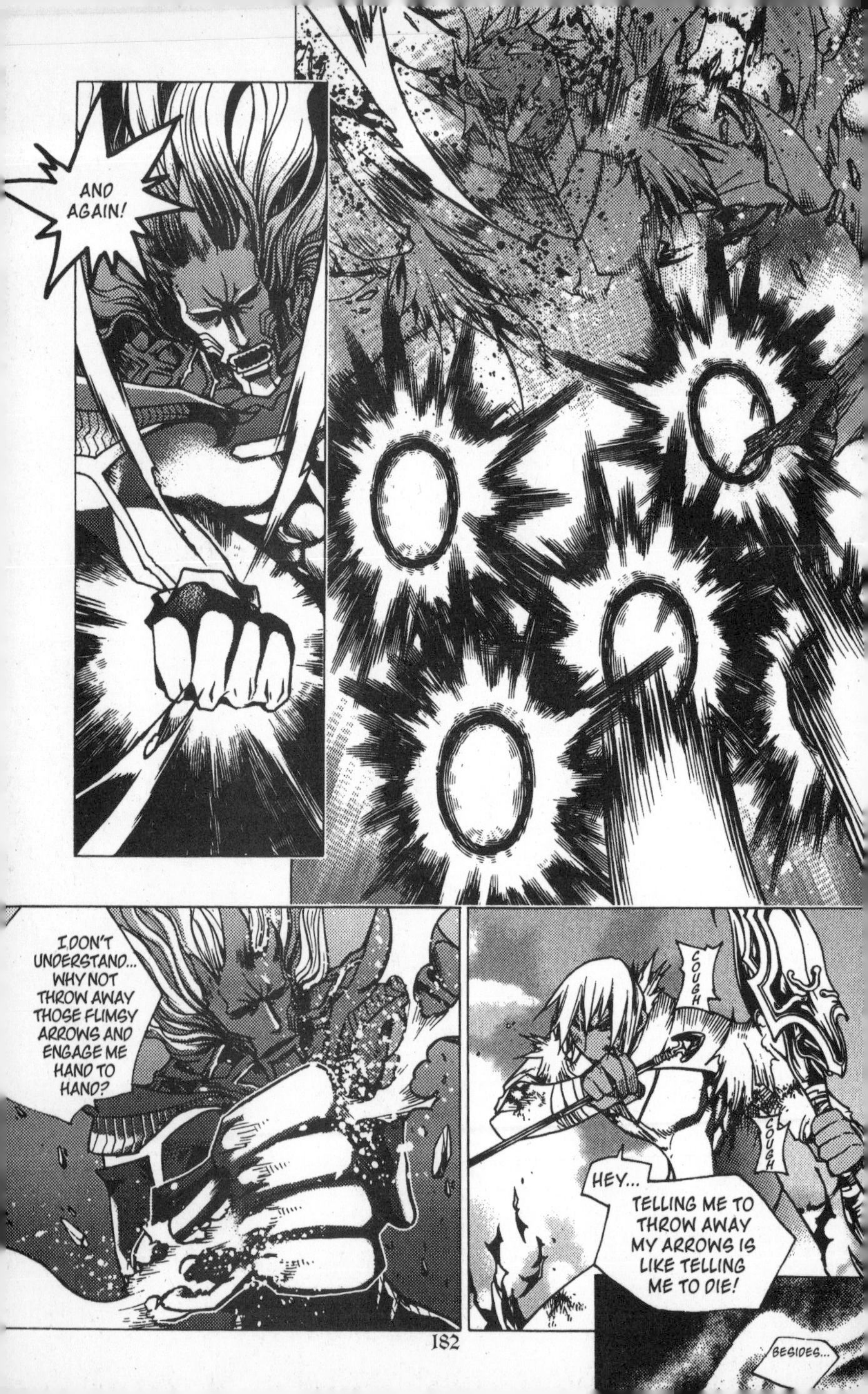
AND AGAIN!
COUGH
COUGH
HEY...
TELLING ME TO THROW AWAY MY ARROWS IS LIKE TELLING ME TO DIE!
I DON'T UNDERSTAND... WHY NOT THROW AWAY THOSE FLIMSY ARROWS AND ENGAGE ME HAND TO HAND?
BESIDES...

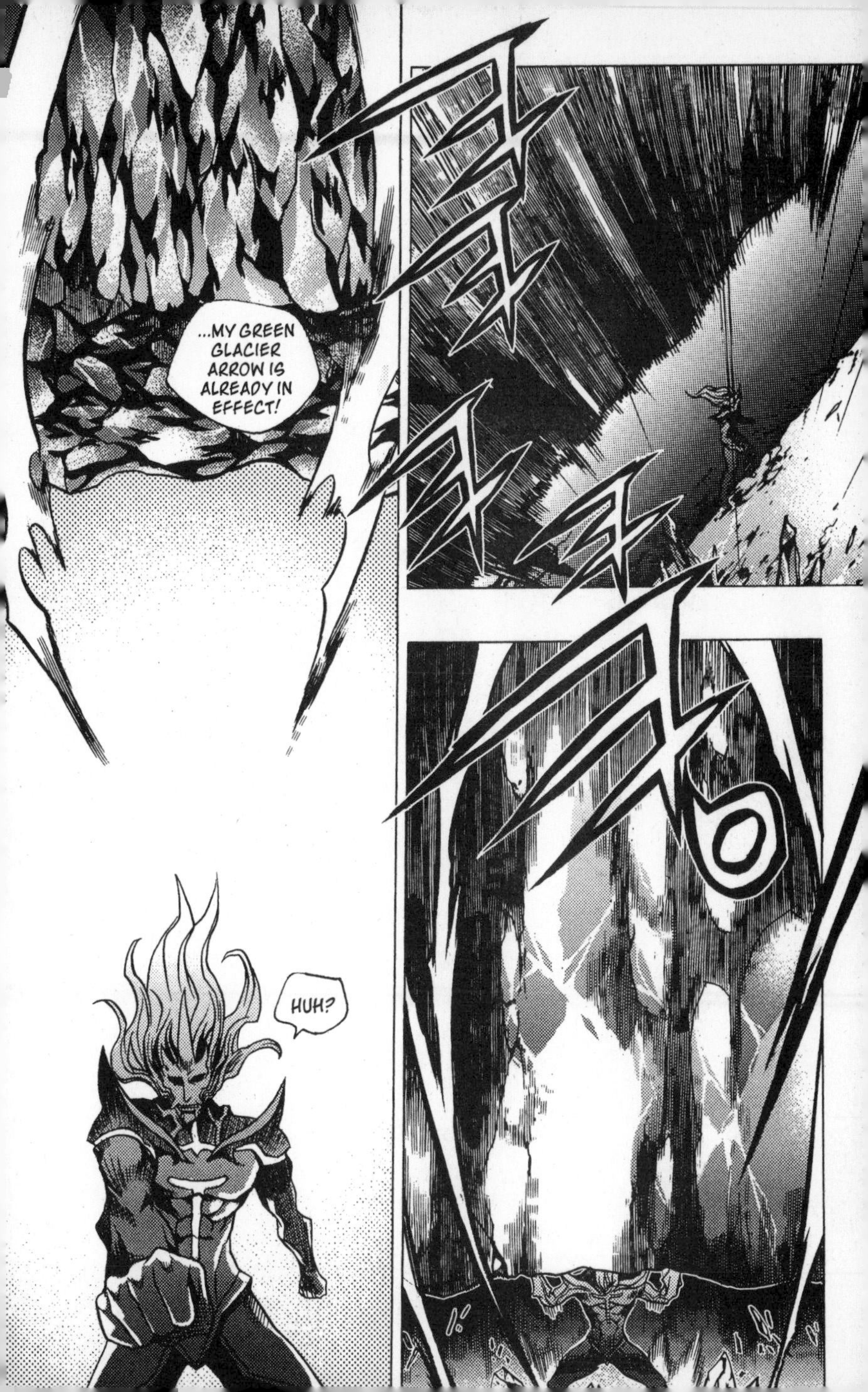
...MY GREEN GLACIER ARROW IS ALREADY IN EFFECT!
HUH?

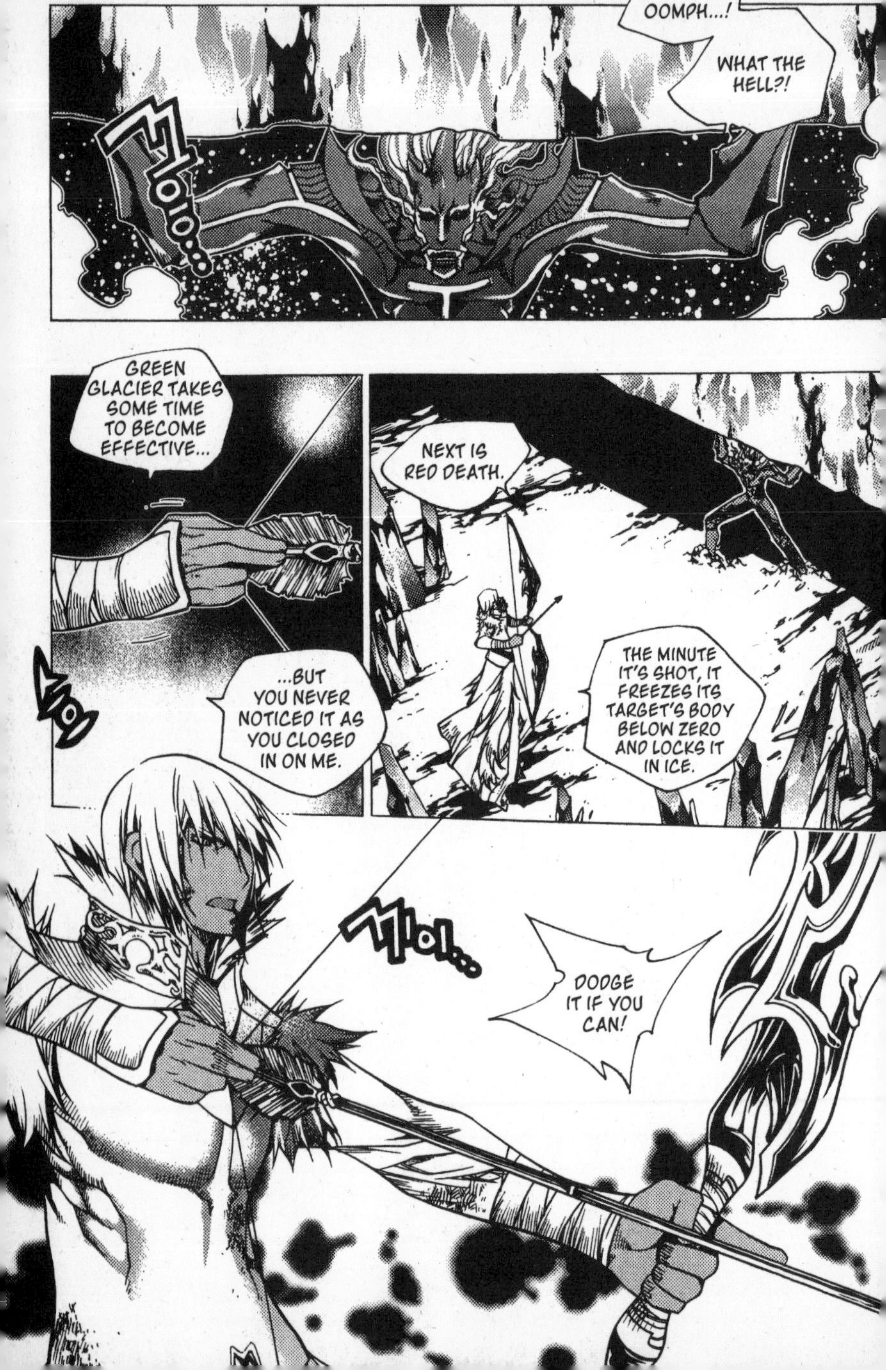
OOMPH...!
WHAT THE HELL?!
GREEN GLACIER TAKES SOME TIME TO BECOME EFFECTIVE...
...BUT YOU NEVER NOTICED IT AS YOU CLOSED IN ON ME.
NEXT IS RED DEATH.
THE MINUTE IT'S SHOT, IT FREEZES ITS TARGET'S BODY BELOW ZERO AND LOCKS IT IN ICE.
DODGE IT IF YOU CAN!

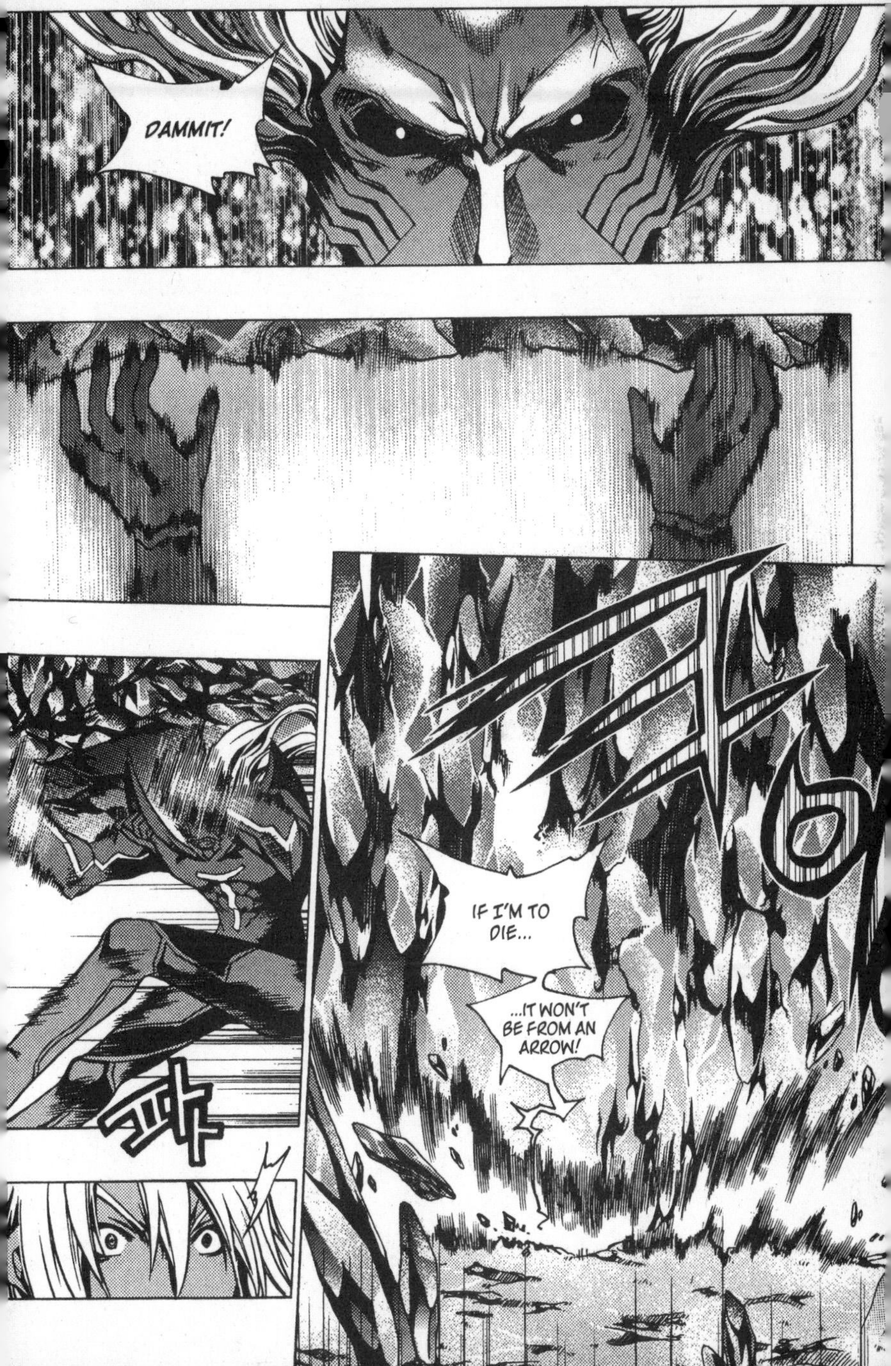
DAMMIT!
IF I'M TO DIE...
...IT WON'T BE FROM AN ARROW!

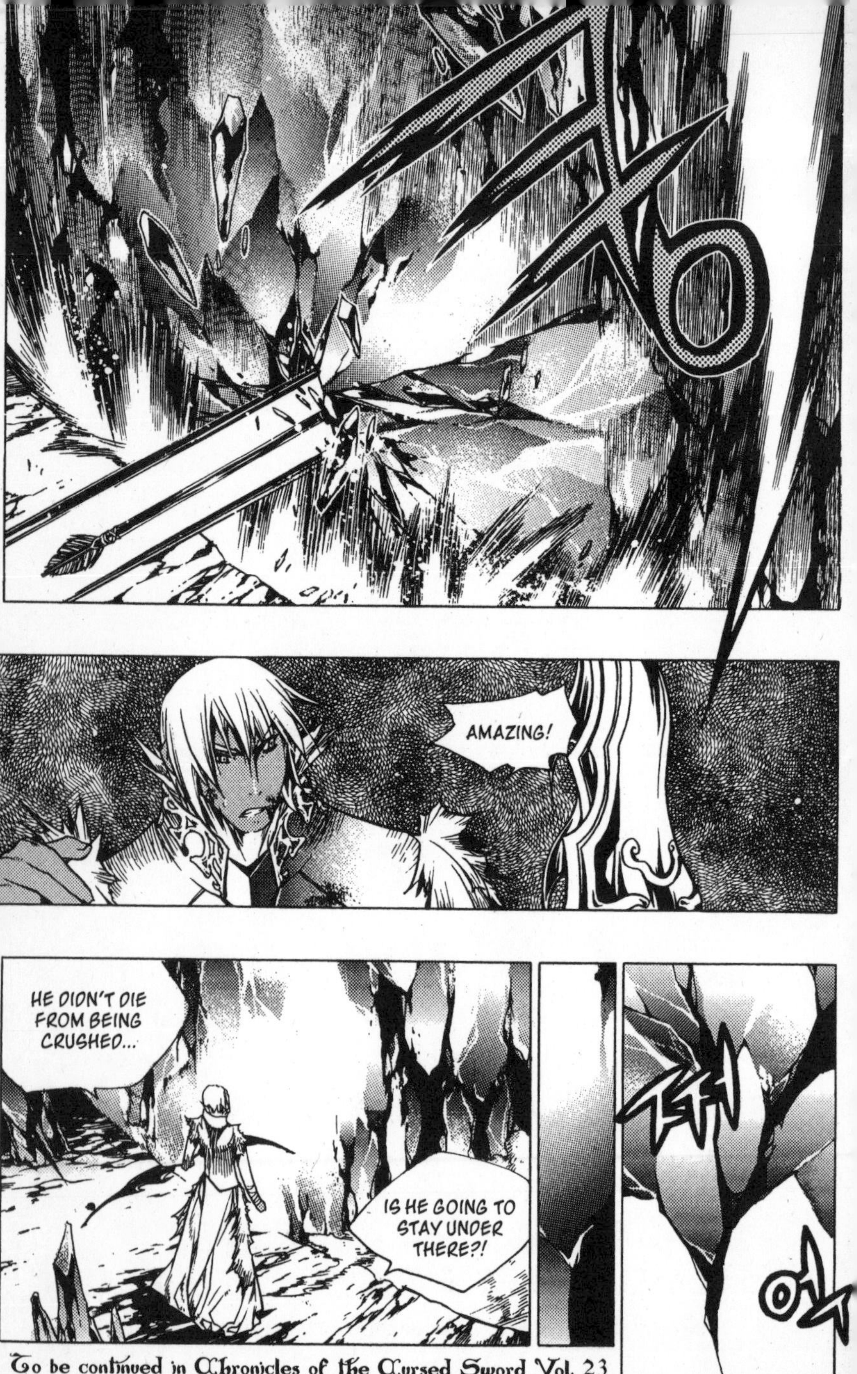
AMAZING!
HE DIDN'T DIE FROM BEING CRUSHED...
IS HE GOING TO STAY UNDER THERE?!

To be continued in Chronicles of the Cursed Sword Vol. 23

NEXT VOLUME:

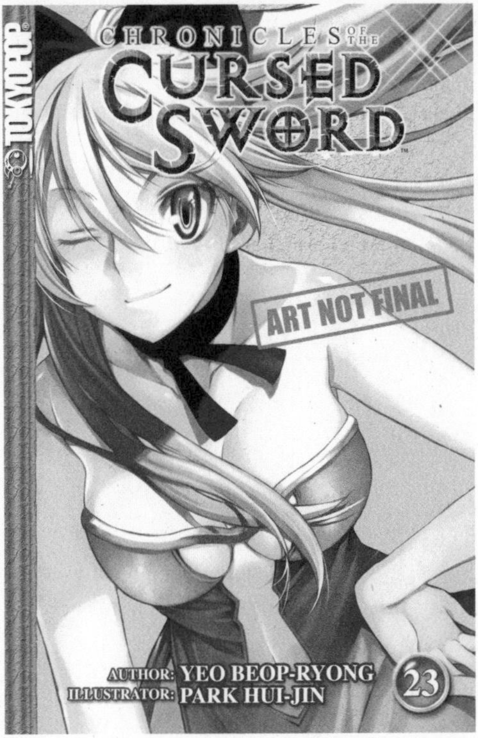
TOKYOPOP
CHRONICLES OF THE
CURSED SWORD
ART NOT FINAL
AUTHOR: YEO BEOP-RYONG
ILLUSTRATOR: PARK HUI-JIN
23

Behind the Heavenly Realm's plot to seal the Human Realm and end all life on Earth lies a shocking truth! Among the rulers of Heaven, brother has fought against brother, and the current plan is the work of the second prince and his sinister supporters. Can Hyacia and Rey form an alliance with those who favor the exiled third prince, and restore order to the rule of Heaven while saving millions of lives?

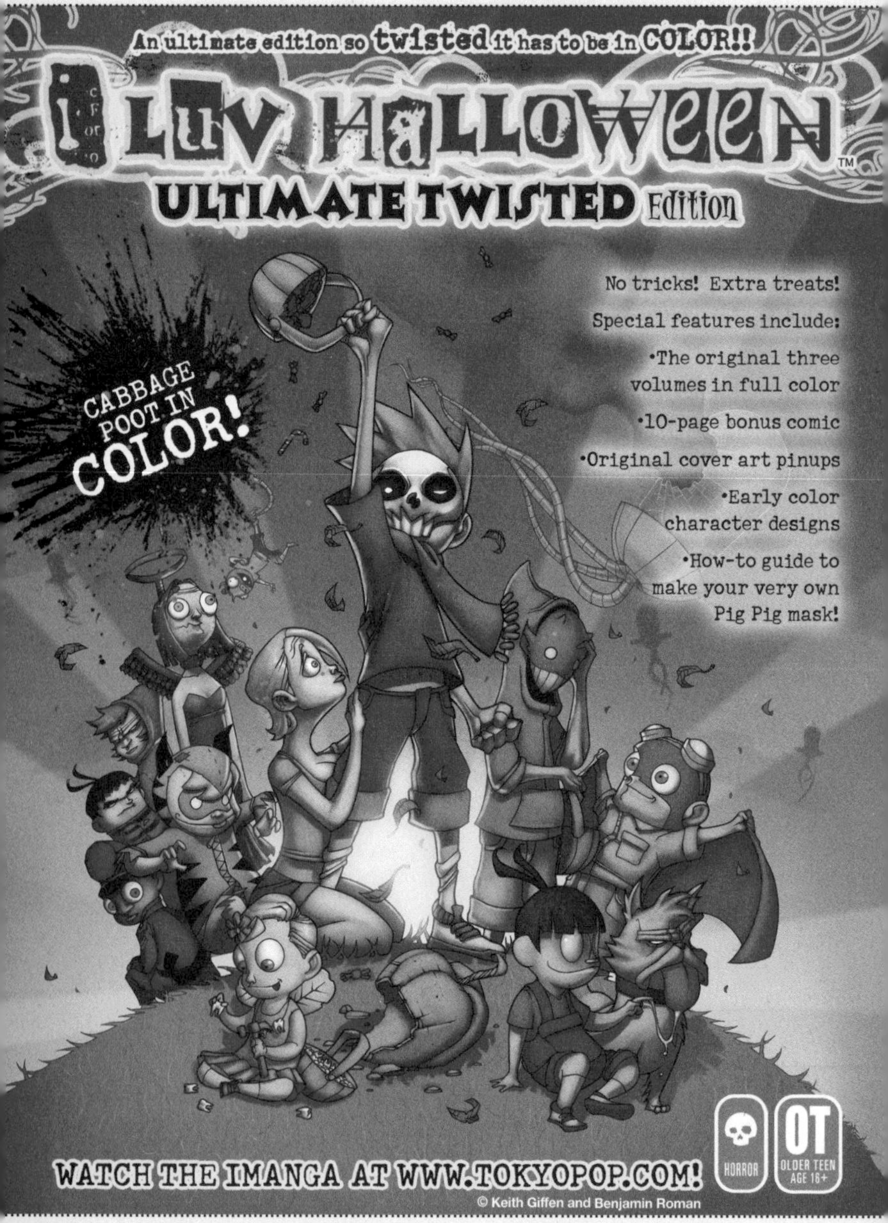
An ultimate edition so twisted it has to be in COLOR!!
I LUV HALLOWEEN™
ULTIMATE TWISTED Edition
No tricks! Extra treats!
Special features include:
•The original three volumes in full color
•10-page bonus comic
•Original cover art pinups
•Early color character designs
•How-to guide to make your very own Pig Pig mask!
CABBAGE POOT IN COLOR!
HORROR
OT OLDER TEEN AGE 16+
WATCH THE IMANGA AT WWW.TOKYOPOP.COM!
© Keith Giffen and Benjamin Roman